Takeshi Obata

ART

Tsugumi Ohba

STORY

Platinum End

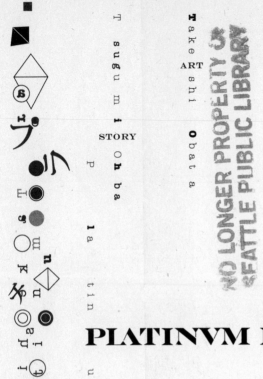

PLATINVM END

7

CHARACTERS

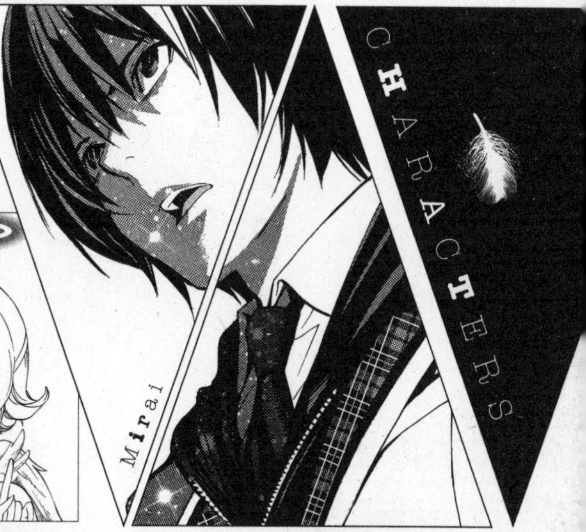
Mirai

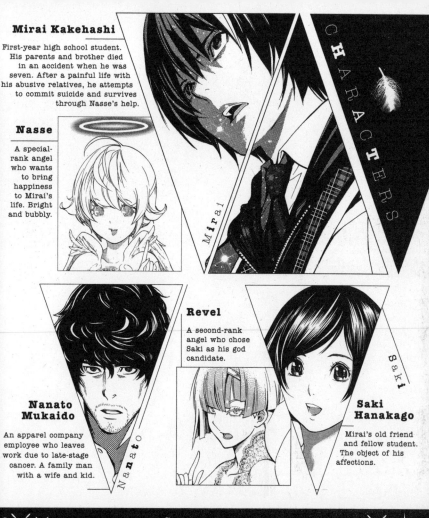

Mirai Kakehashi

First-year high school student. His parents and brother died in an accident when he was seven. After a painful life with his abusive relatives, he attempts to commit suicide and survives through Nasse's help.

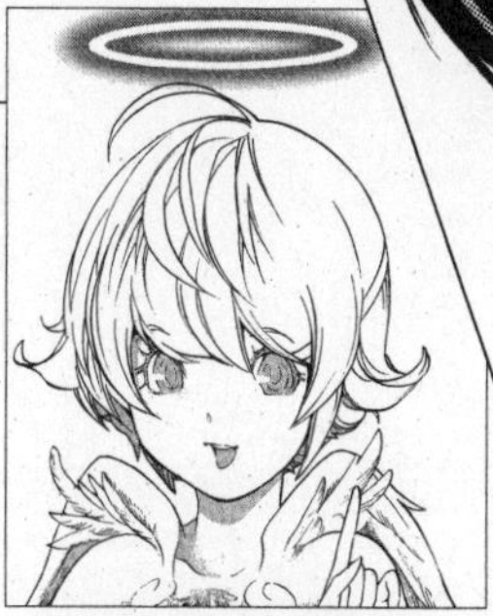

Nasse

A special-rank angel who wants to bring happiness to Mirai's life. Bright and bubbly.

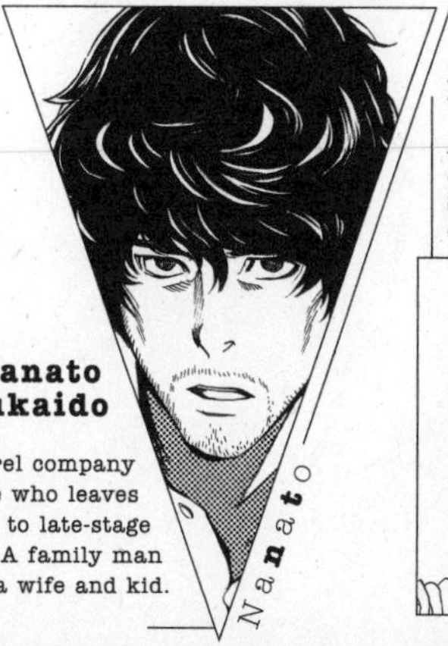
Nanato

Nanato Mukaido

An apparel company employee who leaves work due to late-stage cancer. A family man with a wife and kid.

Revel

A second-rank angel who chose Saki as his god candidate.

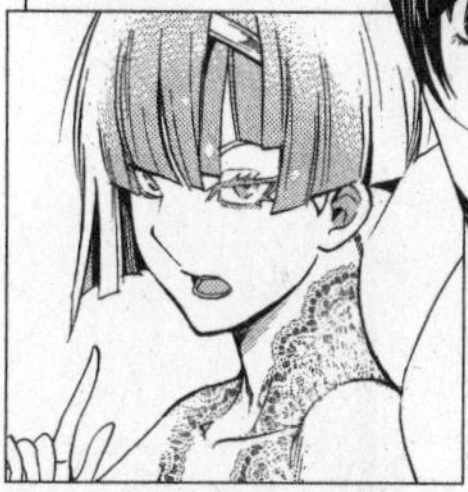

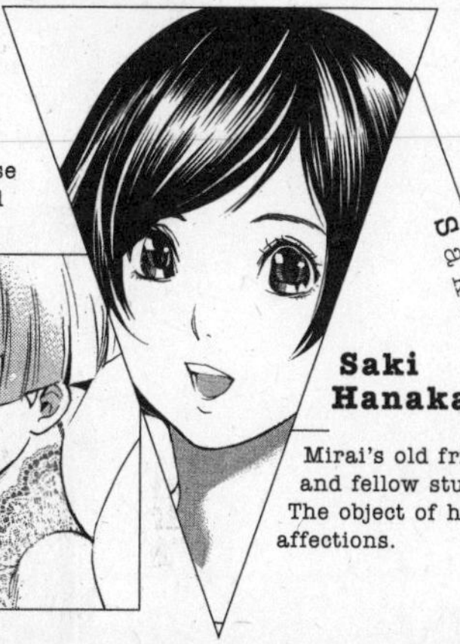
Saki

Saki Hanakago

Mirai's old friend and fellow student. The object of his affections.

Story

"My time has come. I leave the seat of god to the next human.
To a younger, fresher power.

The next god shall be chosen from the 13 humans chosen by you 13 angels.When the chosen human is made the next god, your angelic duty is finished,and you may live beside that god in peace.

You have 999 days remaining..."

CHARACTERS

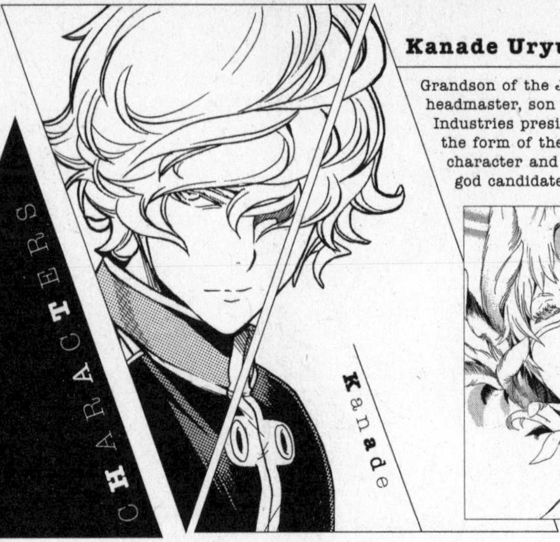
Kanade

Kanade Uryu

Grandson of the Joso Academy headmaster, son of the Joso Industries president. He assumes the form of the Metropoliman character and purges the other god candidates.

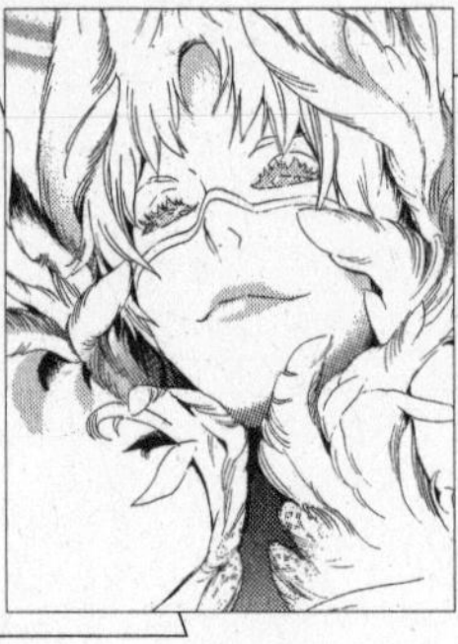

Meyza

The special-ranl angel who chos Kanade. For unknown reasor she was elevate from rankless t the top special rank.

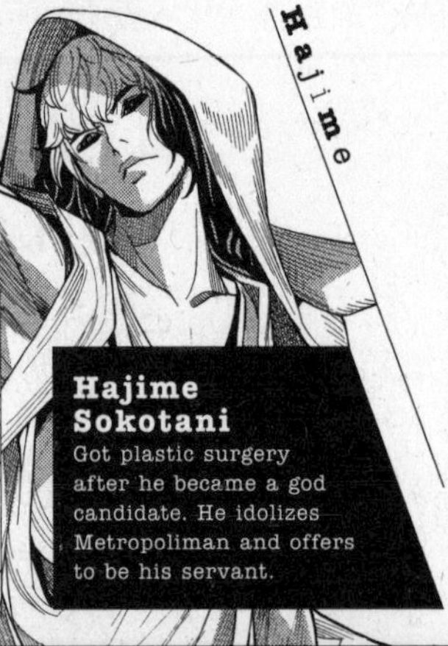
Hajime

Baret

The first-rank angel who chose Mukaido. Possesses great knowledge about the celestial world.

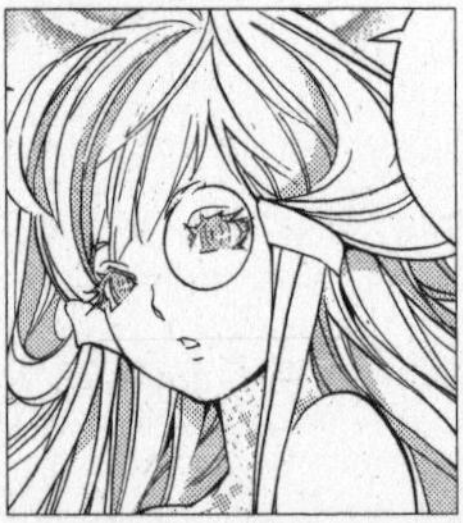

Balta

The first-rank angel who chose Hajime. The Angel of Intuition.

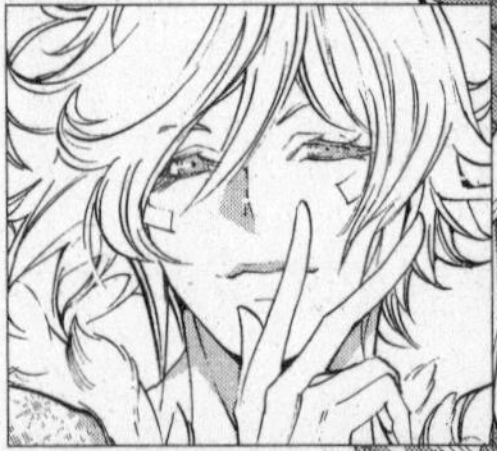

Hajime Sokotani

Got plastic surgery after he became a god candidate. He idolizes Metropoliman and offers to be his servant.

Story

FACE OFF

They escape through the gash created by Hajime's katana. But then Metropoliman appears with some companions...

ESCAPE

Saki finds the chance to hit Hajime with a red arrow. He turns his katana on the building where Mirai and Mukaido are trapped.

ANGEL TEARS

Revel sheds tears for the first time as an angel when he sees Saki blaming herself. He gets promoted to the first-rank Angel of Emotion.

CONTENTS

Prologue 001

Paranormalium 08

7

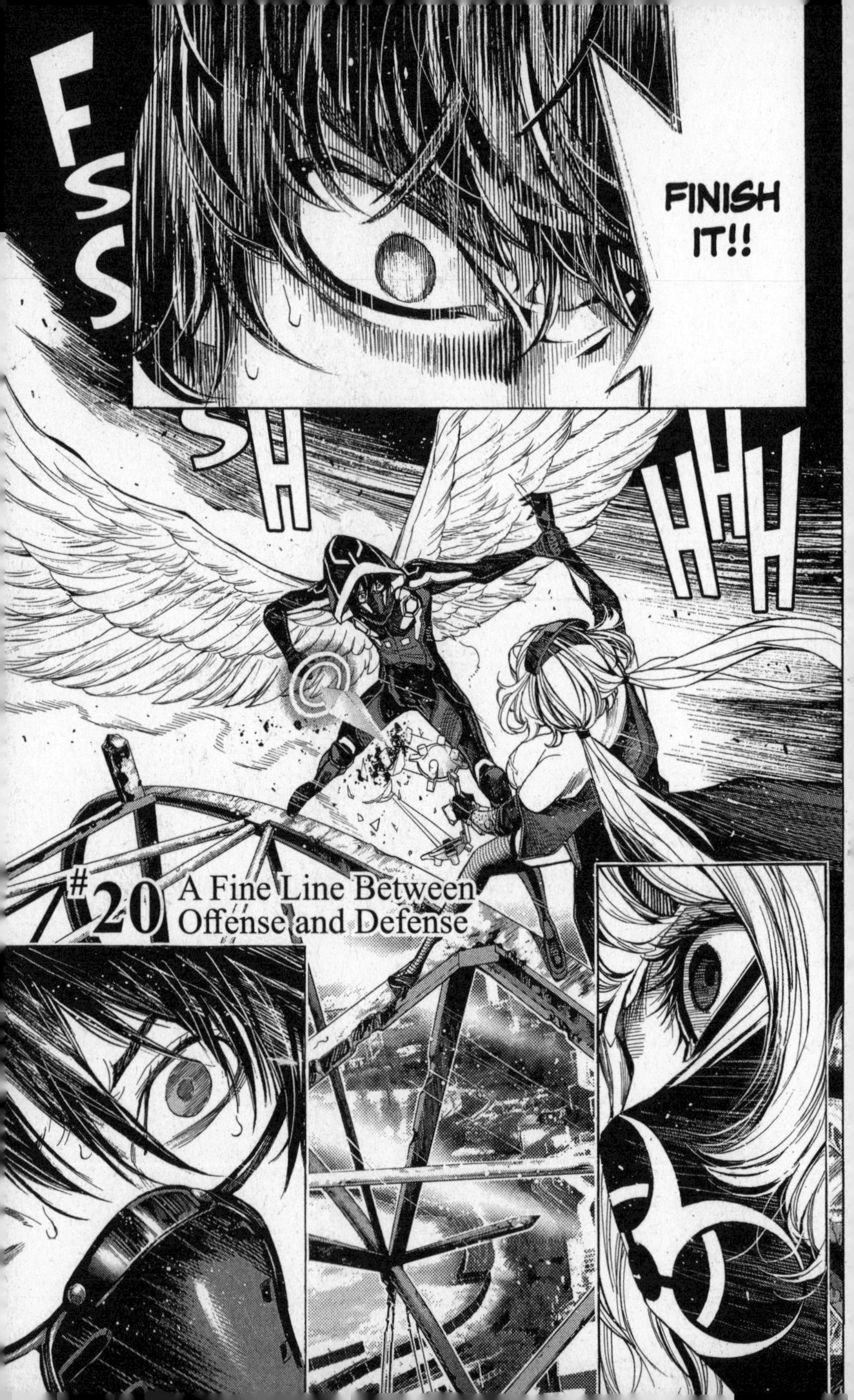
FINISH IT!!
FSSSHHHHH
#20 A Fine Line Between Offense and Defense

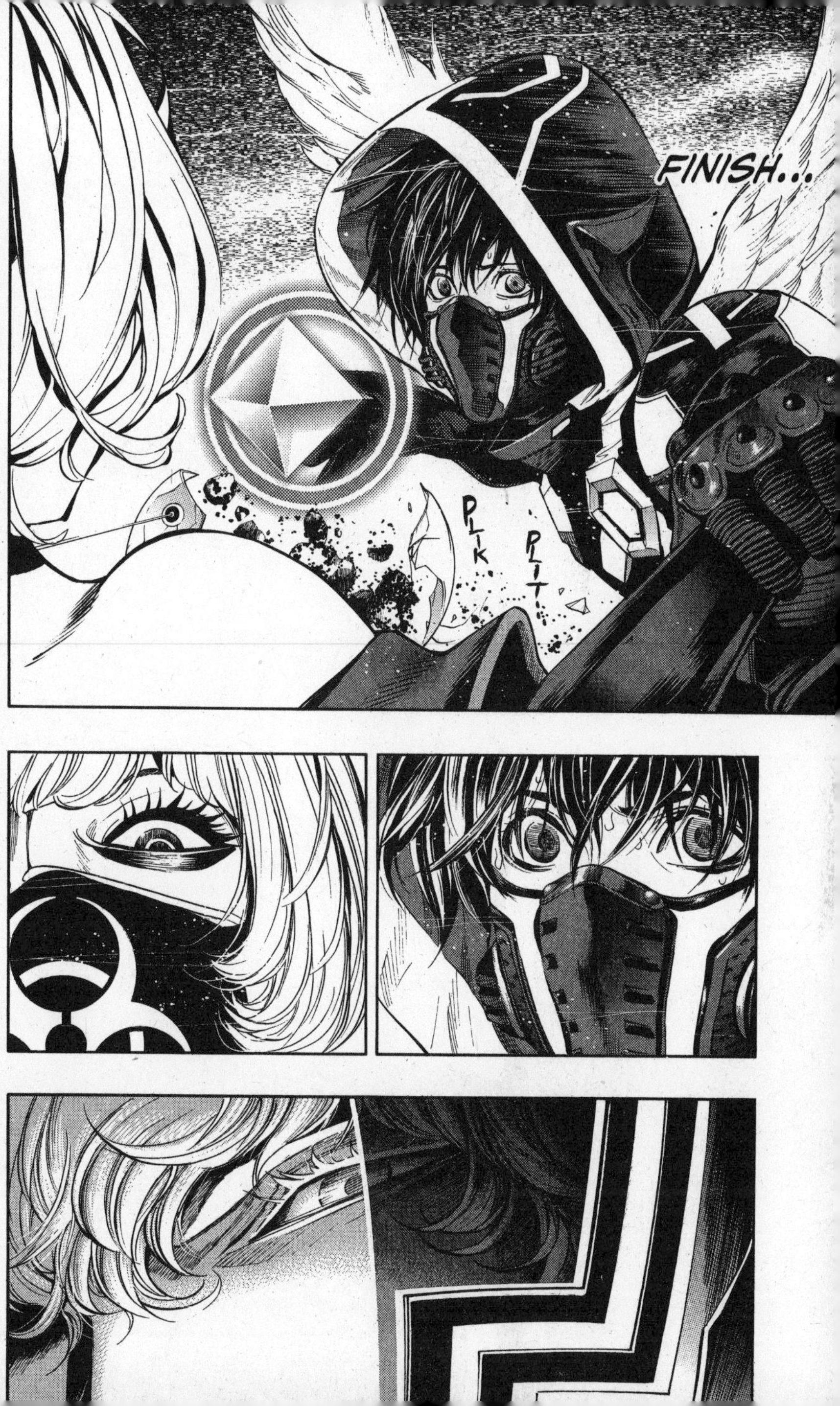
FINISH...
PLIK
PLIT

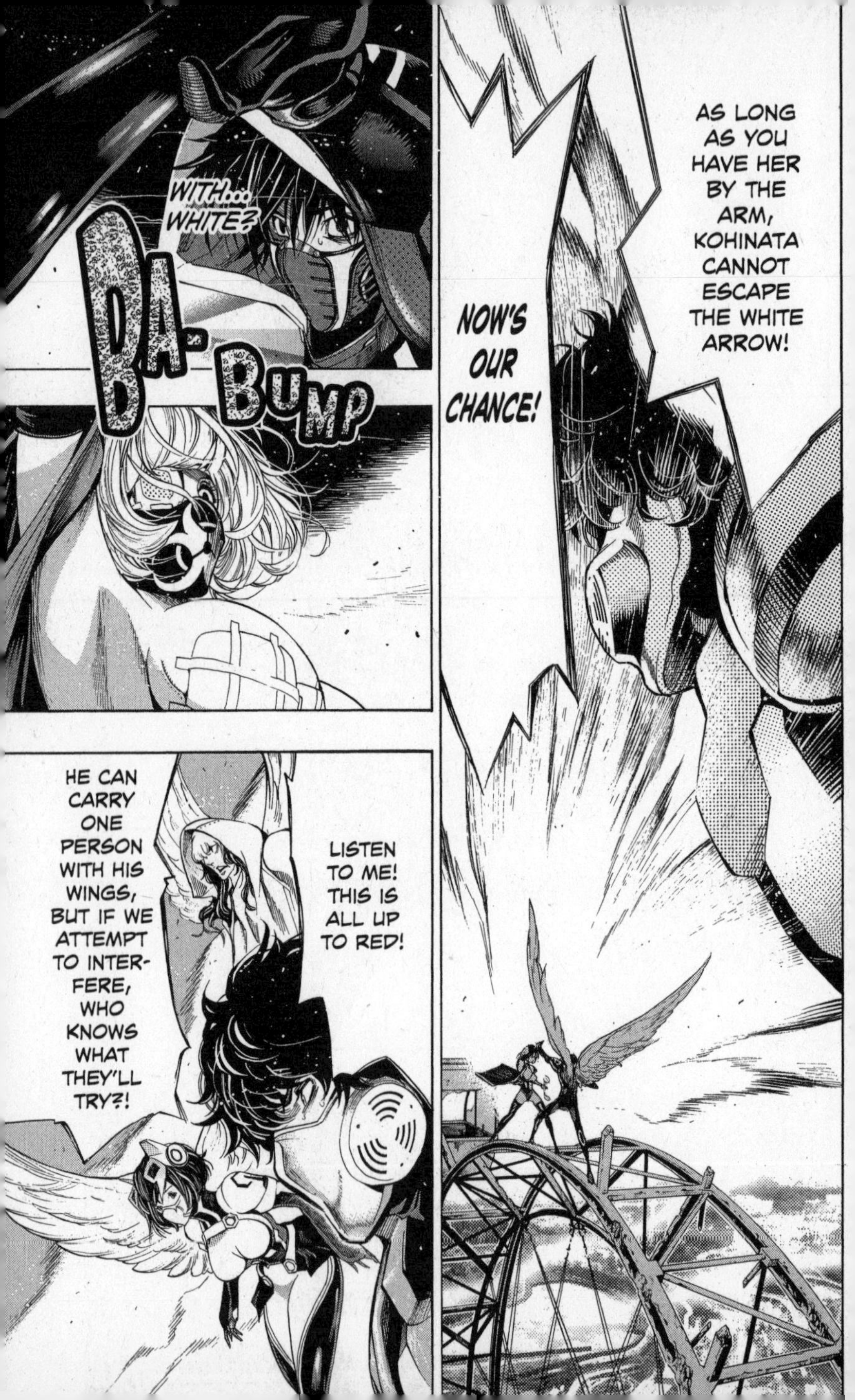
AS LONG AS YOU HAVE HER BY THE ARM, KOHINATA CANNOT ESCAPE THE WHITE ARROW!
NOW'S OUR CHANCE!
WITH... WHITE?
DA-BUMP
LISTEN TO ME! THIS IS ALL UP TO RED!
HE CAN CARRY ONE PERSON WITH HIS WINGS, BUT IF WE ATTEMPT TO INTER-FERE, WHO KNOWS WHAT THEY'LL TRY?!

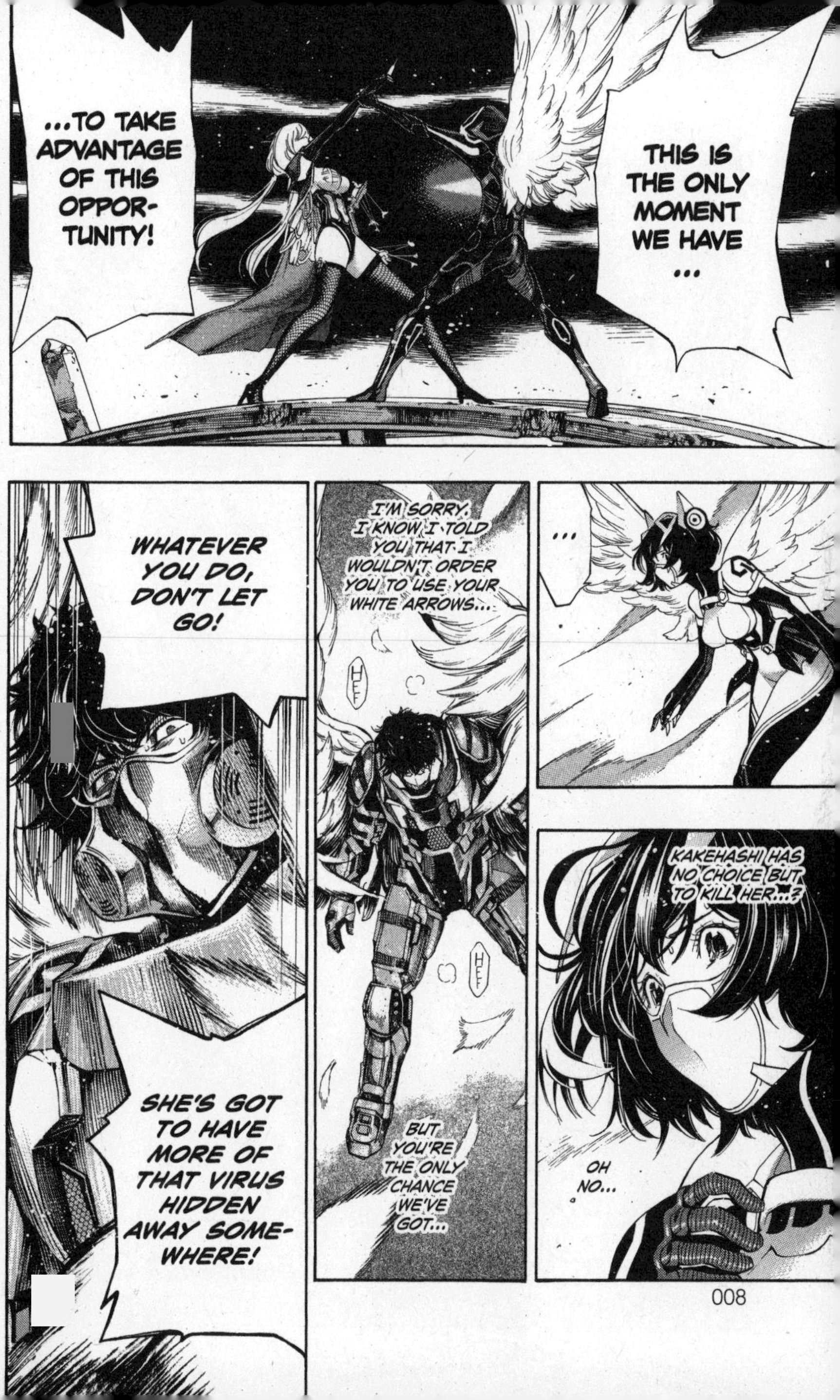
THIS IS THE ONLY MOMENT WE HAVE...
...TO TAKE ADVANTAGE OF THIS OPPORTUNITY!
...
KAKEHASHI HAS NO CHOICE BUT TO KILL HER...?
OH NO...
I'M SORRY. I KNOW I TOLD YOU THAT I WOULDN'T ORDER YOU TO USE YOUR WHITE ARROWS...
HEF
HEF
BUT YOU'RE THE ONLY CHANCE WE'VE GOT...
WHATEVER YOU DO, DON'T LET GO!
SHE'S GOT TO HAVE MORE OF THAT VIRUS HIDDEN AWAY SOMEWHERE!

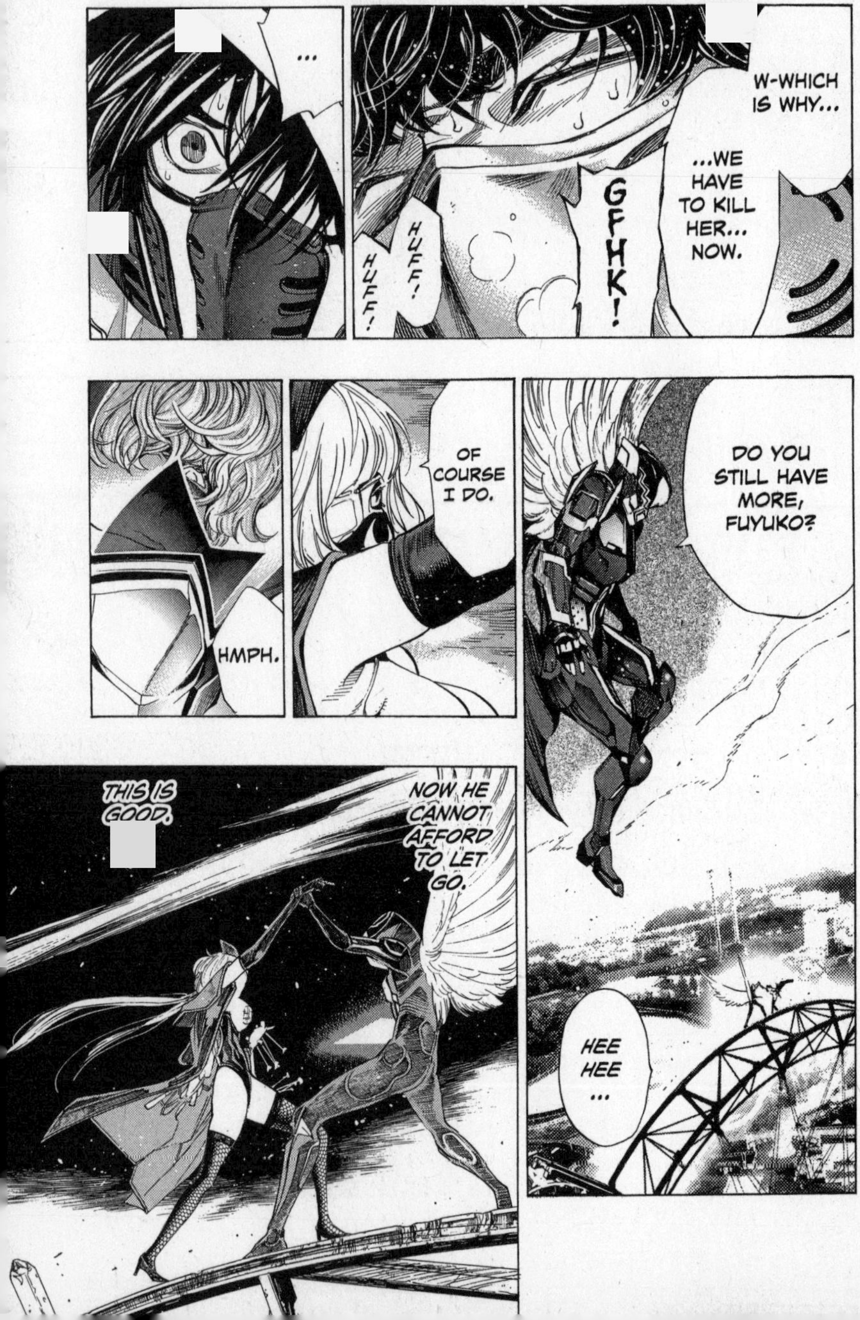
W-WHICH IS WHY...
...WE HAVE TO KILL HER... NOW.
GFHK!
HUFF! HUFF!
...
DO YOU STILL HAVE MORE, FUYUKO?
HEE HEE ...
OF COURSE I DO.
HMPH.
NOW HE CANNOT AFFORD TO LET GO.
THIS IS GOOD.

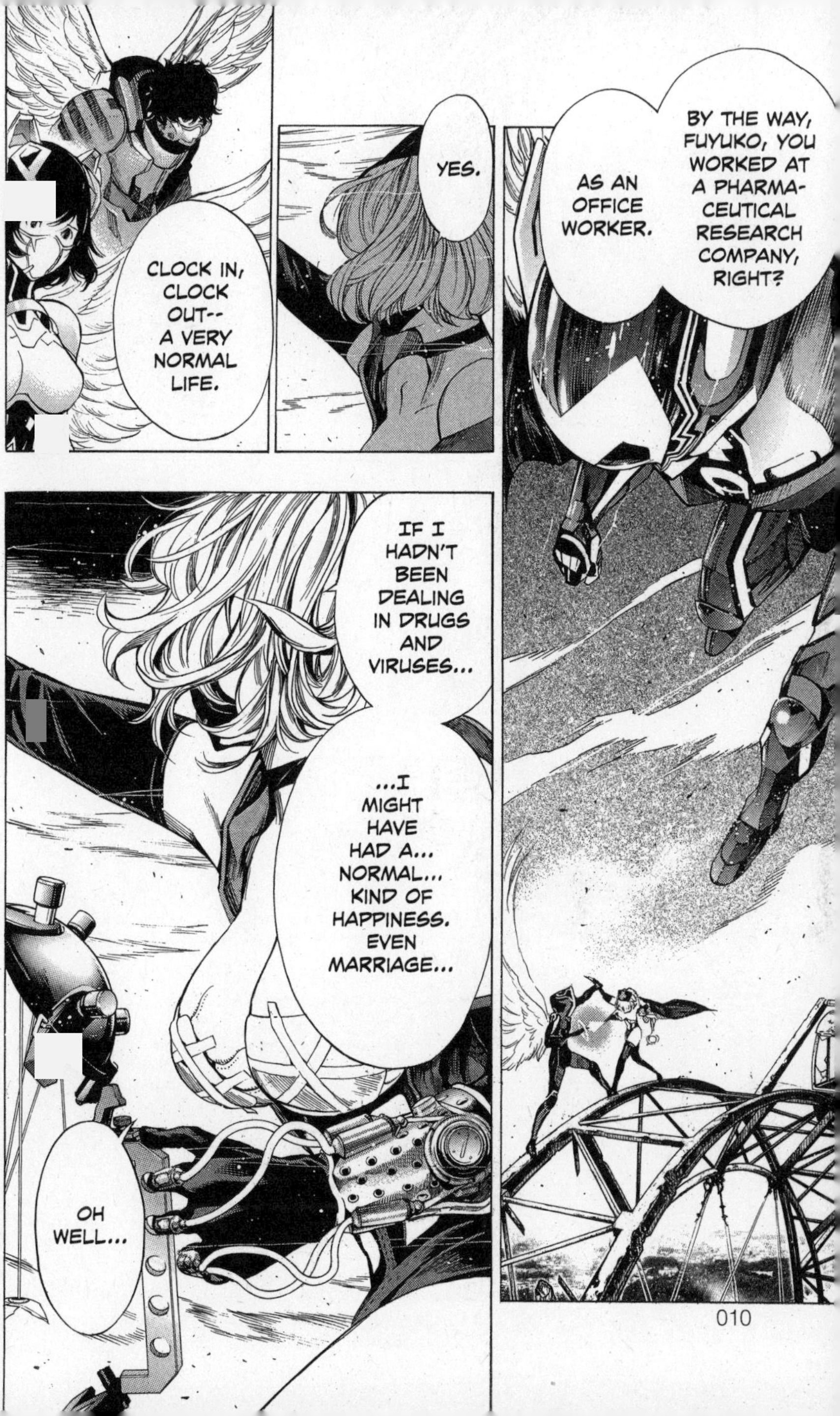
BY THE WAY, FUYUKO, YOU WORKED AT A PHARMA-CEUTICAL RESEARCH COMPANY, RIGHT?
AS AN OFFICE WORKER.
YES.
CLOCK IN, CLOCK OUT-- A VERY NORMAL LIFE.
IF I HADN'T BEEN DEALING IN DRUGS AND VIRUSES...
...I MIGHT HAVE HAD A... NORMAL... KIND OF HAPPINESS. EVEN MARRIAGE...
OH WELL...

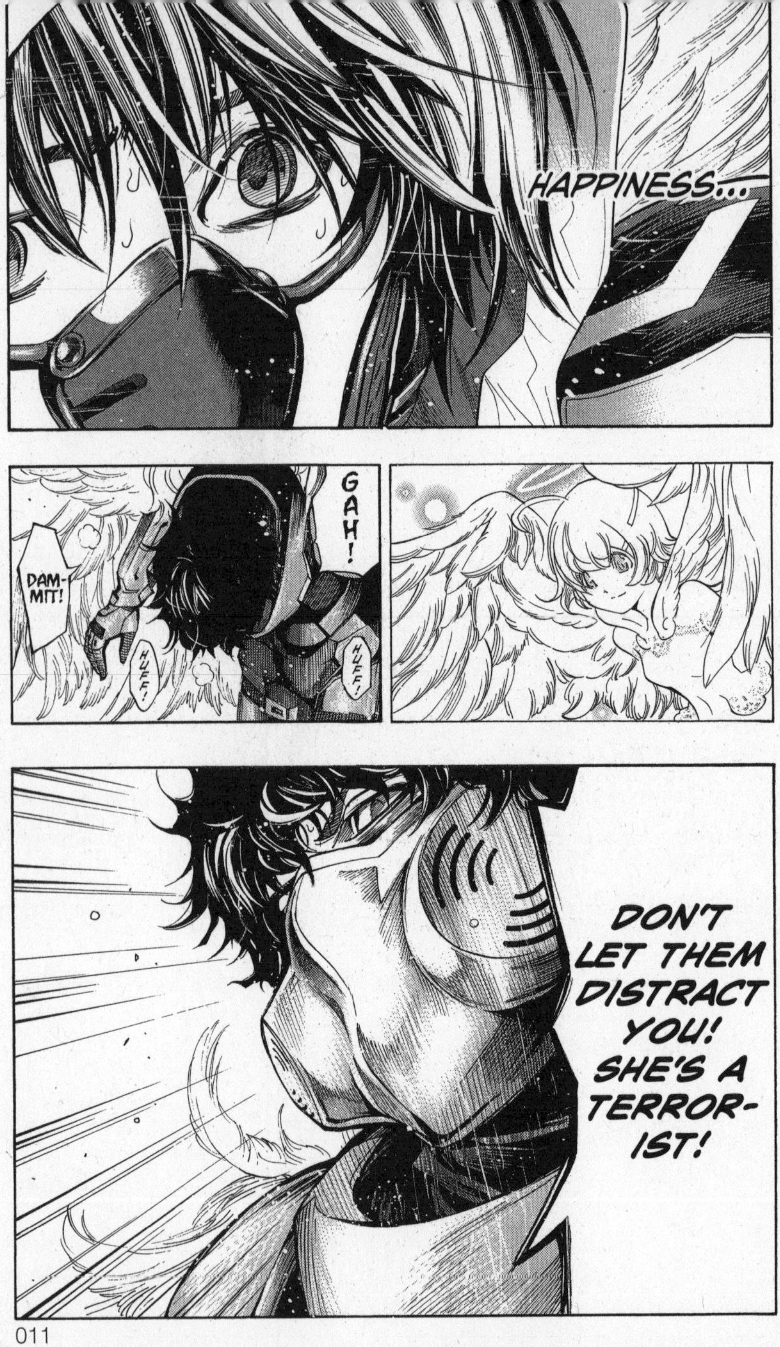
HAPPINESS...
GAH!
HUFF!
DAM-MIT!
HUFF!
DON'T LET THEM DISTRACT YOU! SHE'S A TERROR-IST!

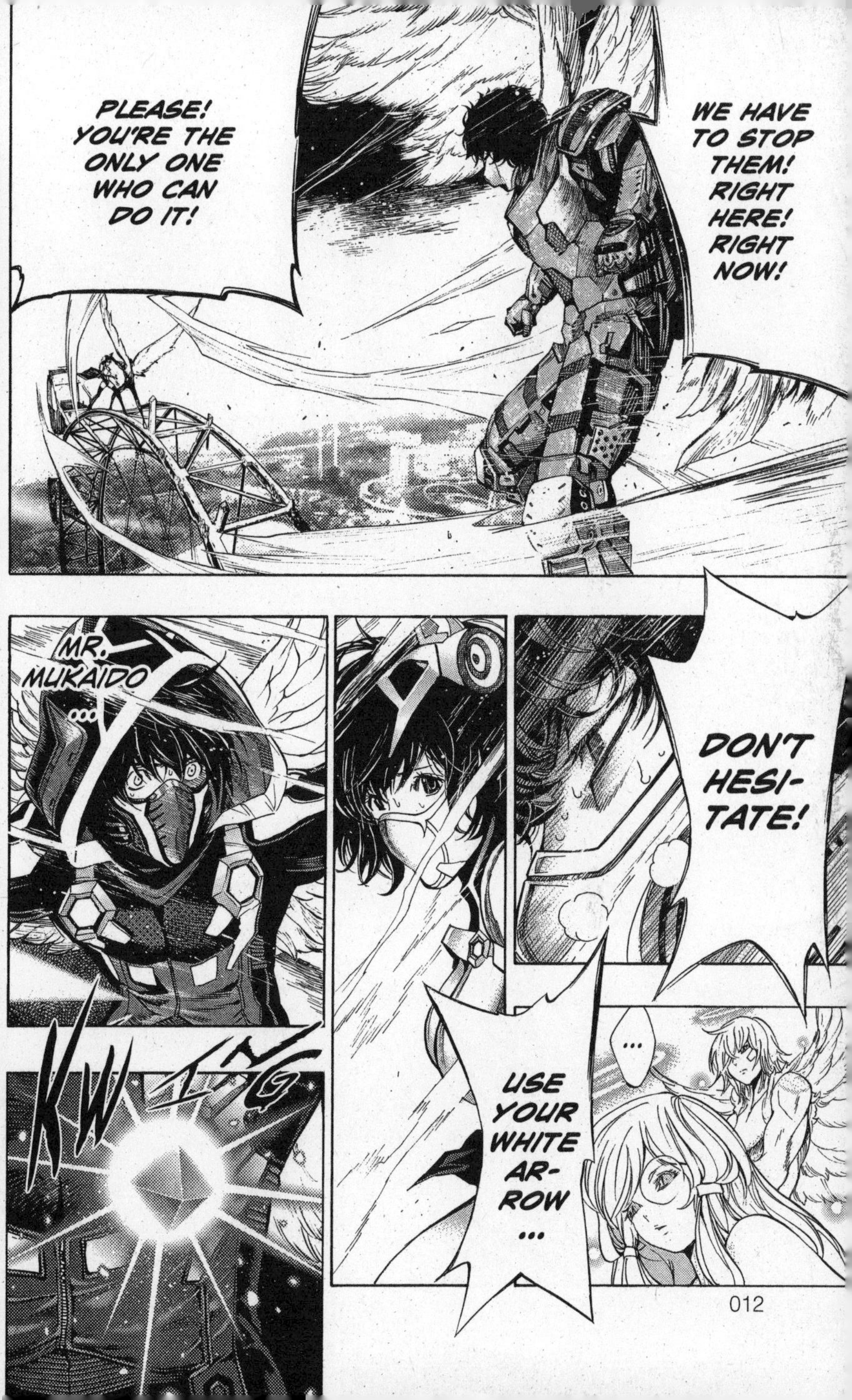
WE HAVE TO STOP THEM! RIGHT HERE! RIGHT NOW!
PLEASE! YOU'RE THE ONLY ONE WHO CAN DO IT!
DON'T HESI-TATE!
...
USE YOUR WHITE AR-ROW...
MR. MUKAIDO...
KWING

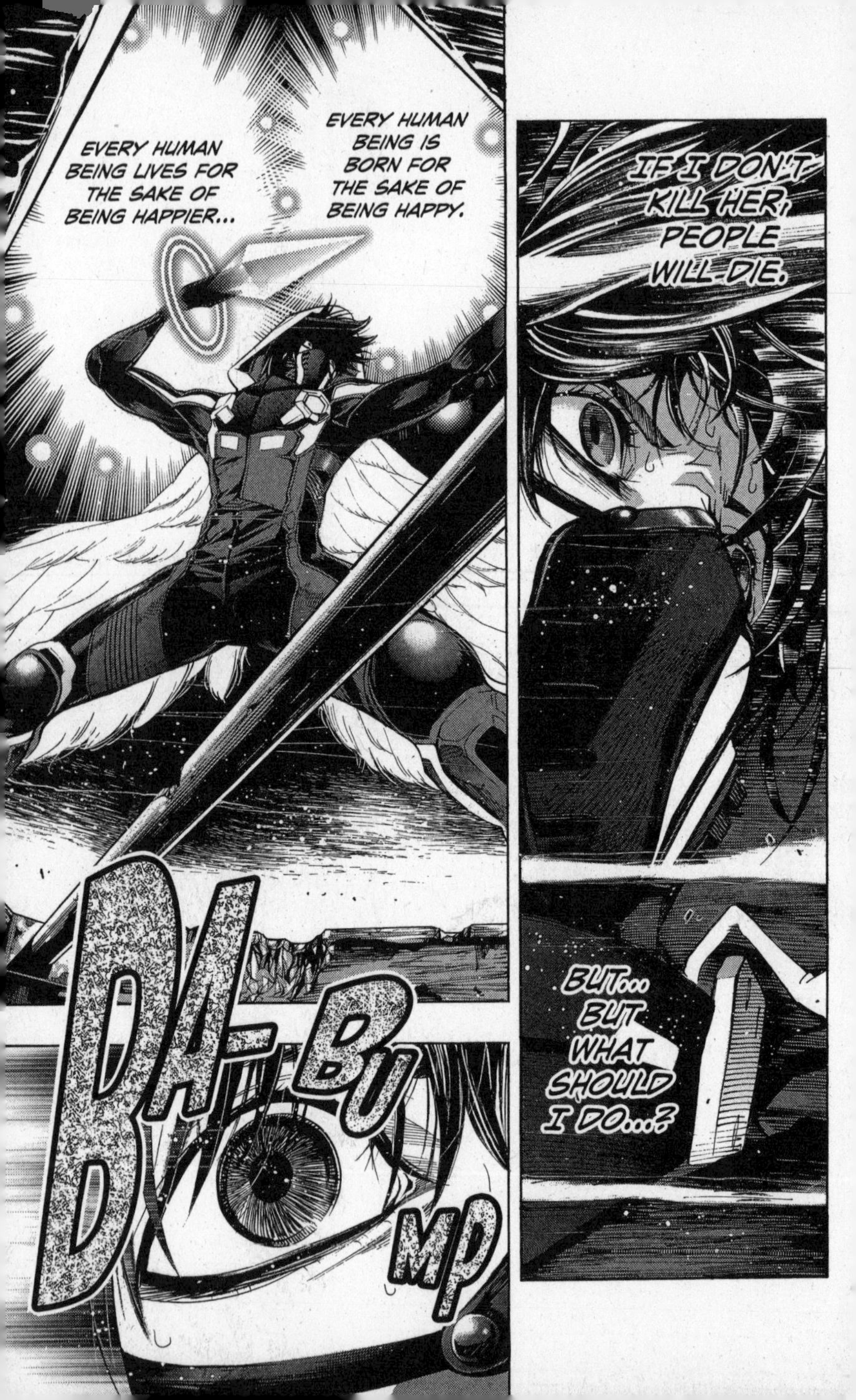
IF I DON'T KILL HER, PEOPLE WILL DIE.
BUT... BUT WHAT SHOULD I DO...?
EVERY HUMAN BEING IS BORN FOR THE SAKE OF BEING HAPPY.
EVERY HUMAN BEING LIVES FOR THE SAKE OF BEING HAPPIER...
DA-BUMP

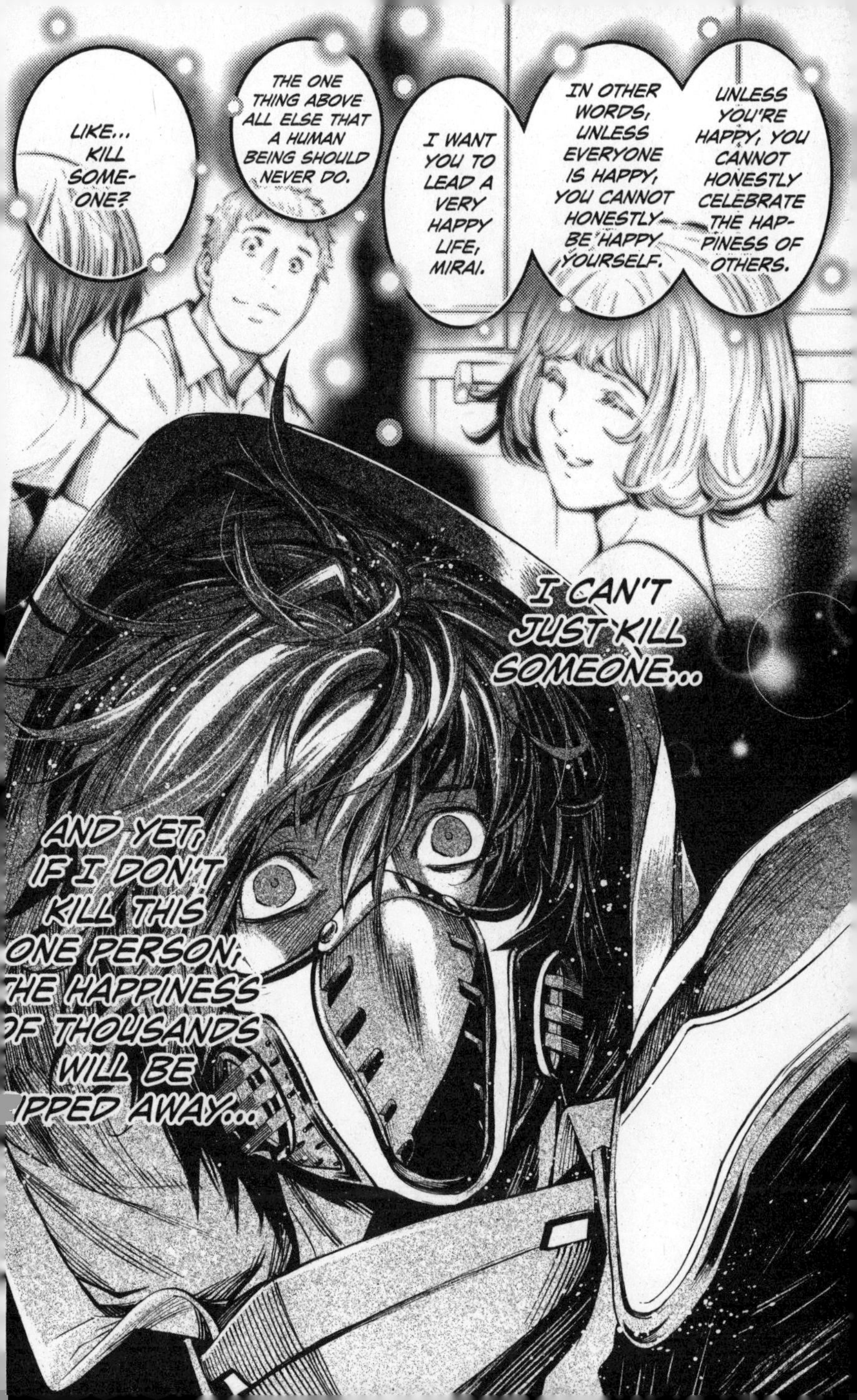
UNLESS YOU'RE HAPPY, YOU CANNOT HONESTLY CELEBRATE THE HAPPINESS OF OTHERS.
IN OTHER WORDS, UNLESS EVERYONE IS HAPPY, YOU CANNOT HONESTLY BE HAPPY YOURSELF.
I WANT YOU TO LEAD A VERY HAPPY LIFE, MIRAI.
THE ONE THING ABOVE ALL ELSE THAT A HUMAN BEING SHOULD NEVER DO.
LIKE... KILL SOMEONE?
I CAN'T JUST KILL SOMEONE...
AND YET, IF I DON'T KILL THIS ONE PERSON, THE HAPPINESS OF THOUSANDS WILL BE IPPED AWAY...

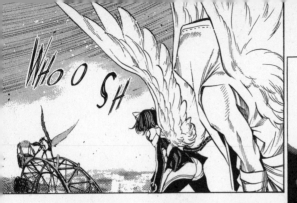

WHOOOSH

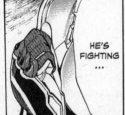

HE'S FIGHTING...

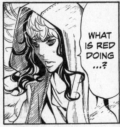

WHAT IS RED DOING...?

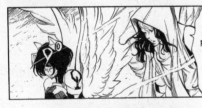

F-FIGHTING...? HOW...?

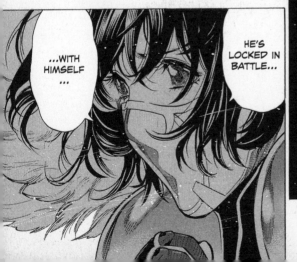

...WITH HIMSELF...

HE'S LOCKED IN BATTLE...

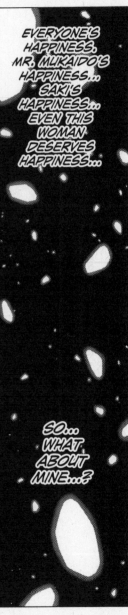

EVERYONE'S HAPPINESS. MR. MUKAIDO'S HAPPINESS... SAKI'S HAPPINESS... EVEN THIS WOMAN DESERVES HAPPINESS...

SO... WHAT ABOUT MINE...?

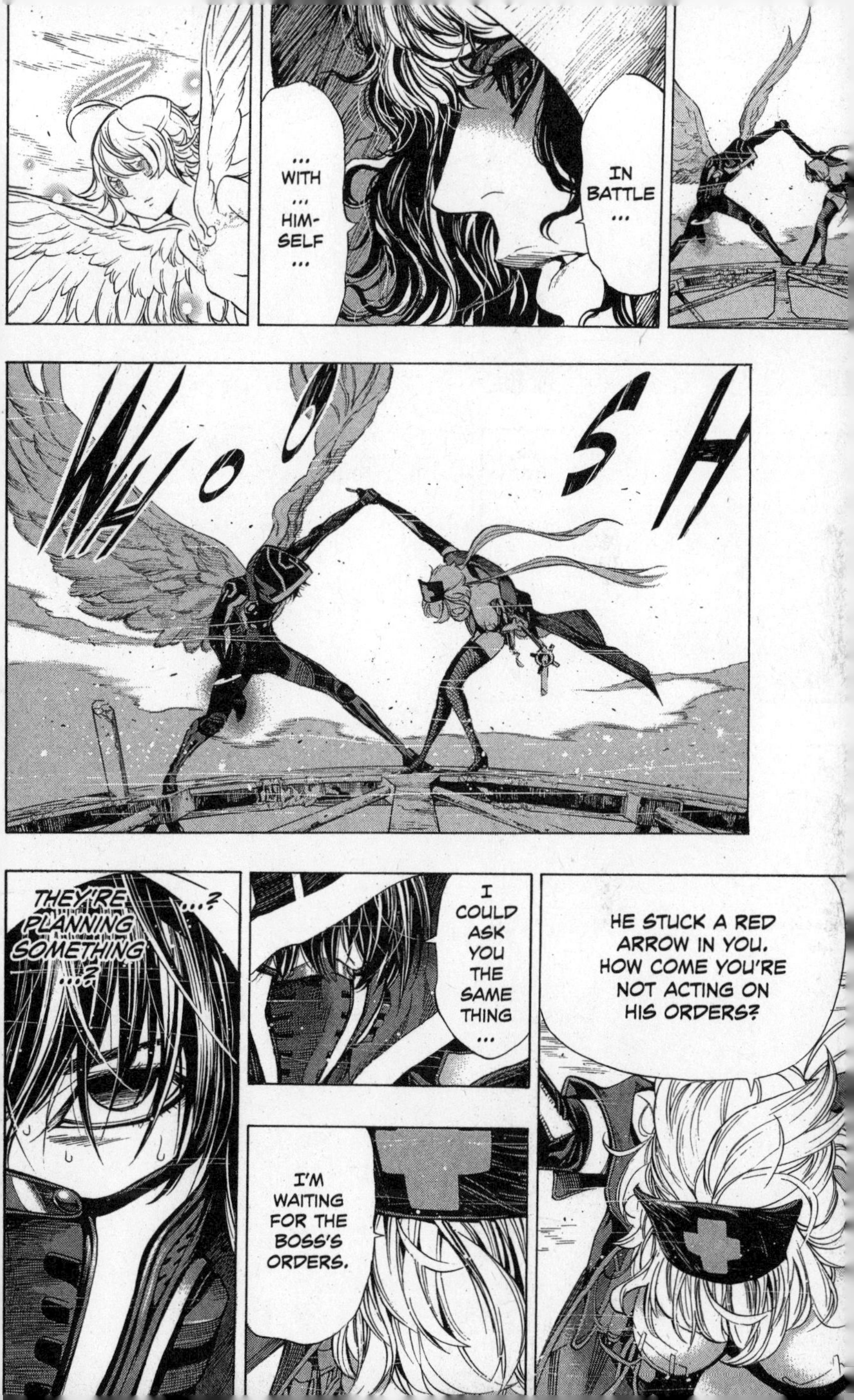
IN BATTLE ...
... WITH ... HIM-SELF ...
WHOOSH
HE STUCK A RED ARROW IN YOU. HOW COME YOU'RE NOT ACTING ON HIS ORDERS?
I COULD ASK YOU THE SAME THING ...
I'M WAITING FOR THE BOSS'S ORDERS.
...?
THEY'RE PLANNING SOMETHING ...?

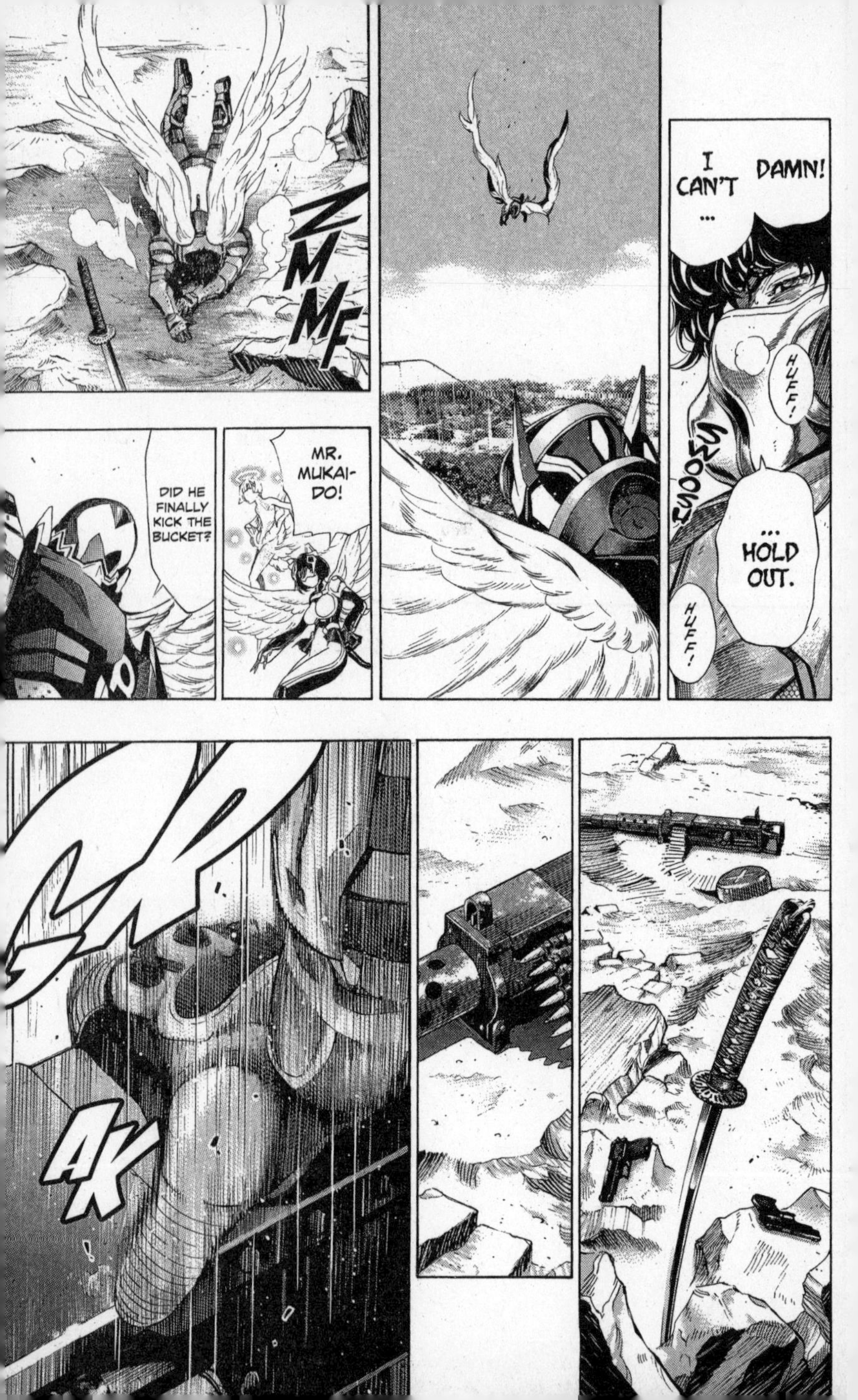
DAMN!
I CAN'T ...
HUFF!
SWOOSH
... HOLD OUT.
HUFF!
ZMMMF
MR. MUKAI-DO!
DID HE FINALLY KICK THE BUCKET?
AK

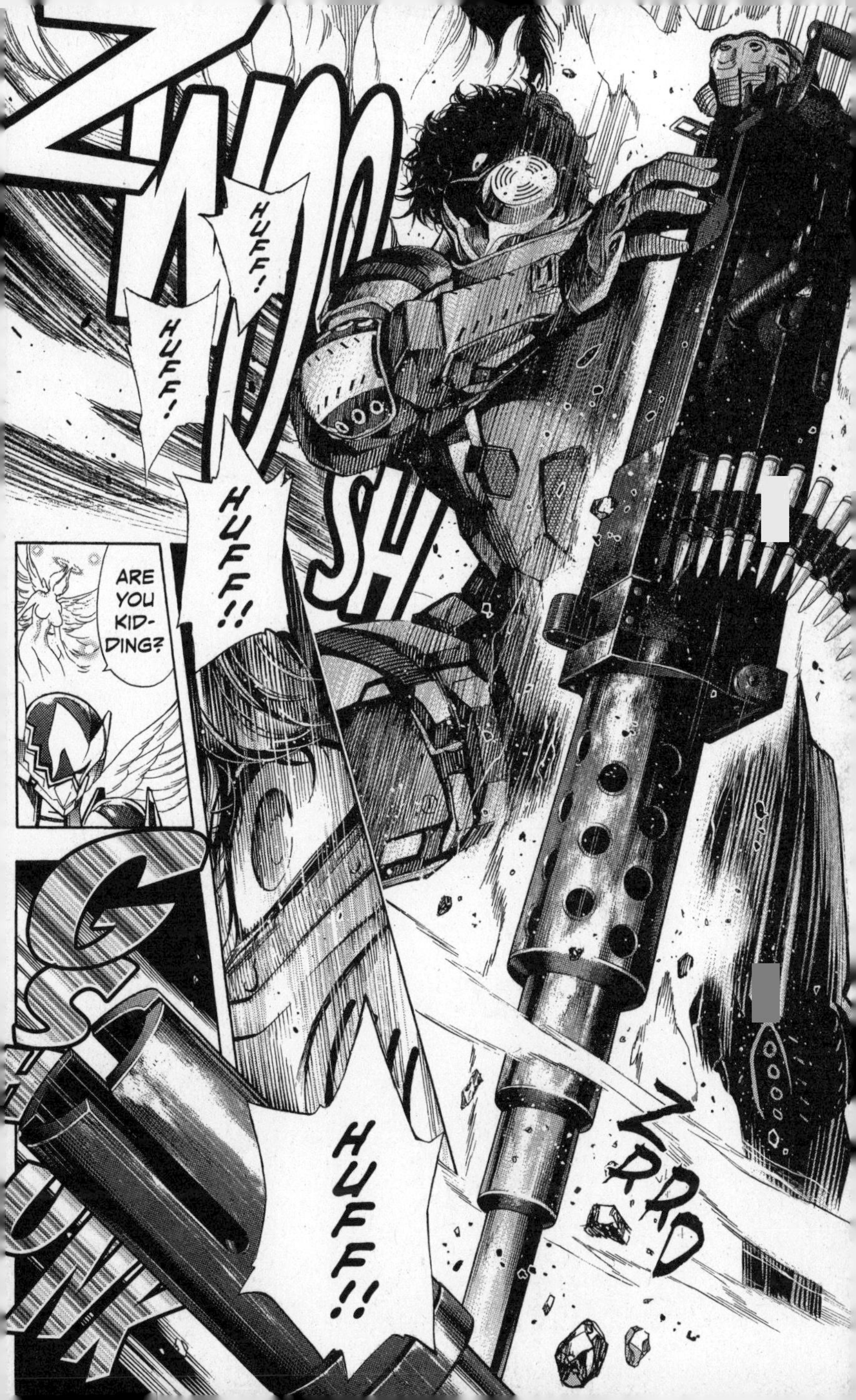

HUFF!
HUFF!
HUFF!!
ARE YOU KID-DING?
HUFF!!
ZRRD

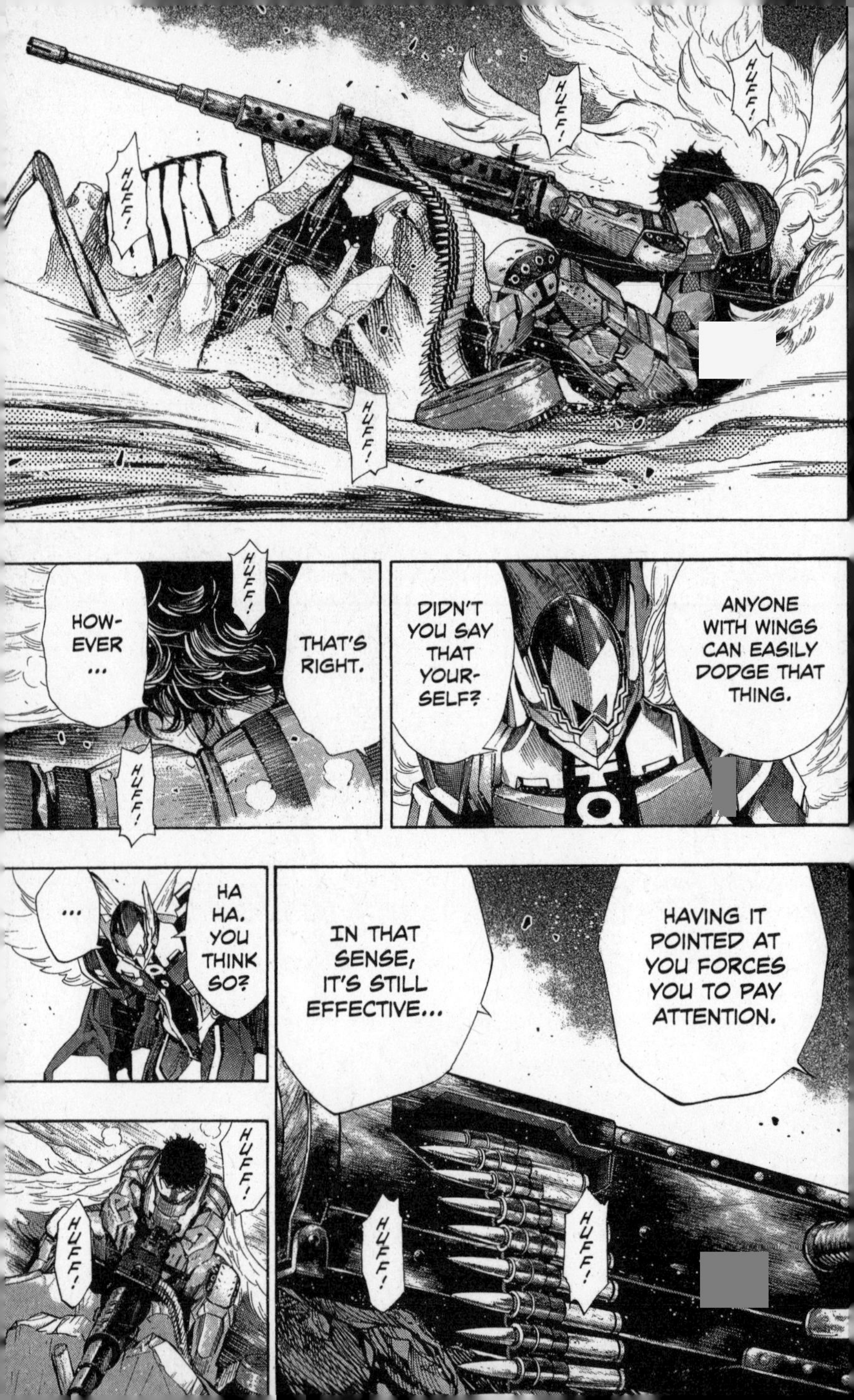
HUFF!
HUFF!
HUFF!
HUFF!
ANYONE WITH WINGS CAN EASILY DODGE THAT THING.
DIDN'T YOU SAY THAT YOURSELF?
THAT'S RIGHT.
HUFF!
HOW-EVER...
HUFF!
HAVING IT POINTED AT YOU FORCES YOU TO PAY ATTENTION.
IN THAT SENSE, IT'S STILL EFFECTIVE...
HUFF!
HUFF!
HA HA. YOU THINK SO?
...
HUFF!
HUFF!

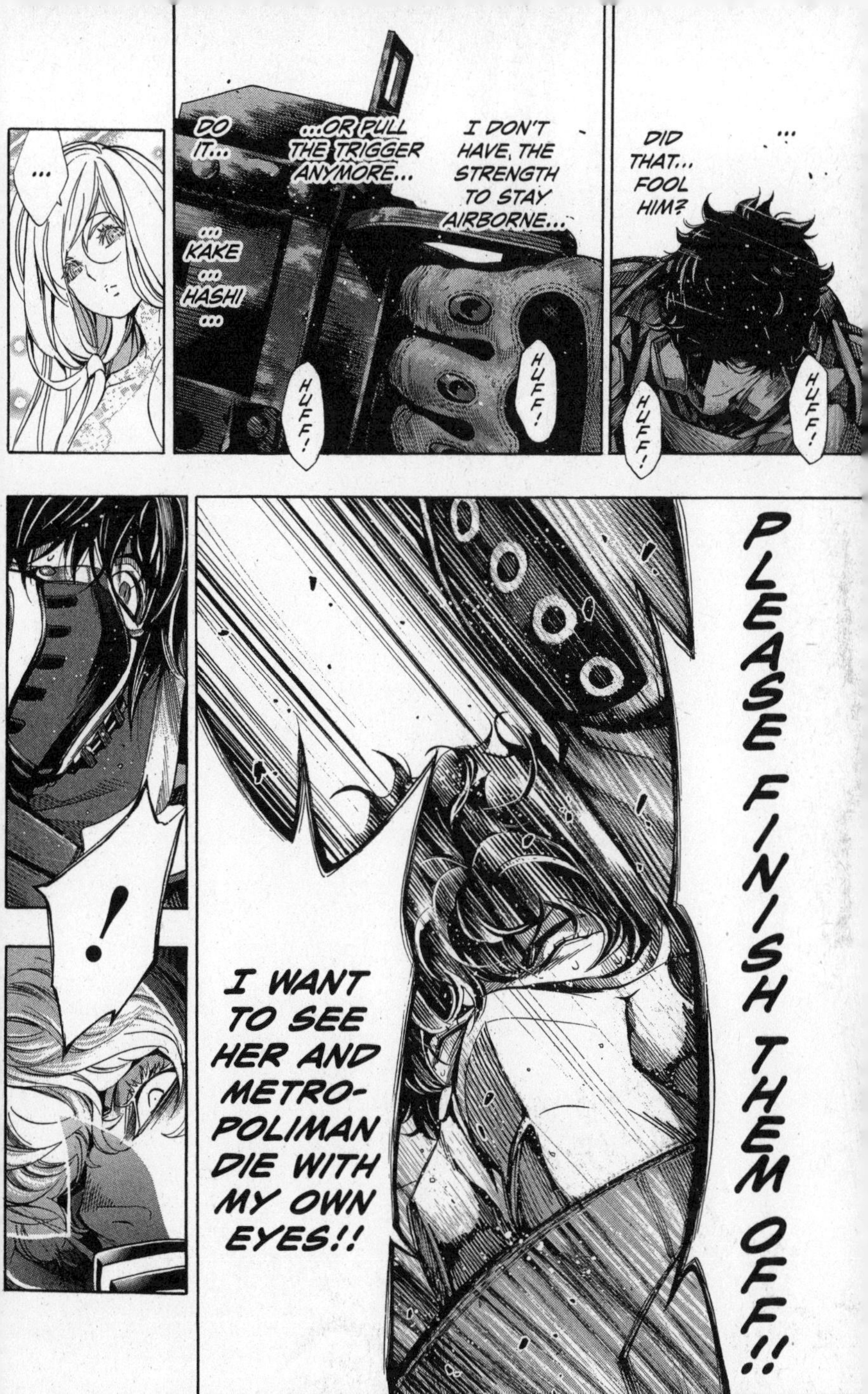
...
DID THAT... FOOL HIM?
HUFF!
HUFF!
I DON'T HAVE THE STRENGTH TO STAY AIRBORNE...
...OR PULL THE TRIGGER ANYMORE...
DO IT...
...KAKE...HASHI...
HUFF!
HUFF!
...
PLEASE FINISH THEM OFF!!
I WANT TO SEE HER AND METRO-POLIMAN DIE WITH MY OWN EYES!!
!

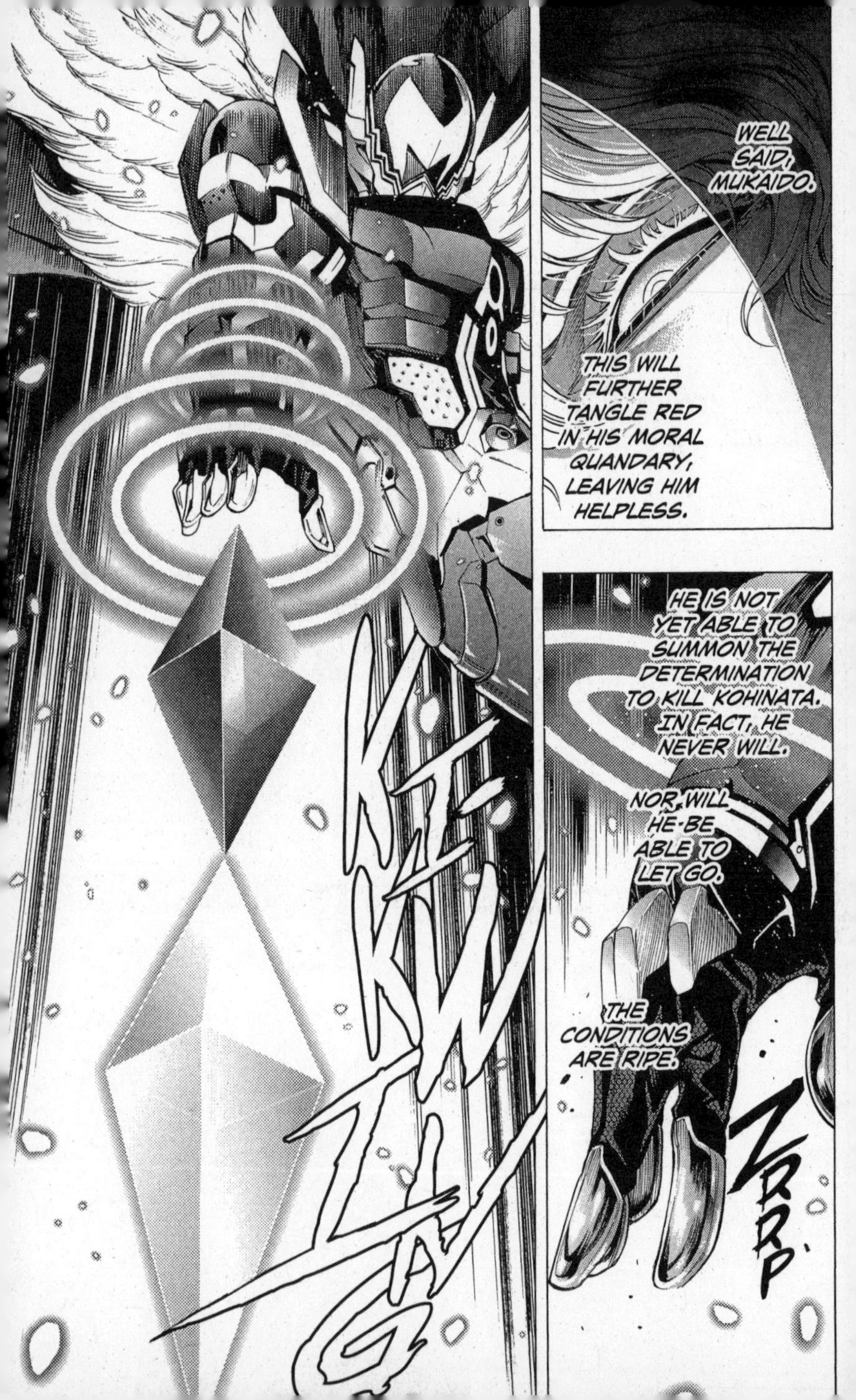
WELL SAID, MUKAIDO.
THIS WILL FURTHER TANGLE RED IN HIS MORAL QUANDARY, LEAVING HIM HELPLESS.
HE IS NOT YET ABLE TO SUMMON THE DETERMINATION TO KILL KOHINATA. IN FACT, HE NEVER WILL.
NOR WILL HE BE ABLE TO LET GO.
THE CONDITIONS ARE RIPE.

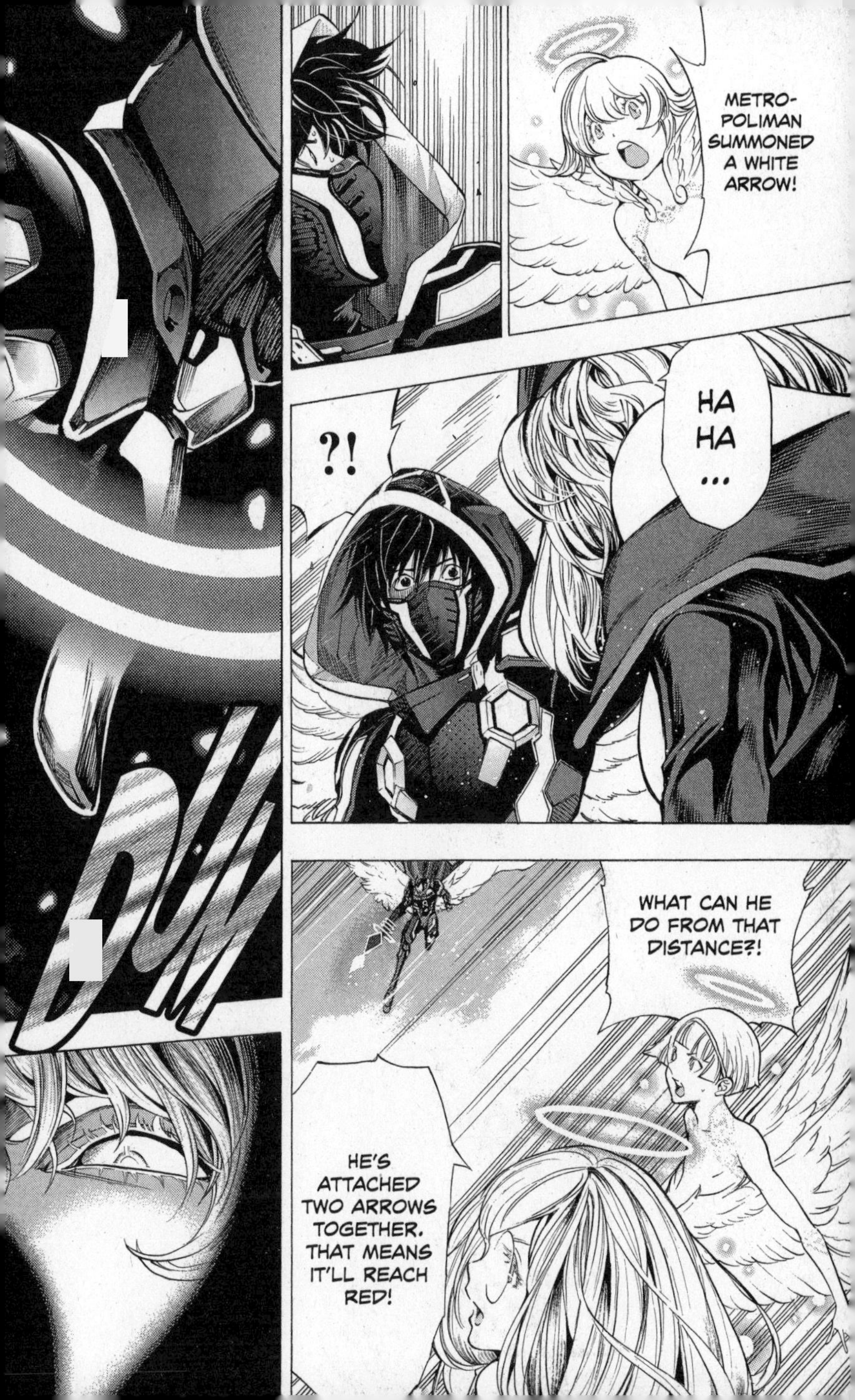
METRO-POLIMAN SUMMONED A WHITE ARROW!
HA HA ...
?!
WHAT CAN HE DO FROM THAT DISTANCE?!
HE'S ATTACHED TWO ARROWS TOGETHER. THAT MEANS IT'LL REACH RED!

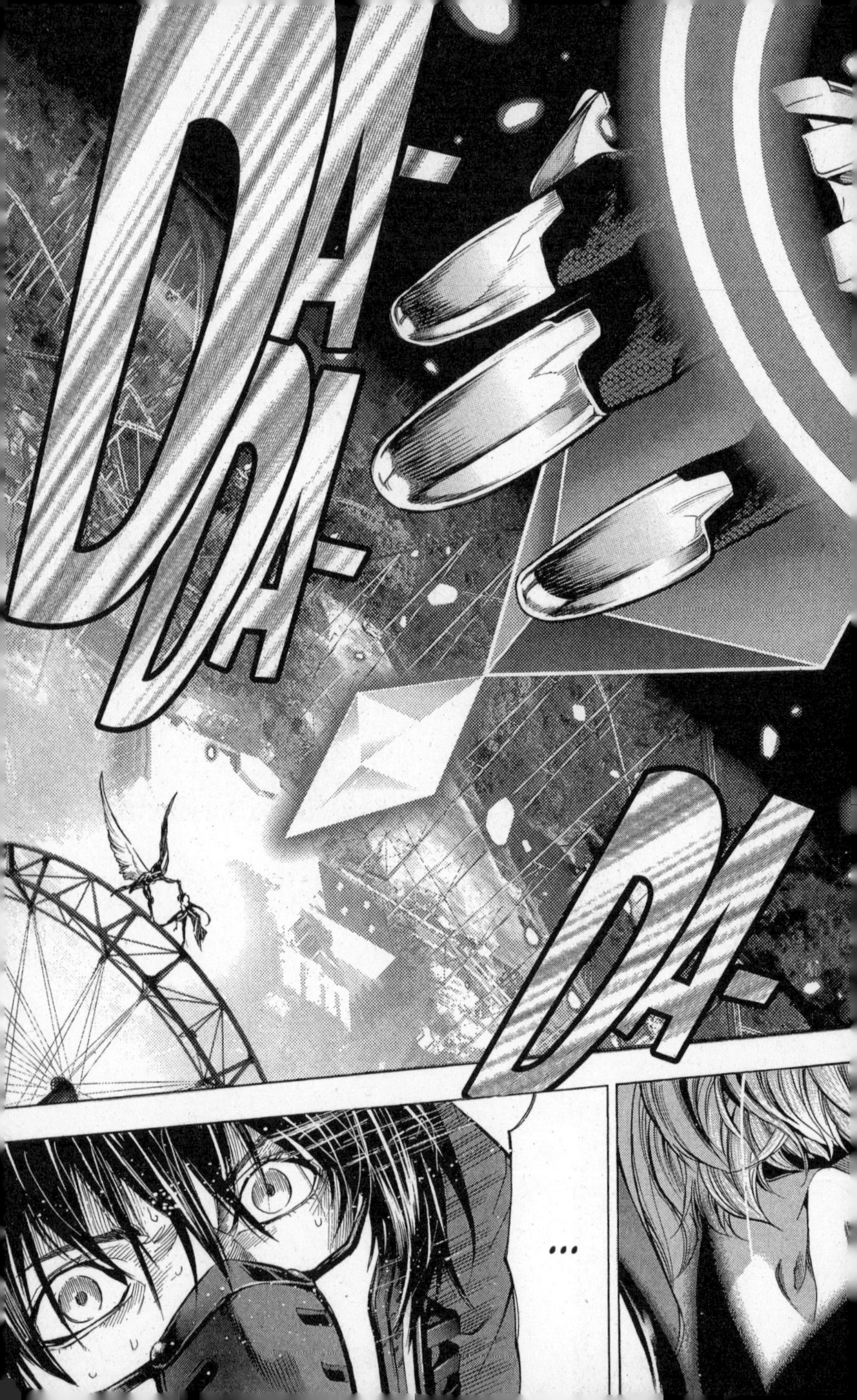
DA-DA-
DA-
...

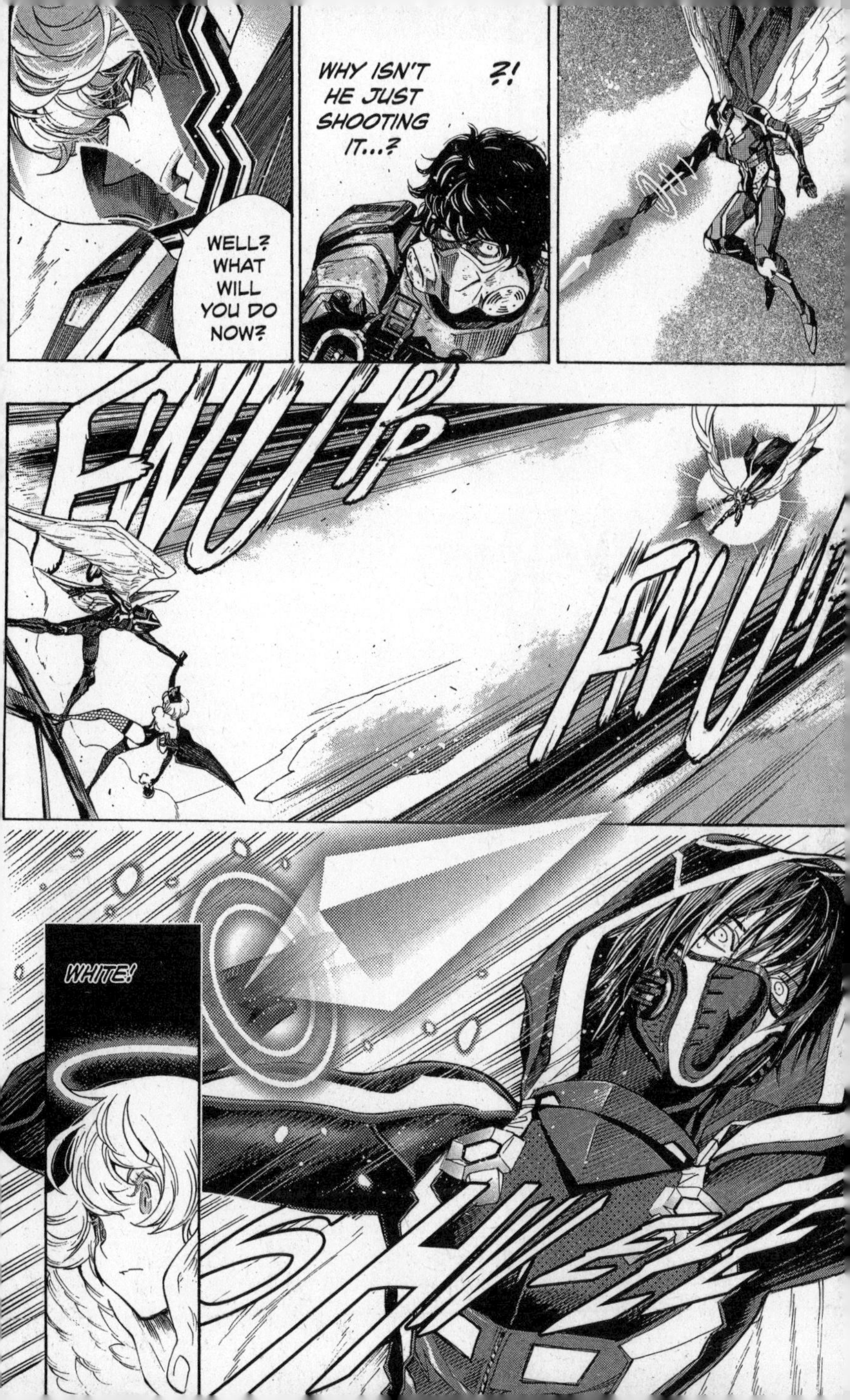
?!
WHY ISN'T HE JUST SHOOTING IT...?
WELL? WHAT WILL YOU DO NOW?
WHITE!

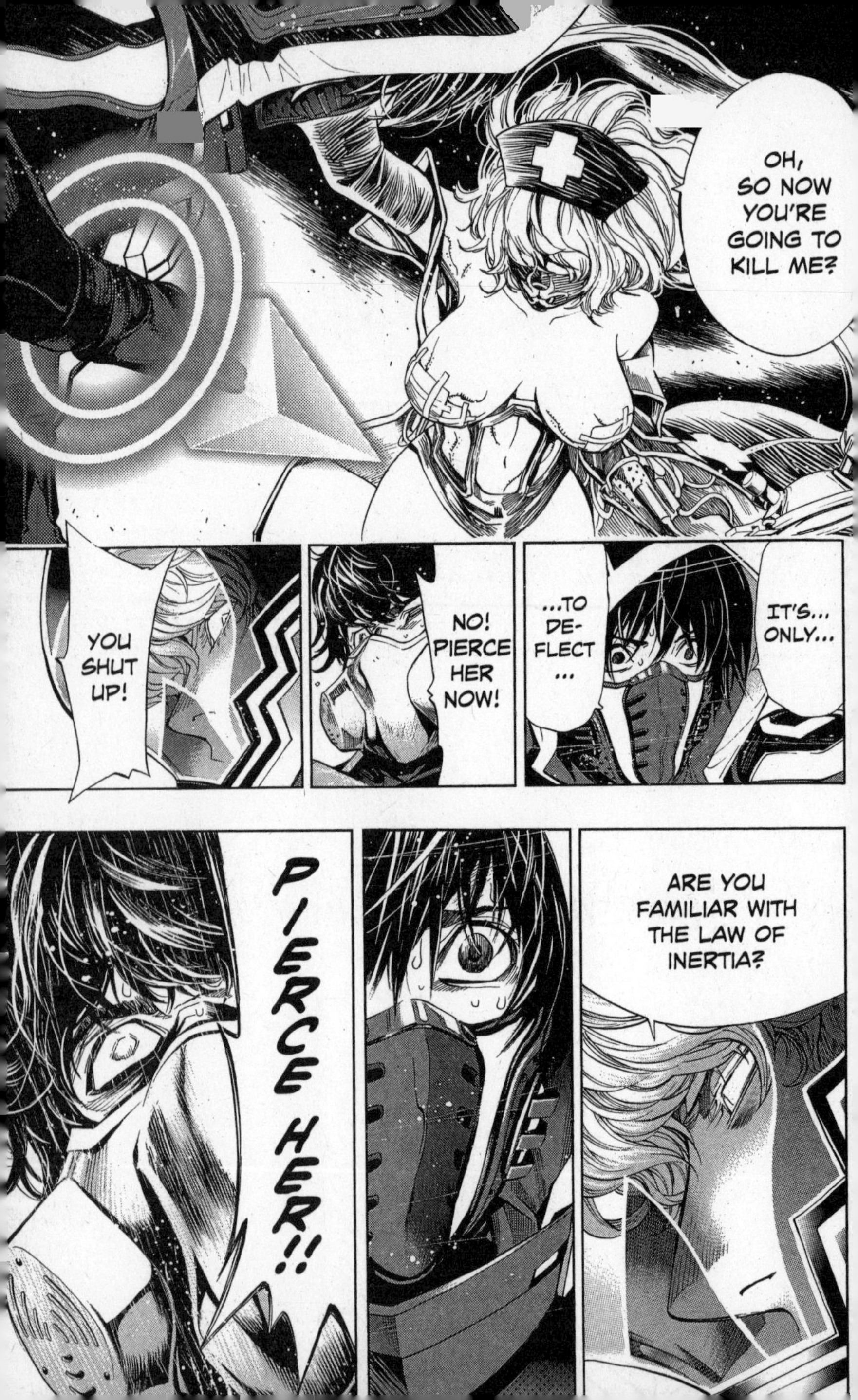
OH, SO NOW YOU'RE GOING TO KILL ME?
IT'S... ONLY...
...TO DE-FLECT ...
NO! PIERCE HER NOW!
YOU SHUT UP!
ARE YOU FAMILIAR WITH THE LAW OF INERTIA?
PIERCE HER!!

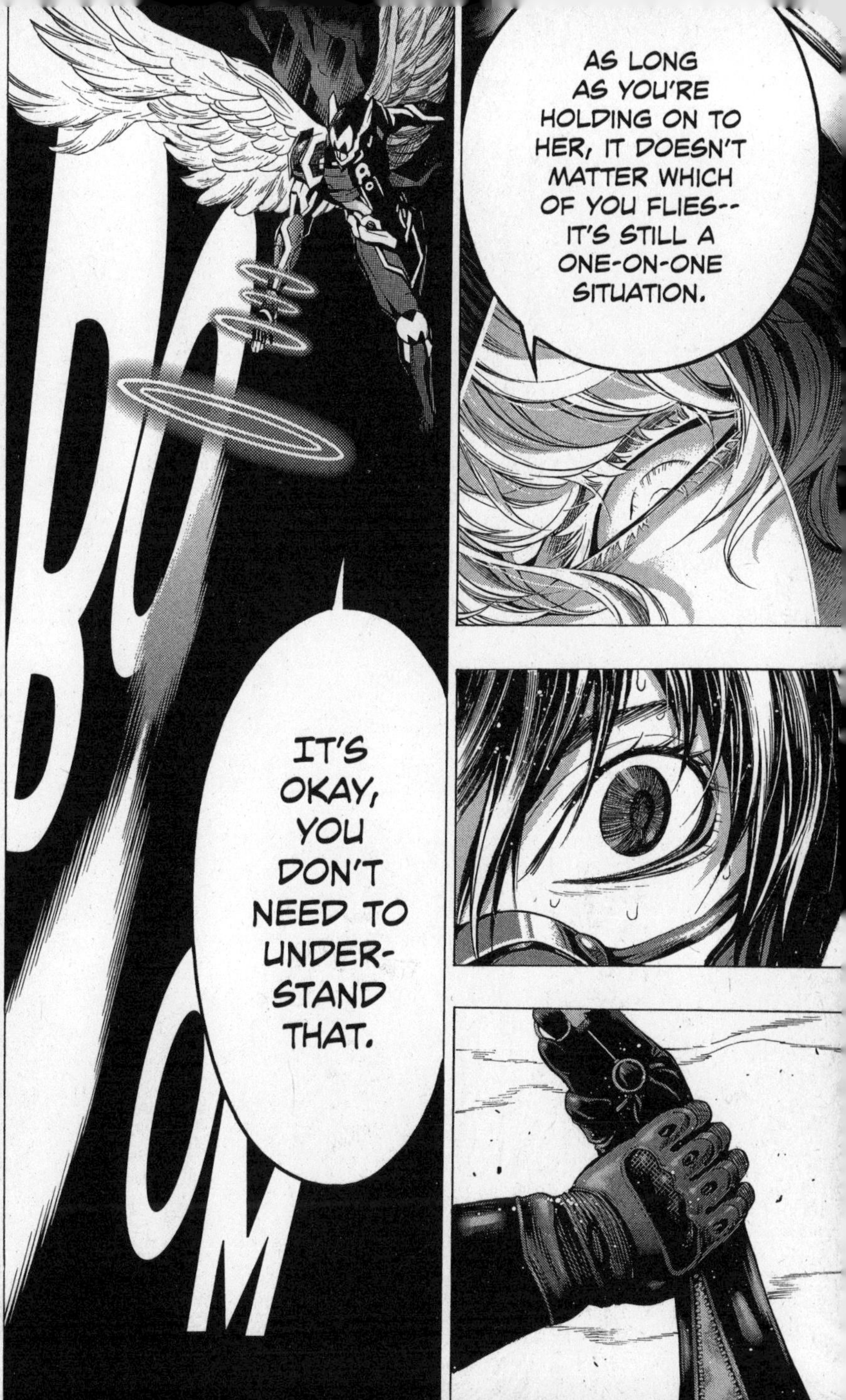
AS LONG AS YOU'RE HOLDING ON TO HER, IT DOESN'T MATTER WHICH OF YOU FLIES-- IT'S STILL A ONE-ON-ONE SITUATION.
IT'S OKAY, YOU DON'T NEED TO UNDER-STAND THAT.
BOOM

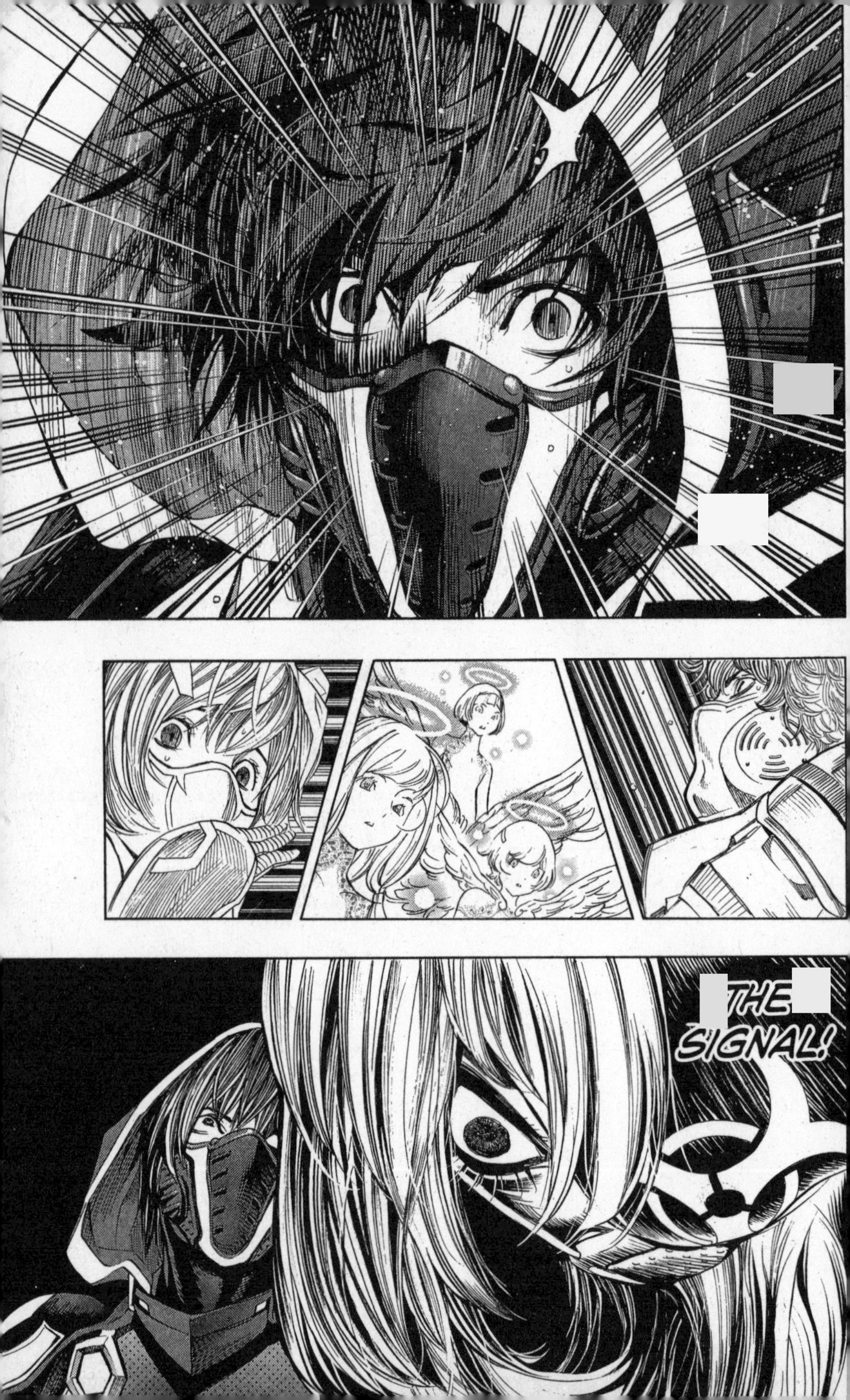
THE
SIGNAL!

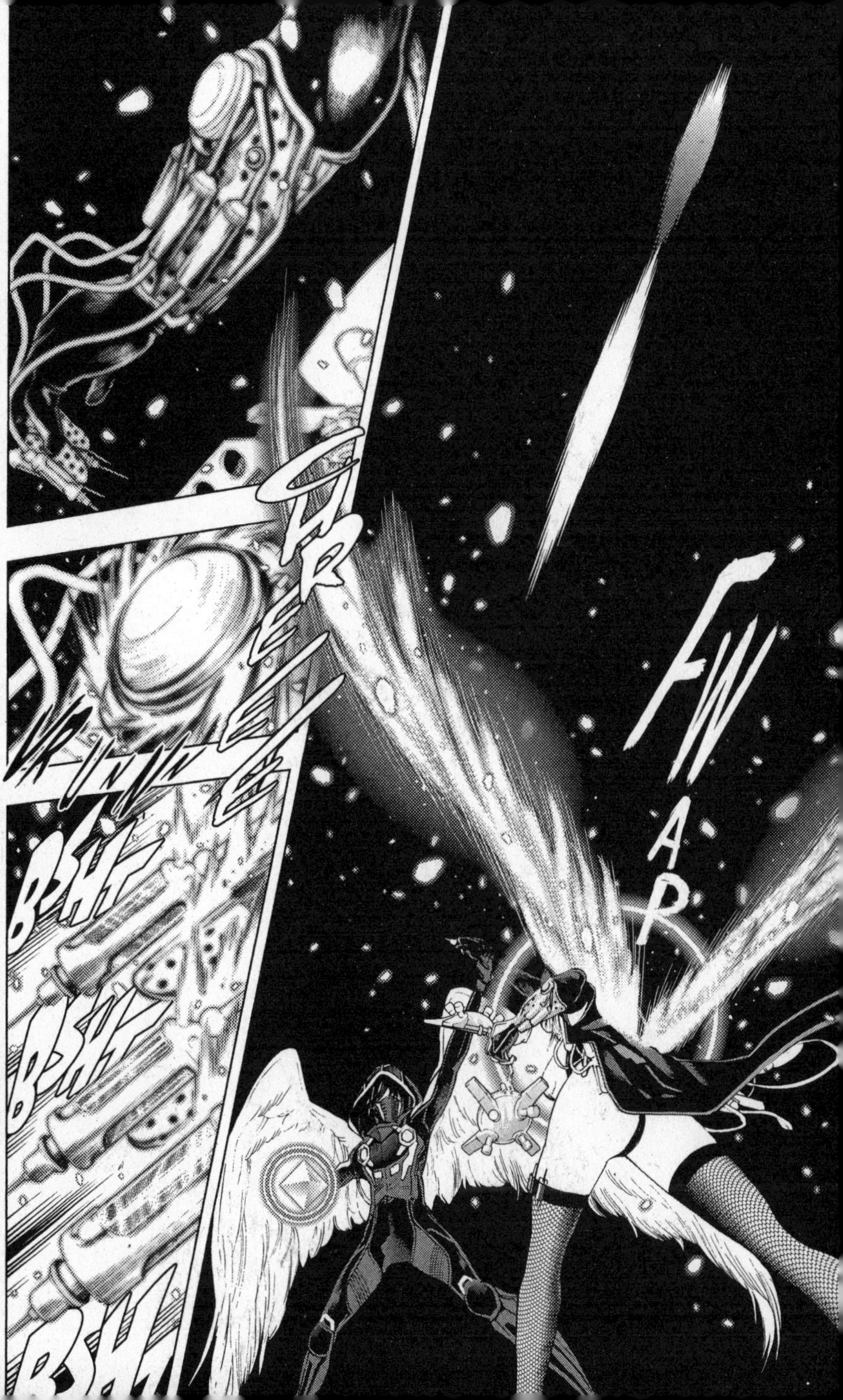
FWAP

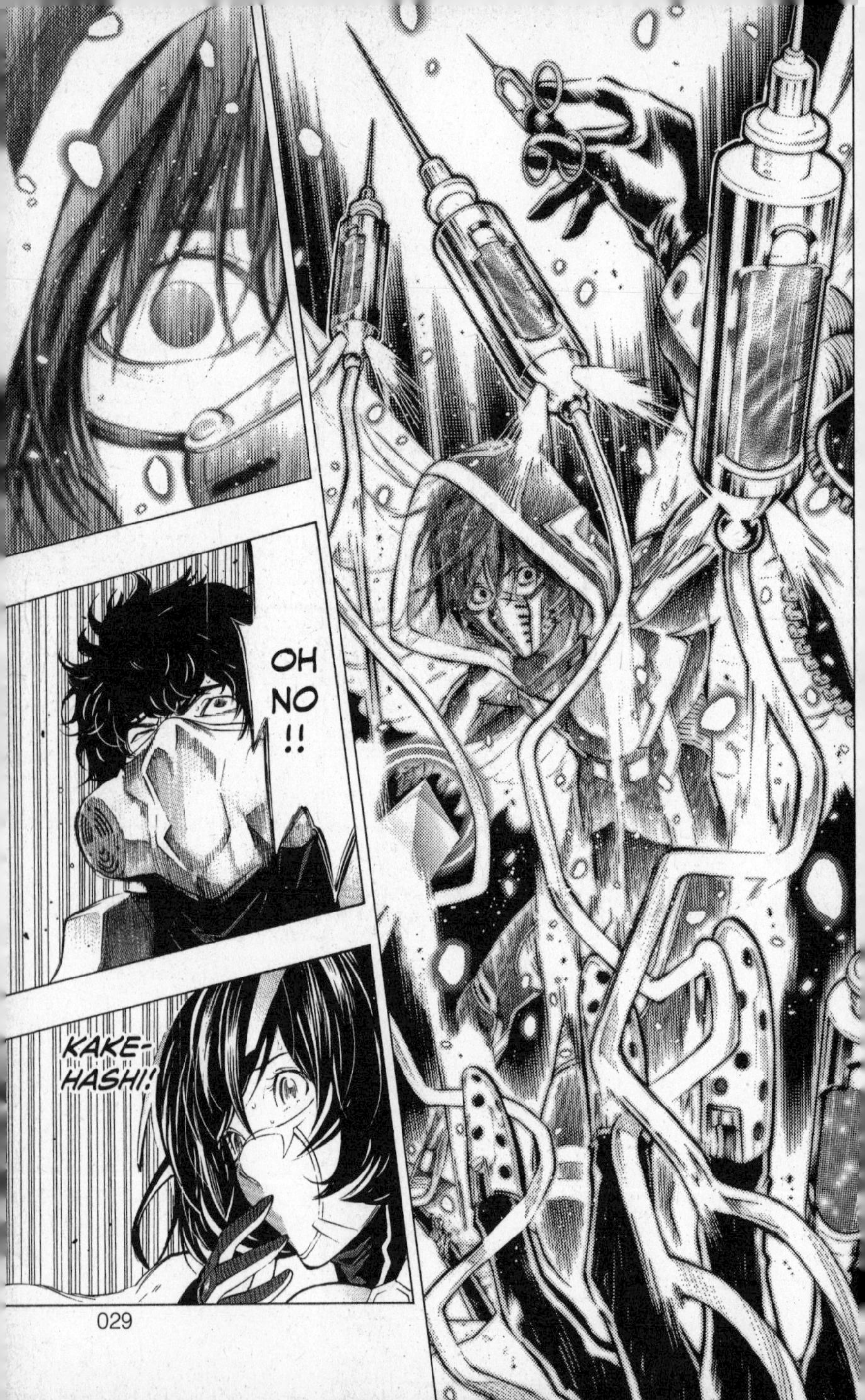
OH NO !!
KAKE-HASHI!

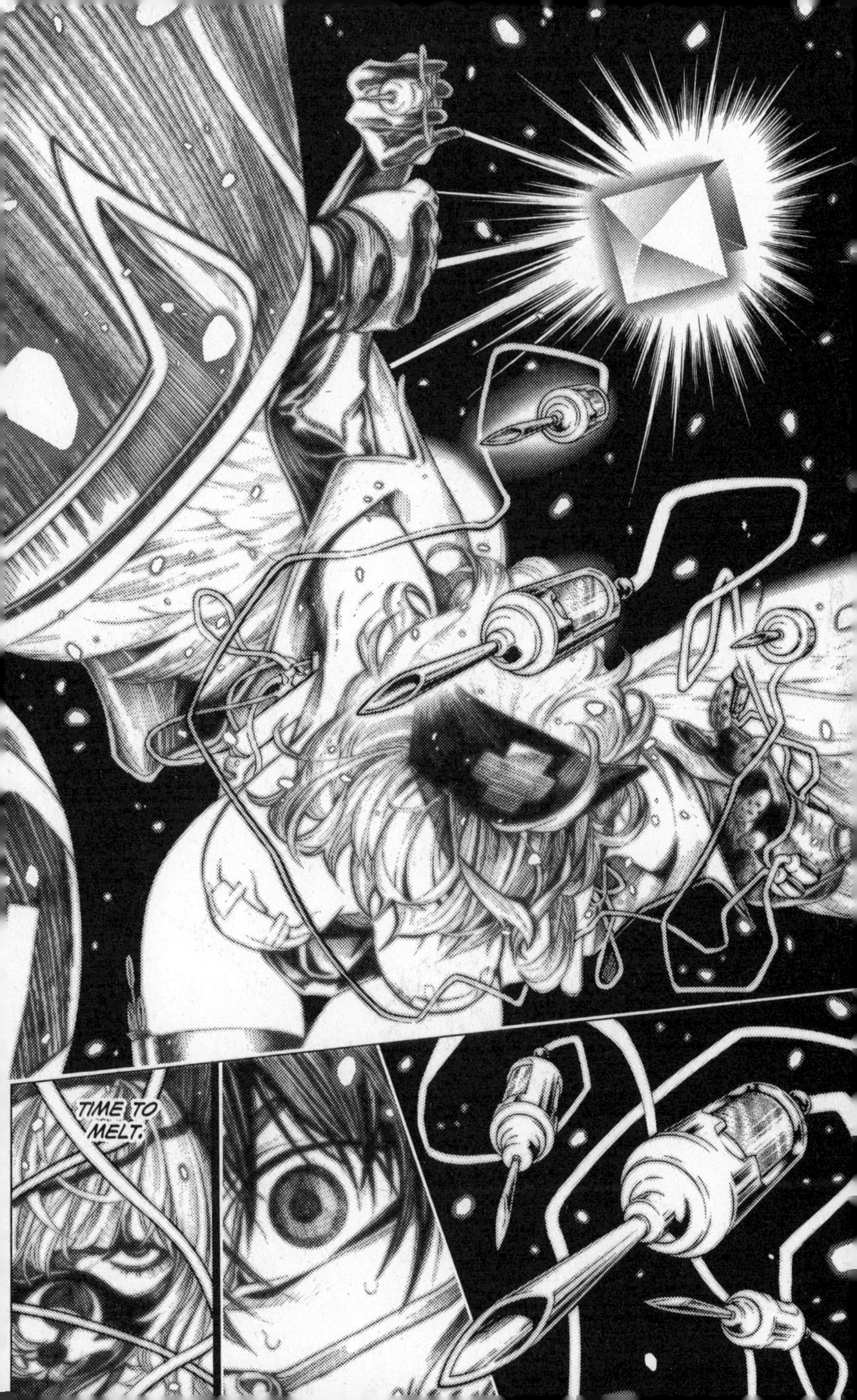
TIME TO MELT.

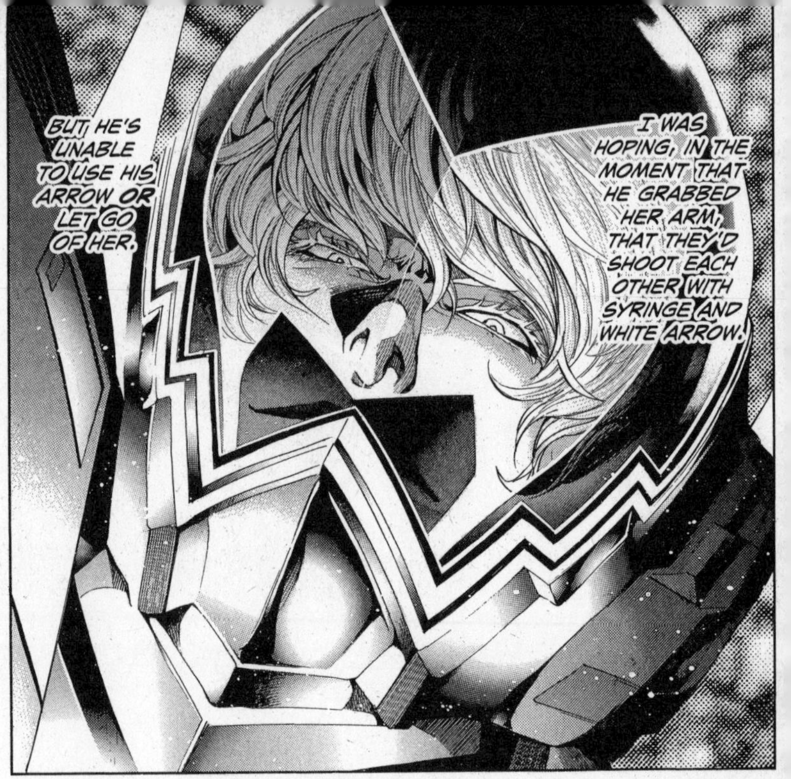
I WAS HOPING, IN THE MOMENT THAT HE GRABBED HER ARM, THAT THEY'D SHOOT EACH OTHER WITH SYRINGE AND WHITE ARROW.
BUT HE'S UNABLE TO USE HIS ARROW OR LET GO OF HER.

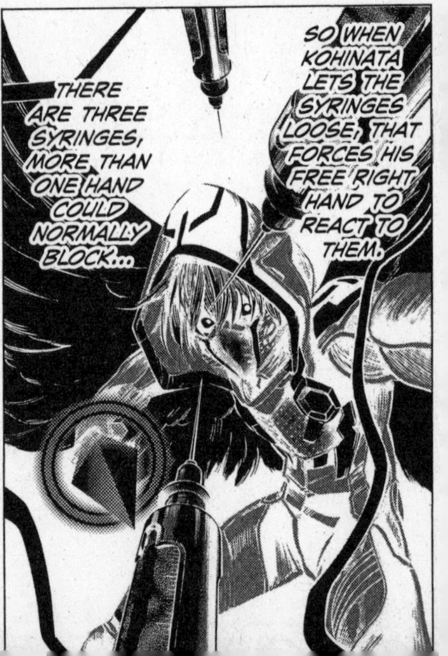
SO WHEN KOHINATA LETS THE SYRINGES LOOSE, THAT FORCES HIS FREE RIGHT HAND TO REACT TO THEM.
THERE ARE THREE SYRINGES, MORE THAN ONE HAND COULD NORMALLY BLOCK...

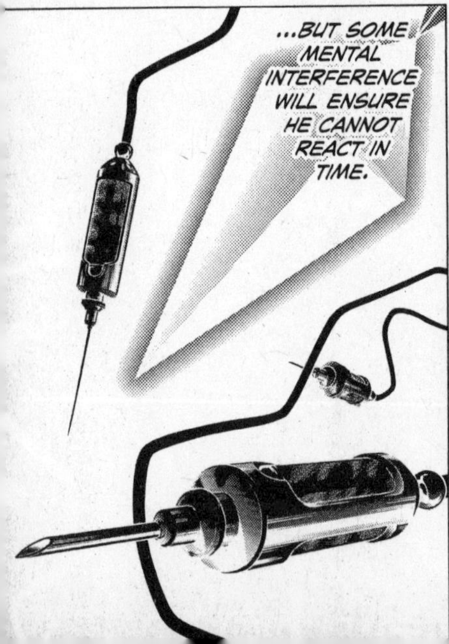
...BUT SOME MENTAL INTERFERENCE WILL ENSURE HE CANNOT REACT IN TIME.

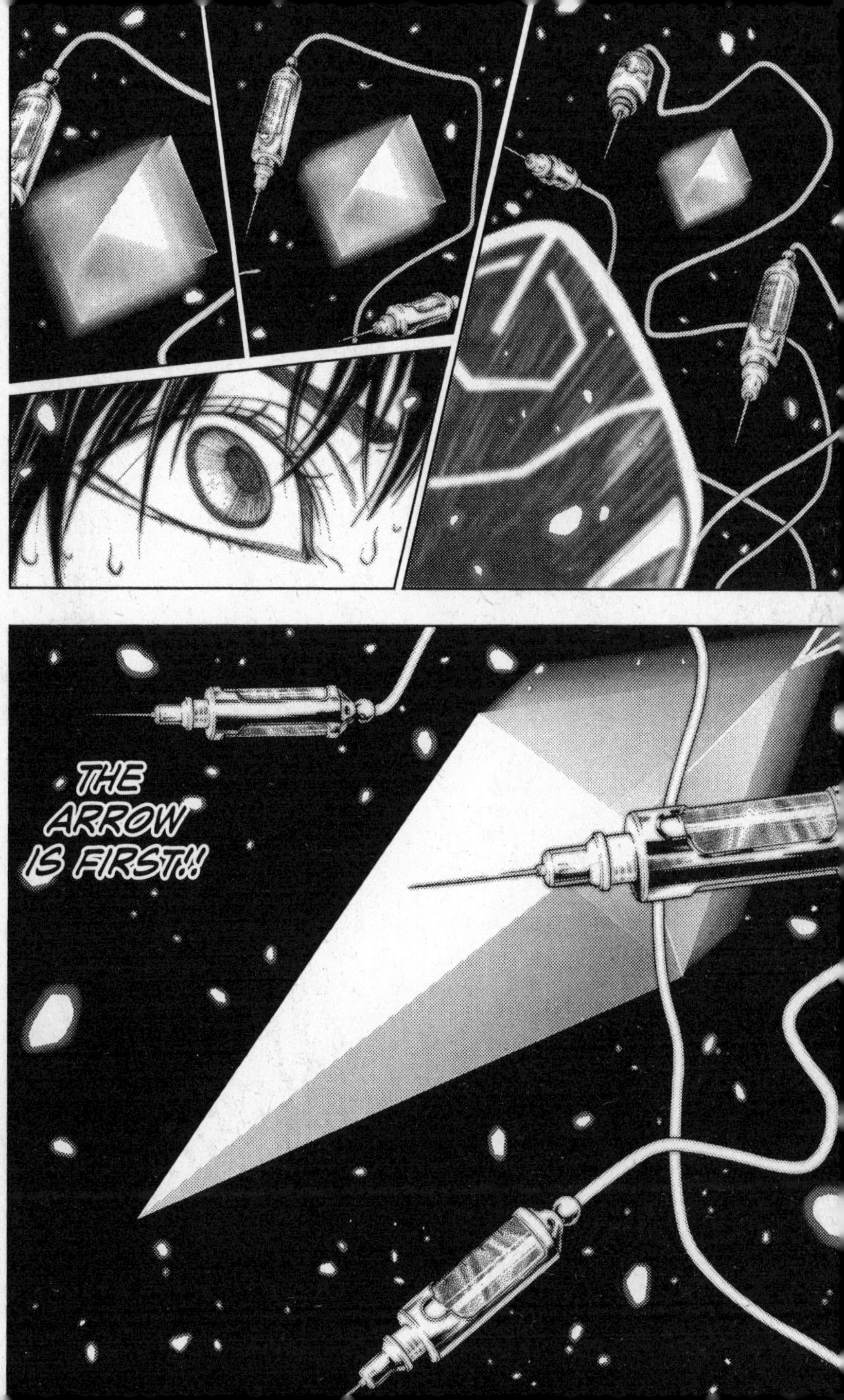
THE ARROW IS FIRST!!

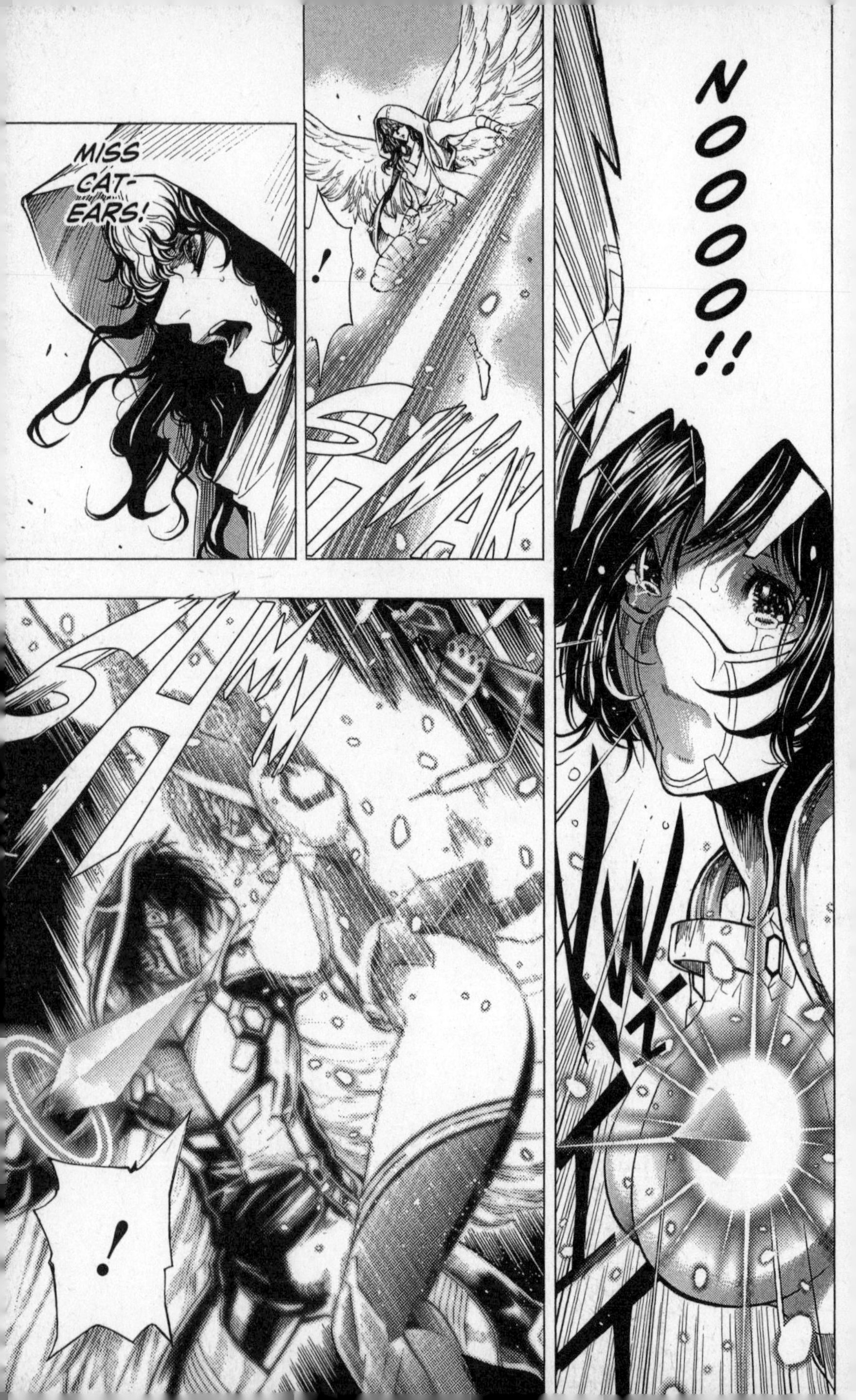
NOOOO!!
!
MISS CAT-EARS!
!

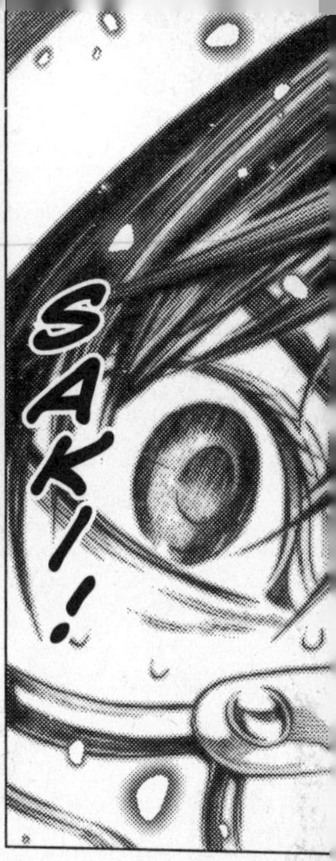
SAKI!!
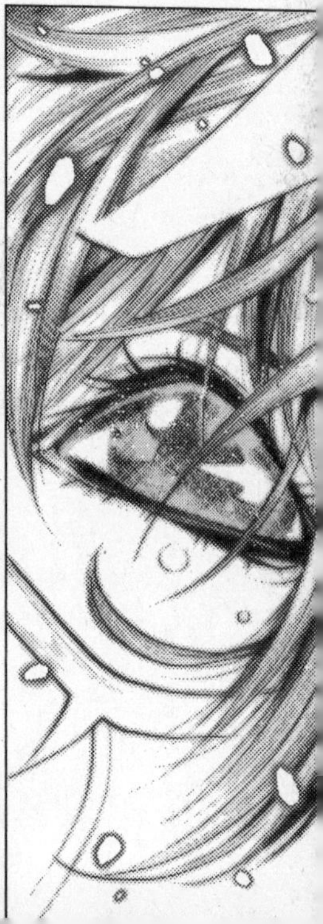
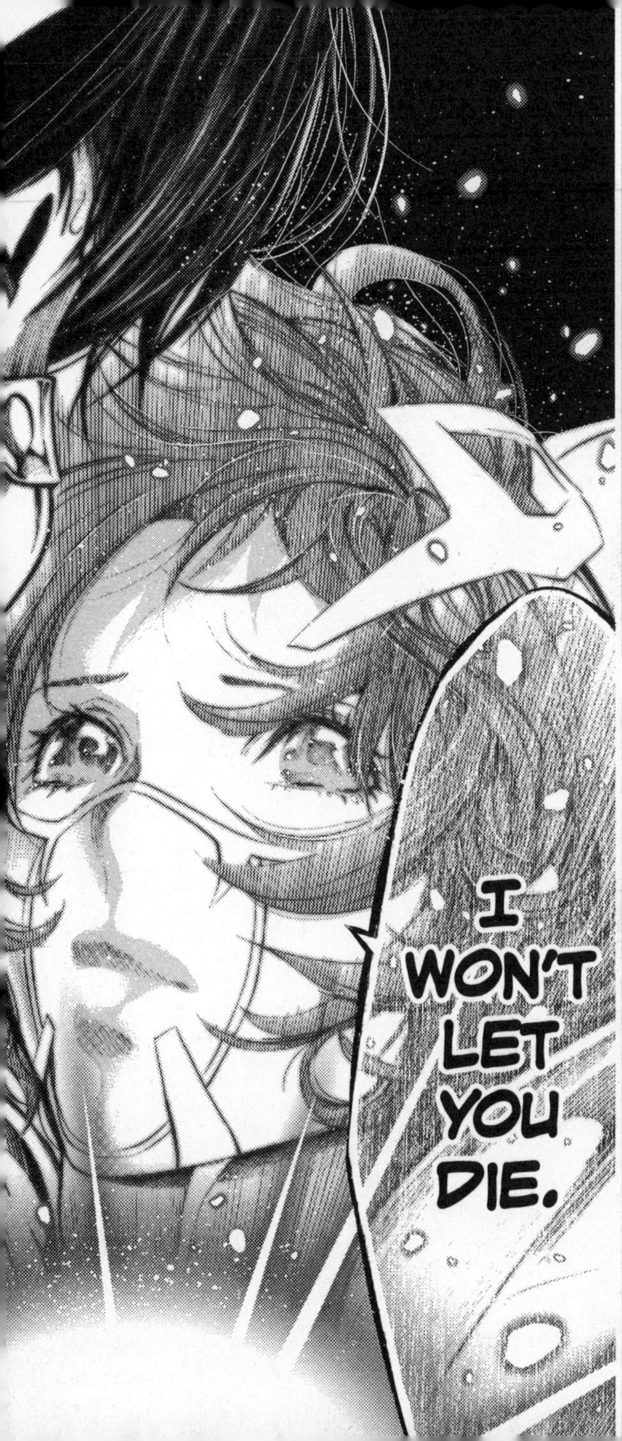
I WON'T LET YOU DIE.

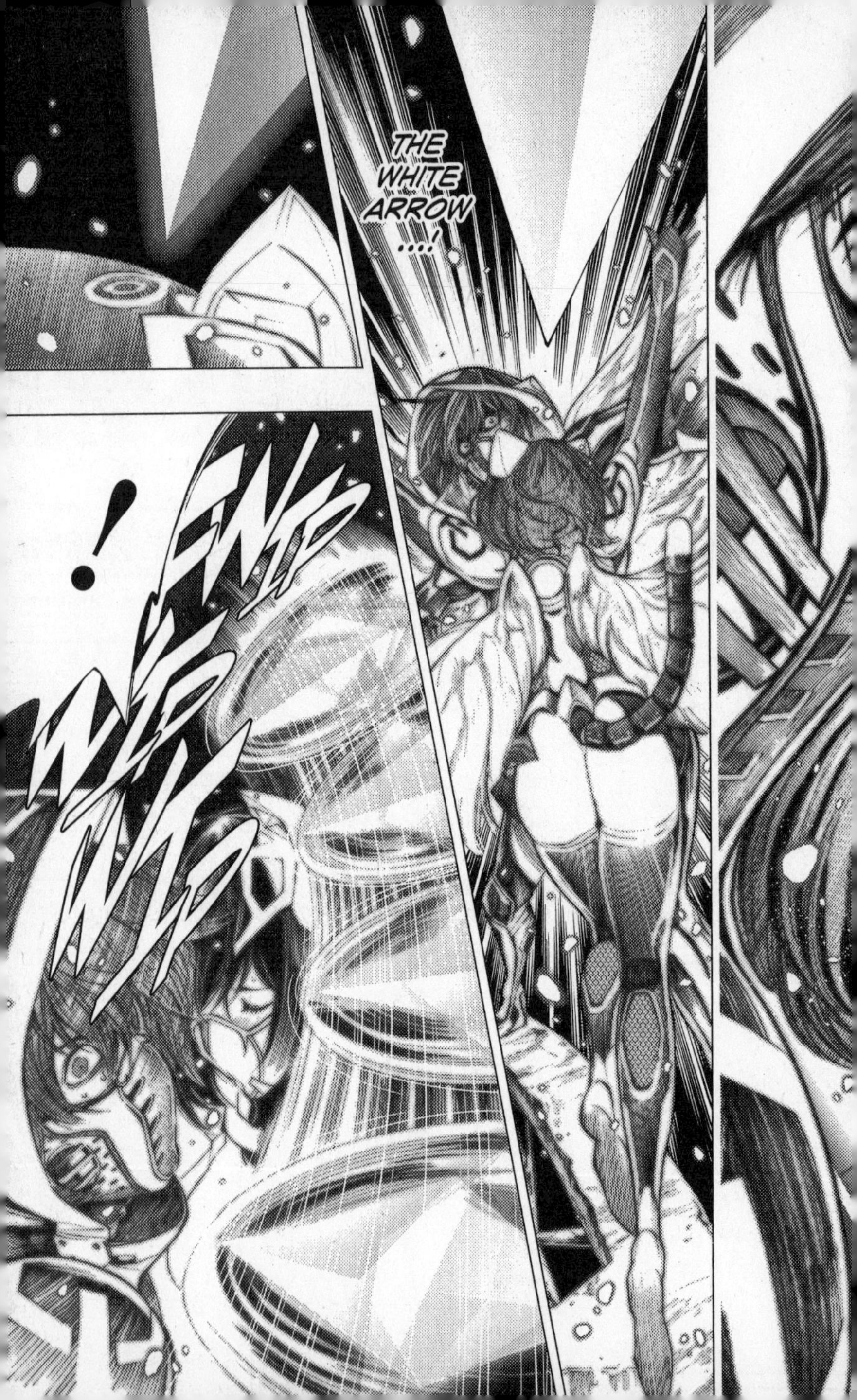
THE WHITE ARROW ...!
!

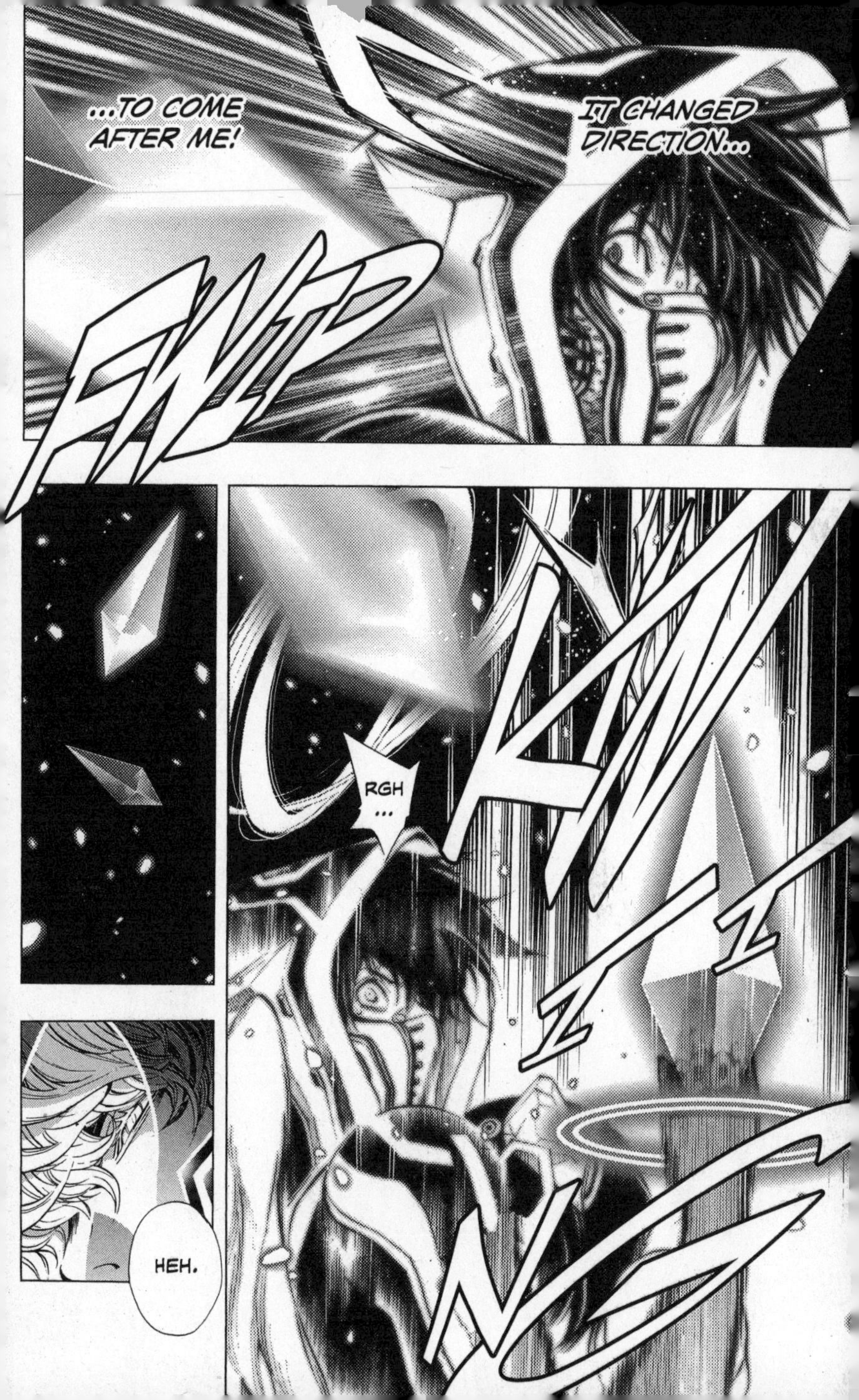
IT CHANGED DIRECTION...
...TO COME AFTER ME!
FWIP
RGH ...
HEH.

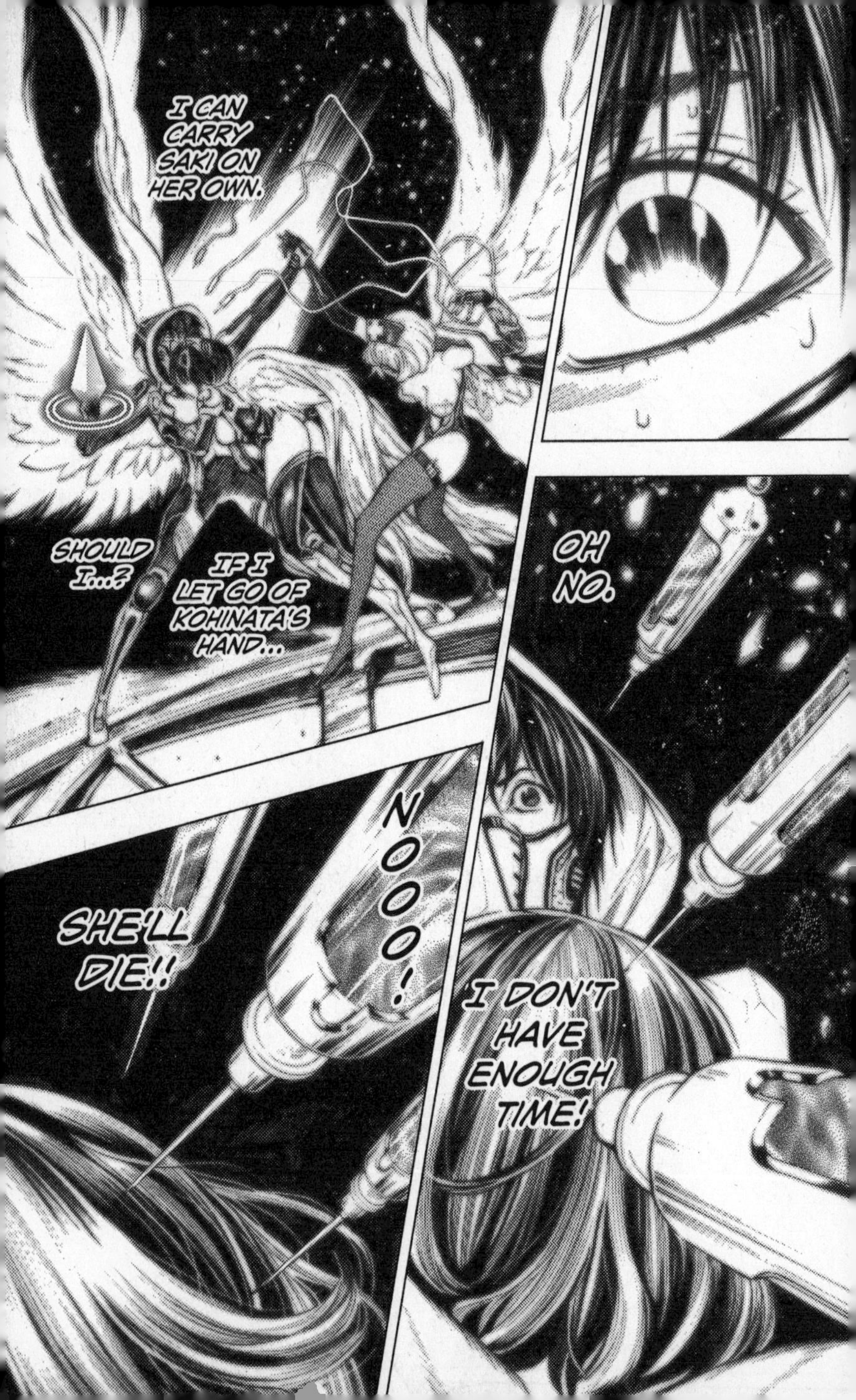

I CAN CARRY SAKI ON HER OWN.
IF I LET GO OF KOHINATA'S HAND...
SHOULD I...?
OH NO.
I DON'T HAVE ENOUGH TIME!
NOOOO!
SHE'LL DIE!!

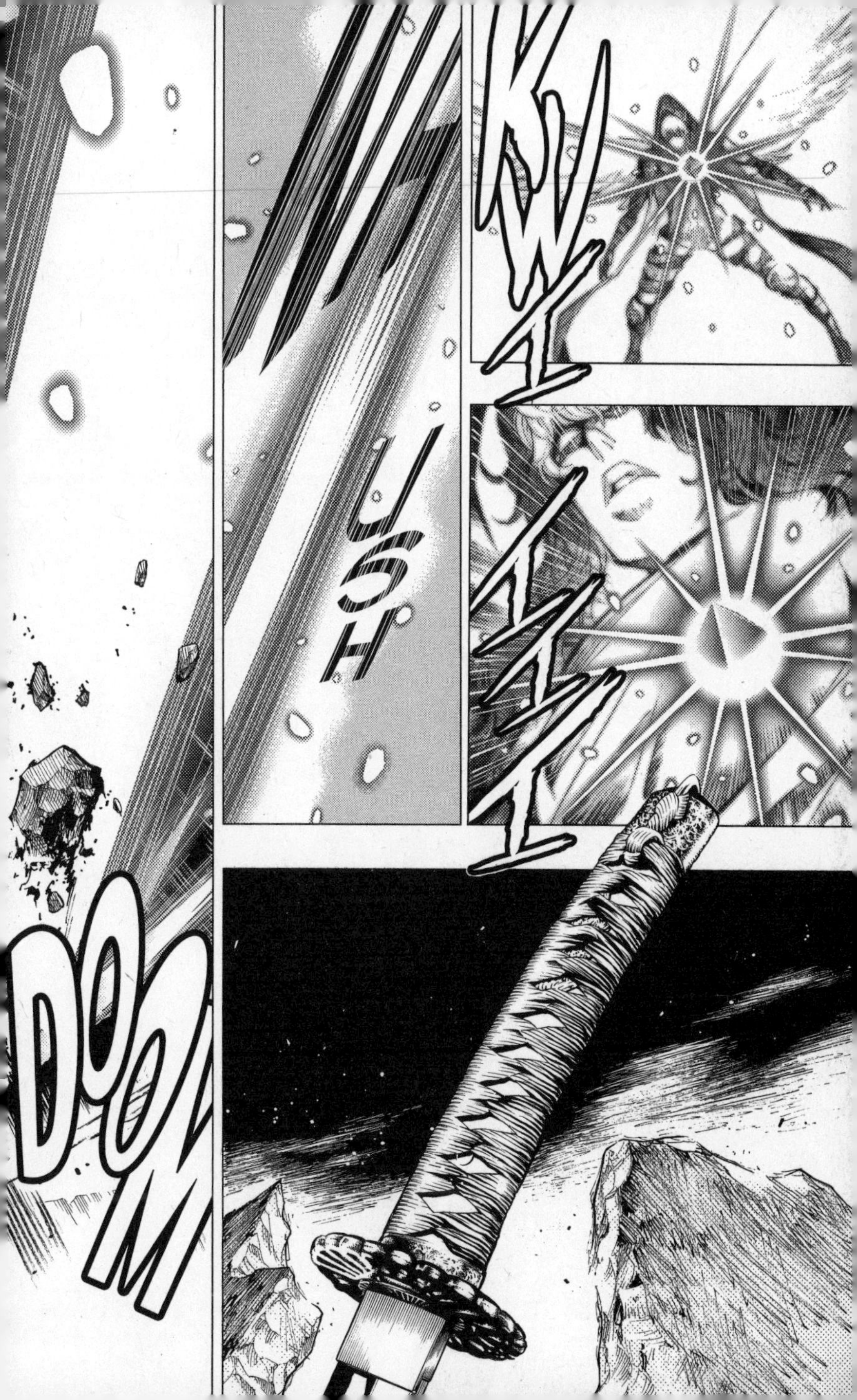
KWIIIII
USH
DOOOM

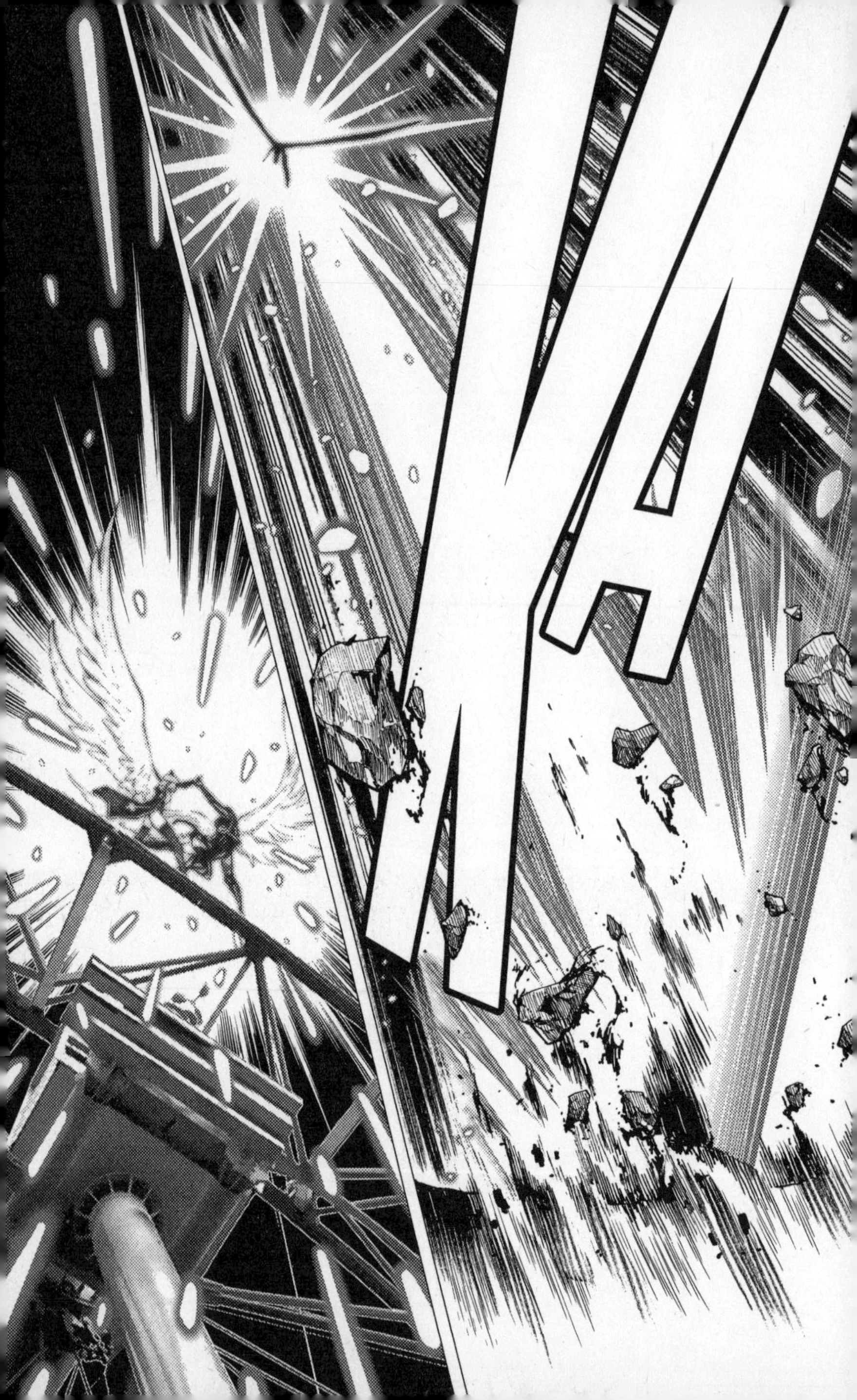
KA

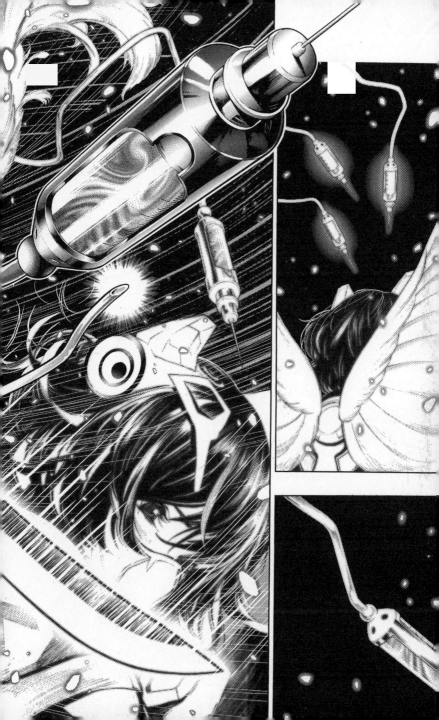

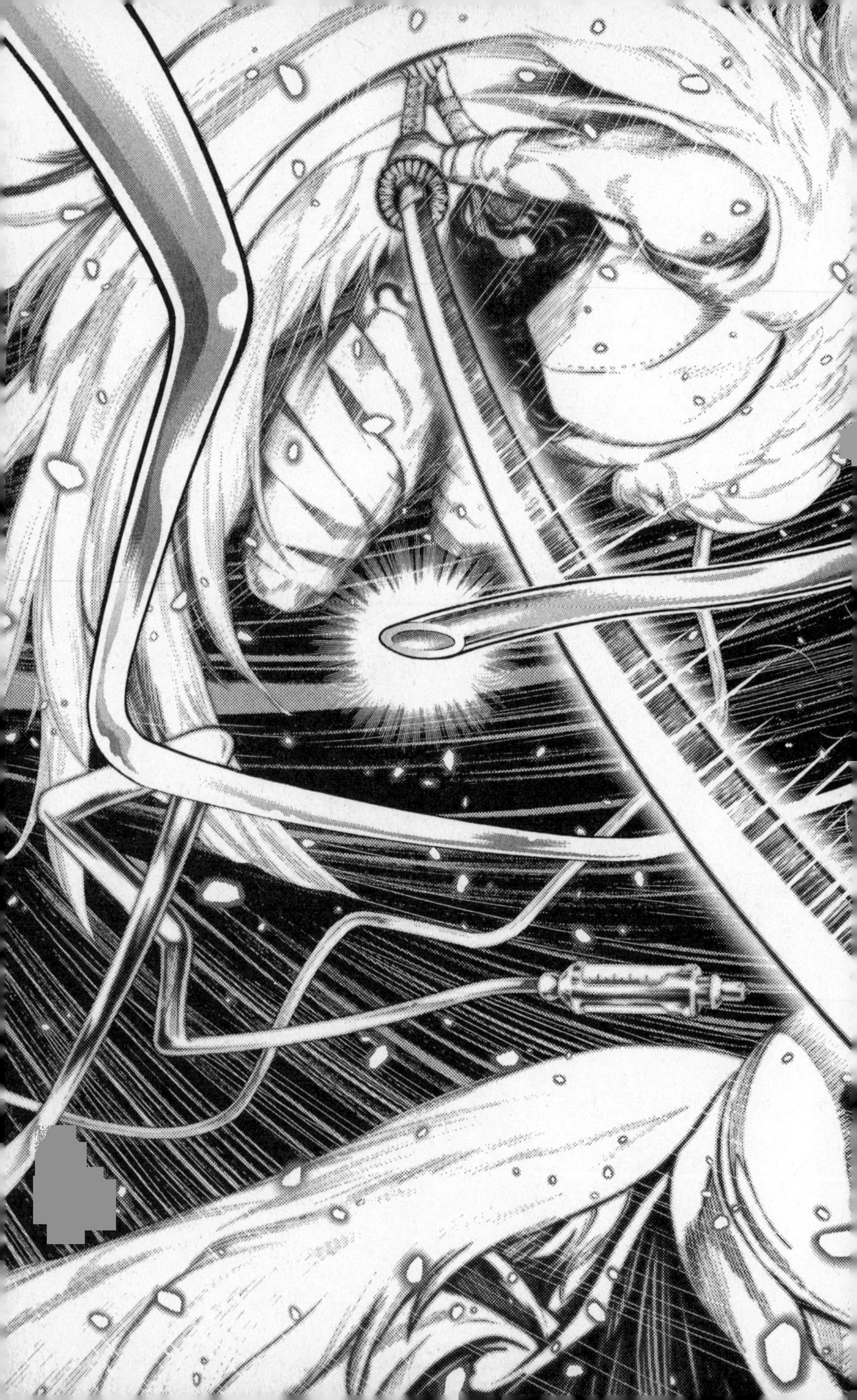

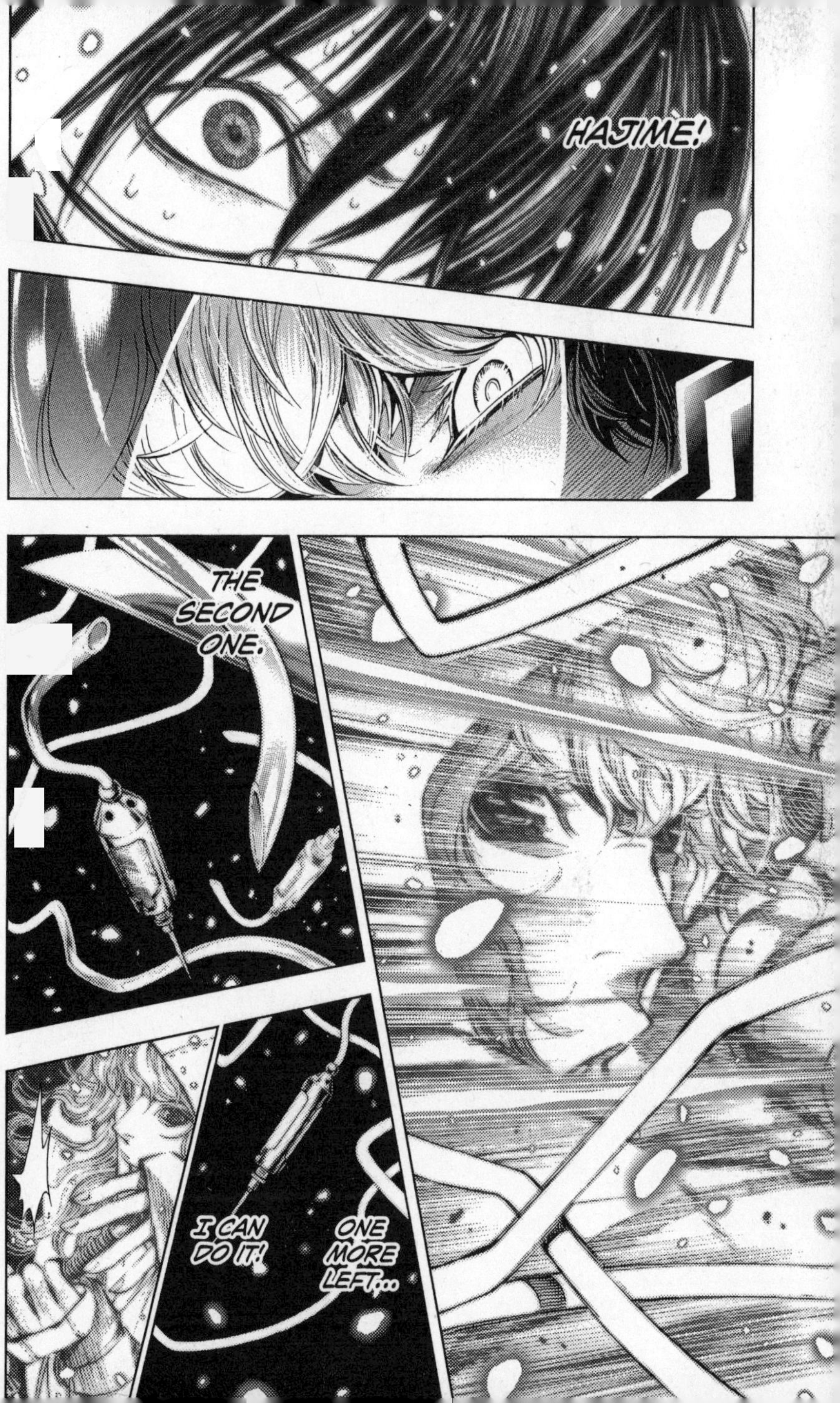
HAJIME!
THE SECOND ONE.
ONE MORE LEFT...
I CAN DO IT!

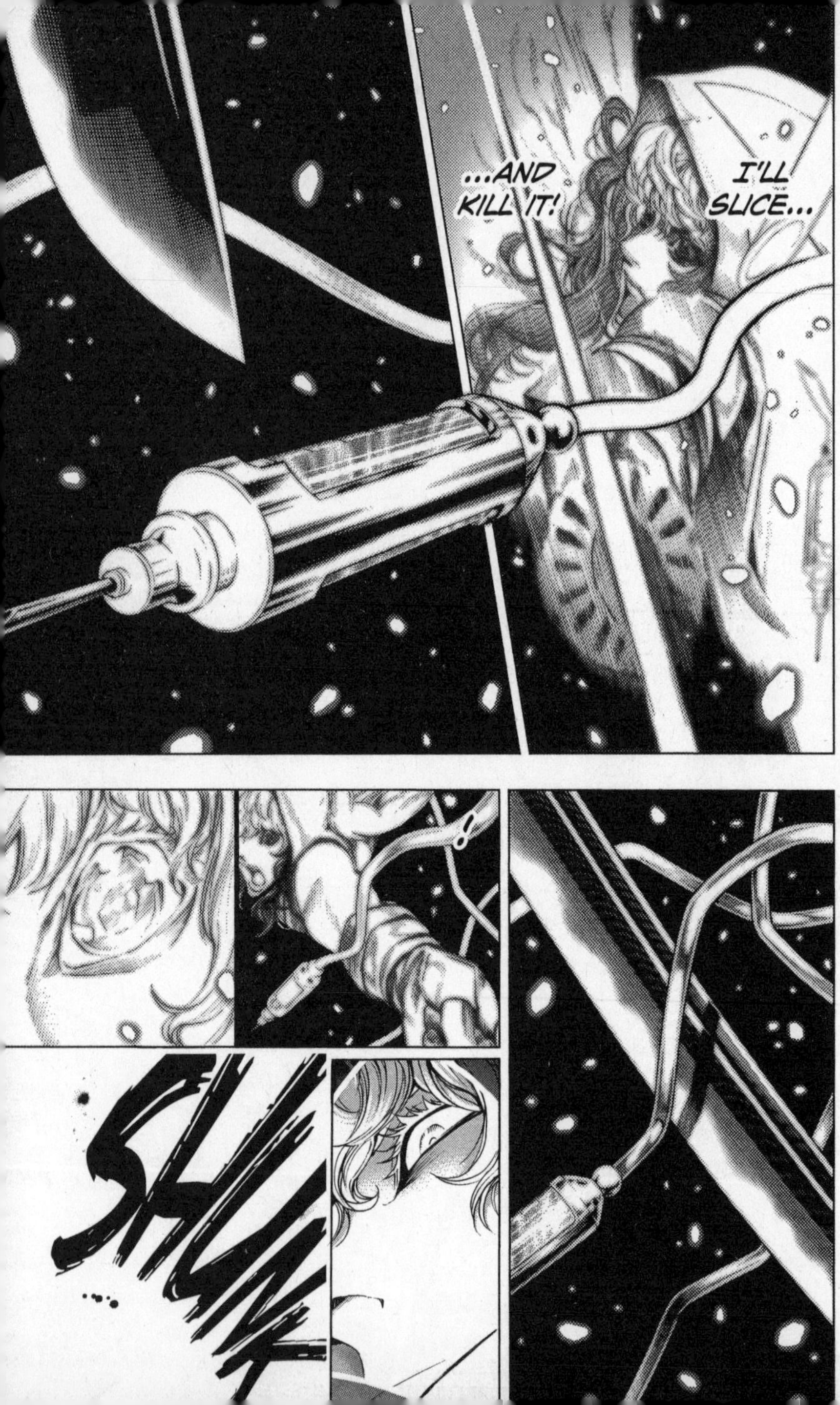
I'LL SLICE...
...AND KILL IT!
!
SHUNK

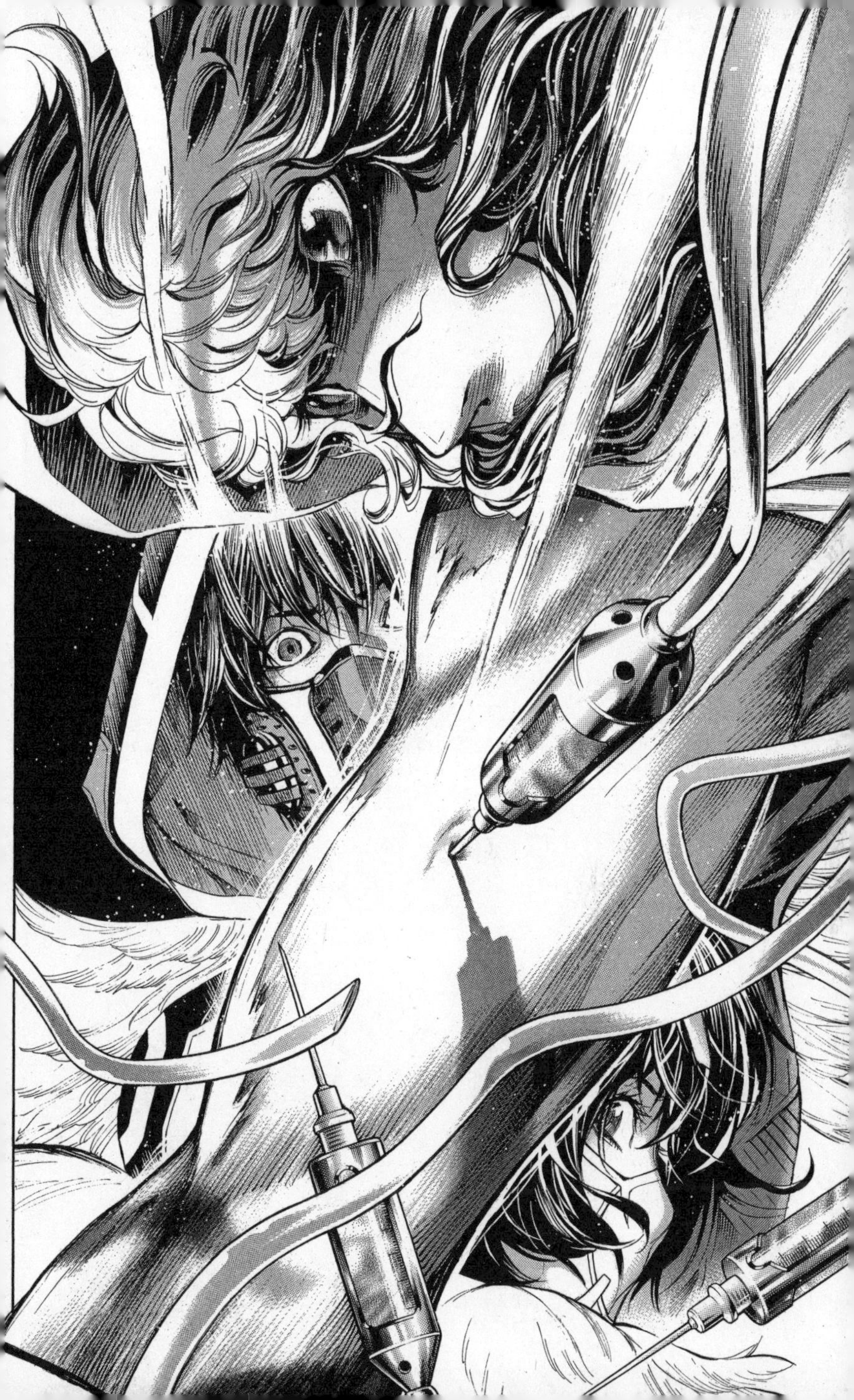

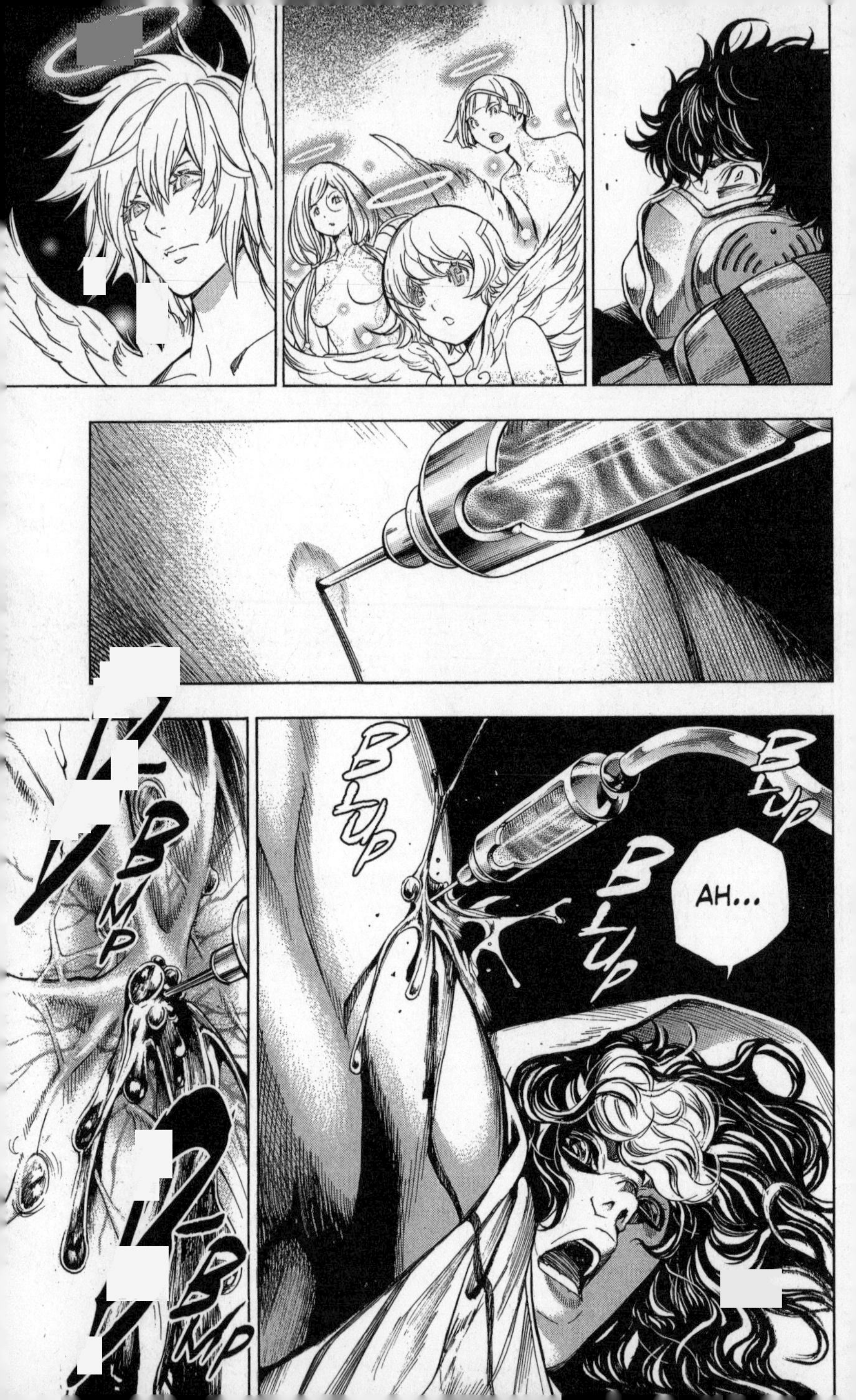
BLUP
BLUP
AH...
BLUP
BUMP

AHHHH!!
AAAAH!
SPLURK
ZLUBP
!!
YES! YES!
OOOH, LOOK AT IT DRIP!
HUH?

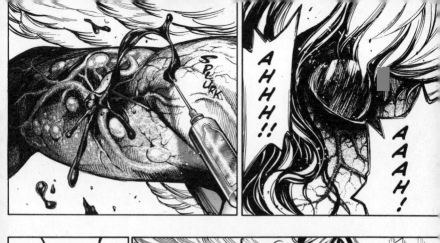

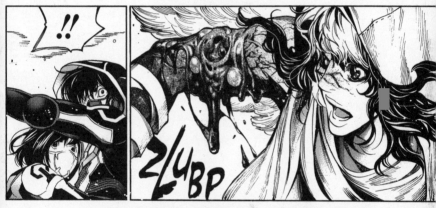

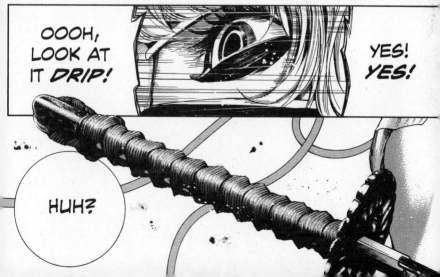

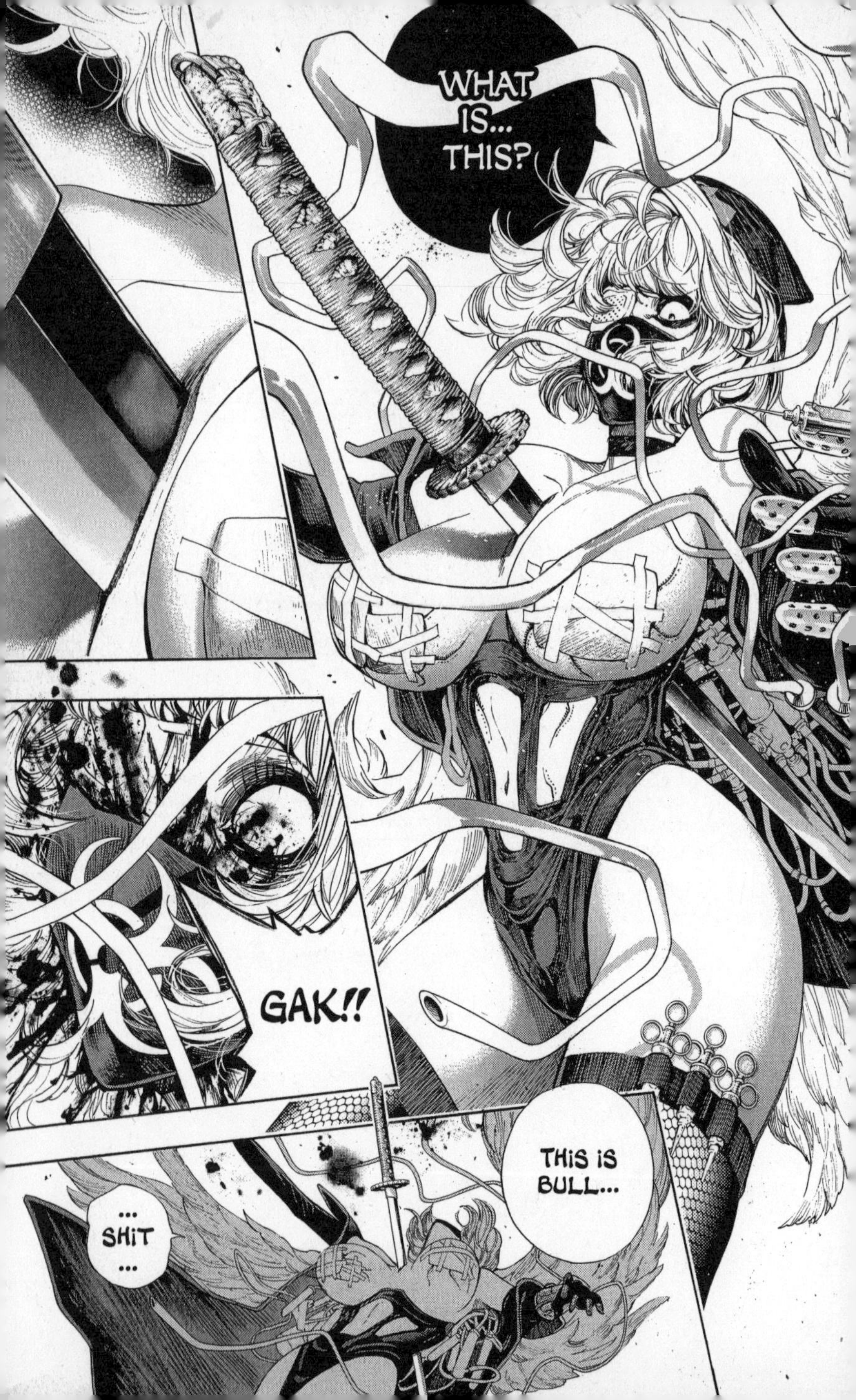
WHAT IS... THIS?
GAK!!
THIS IS BULL...
... SHIT ...

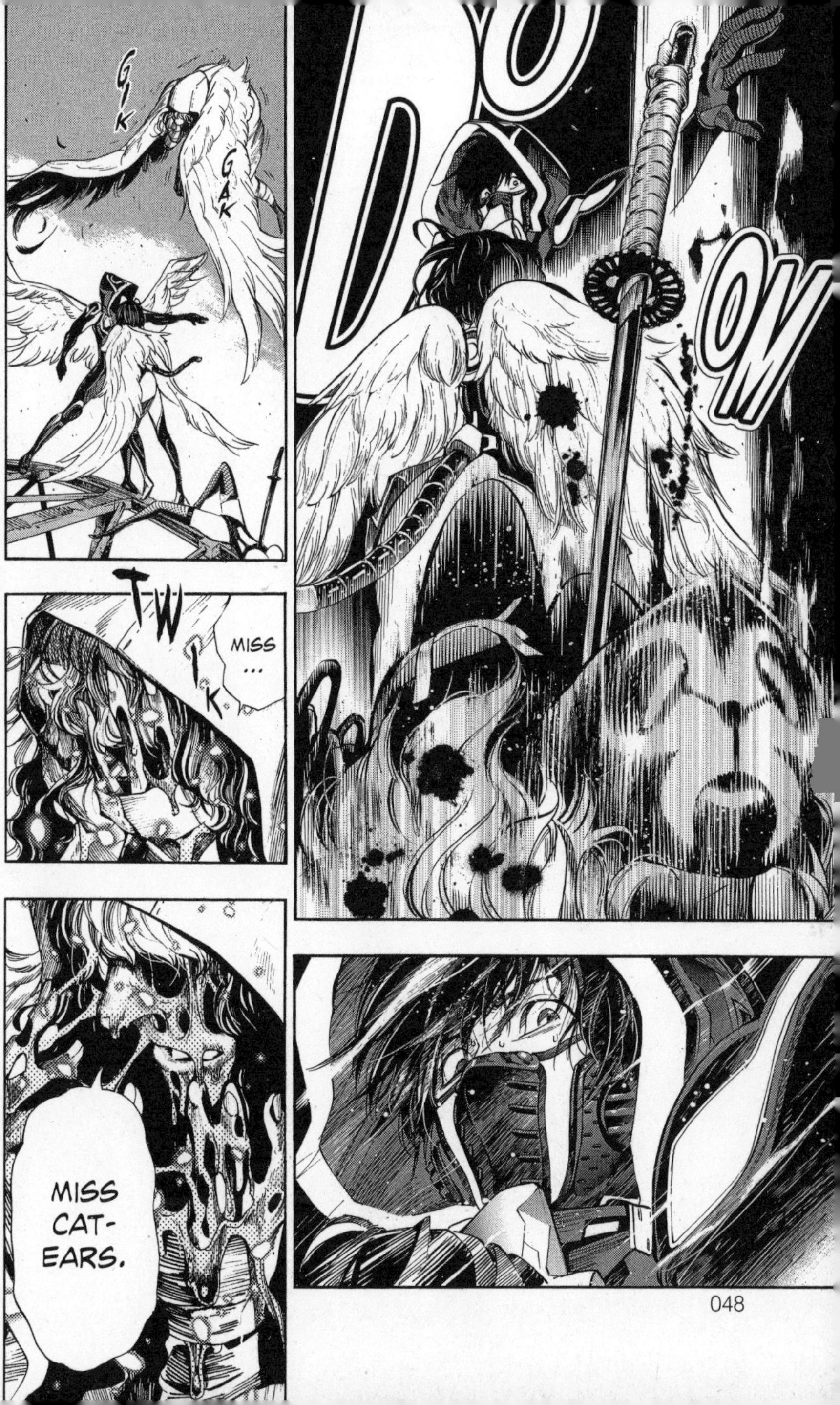
DOOM
GIK
GAK
TWIK
MISS...
MISS CAT-EARS.

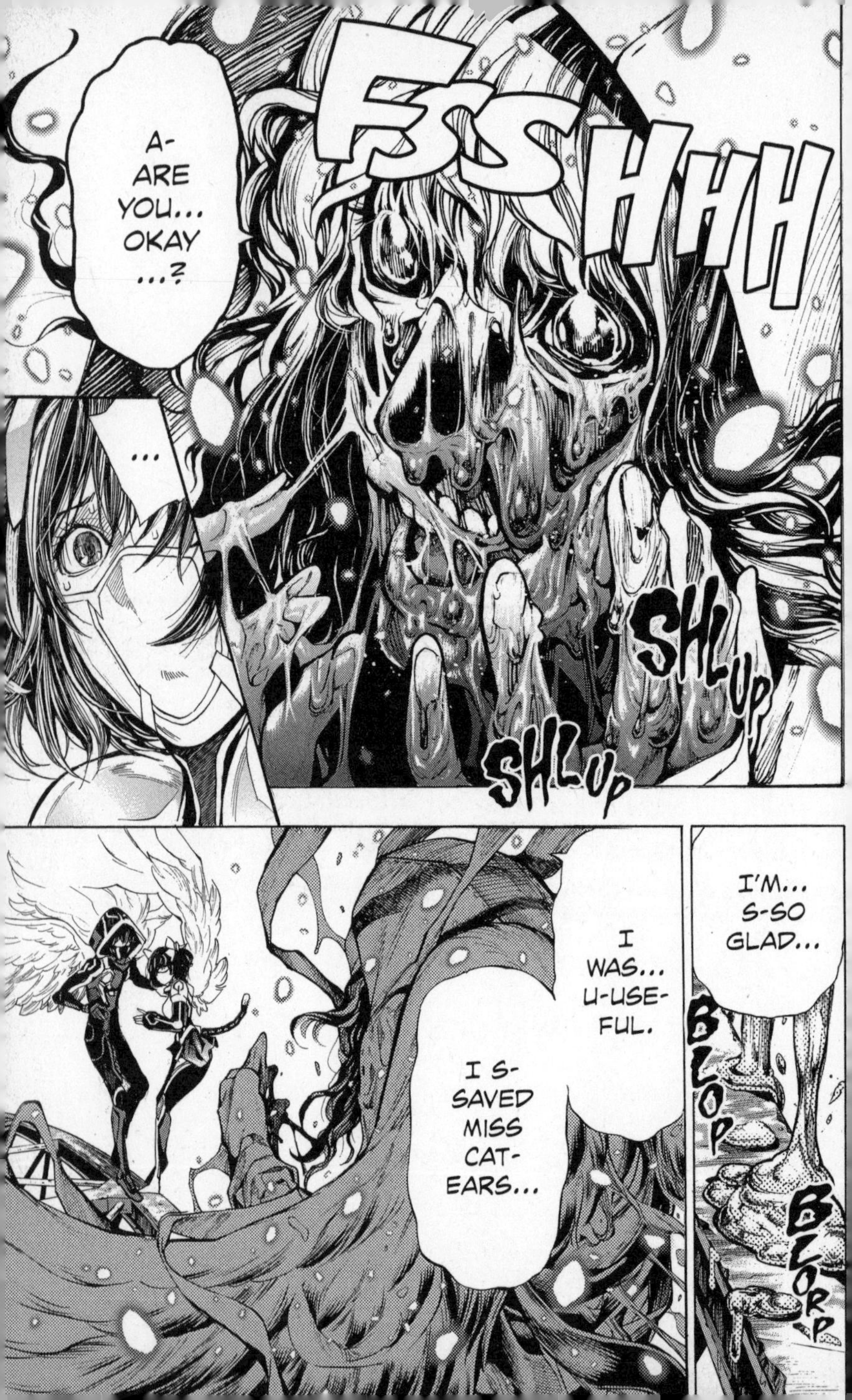
FSSHHH
A- ARE YOU... OKAY ...?
SHLUP
SHLUP
...
I'M... S-SO GLAD...
BLOP
BLORP
I WAS... U-USE-FUL.
I S-SAVED MISS CAT-EARS...

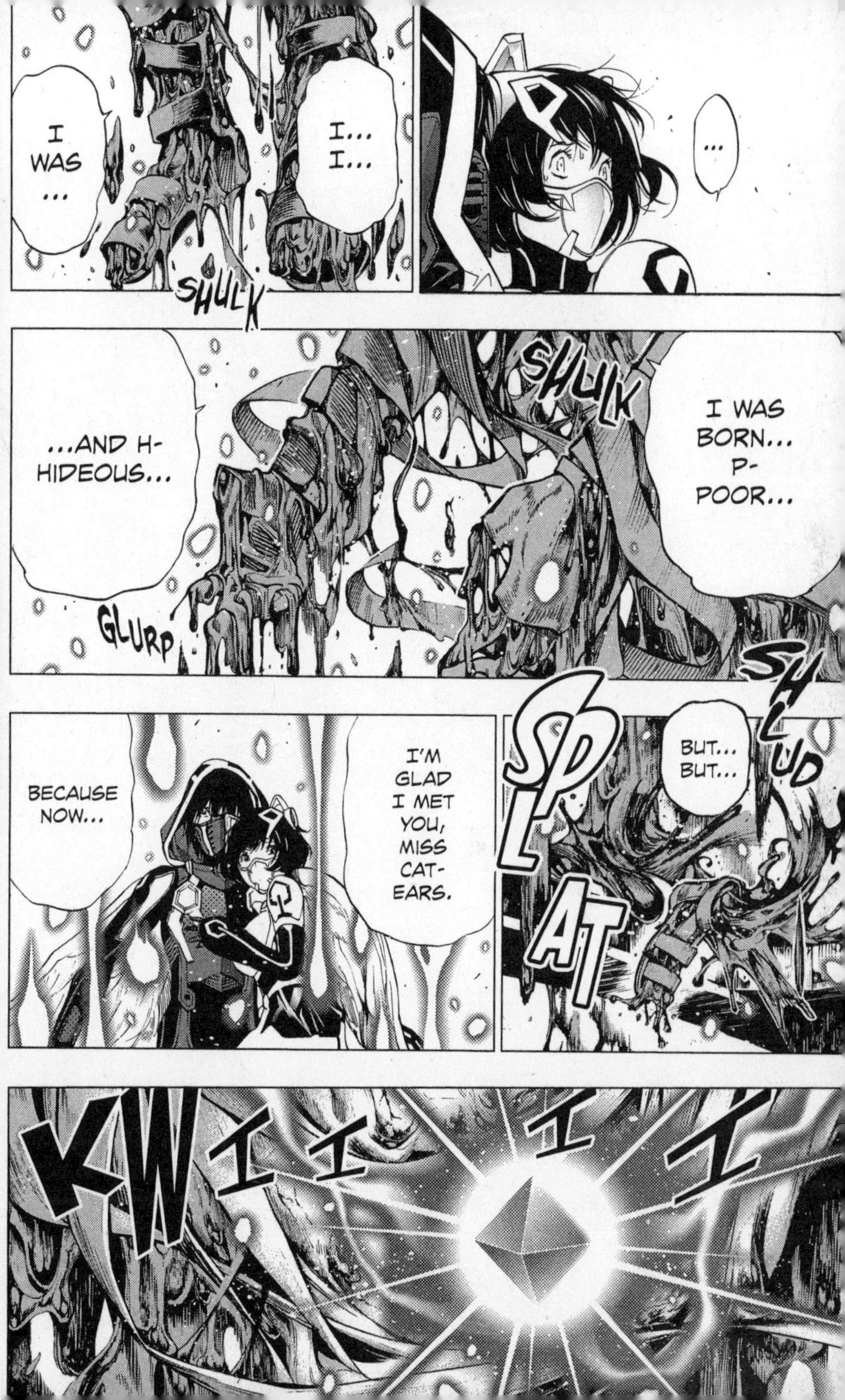
...
I... I...
I WAS ...
SHULK
I WAS BORN... P-POOR...
SHULK
...AND H-HIDEOUS...
GLURP
SHLUD
BUT... BUT...
SPLAT
I'M GLAD I MET YOU, MISS CAT-EARS.
BECAUSE NOW...
KWIIII

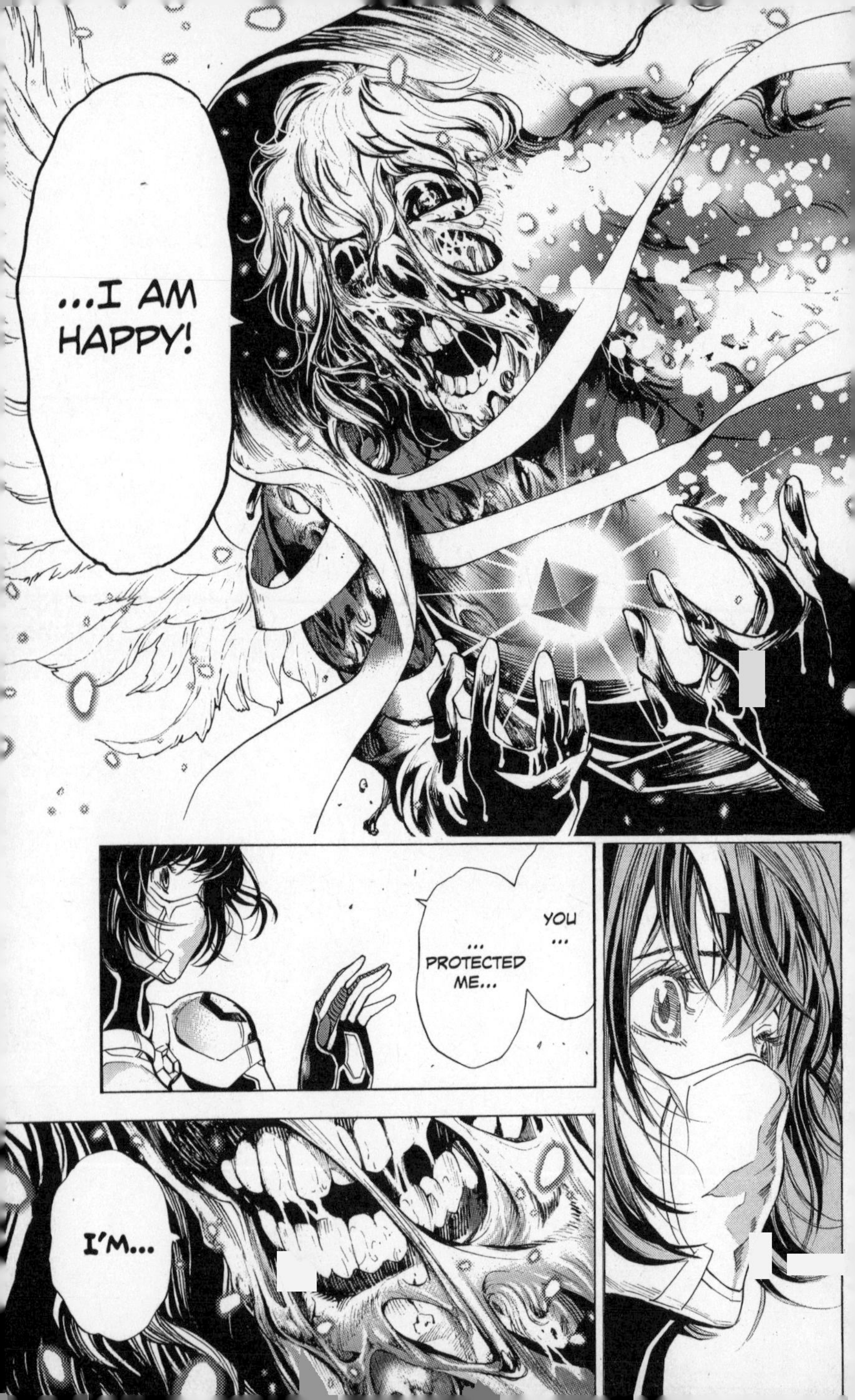
...I AM HAPPY!
YOU ... ... PROTECTED ME...
I'M...

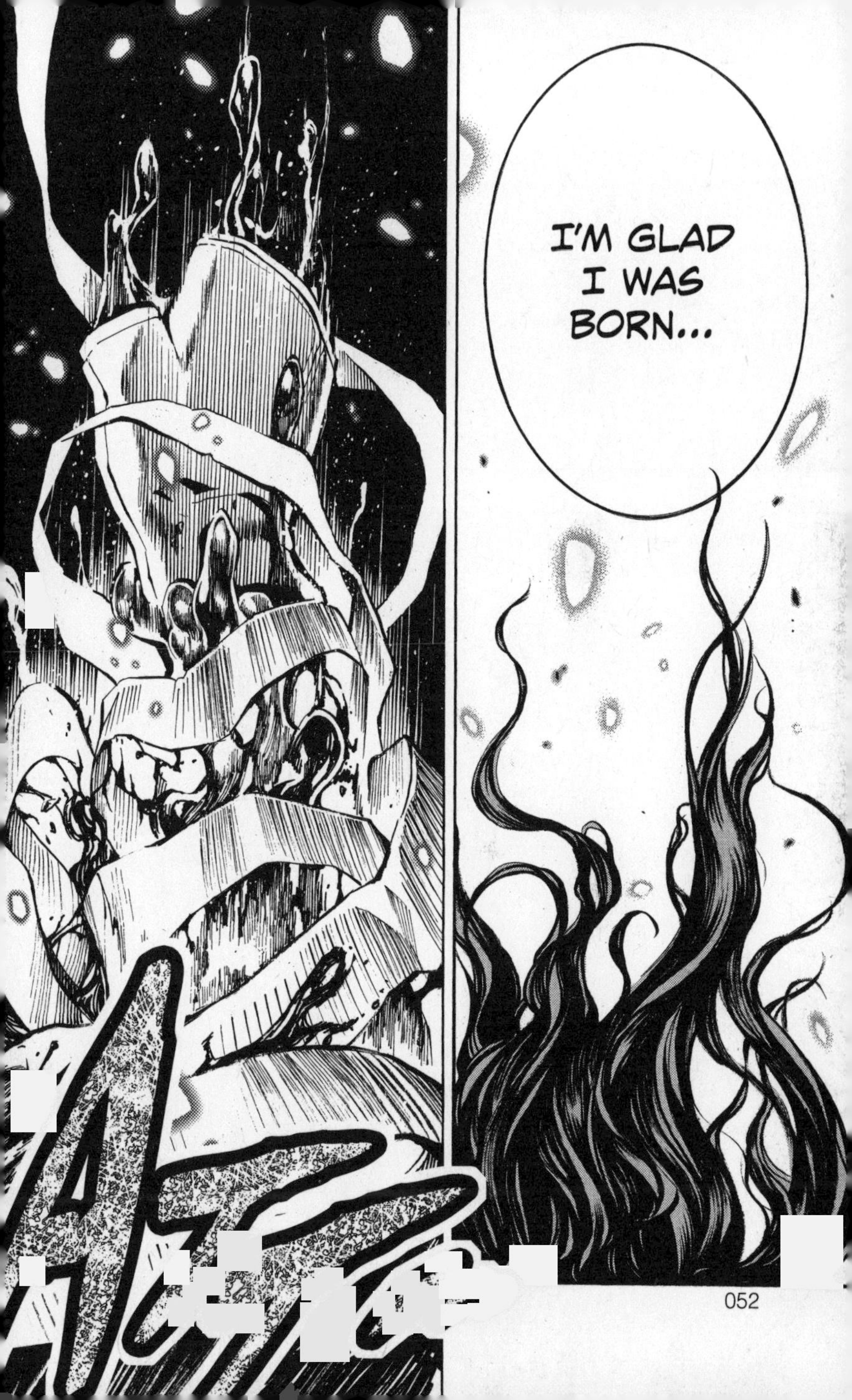
I'M GLAD I WAS BORN...

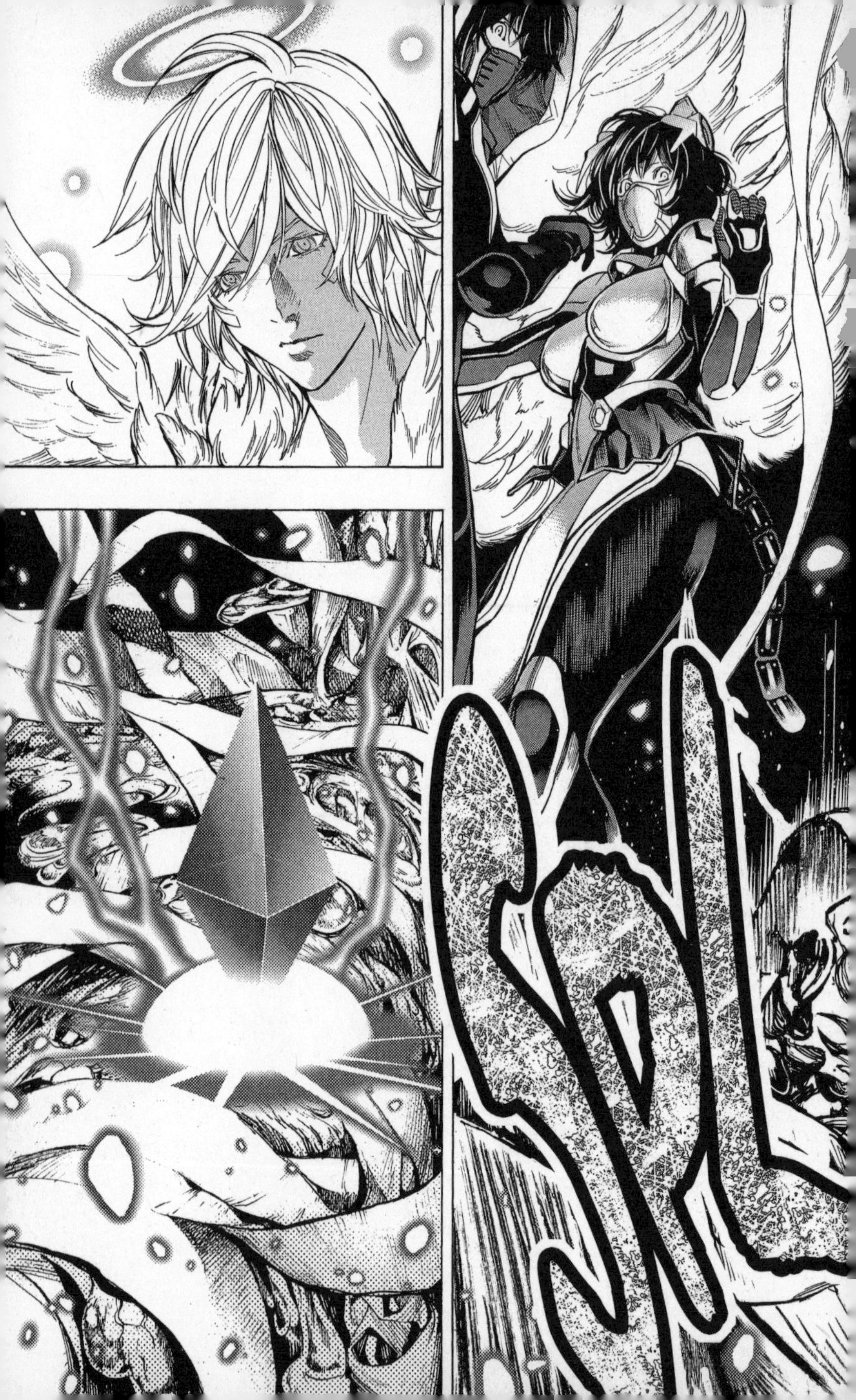

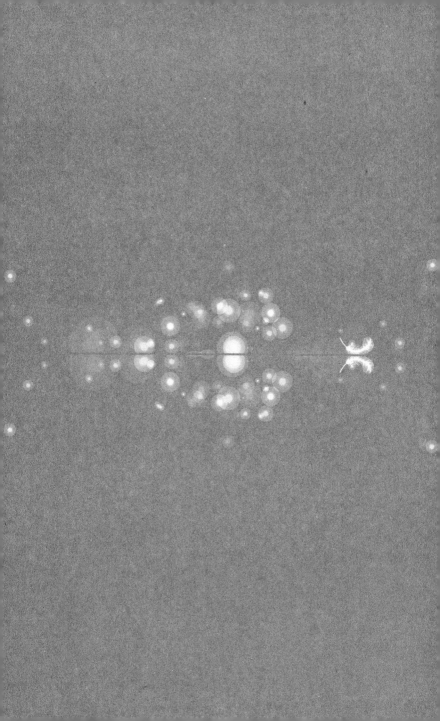

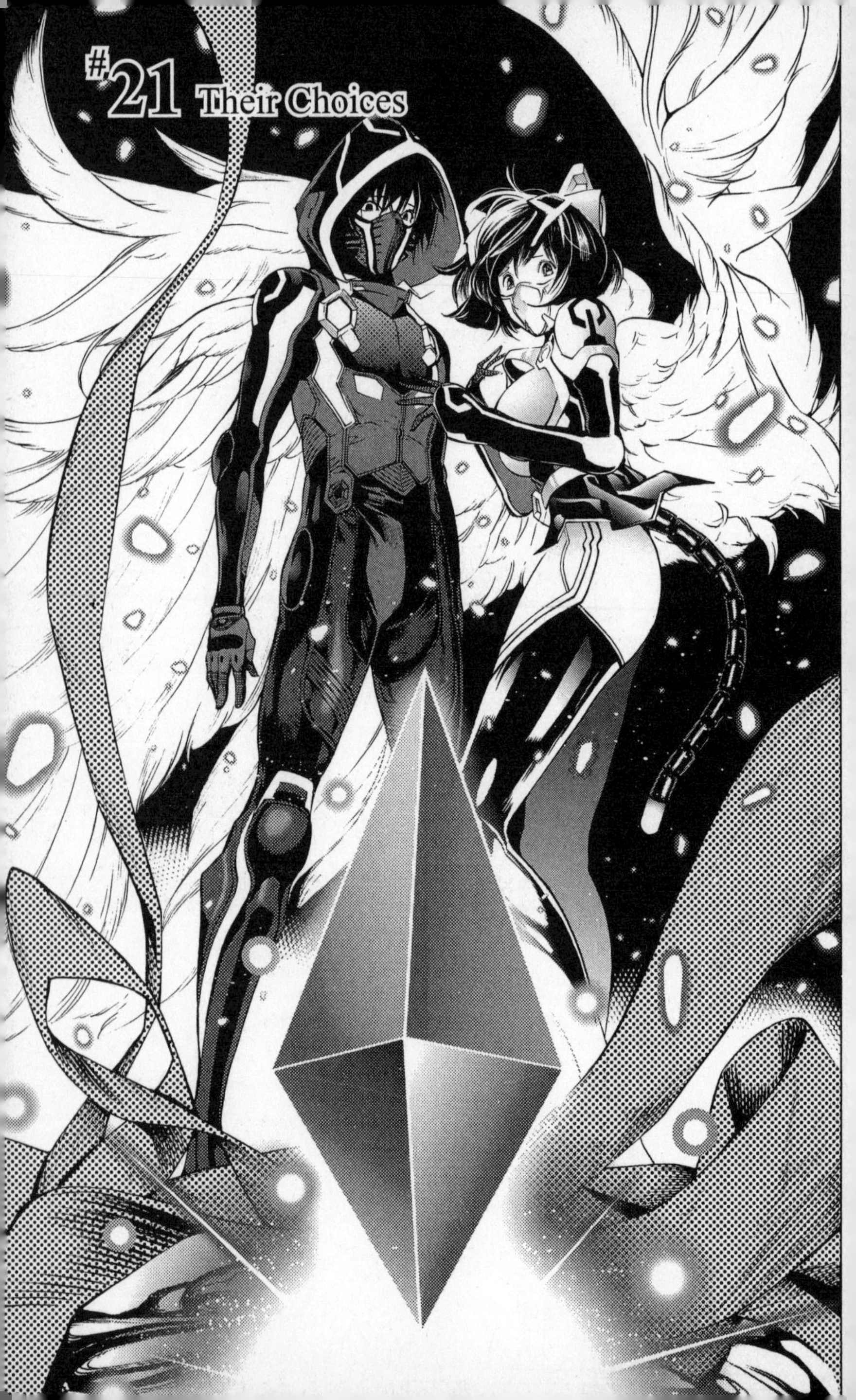
#21 Their Choices

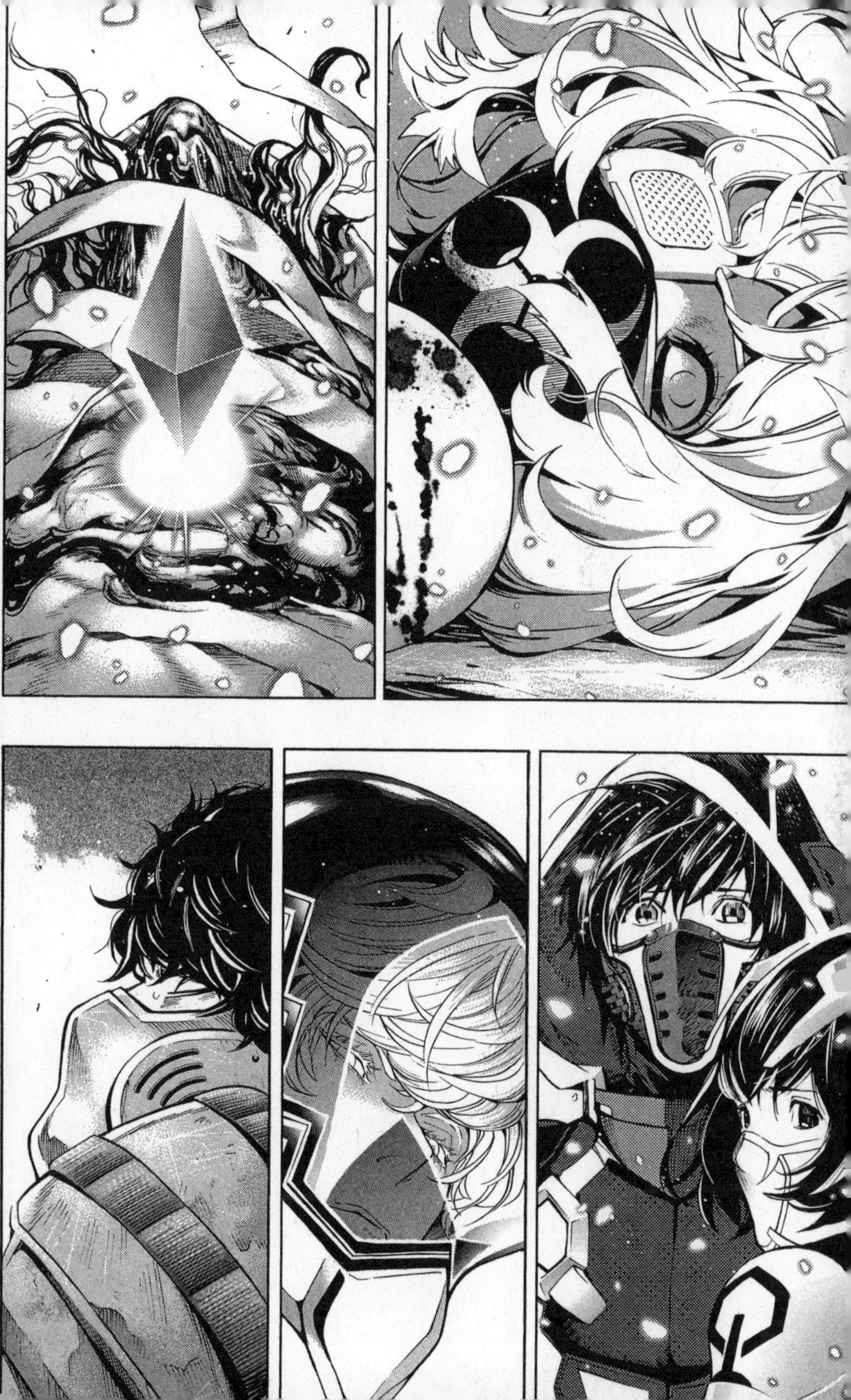

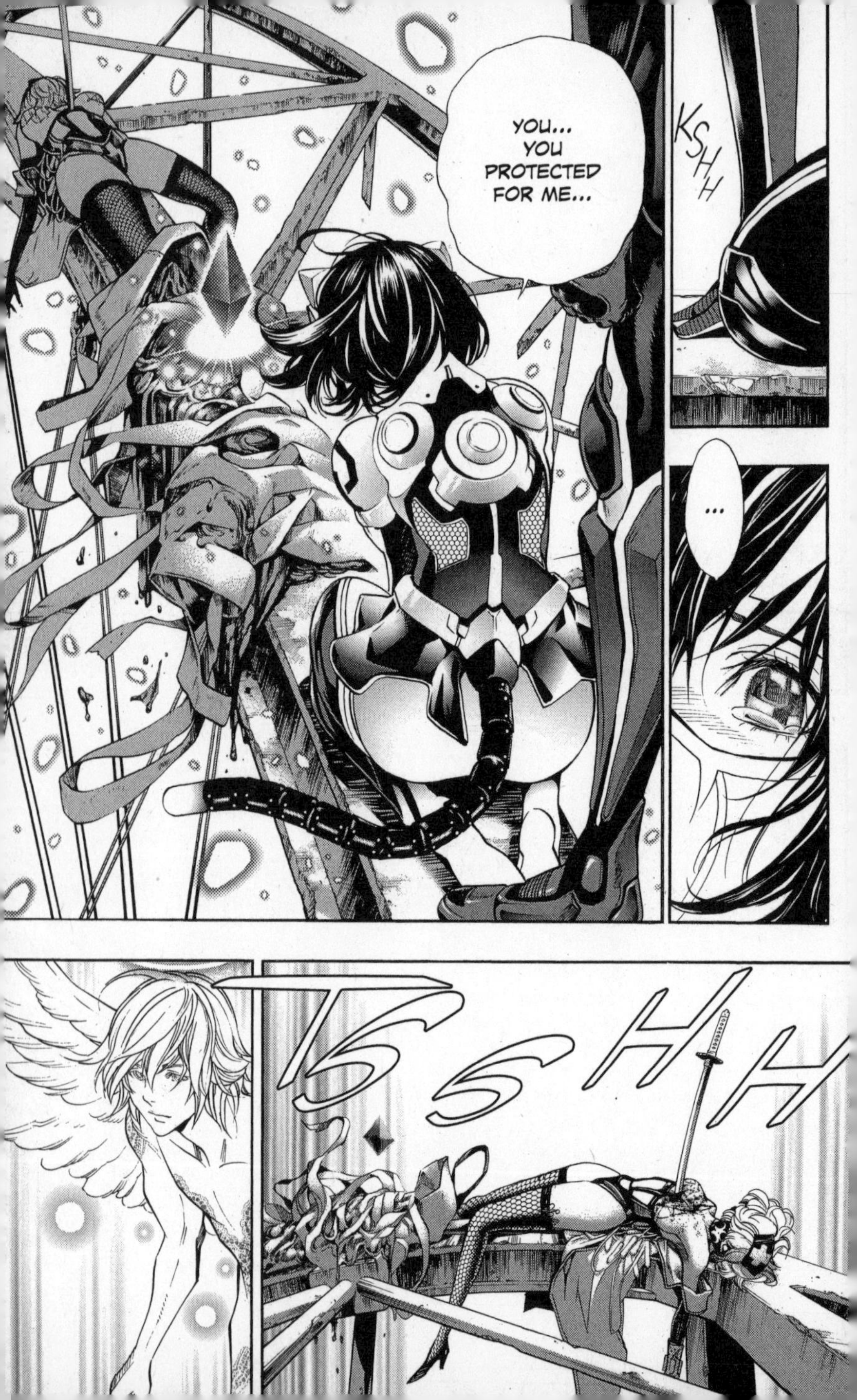
KSHH
...
YOU... YOU PROTECTED FOR ME...
TSSHH

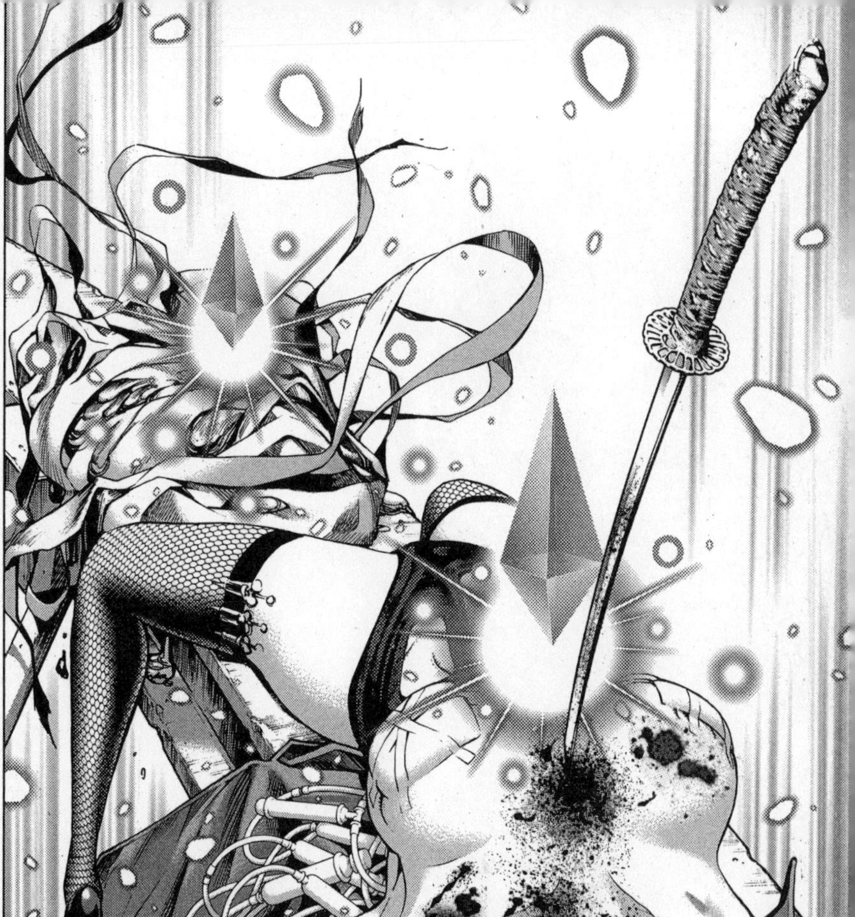
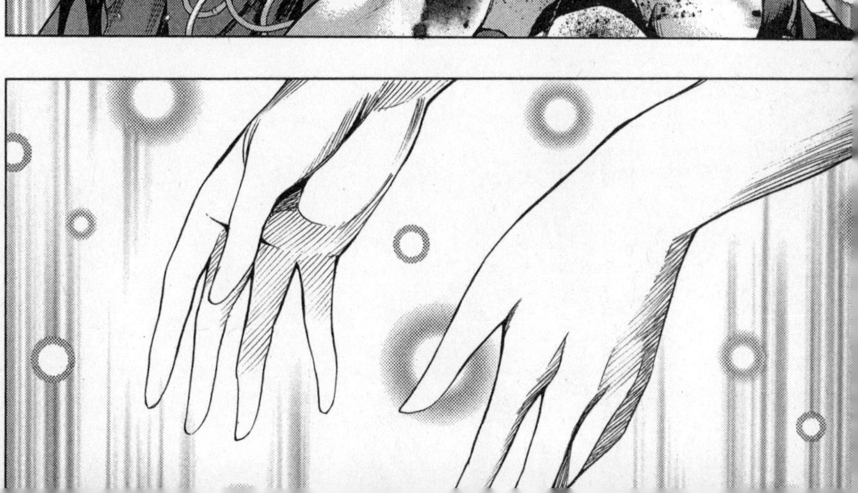

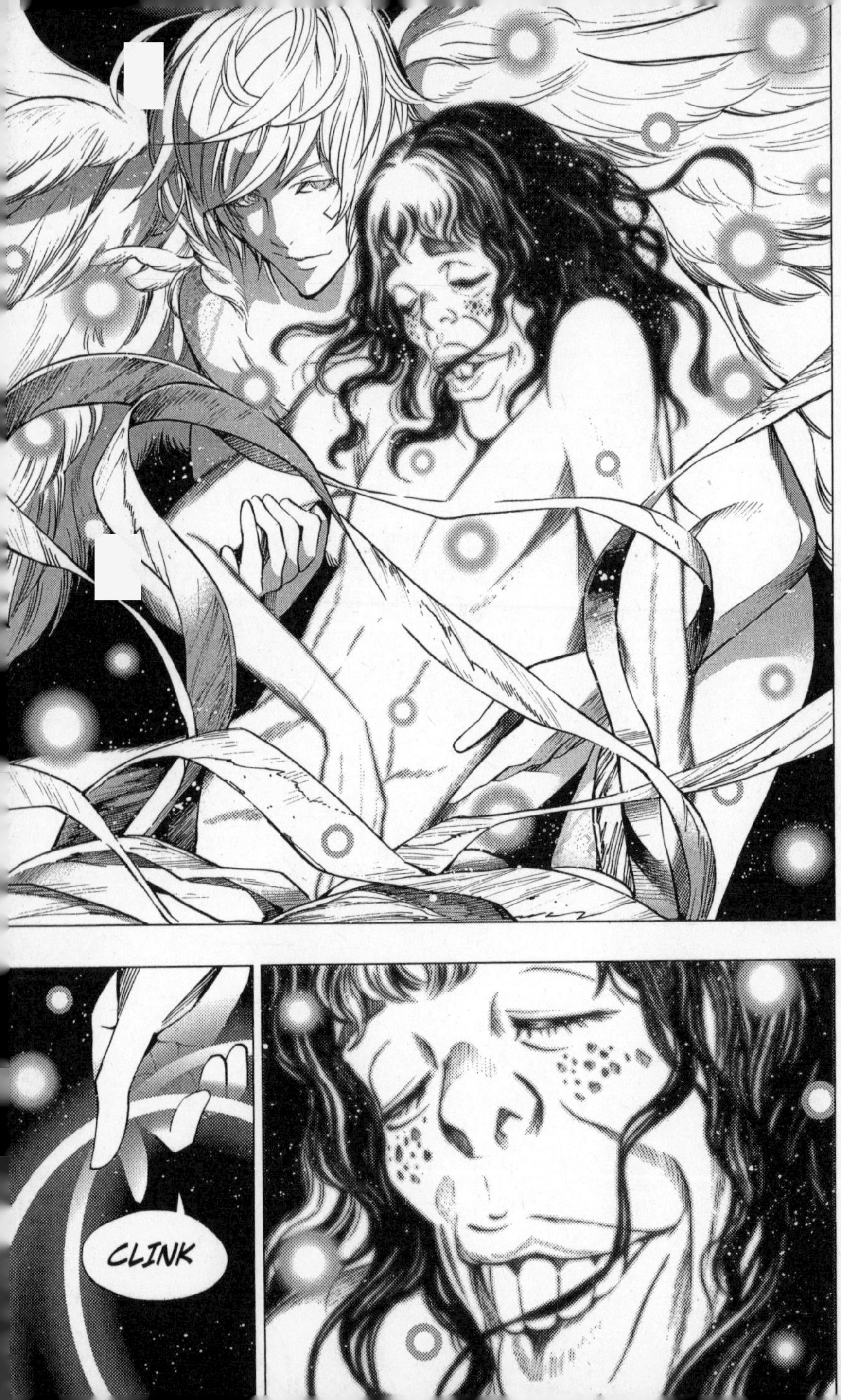
CLINK

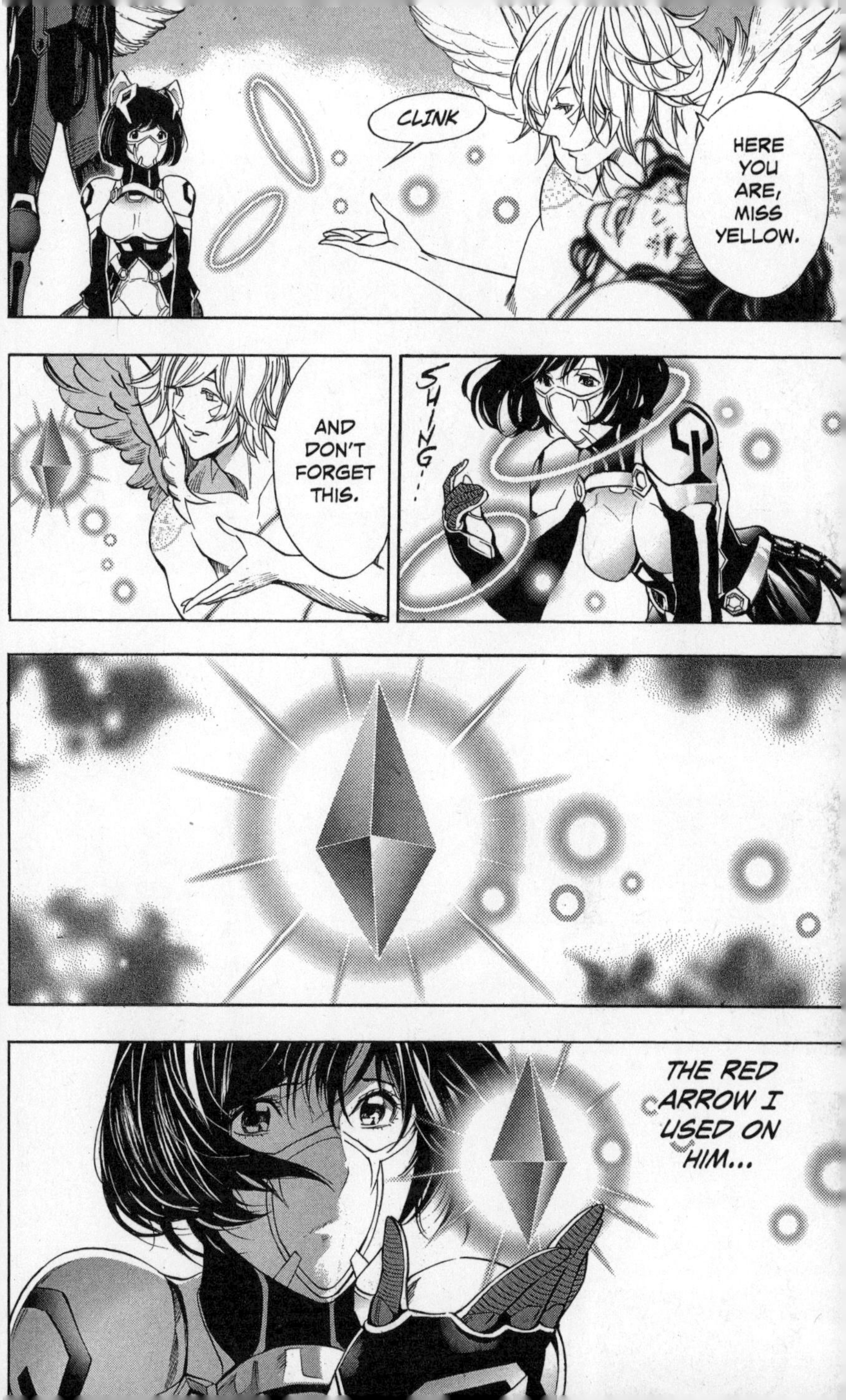
HERE YOU ARE, MISS YELLOW.
CLINK
SHING...
AND DON'T FORGET THIS.
THE RED ARROW I USED ON HIM...

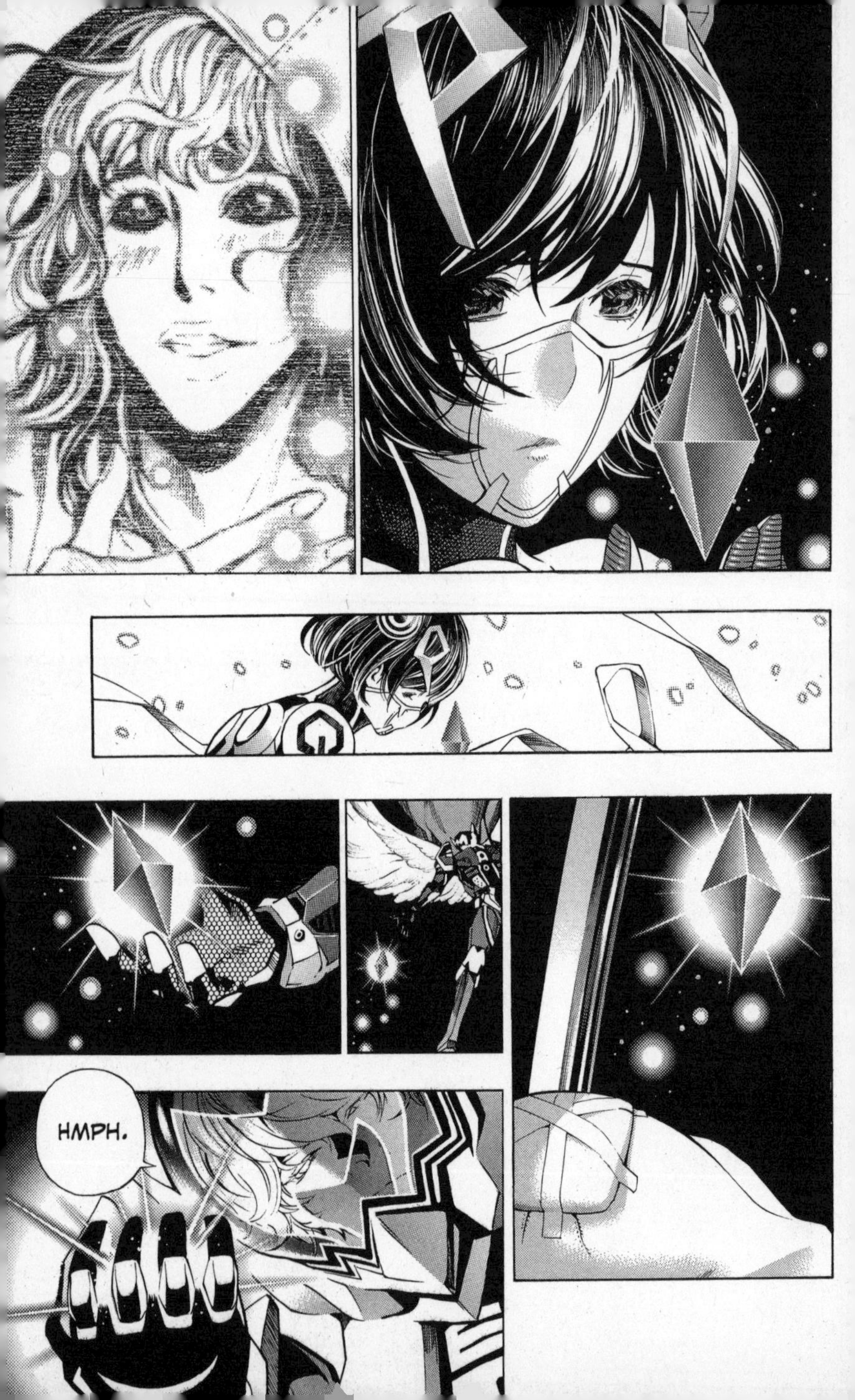
HMPH.

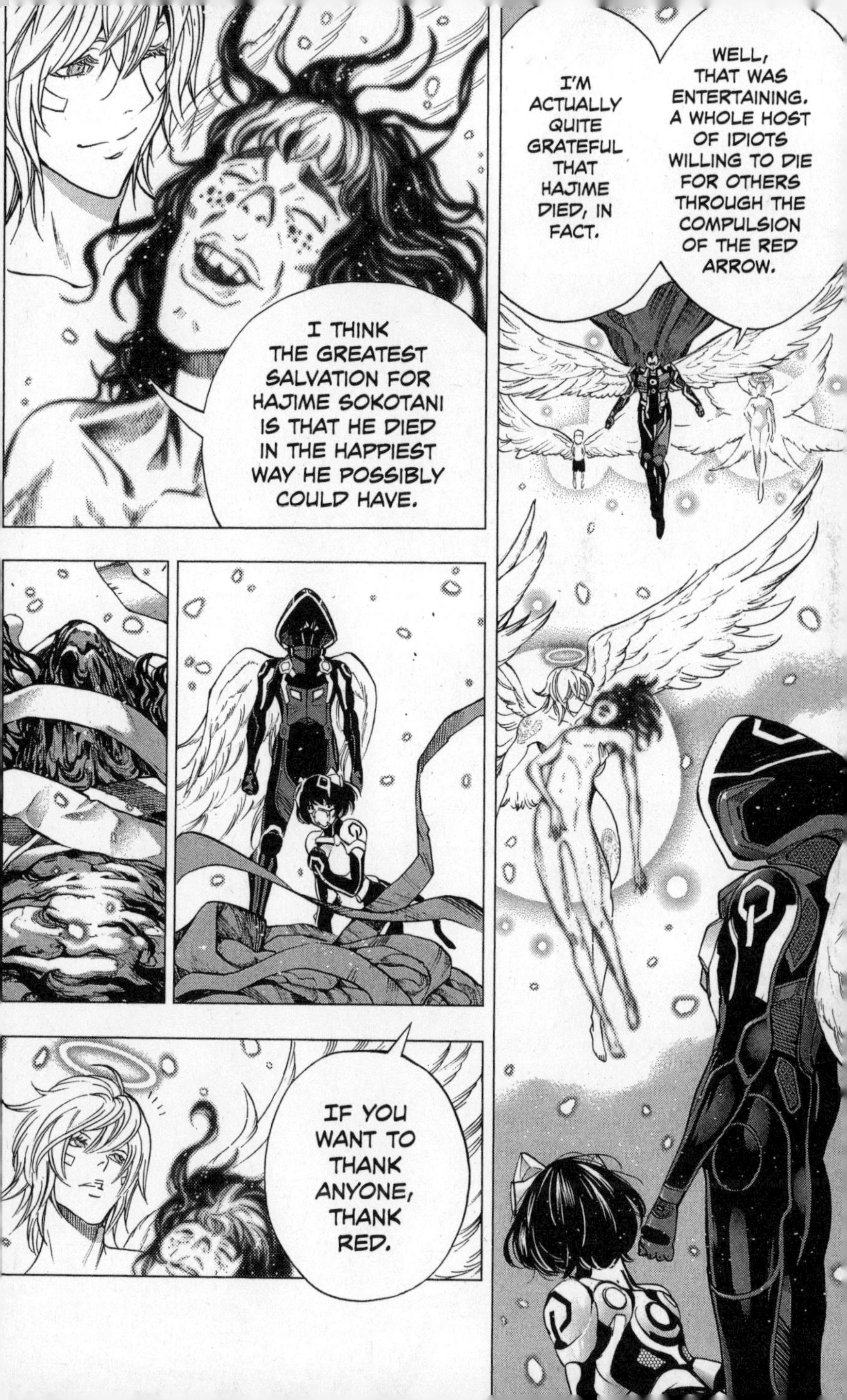
WELL, THAT WAS ENTERTAINING. A WHOLE HOST OF IDIOTS WILLING TO DIE FOR OTHERS THROUGH THE COMPULSION OF THE RED ARROW.
I'M ACTUALLY QUITE GRATEFUL THAT HAJIME DIED, IN FACT.
I THINK THE GREATEST SALVATION FOR HAJIME SOKOTANI IS THAT HE DIED IN THE HAPPIEST WAY HE POSSIBLY COULD HAVE.
IF YOU WANT TO THANK ANYONE, THANK RED.

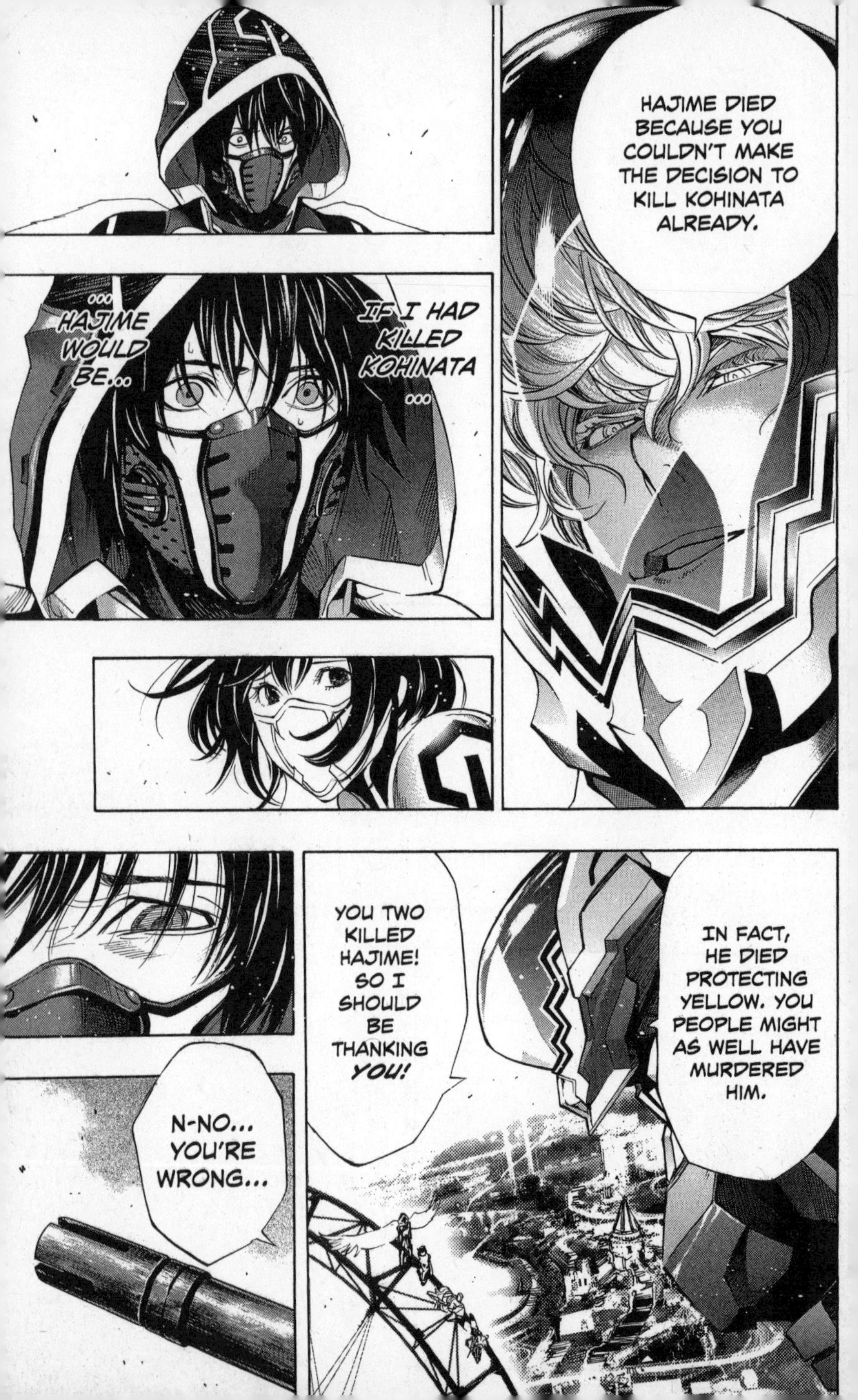
HAJIME DIED BECAUSE YOU COULDN'T MAKE THE DECISION TO KILL KOHINATA ALREADY.
IF I HAD KILLED KOHINATA...
...HAJIME WOULD BE...
IN FACT, HE DIED PROTECTING YELLOW. YOU PEOPLE MIGHT AS WELL HAVE MURDERED HIM.
YOU TWO KILLED HAJIME! SO I SHOULD BE THANKING *YOU!*
N-NO... YOU'RE WRONG...

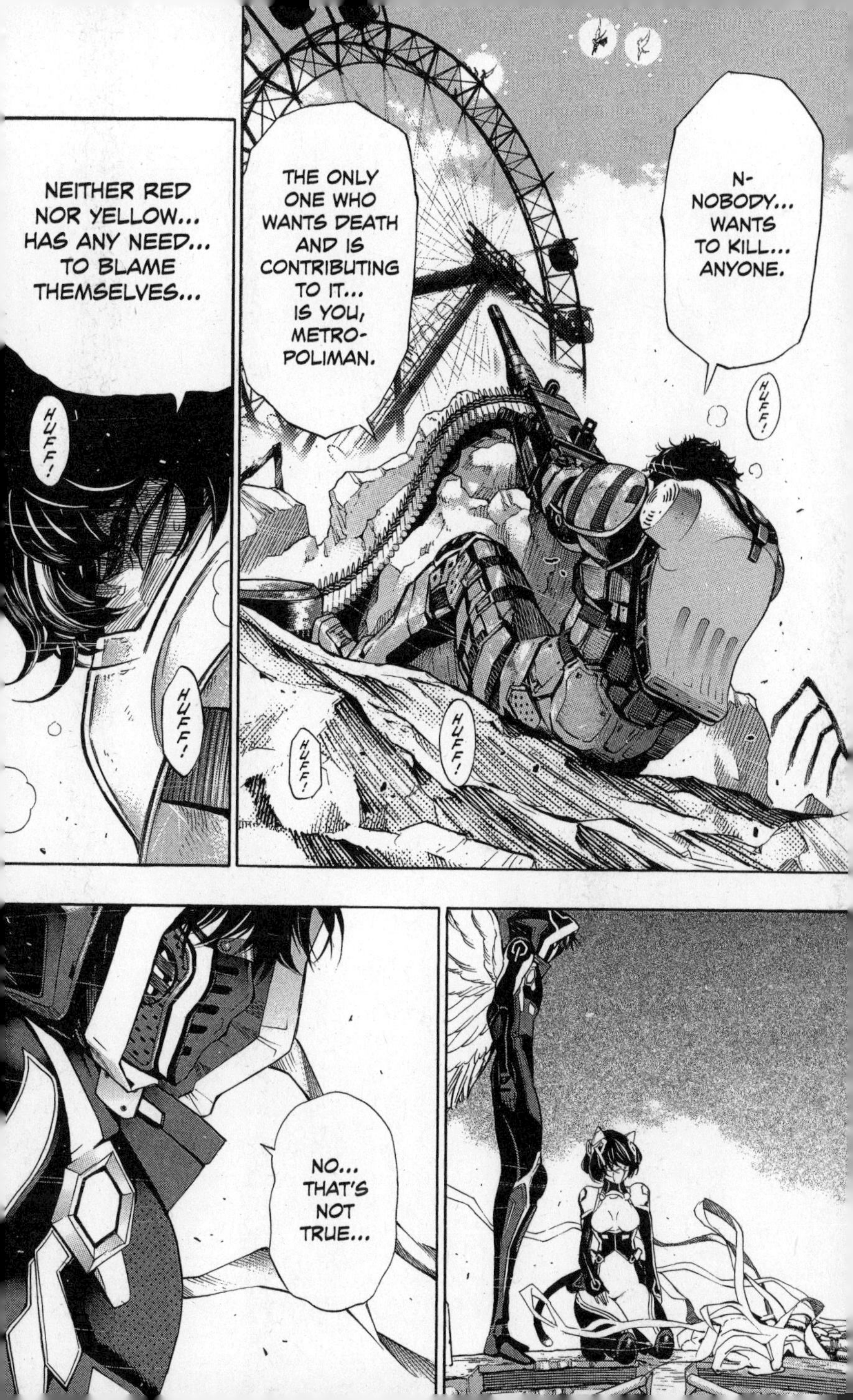
N- NOBODY... WANTS TO KILL... ANYONE.
HUFF!
THE ONLY ONE WHO WANTS DEATH AND IS CONTRIBUTING TO IT... IS YOU, METRO-POLIMAN.
HUFF!
HUFF!
NEITHER RED NOR YELLOW... HAS ANY NEED... TO BLAME THEMSELVES...
HUFF!
HUFF!
NO... THAT'S NOT TRUE...

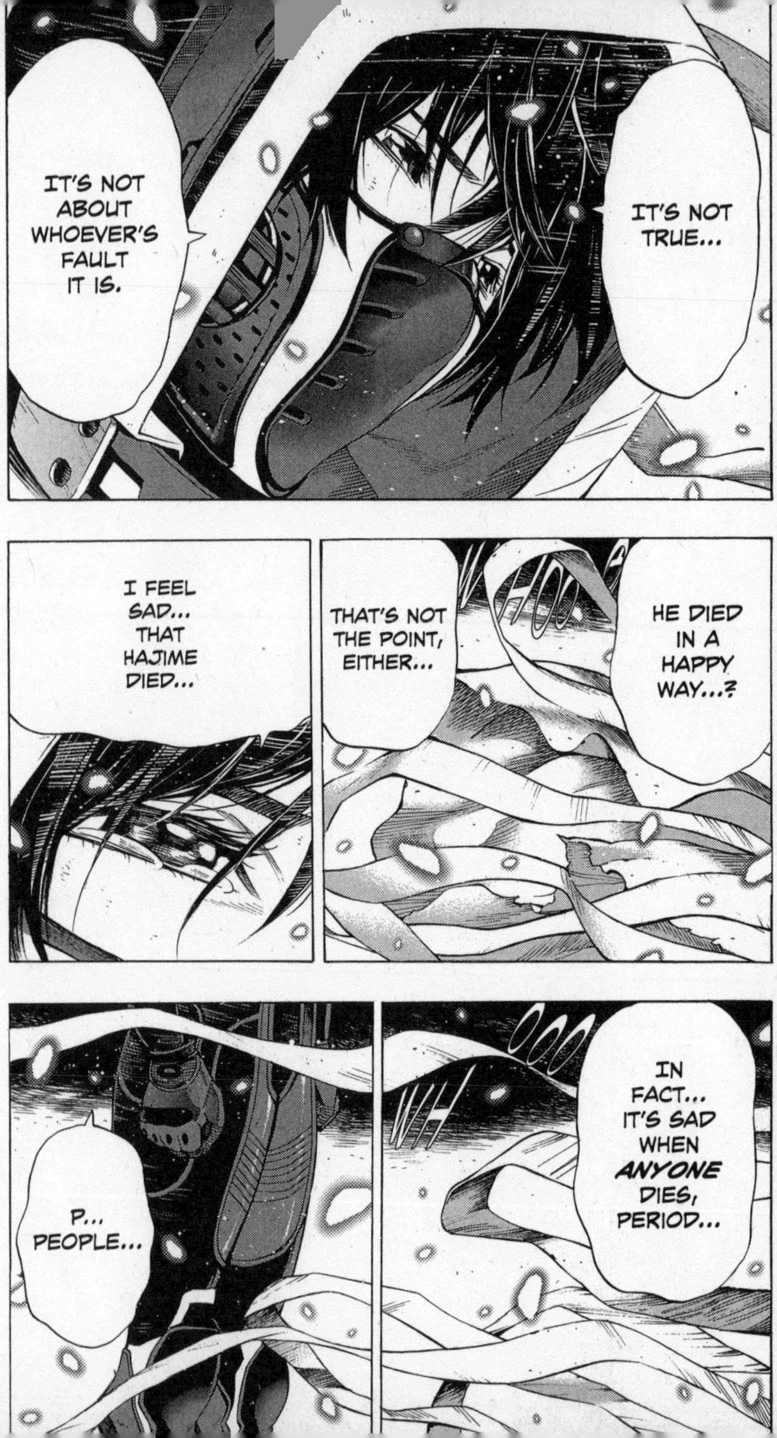
IT'S NOT TRUE...
IT'S NOT ABOUT WHOEVER'S FAULT IT IS.
HE DIED IN A HAPPY WAY...?
THAT'S NOT THE POINT, EITHER...
I FEEL SAD... THAT HAJIME DIED...
IN FACT... IT'S SAD WHEN ANYONE DIES, PERIOD...
P... PEOPLE...

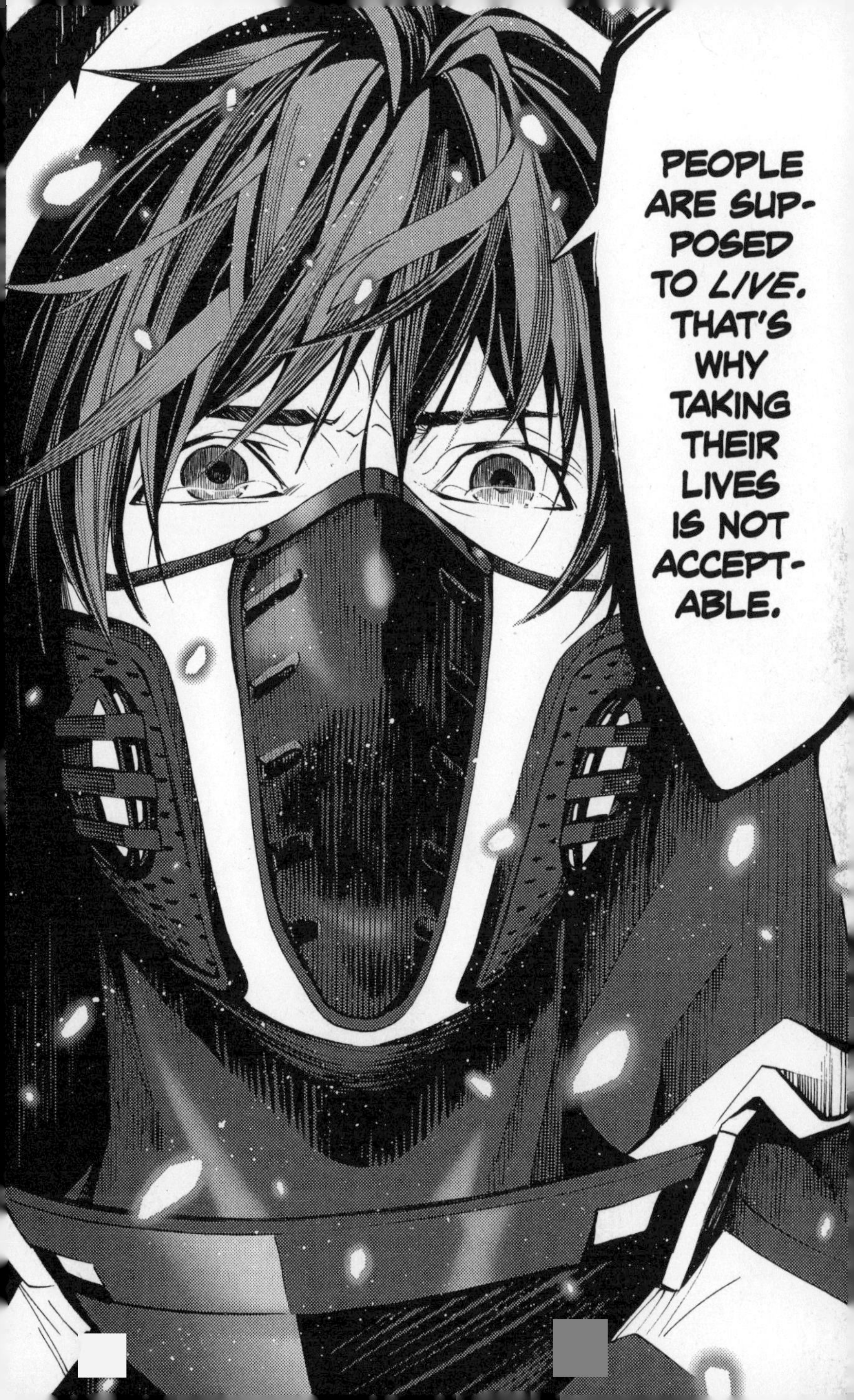
PEOPLE ARE SUP-POSED TO *LIVE*. THAT'S WHY TAKING THEIR LIVES IS NOT ACCEPT-ABLE.

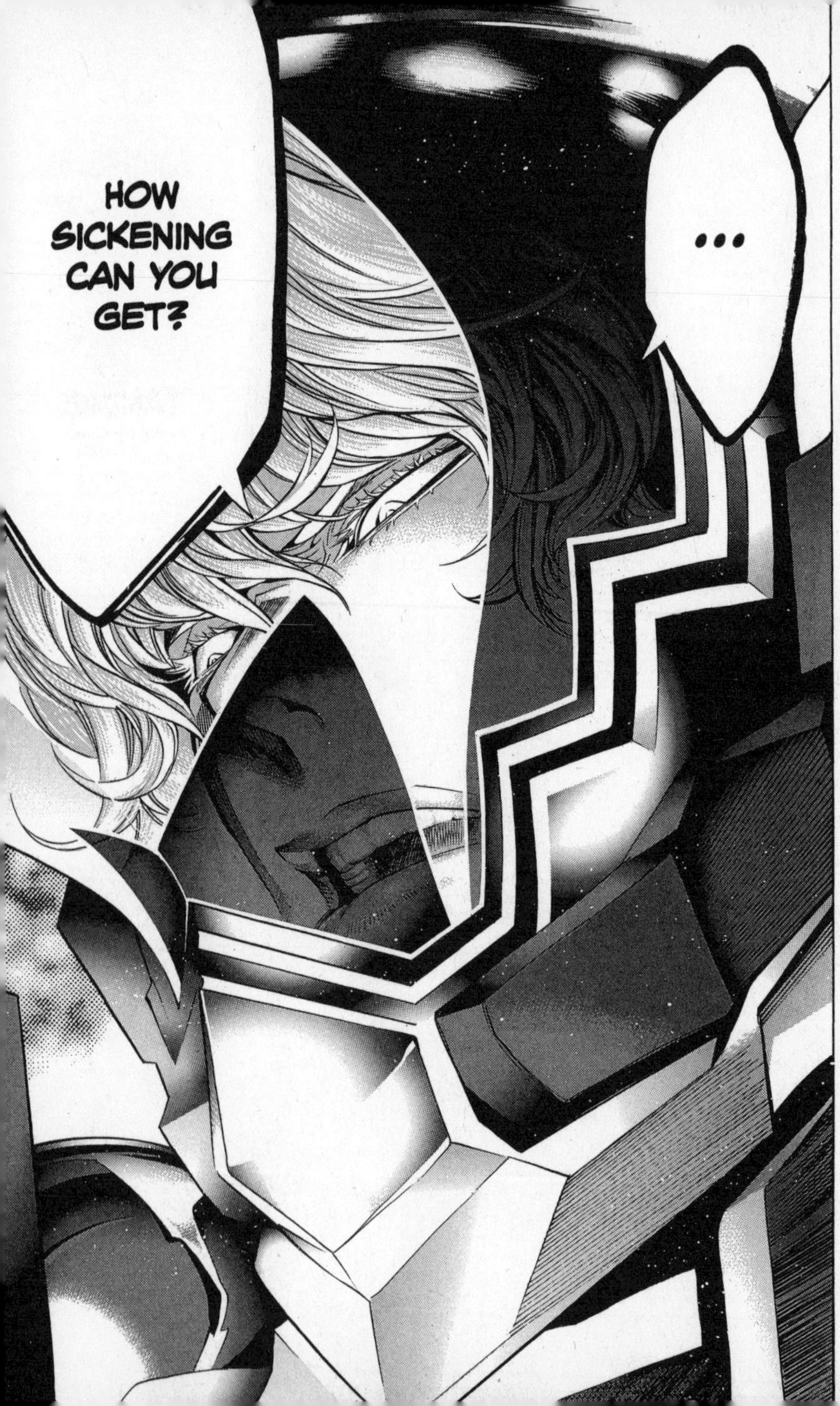
...
HOW SICKENING CAN YOU GET?

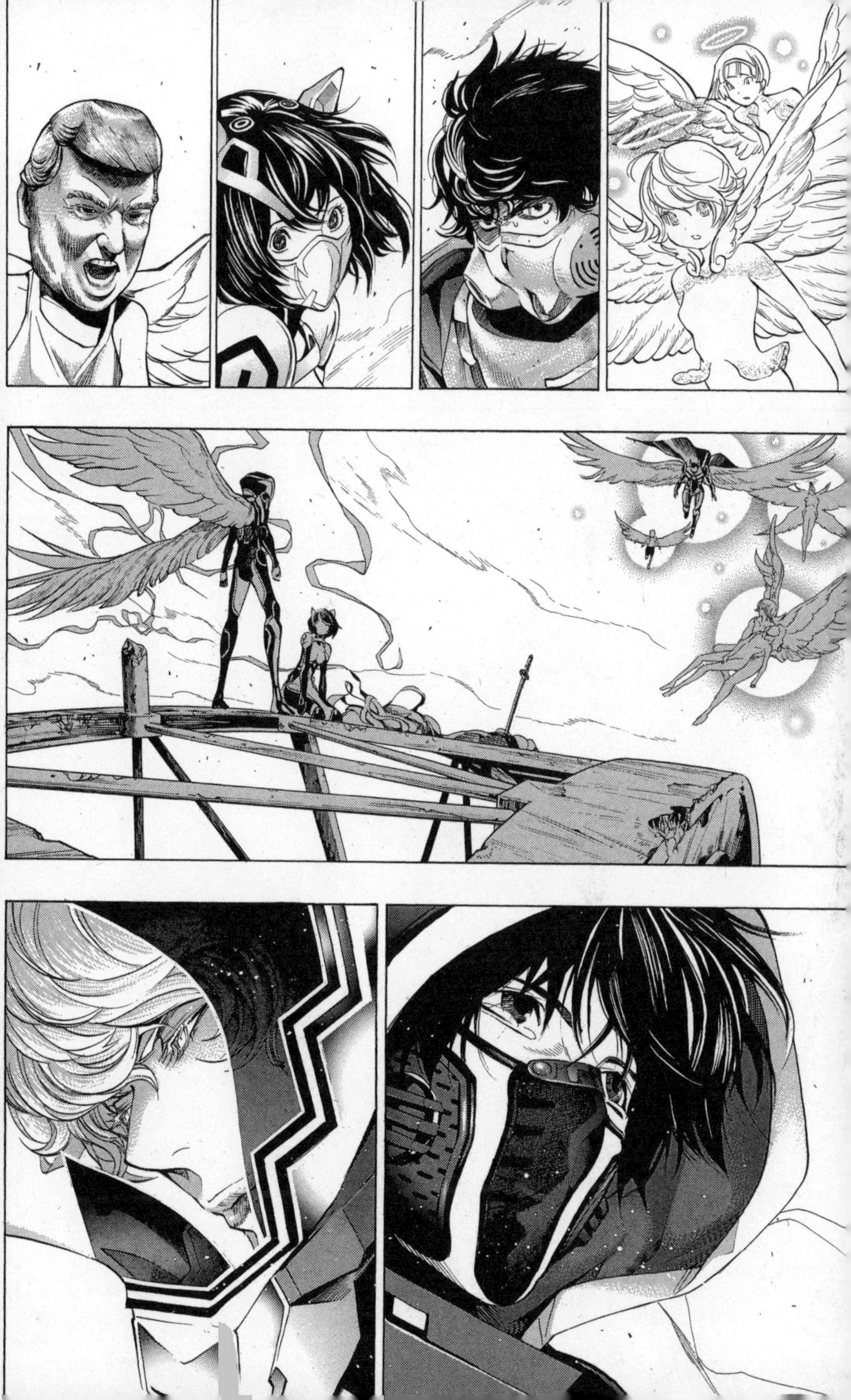

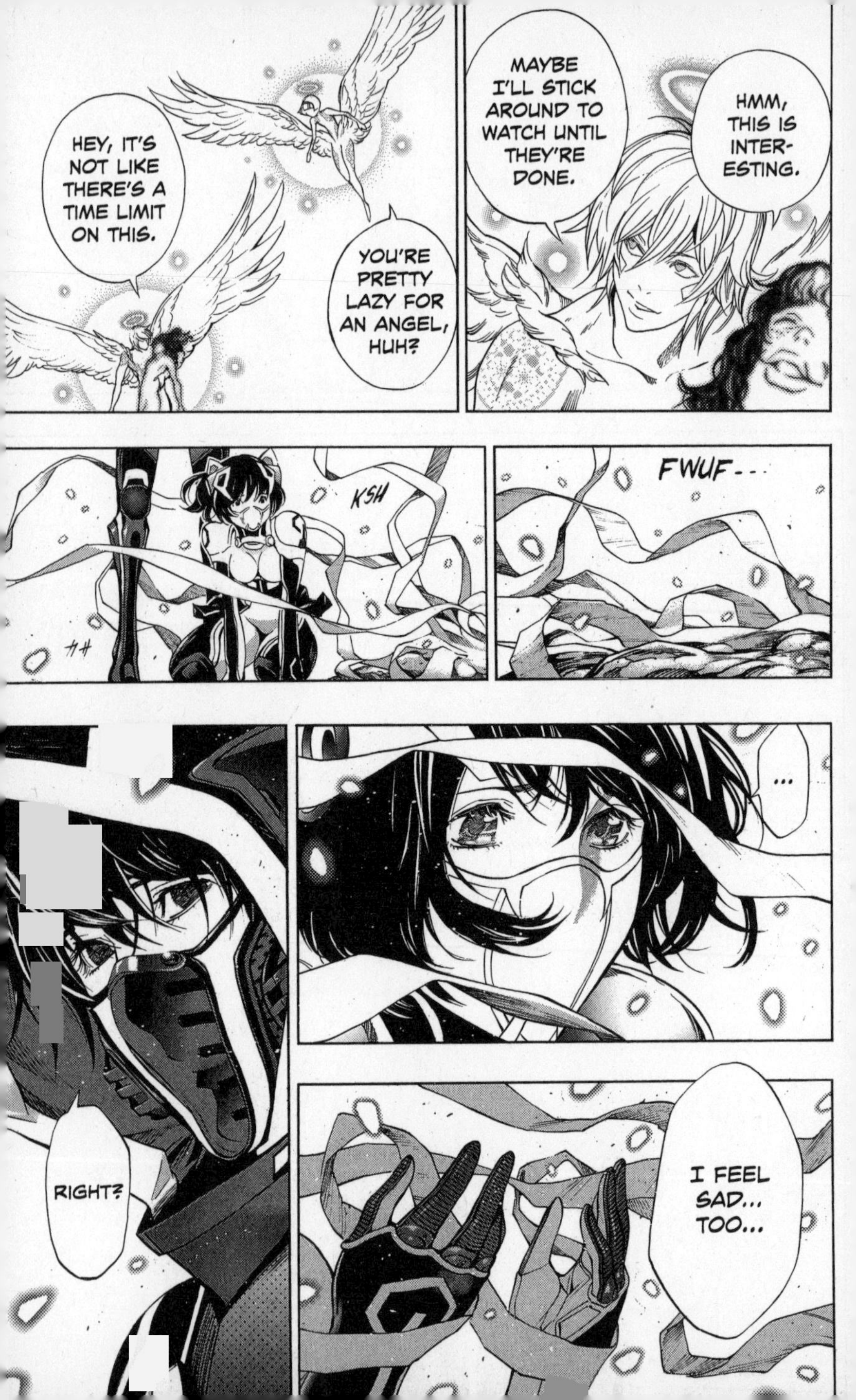
HMM, THIS IS INTER-ESTING.
MAYBE I'LL STICK AROUND TO WATCH UNTIL THEY'RE DONE.
YOU'RE PRETTY LAZY FOR AN ANGEL, HUH?
HEY, IT'S NOT LIKE THERE'S A TIME LIMIT ON THIS.
FWUF...
KSH
...
I FEEL SAD... TOO...
RIGHT?

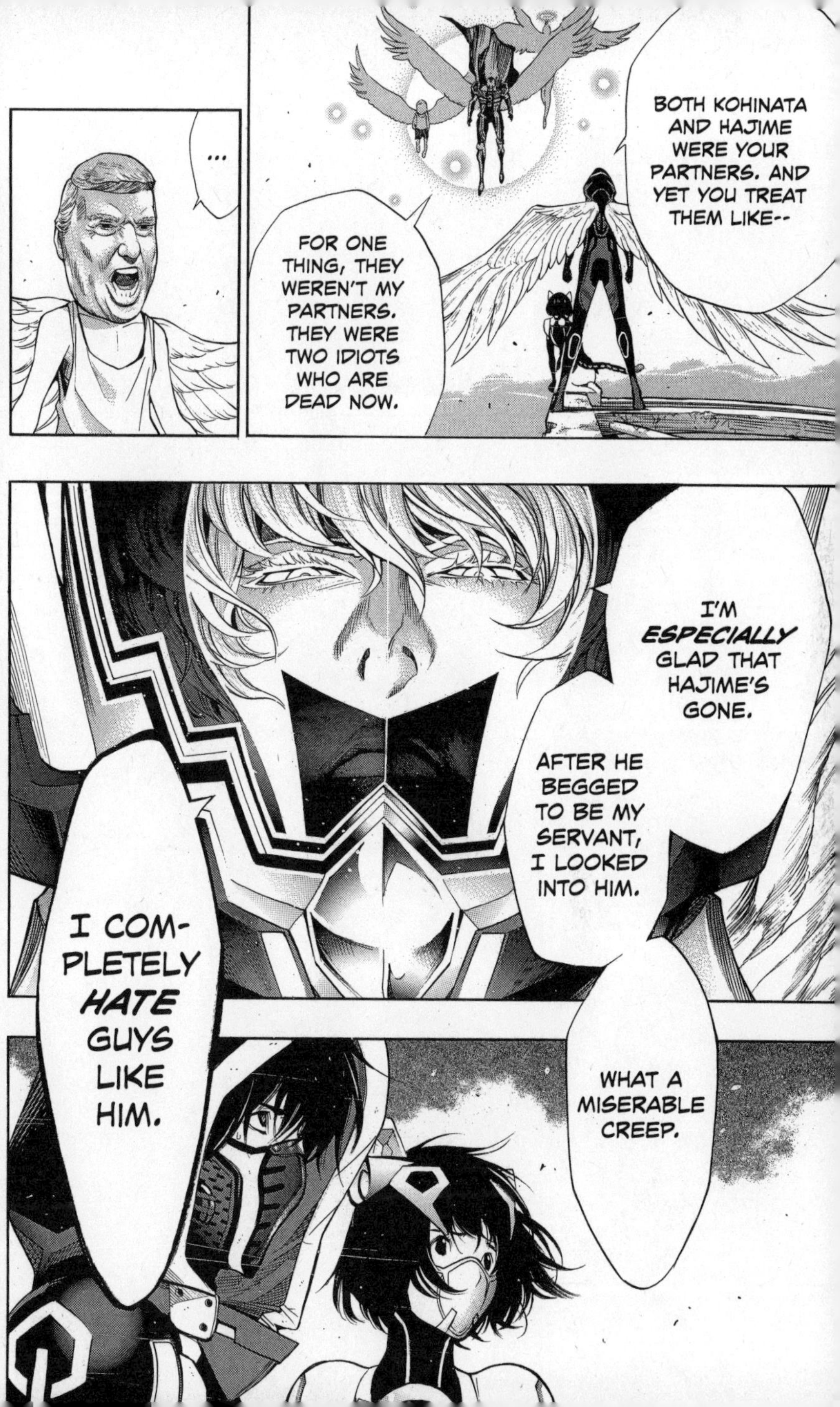
BOTH KOHINATA AND HAJIME WERE YOUR PARTNERS. AND YET YOU TREAT THEM LIKE--
FOR ONE THING, THEY WEREN'T MY PARTNERS. THEY WERE TWO IDIOTS WHO ARE DEAD NOW.
...
I'M *ESPECIALLY* GLAD THAT HAJIME'S GONE.
AFTER HE BEGGED TO BE MY SERVANT, I LOOKED INTO HIM.
WHAT A MISERABLE CREEP.
I COMPLETELY *HATE* GUYS LIKE HIM.

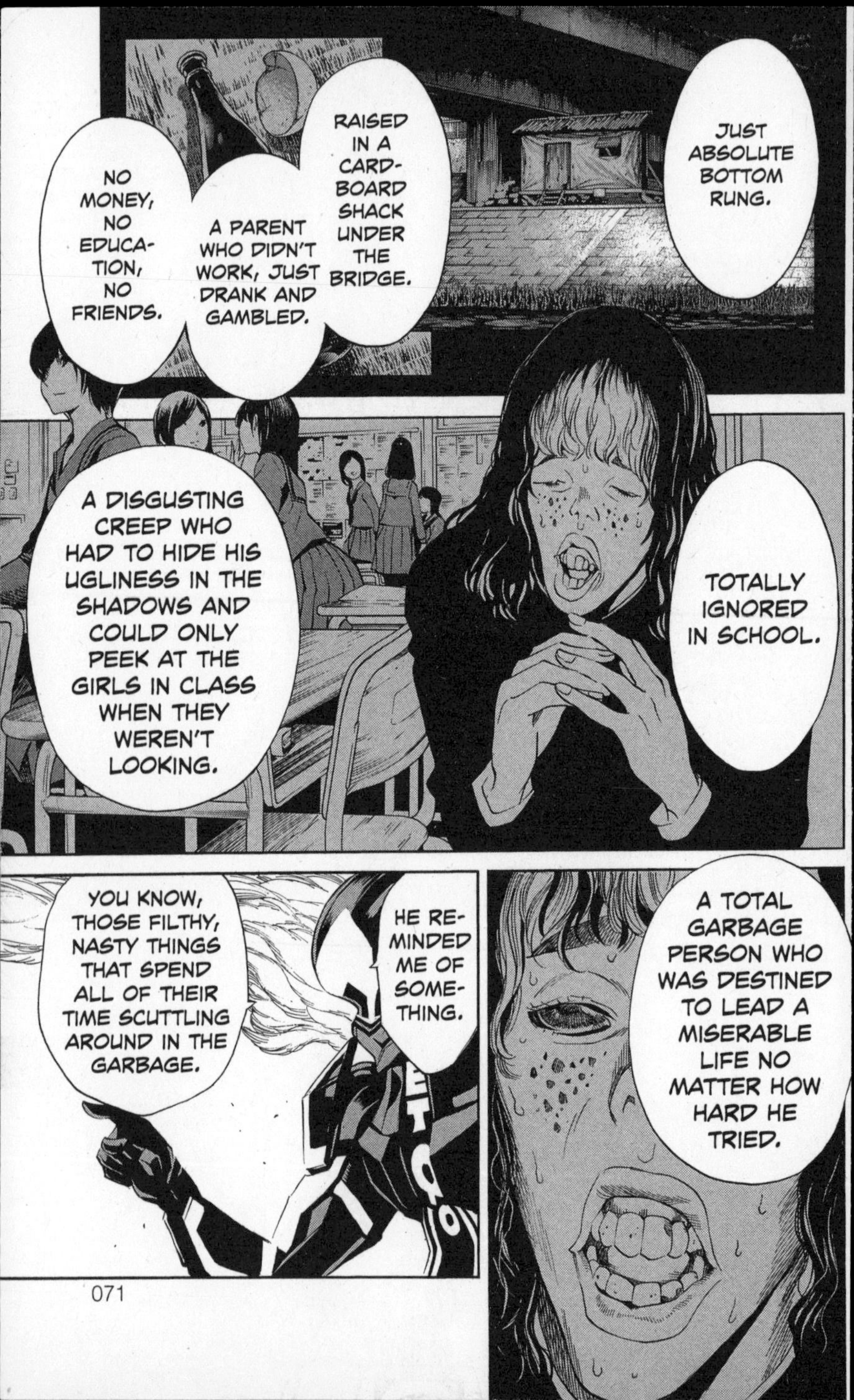
RAISED IN A CARD-BOARD SHACK UNDER THE BRIDGE.
A PARENT WHO DIDN'T WORK, JUST DRANK AND GAMBLED.
NO MONEY, NO EDUCA-TION, NO FRIENDS.
JUST ABSOLUTE BOTTOM RUNG.
TOTALLY IGNORED IN SCHOOL.
A DISGUSTING CREEP WHO HAD TO HIDE HIS UGLINESS IN THE SHADOWS AND COULD ONLY PEEK AT THE GIRLS IN CLASS WHEN THEY WEREN'T LOOKING.
A TOTAL GARBAGE PERSON WHO WAS DESTINED TO LEAD A MISERABLE LIFE NO MATTER HOW HARD HE TRIED.
HE RE-MINDED ME OF SOME-THING.
YOU KNOW, THOSE FILTHY, NASTY THINGS THAT SPEND ALL OF THEIR TIME SCUTTLING AROUND IN THE GARBAGE.

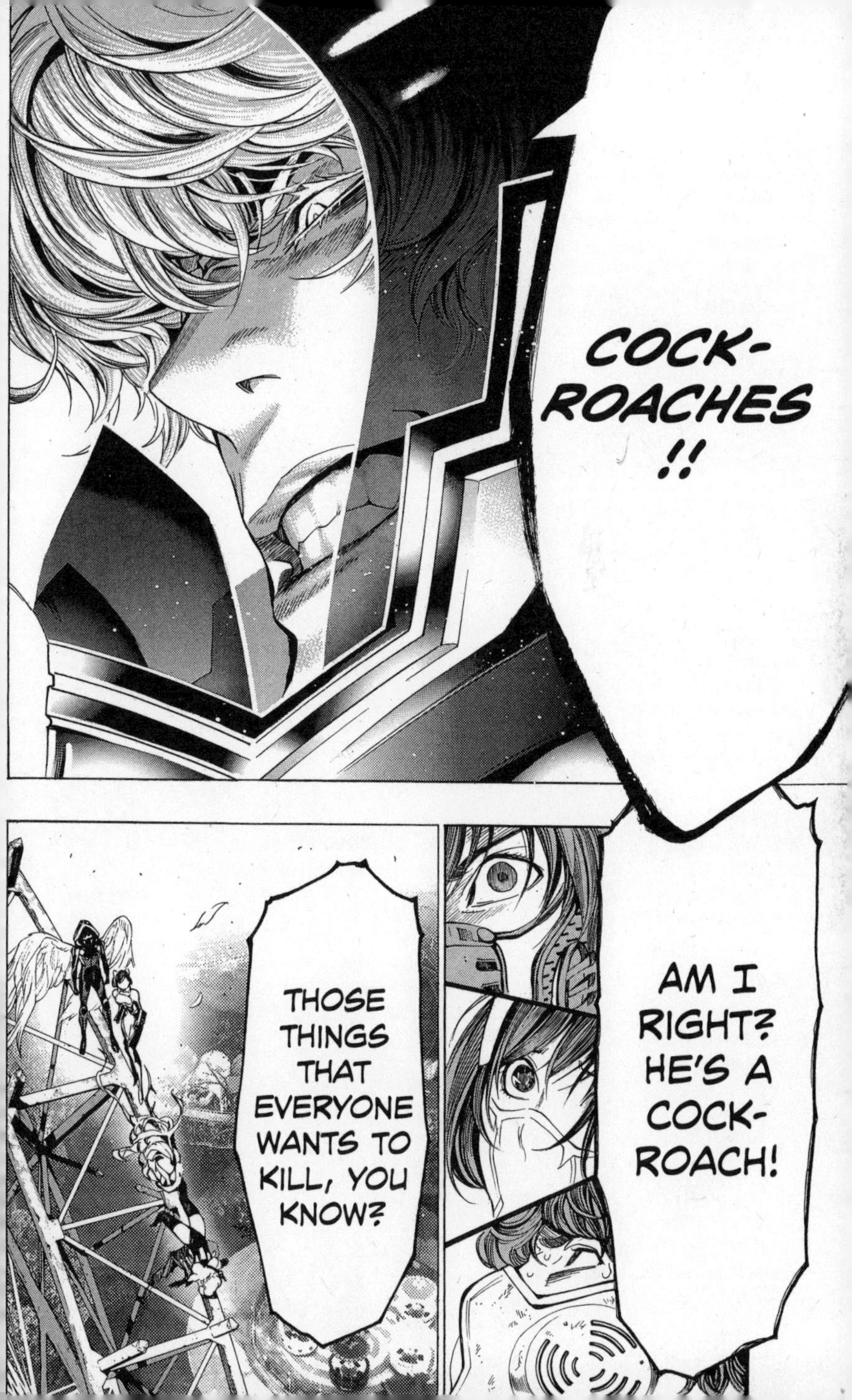
COCK-
ROACHES
!!
AM I RIGHT? HE'S A COCK-ROACH!
THOSE THINGS THAT EVERYONE WANTS TO KILL, YOU KNOW?

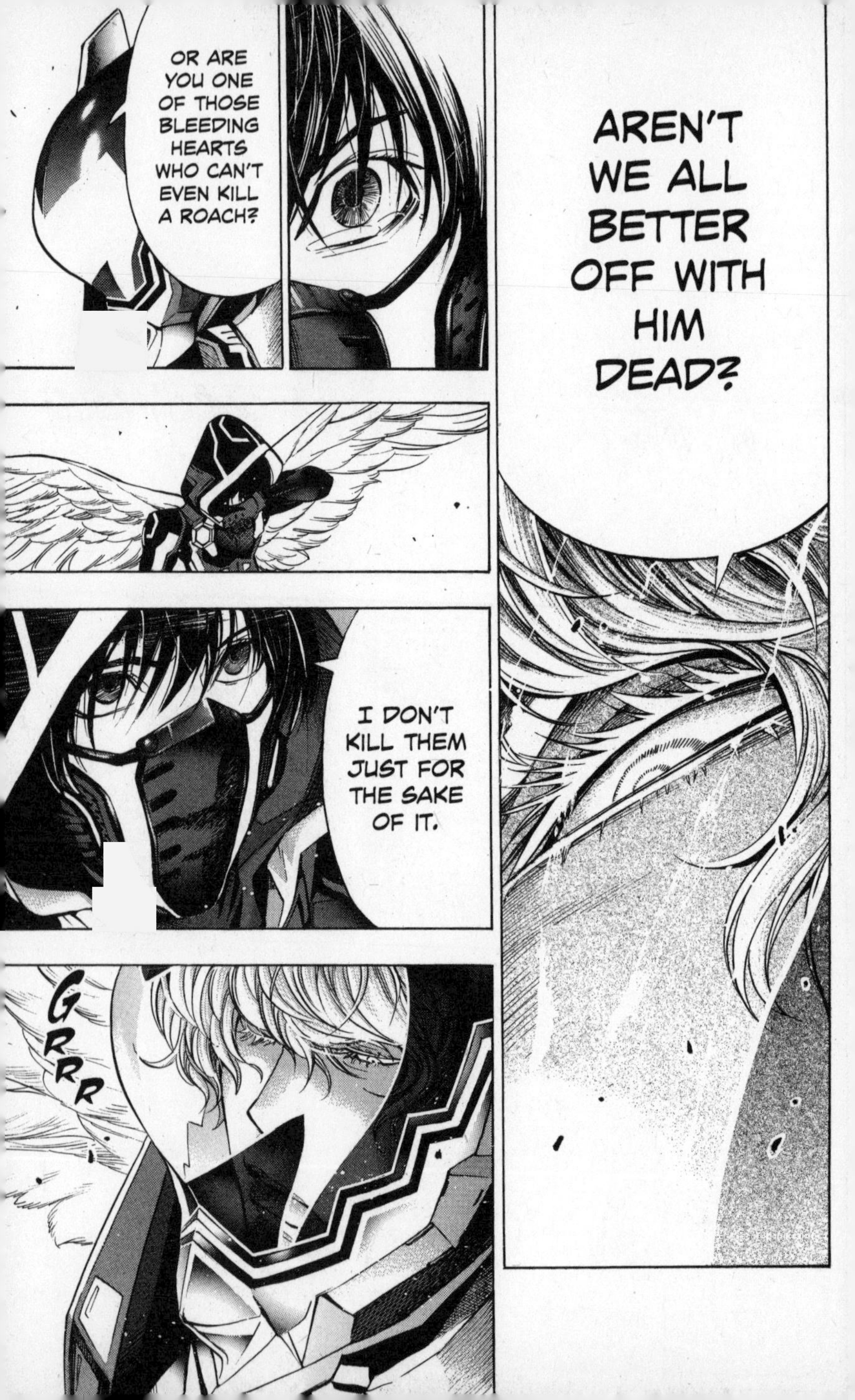
AREN'T WE ALL BETTER OFF WITH HIM DEAD?
OR ARE YOU ONE OF THOSE BLEEDING HEARTS WHO CAN'T EVEN KILL A ROACH?
I DON'T KILL THEM JUST FOR THE SAKE OF IT.
GRRR

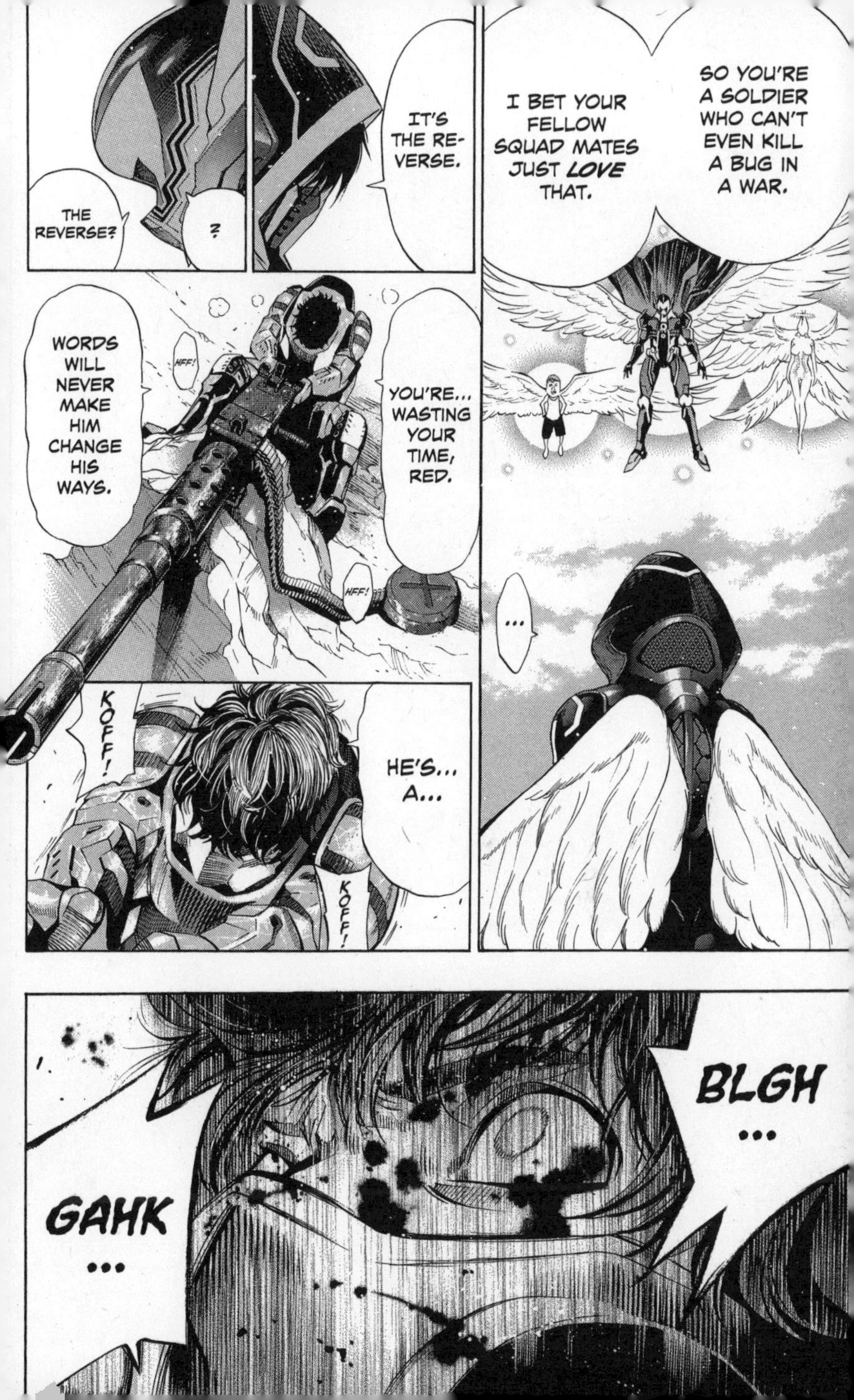
SO YOU'RE A SOLDIER WHO CAN'T EVEN KILL A BUG IN A WAR.
I BET YOUR FELLOW SQUAD MATES JUST *LOVE* THAT.
...
IT'S THE RE-VERSE.
?
THE REVERSE?
HFF!
YOU'RE... WASTING YOUR TIME, RED.
HFF!
WORDS WILL NEVER MAKE HIM CHANGE HIS WAYS.
HE'S... A...
KOFF!
KOFF!
BLGH ...
GAHK ...

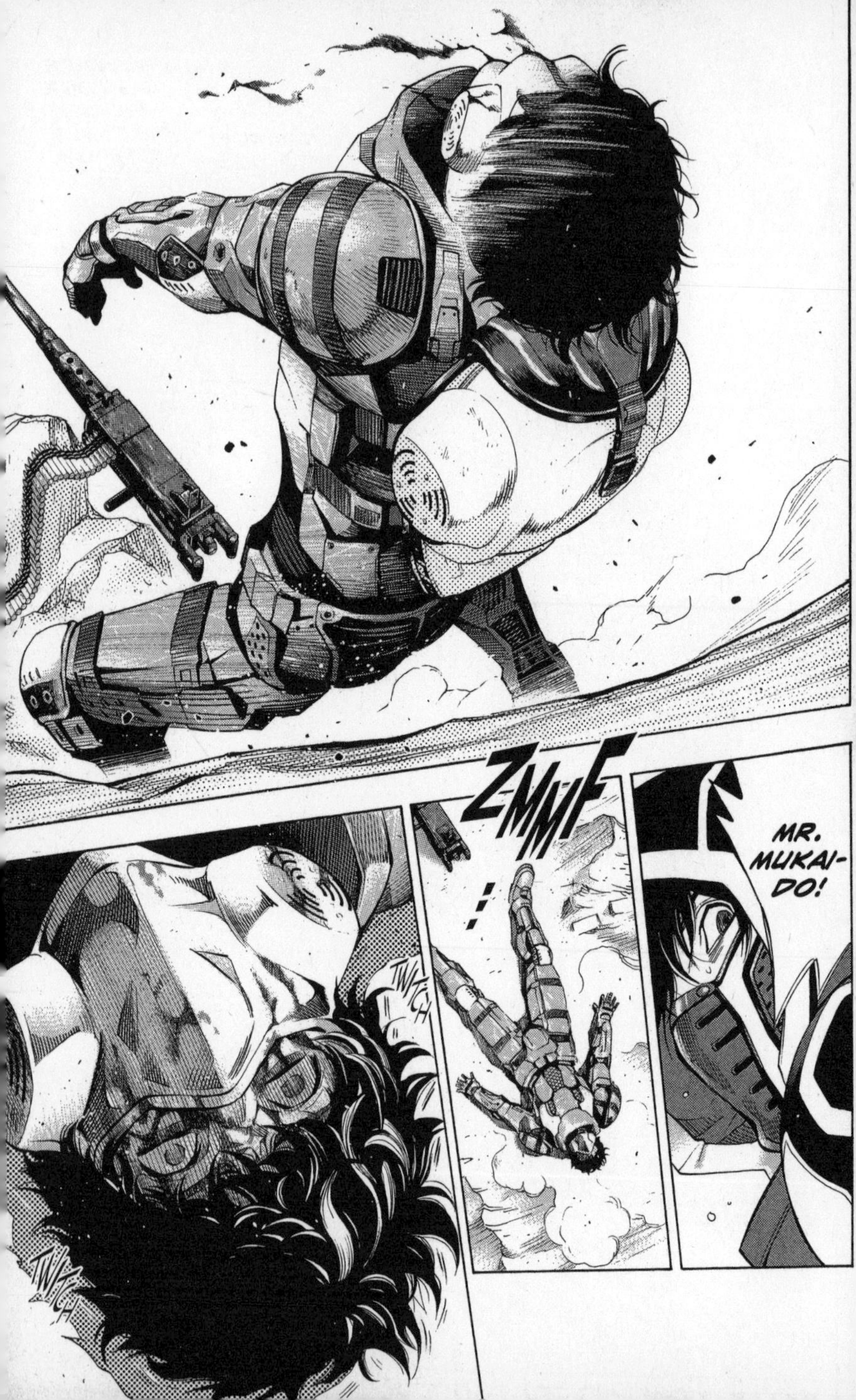
MR. MUKAI-DO!
ZMMF
TWITCH
TWITCH

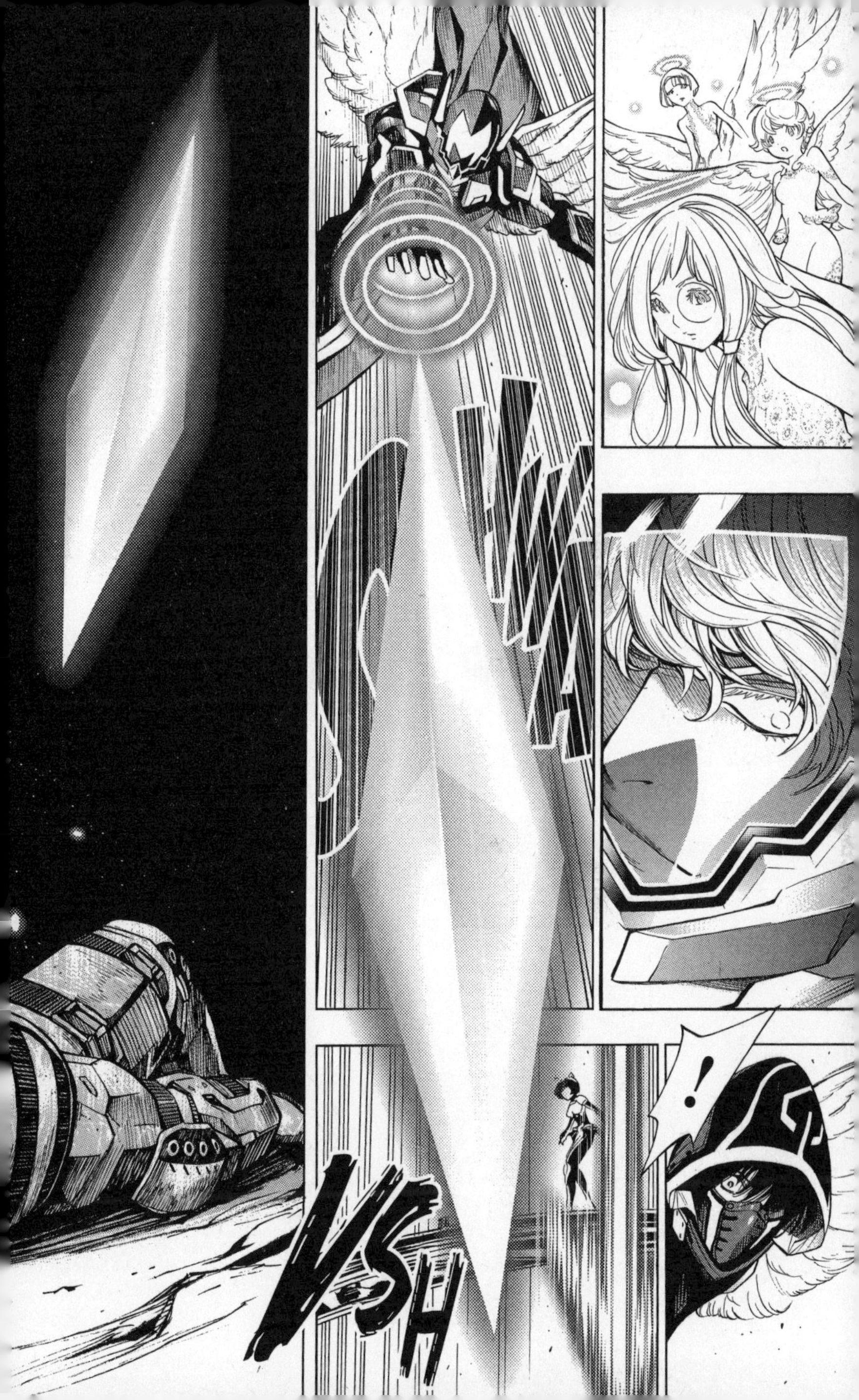
!
VSH

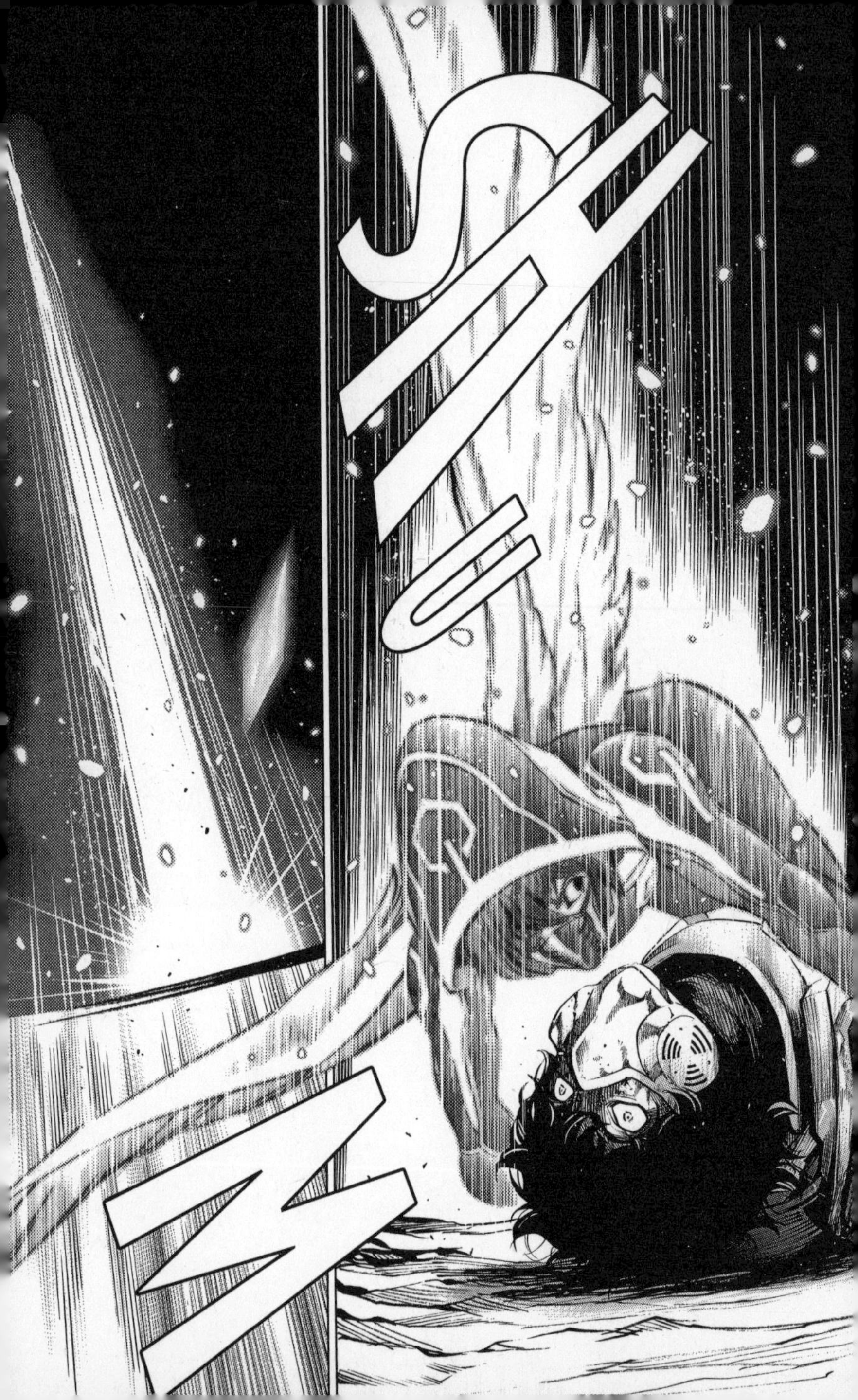
SHUN

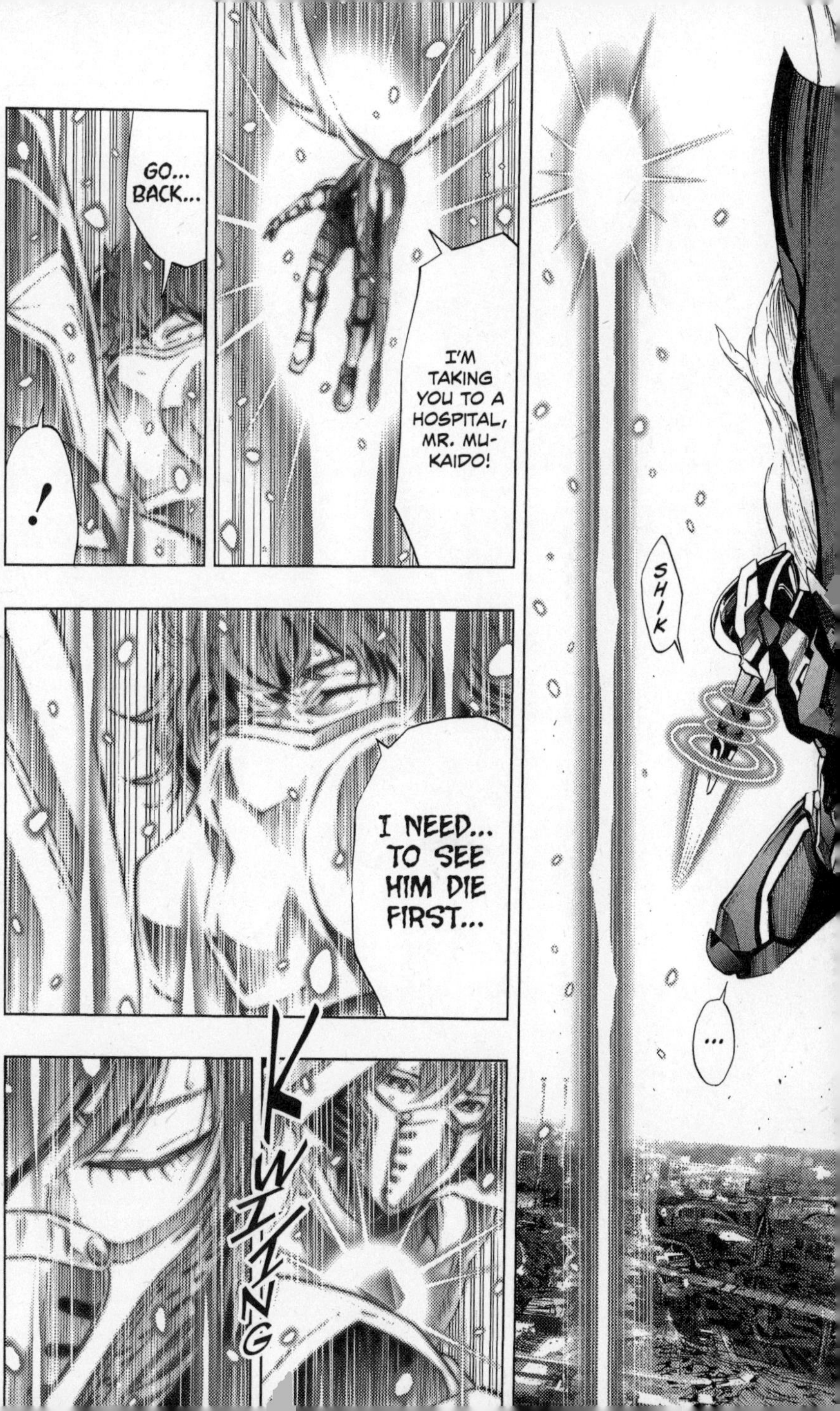
SHIK
...
I'M TAKING YOU TO A HOSPITAL, MR. MU-KAIDO!
GO... BACK...
!
I NEED... TO SEE HIM DIE FIRST...
KWHING

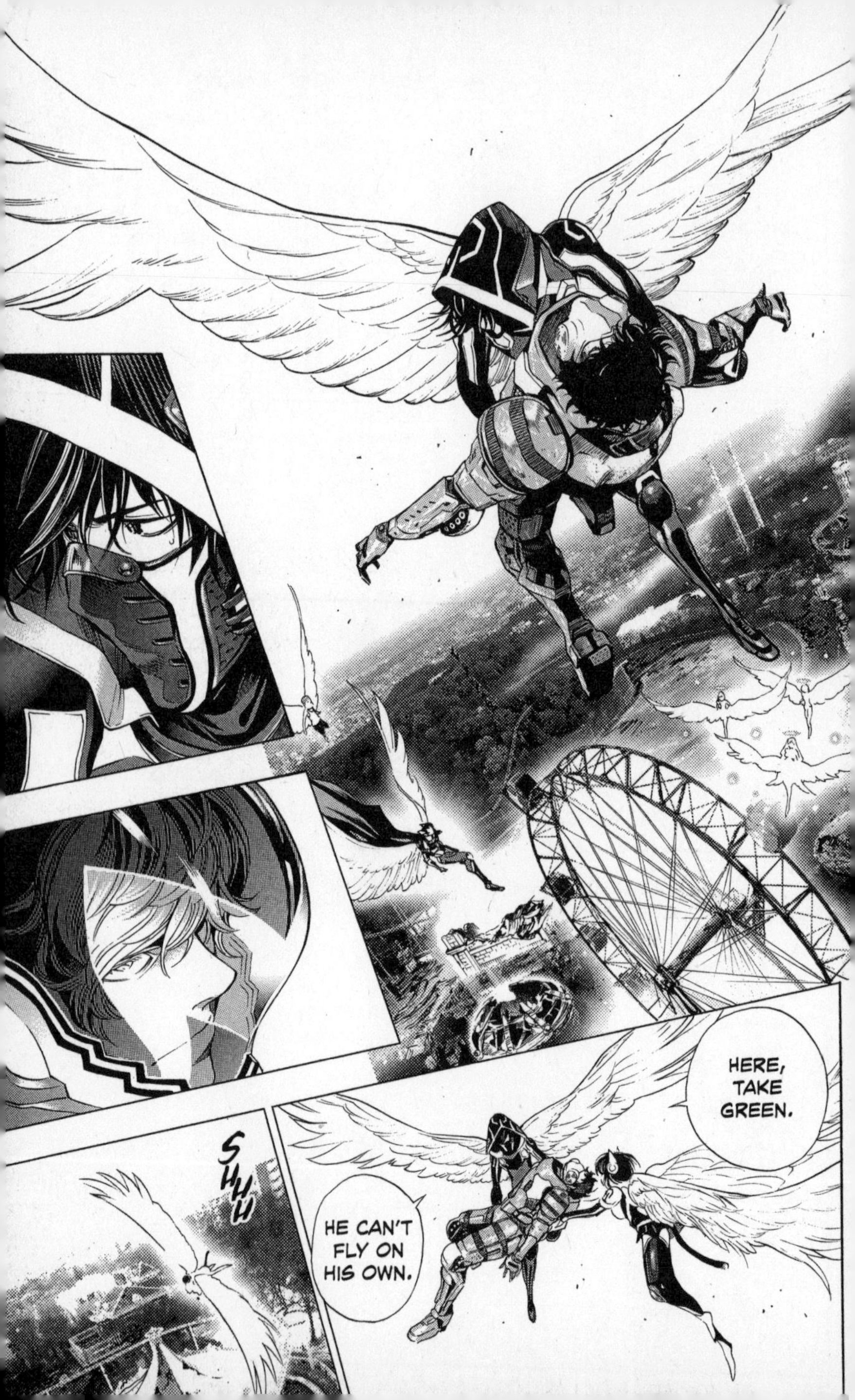
HERE, TAKE GREEN.
HE CAN'T FLY ON HIS OWN.
SHUU

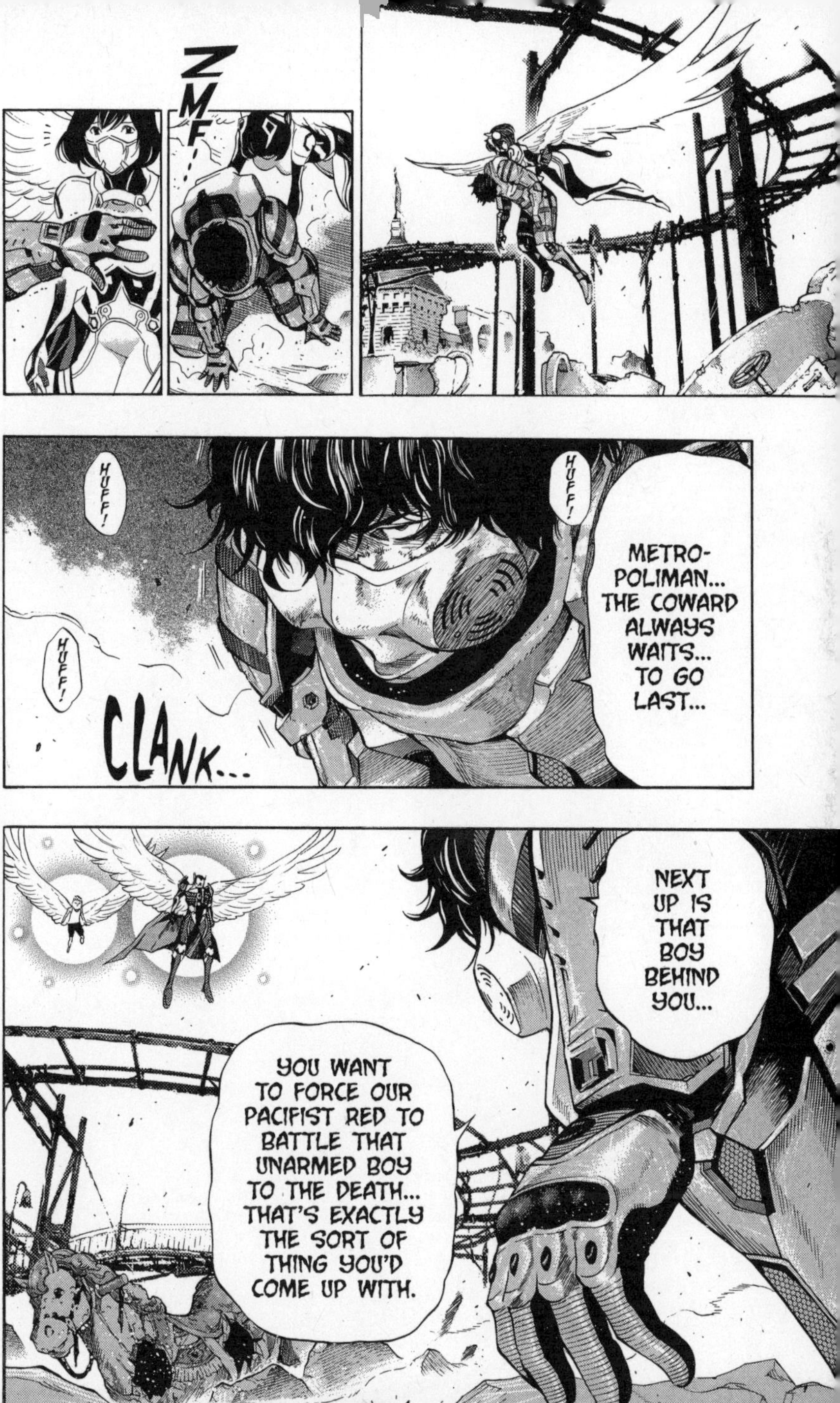
ZMF...
HUFF!
HUFF!
HUFF!
METRO-POLIMAN... THE COWARD ALWAYS WAITS... TO GO LAST...
CLANK...
NEXT UP IS THAT BOY BEHIND YOU...
YOU WANT TO FORCE OUR PACIFIST RED TO BATTLE THAT UNARMED BOY TO THE DEATH... THAT'S EXACTLY THE SORT OF THING YOU'D COME UP WITH.

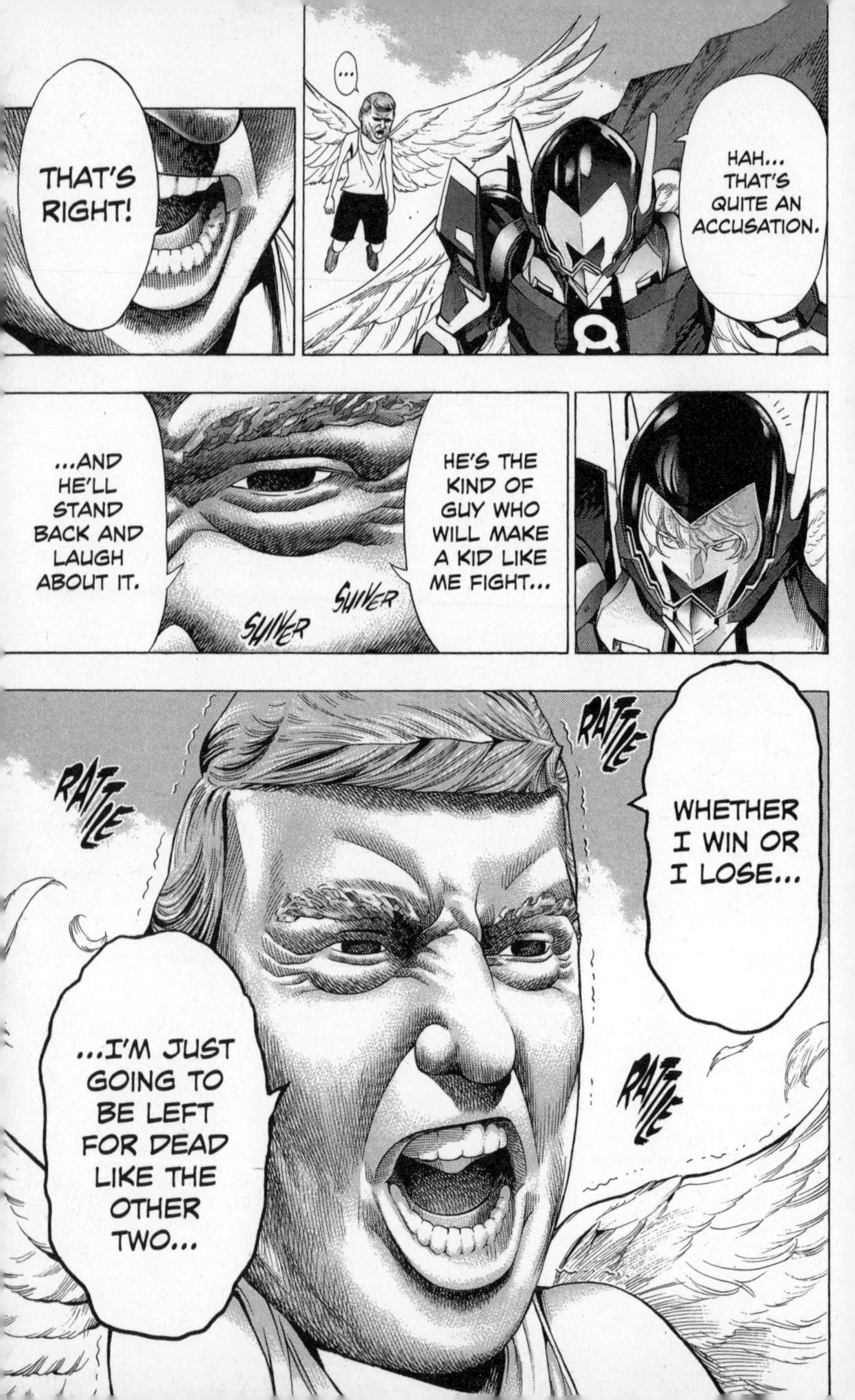
HAH... THAT'S QUITE AN ACCUSATION.
...
THAT'S RIGHT!
HE'S THE KIND OF GUY WHO WILL MAKE A KID LIKE ME FIGHT...
...AND HE'LL STAND BACK AND LAUGH ABOUT IT.
SHIVER
SHIVER
RATTLE
WHETHER I WIN OR I LOSE...
RATTLE
RATTLE
...I'M JUST GOING TO BE LEFT FOR DEAD LIKE THE OTHER TWO...

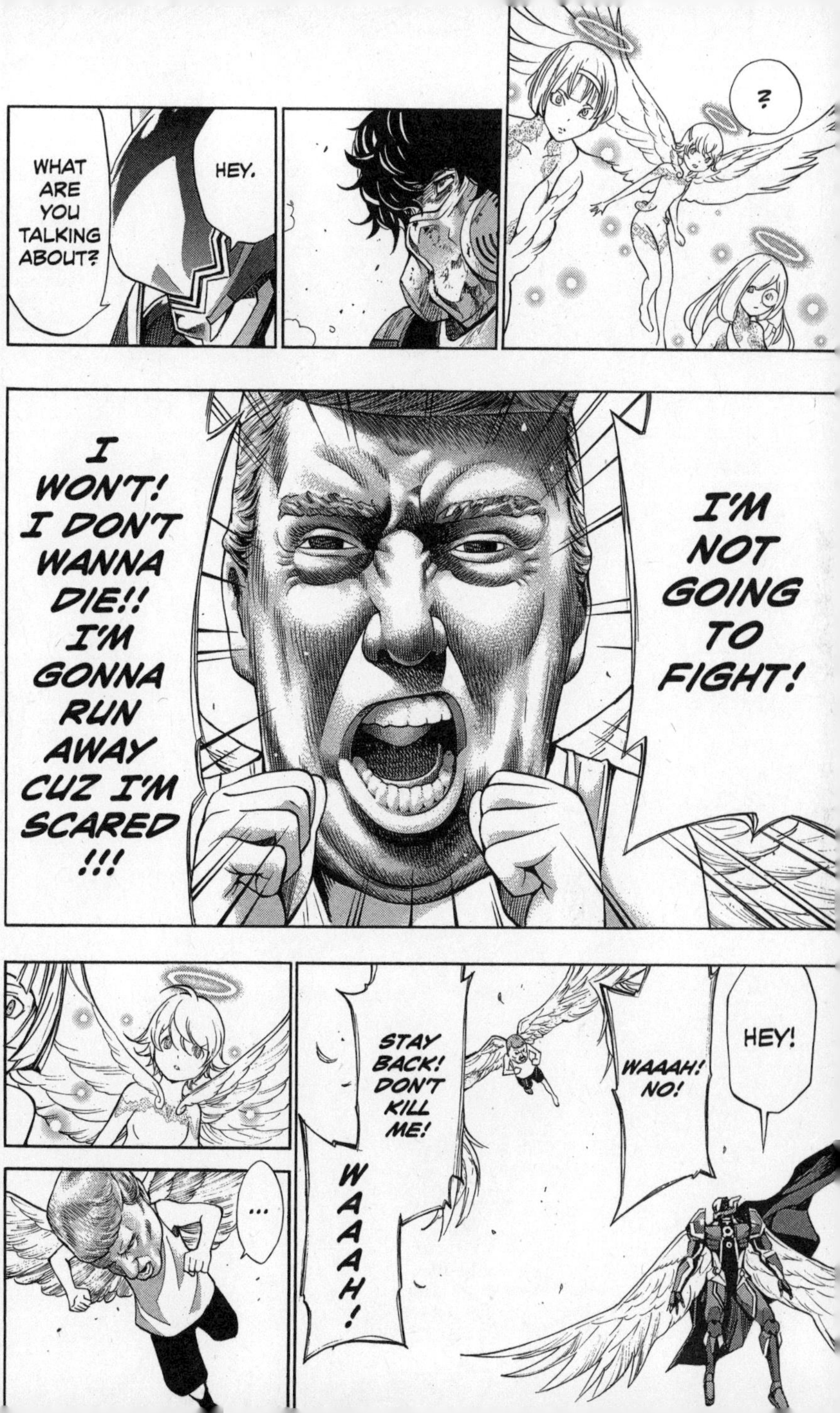
?
HEY.
WHAT ARE YOU TALKING ABOUT?
I'M NOT GOING TO FIGHT!
I WON'T! I DON'T WANNA DIE!! I'M GONNA RUN AWAY CUZ I'M SCARED!!!
HEY!
WAAAH! NO!
STAY BACK! DON'T KILL ME!
WAAAAH!
...

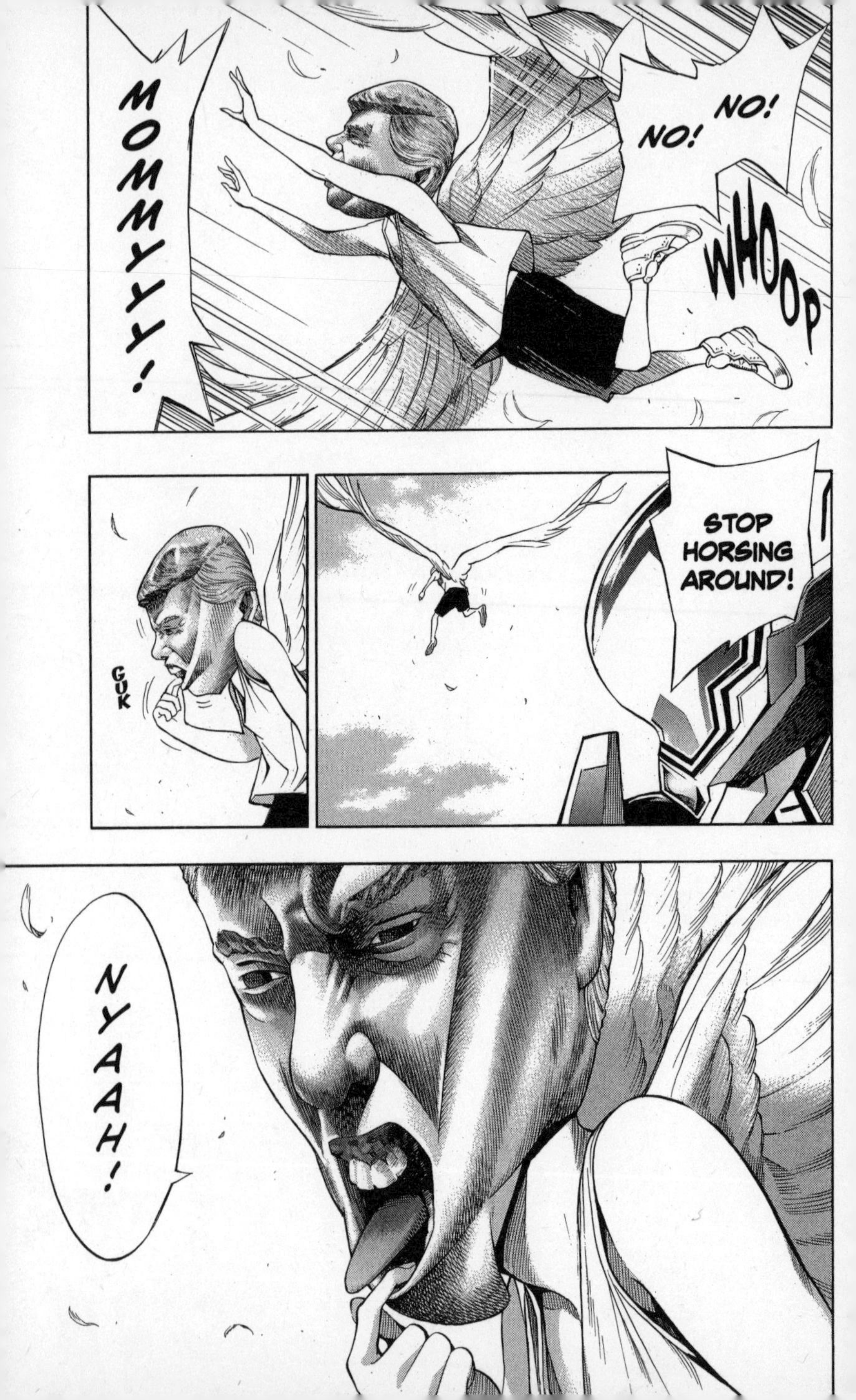
NO! NO!
WHOOP
MOMMYYYY!
STOP HORSING AROUND!
GUK
NYAAH!

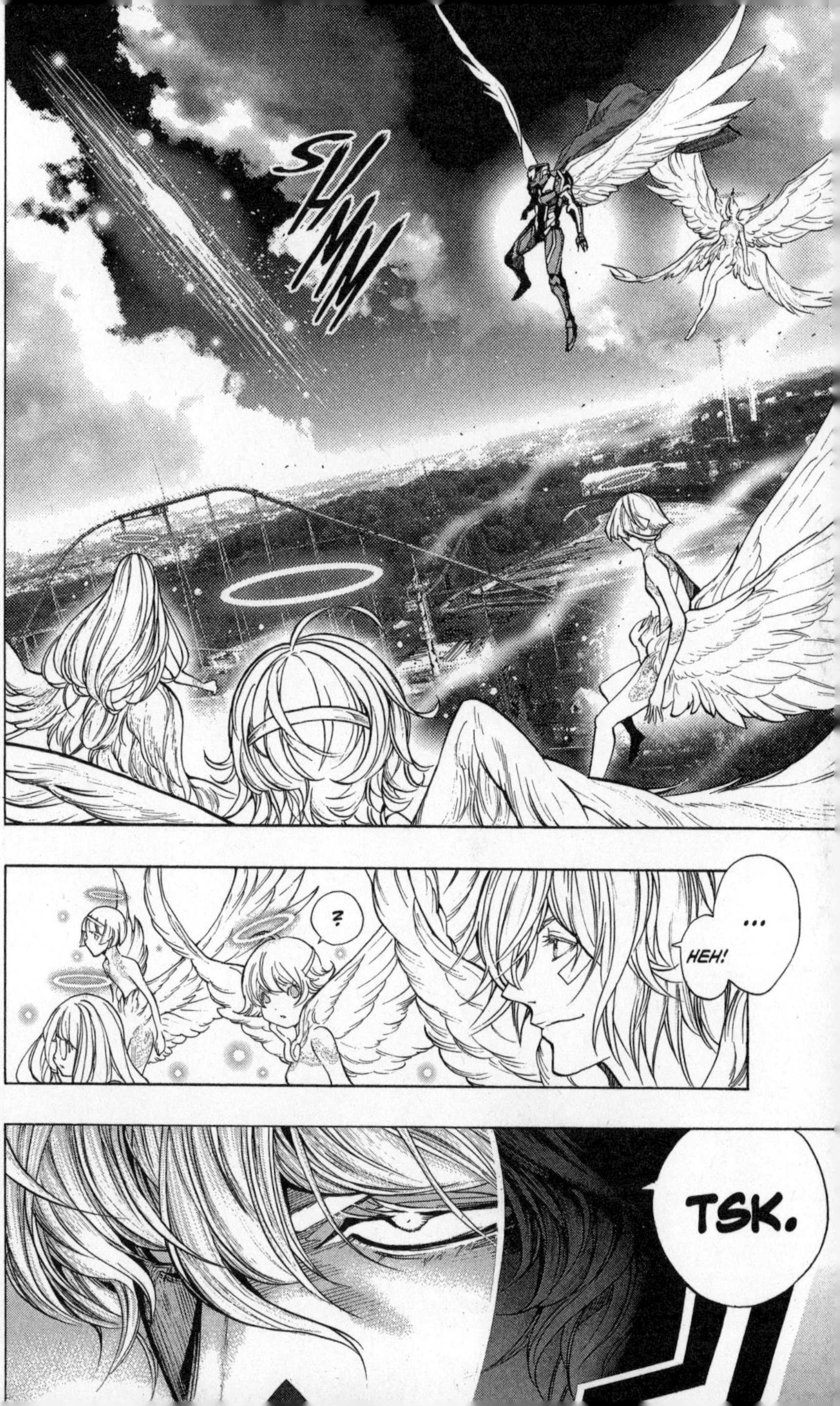
SHMM
?
... HEH!
TSK.

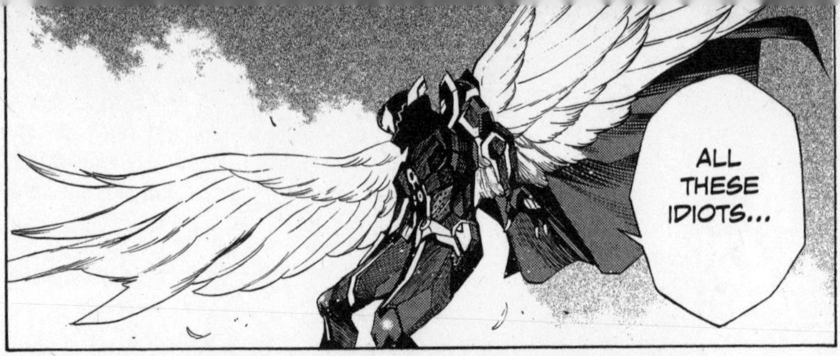
ALL THESE IDIOTS...
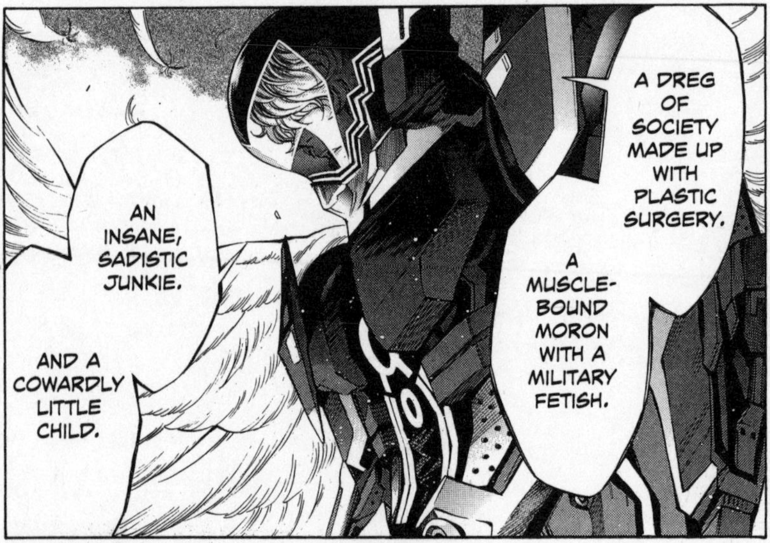
A DREG OF SOCIETY MADE UP WITH PLASTIC SURGERY.
A MUSCLE-BOUND MORON WITH A MILITARY FETISH.
AN INSANE, SADISTIC JUNKIE.
AND A COWARDLY LITTLE CHILD.
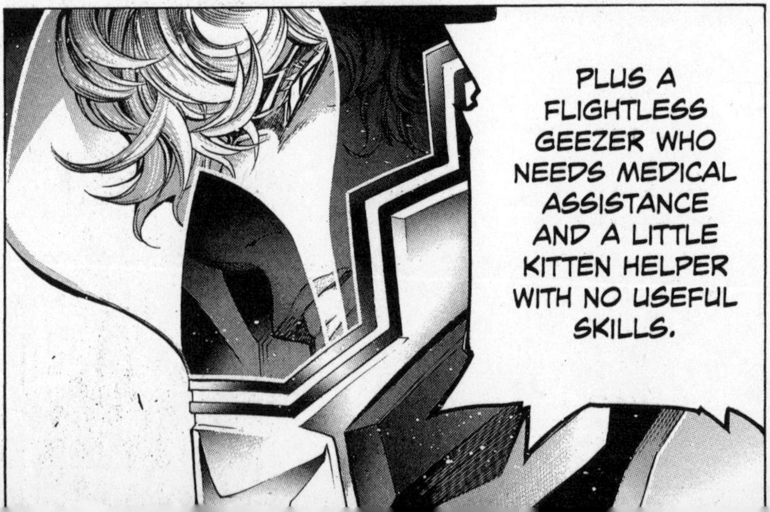
PLUS A FLIGHTLESS GEEZER WHO NEEDS MEDICAL ASSISTANCE AND A LITTLE KITTEN HELPER WITH NO USEFUL SKILLS.

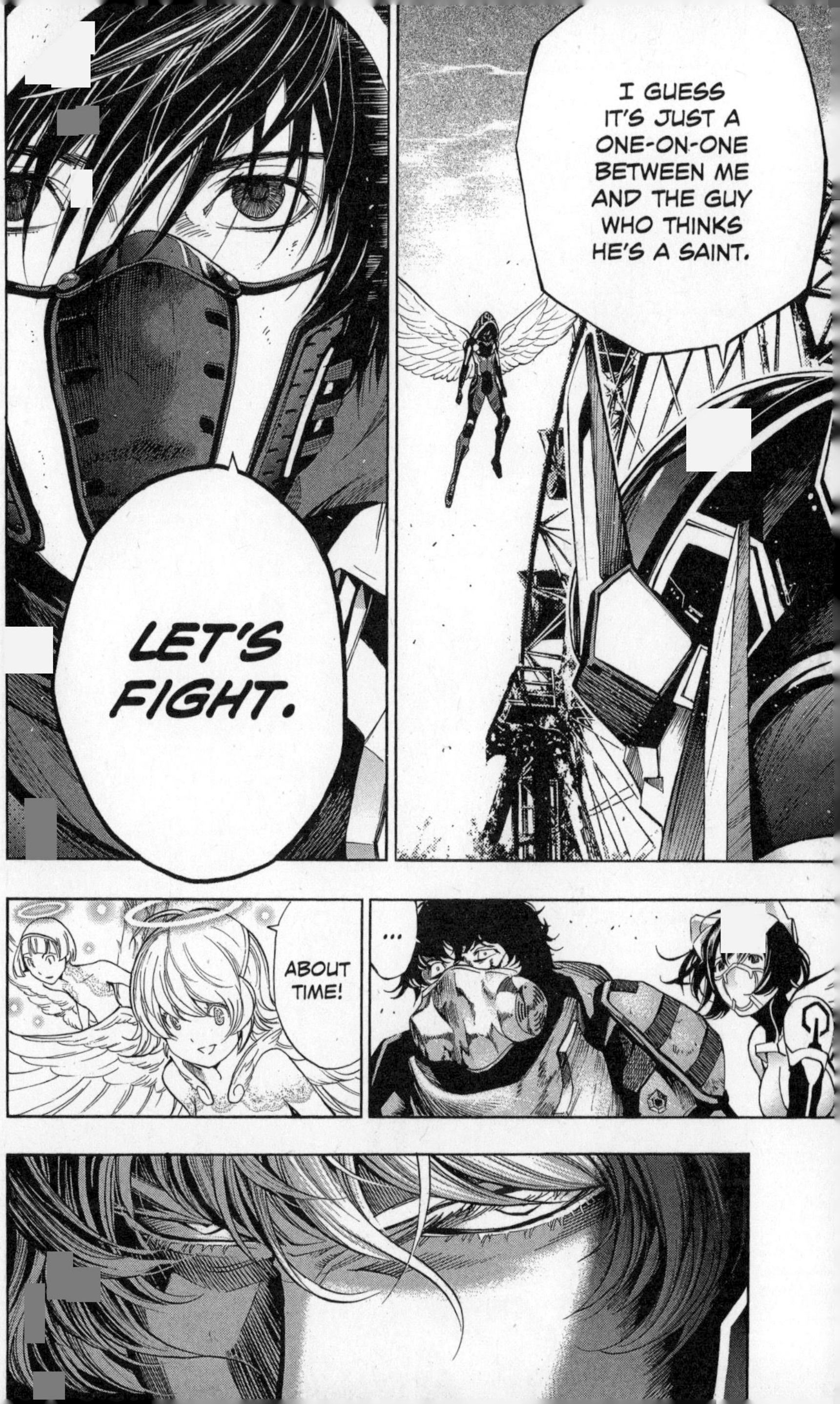
I GUESS IT'S JUST A ONE-ON-ONE BETWEEN ME AND THE GUY WHO THINKS HE'S A SAINT.
LET'S FIGHT.
...
ABOUT TIME!

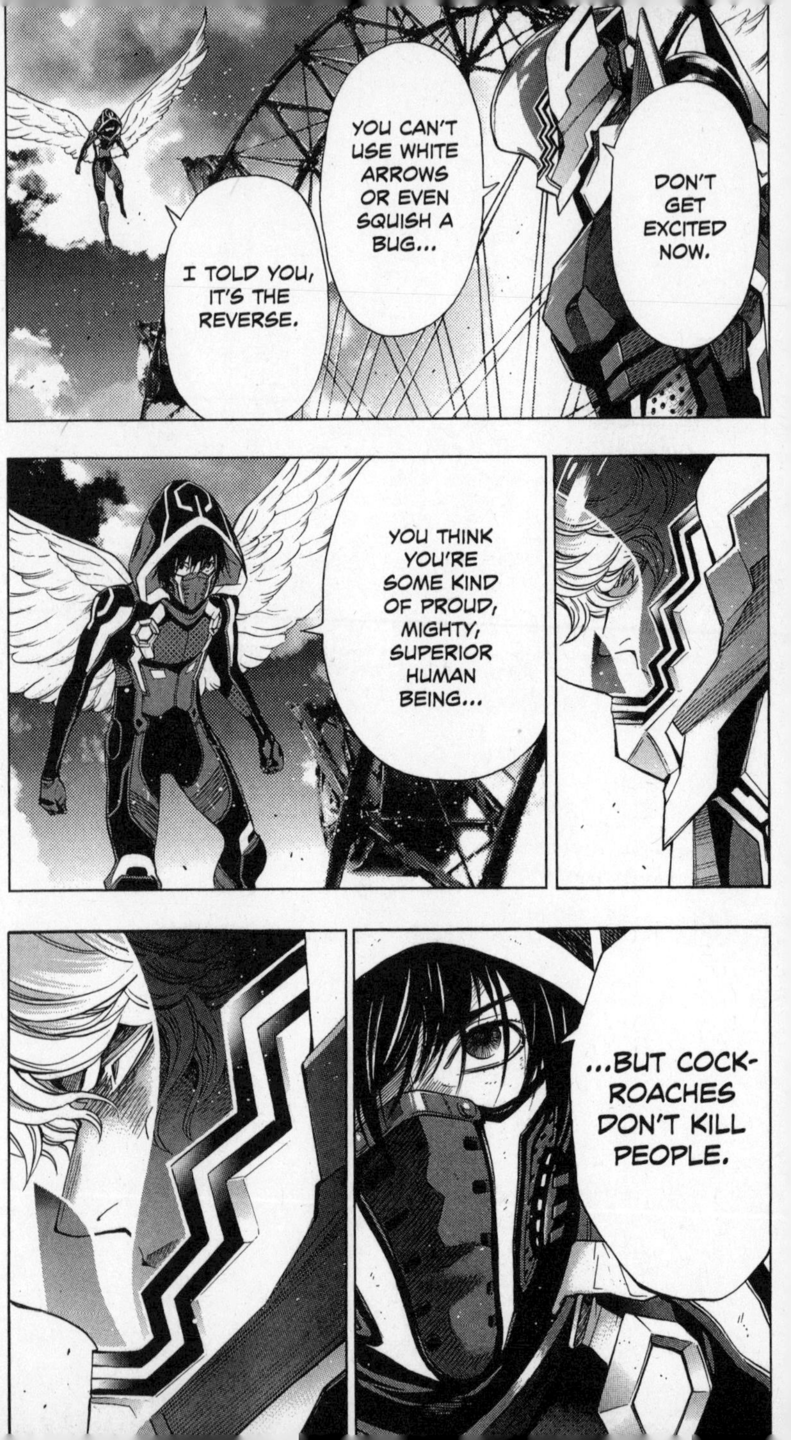
DON'T GET EXCITED NOW.
YOU CAN'T USE WHITE ARROWS OR EVEN SQUISH A BUG...
I TOLD YOU, IT'S THE REVERSE.
YOU THINK YOU'RE SOME KIND OF PROUD, MIGHTY, SUPERIOR HUMAN BEING...
...BUT COCK-ROACHES DON'T KILL PEOPLE.

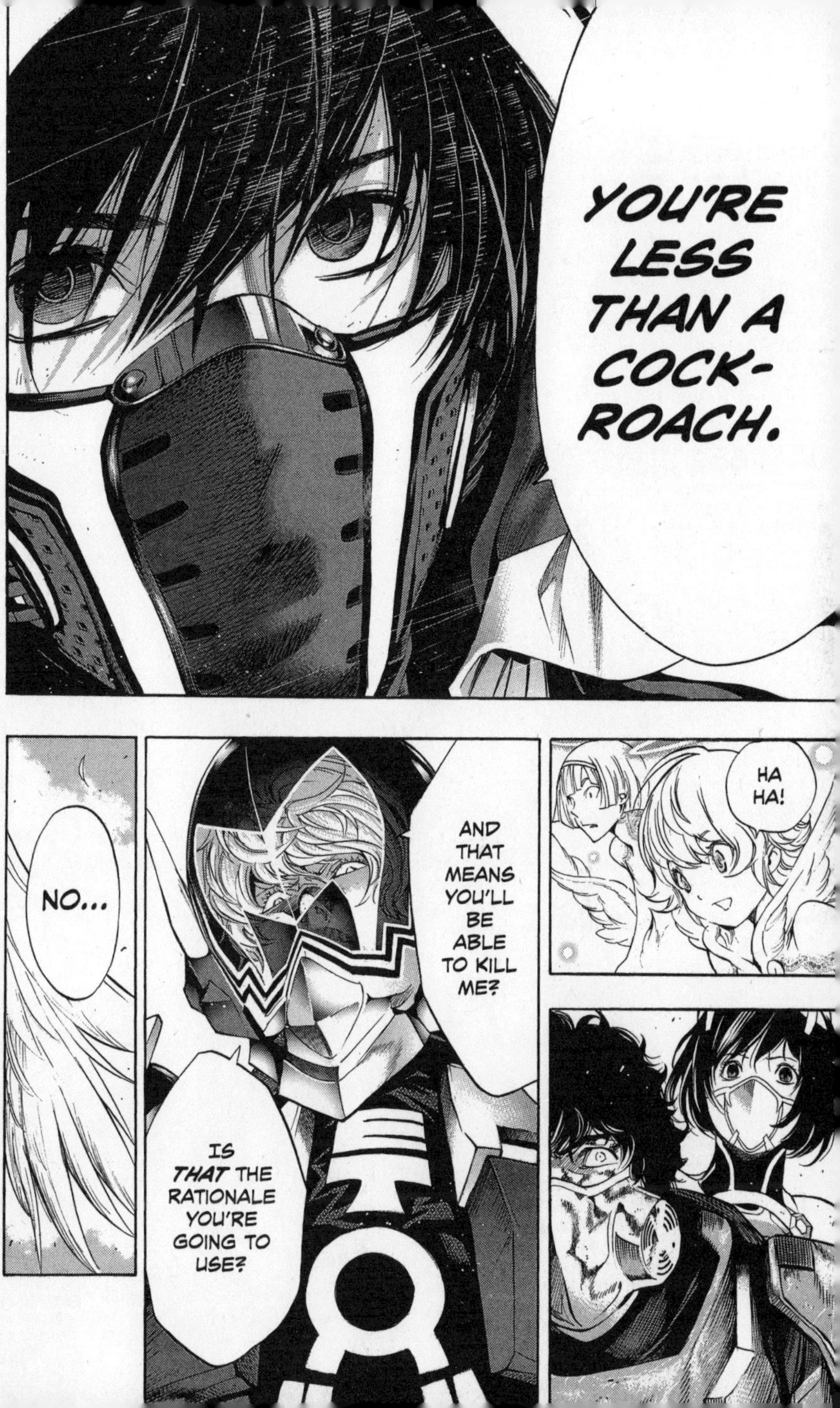
YOU'RE LESS THAN A COCK-ROACH.
HA HA!
AND THAT MEANS YOU'LL BE ABLE TO KILL ME?
IS *THAT* THE RATIONALE YOU'RE GOING TO USE?
NO...

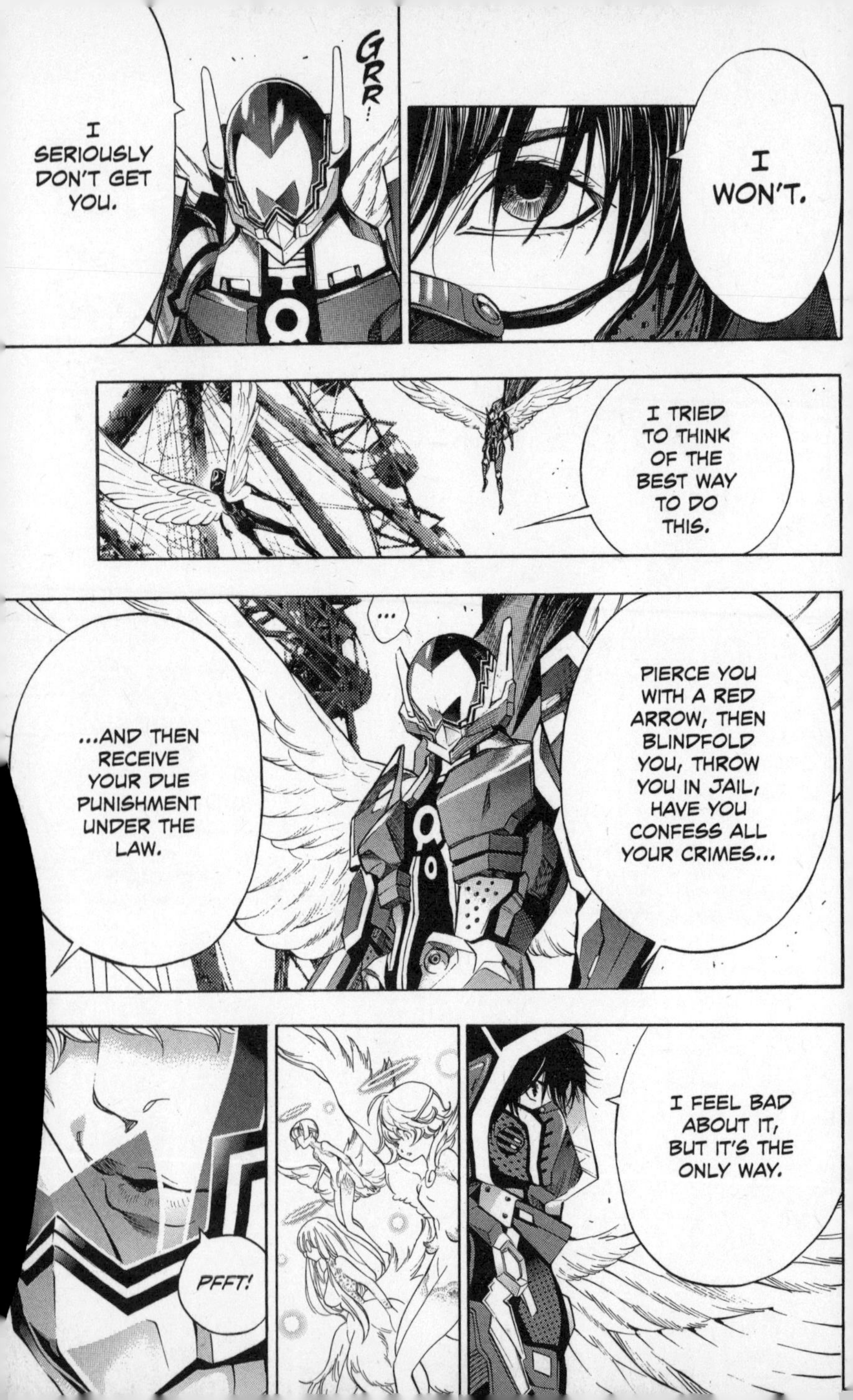
I WON'T.
GRR...
...
I SERIOUSLY DON'T GET YOU.
I TRIED TO THINK OF THE BEST WAY TO DO THIS.
PIERCE YOU WITH A RED ARROW, THEN BLINDFOLD YOU, THROW YOU IN JAIL, HAVE YOU CONFESS ALL YOUR CRIMES...
...
...AND THEN RECEIVE YOUR DUE PUNISHMENT UNDER THE LAW.
I FEEL BAD ABOUT IT, BUT IT'S THE ONLY WAY.
PFFT!

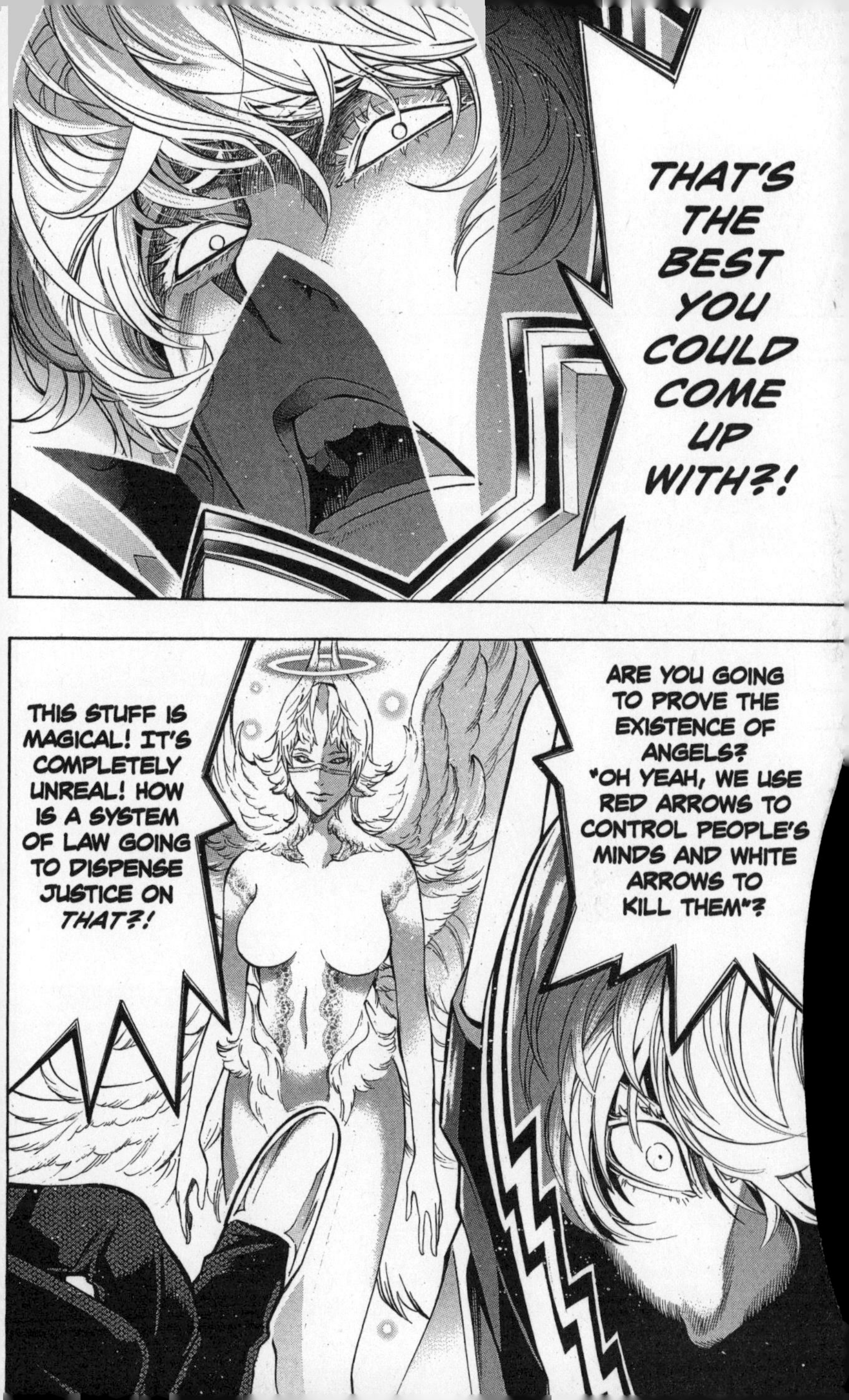
THAT'S THE BEST YOU COULD COME UP WITH?!
ARE YOU GOING TO PROVE THE EXISTENCE OF ANGELS? "OH YEAH, WE USE RED ARROWS TO CONTROL PEOPLE'S MINDS AND WHITE ARROWS TO KILL THEM"?
THIS STUFF IS MAGICAL! IT'S COMPLETELY UNREAL! HOW IS A SYSTEM OF LAW GOING TO DISPENSE JUSTICE ON *THAT*?!

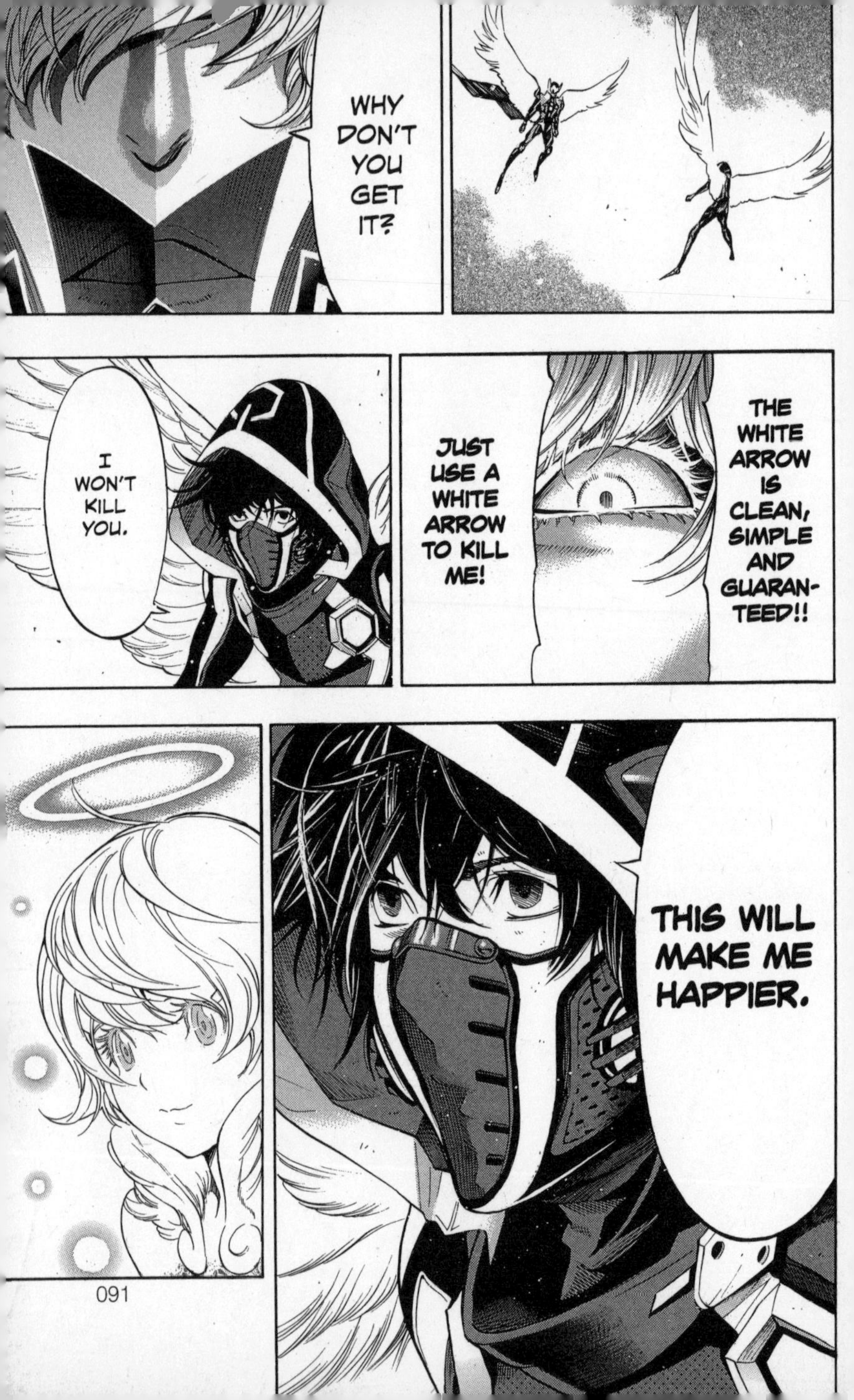
WHY DON'T YOU GET IT?
THE WHITE ARROW IS CLEAN, SIMPLE AND GUARAN-TEED!!
JUST USE A WHITE ARROW TO KILL ME!
I WON'T KILL YOU.
THIS WILL MAKE ME HAPPIER.

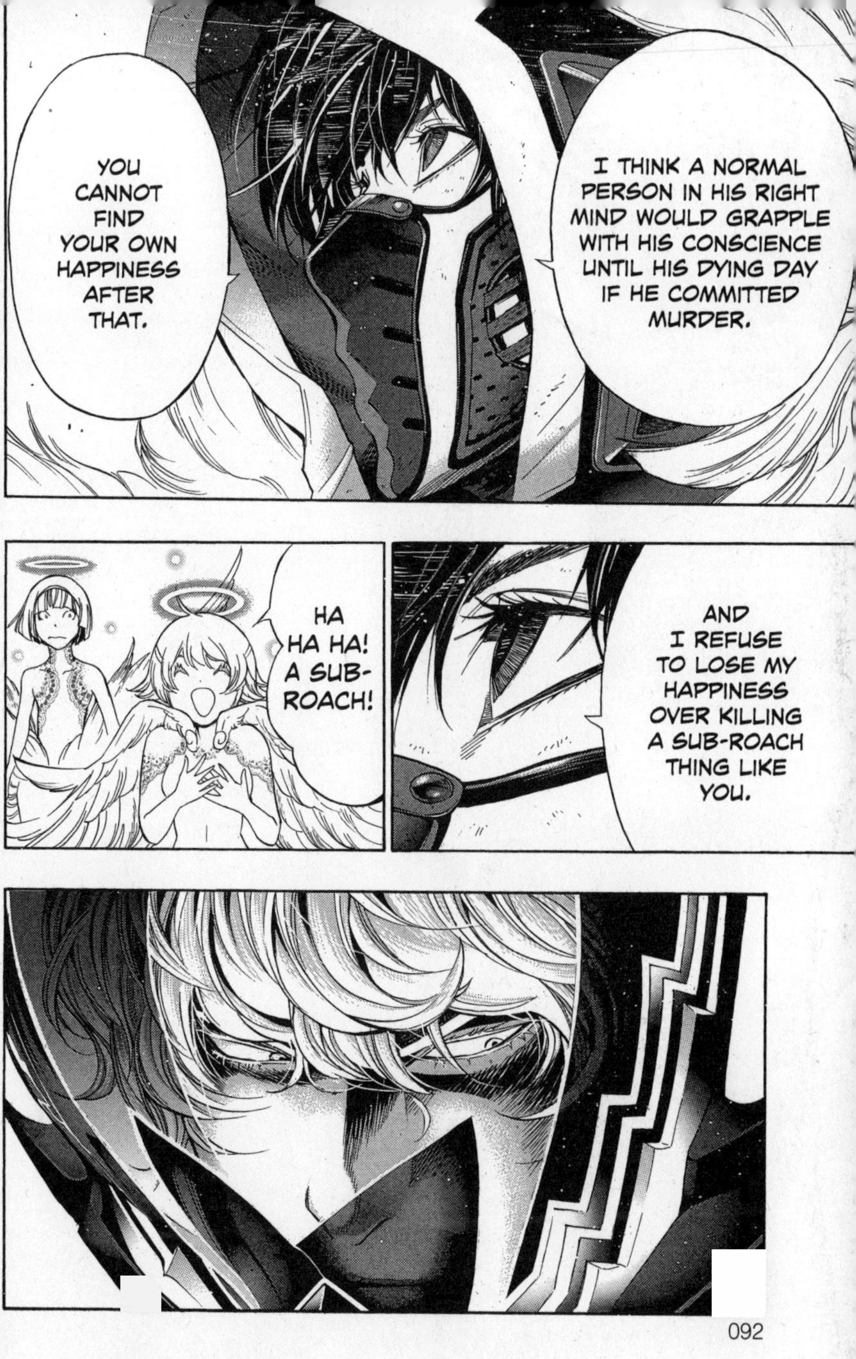
I THINK A NORMAL PERSON IN HIS RIGHT MIND WOULD GRAPPLE WITH HIS CONSCIENCE UNTIL HIS DYING DAY IF HE COMMITTED MURDER.
YOU CANNOT FIND YOUR OWN HAPPINESS AFTER THAT.
AND I REFUSE TO LOSE MY HAPPINESS OVER KILLING A SUB-ROACH THING LIKE YOU.
HA HA HA! A SUB-ROACH!

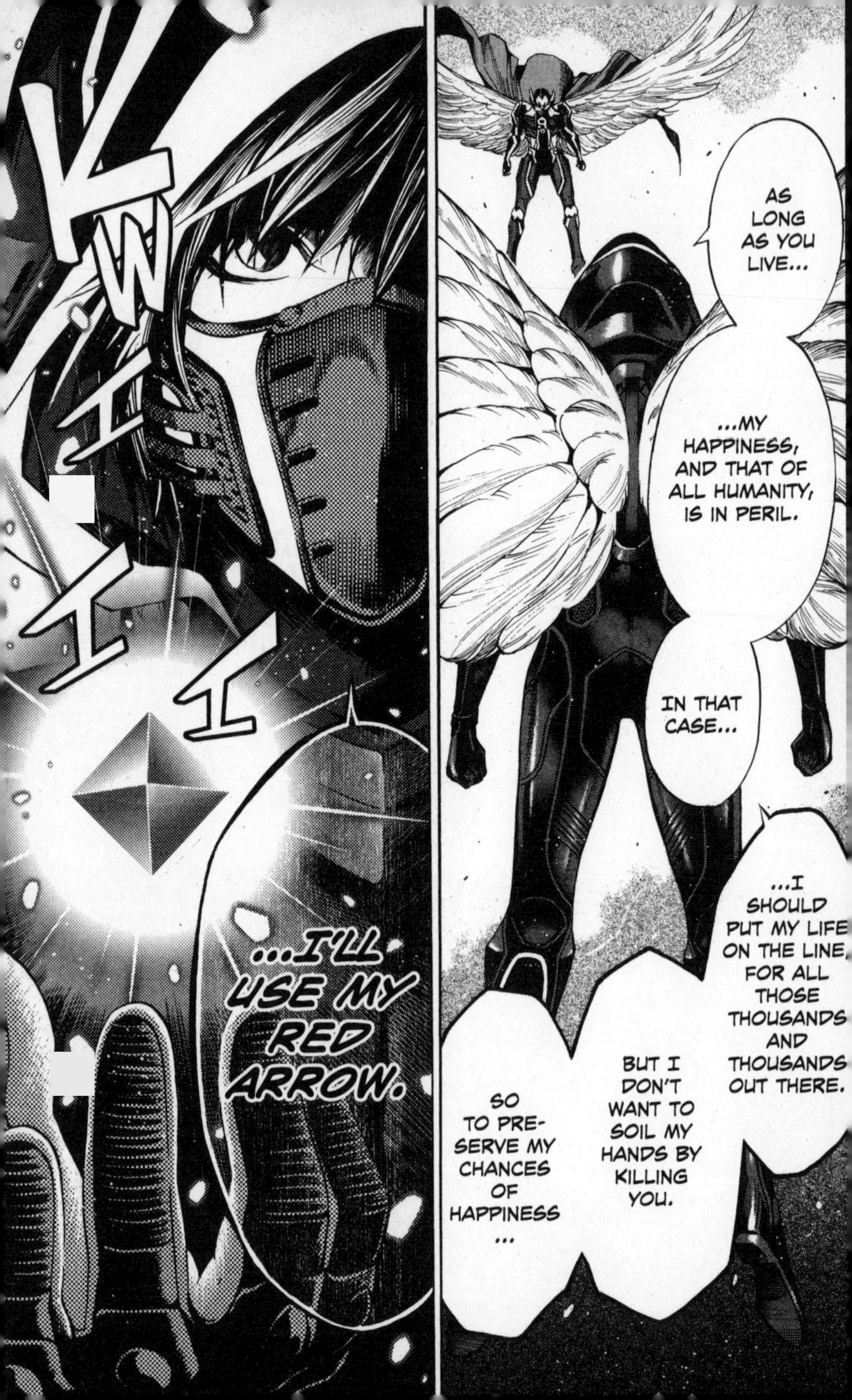
AS LONG AS YOU LIVE...
...MY HAPPINESS, AND THAT OF ALL HUMANITY, IS IN PERIL.
IN THAT CASE...
...I SHOULD PUT MY LIFE ON THE LINE FOR ALL THOSE THOUSANDS AND THOUSANDS OUT THERE.
BUT I DON'T WANT TO SOIL MY HANDS BY KILLING YOU.
SO TO PRE-SERVE MY CHANCES OF HAPPINESS...
KWIII
...I'LL USE MY RED ARROW.

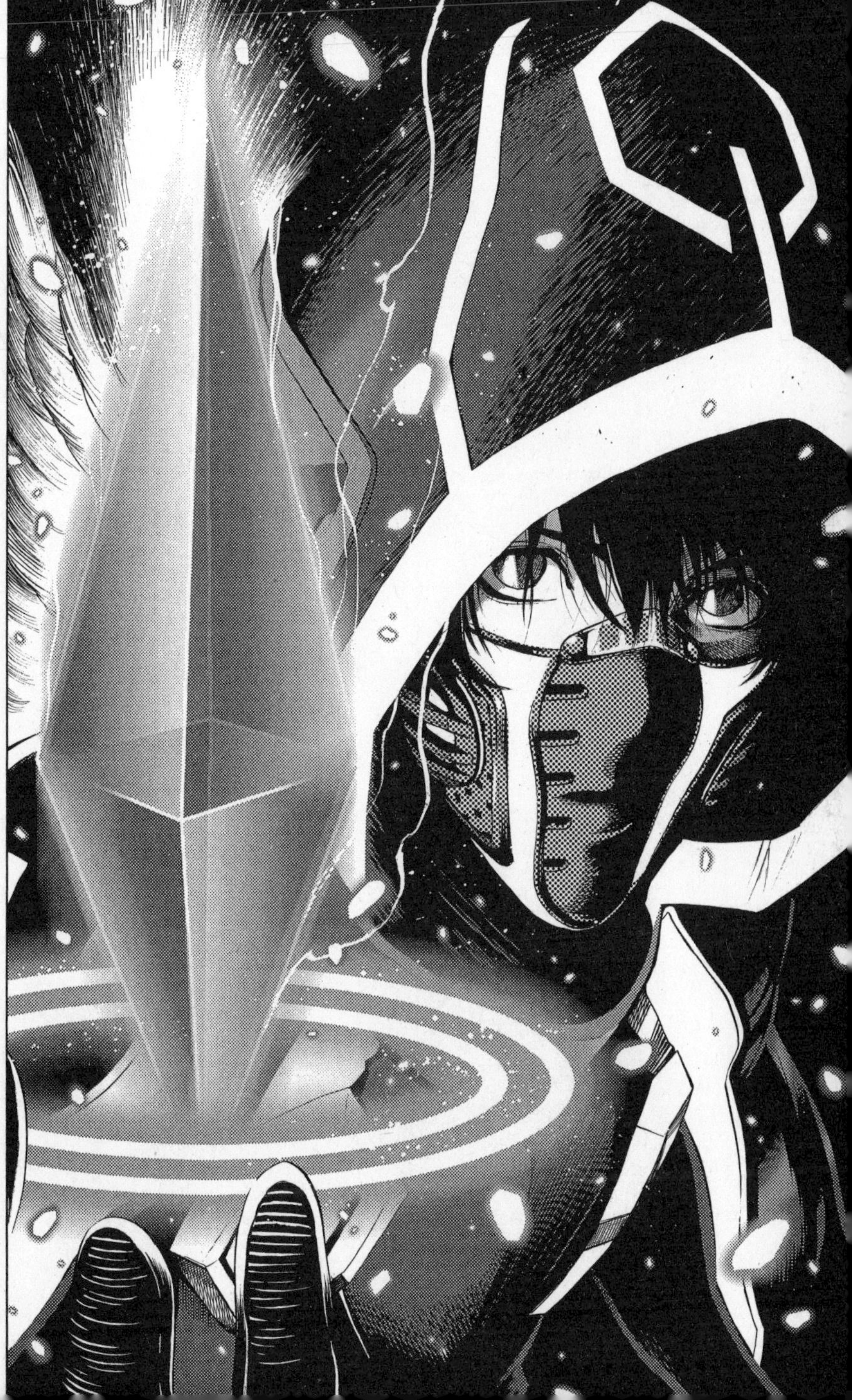

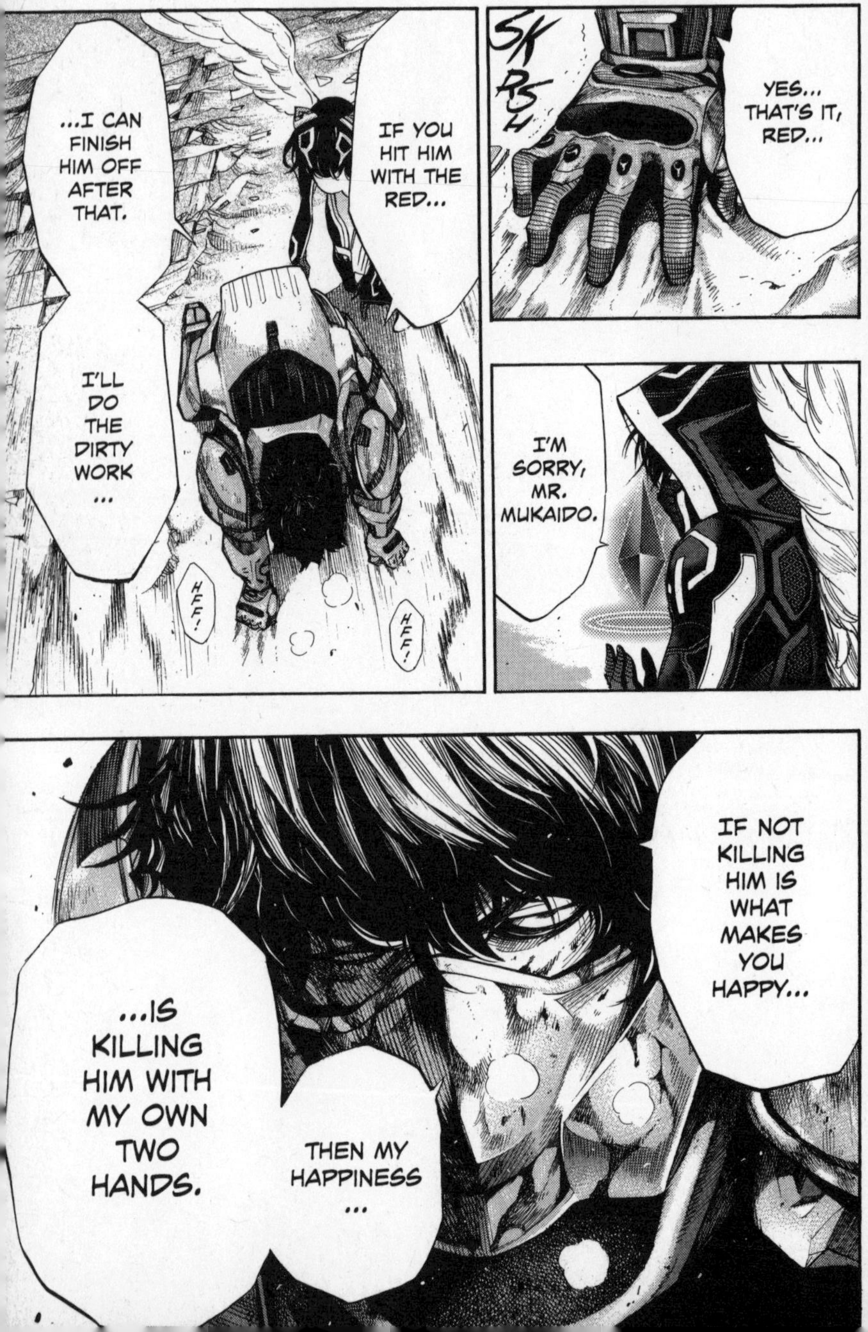
SKRSH
YES... THAT'S IT, RED...
I'M SORRY, MR. MUKAIDO.
IF YOU HIT HIM WITH THE RED...
...I CAN FINISH HIM OFF AFTER THAT.
I'LL DO THE DIRTY WORK...
HFF!
HFF!
IF NOT KILLING HIM IS WHAT MAKES YOU HAPPY...
THEN MY HAPPINESS...
...IS KILLING HIM WITH MY OWN TWO HANDS.

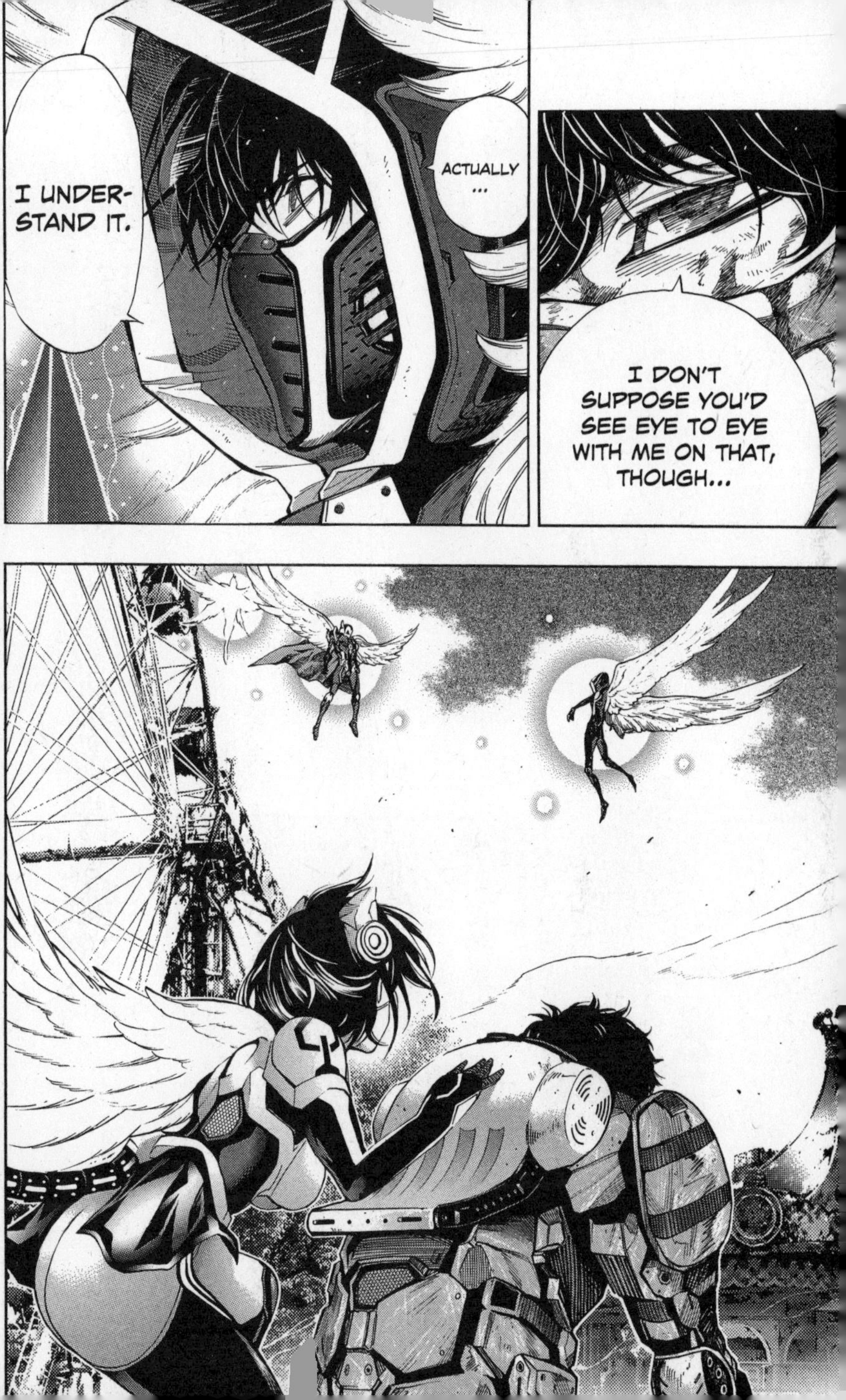

I DON'T SUPPOSE YOU'D SEE EYE TO EYE WITH ME ON THAT, THOUGH...
ACTUALLY...
I UNDER-STAND IT.

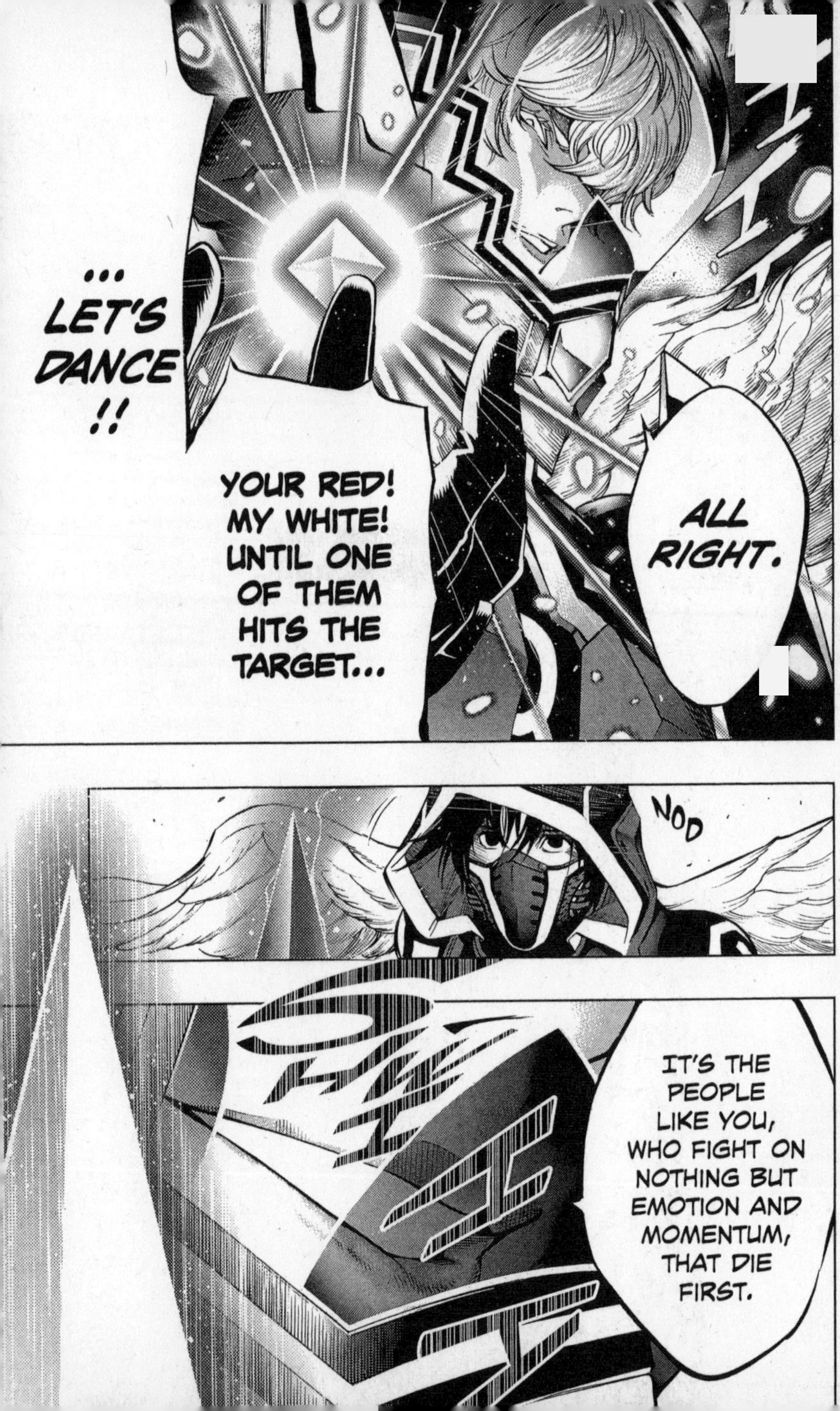
ALL RIGHT.
YOUR RED! MY WHITE! UNTIL ONE OF THEM HITS THE TARGET...
...LET'S DANCE!!
NOD
IT'S THE PEOPLE LIKE YOU, WHO FIGHT ON NOTHING BUT EMOTION AND MOMENTUM, THAT DIE FIRST.

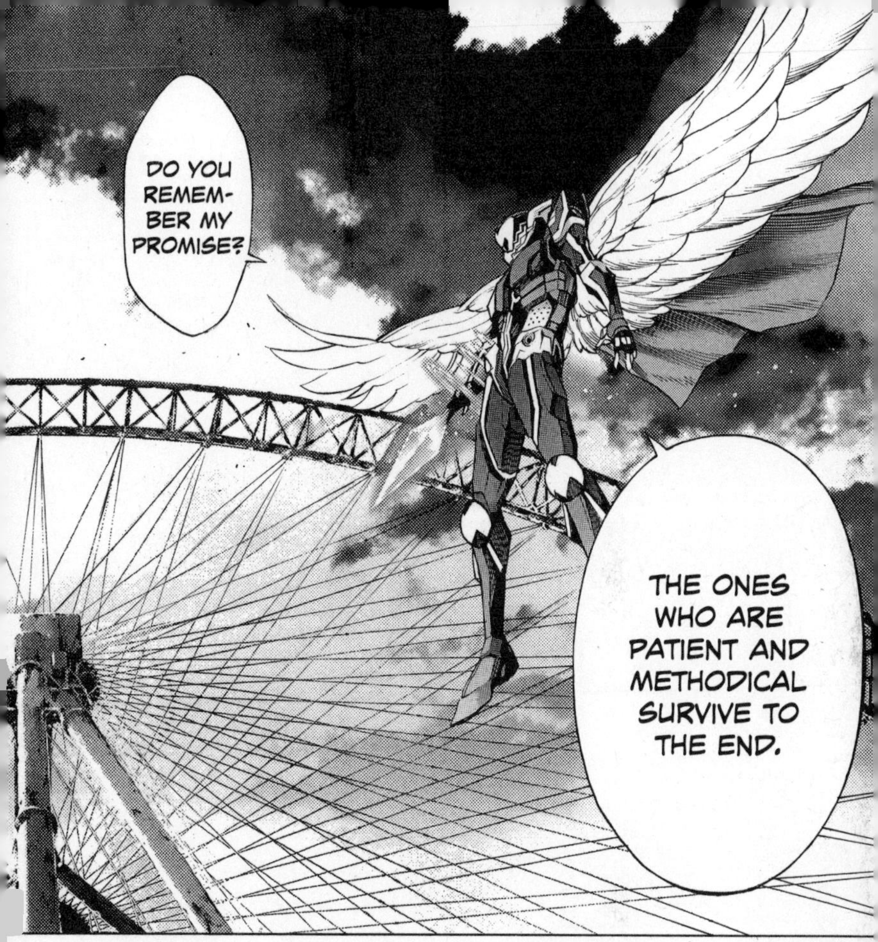
DO YOU REMEMBER MY PROMISE?
THE ONES WHO ARE PATIENT AND METHODICAL SURVIVE TO THE END.
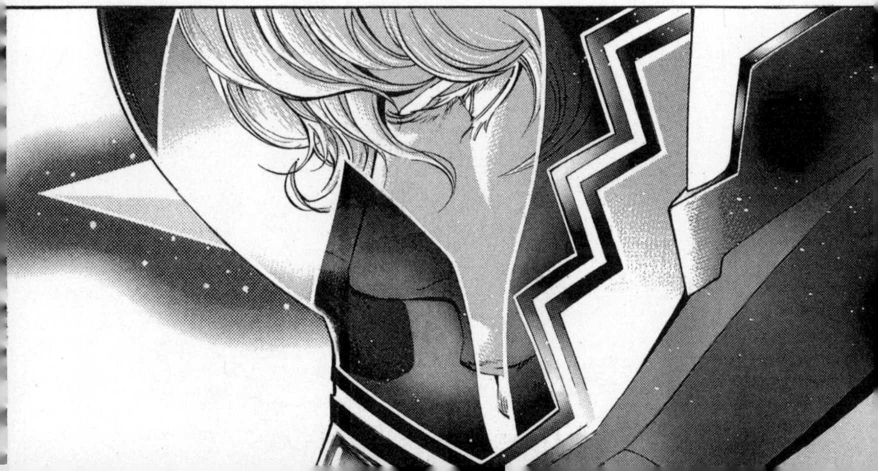

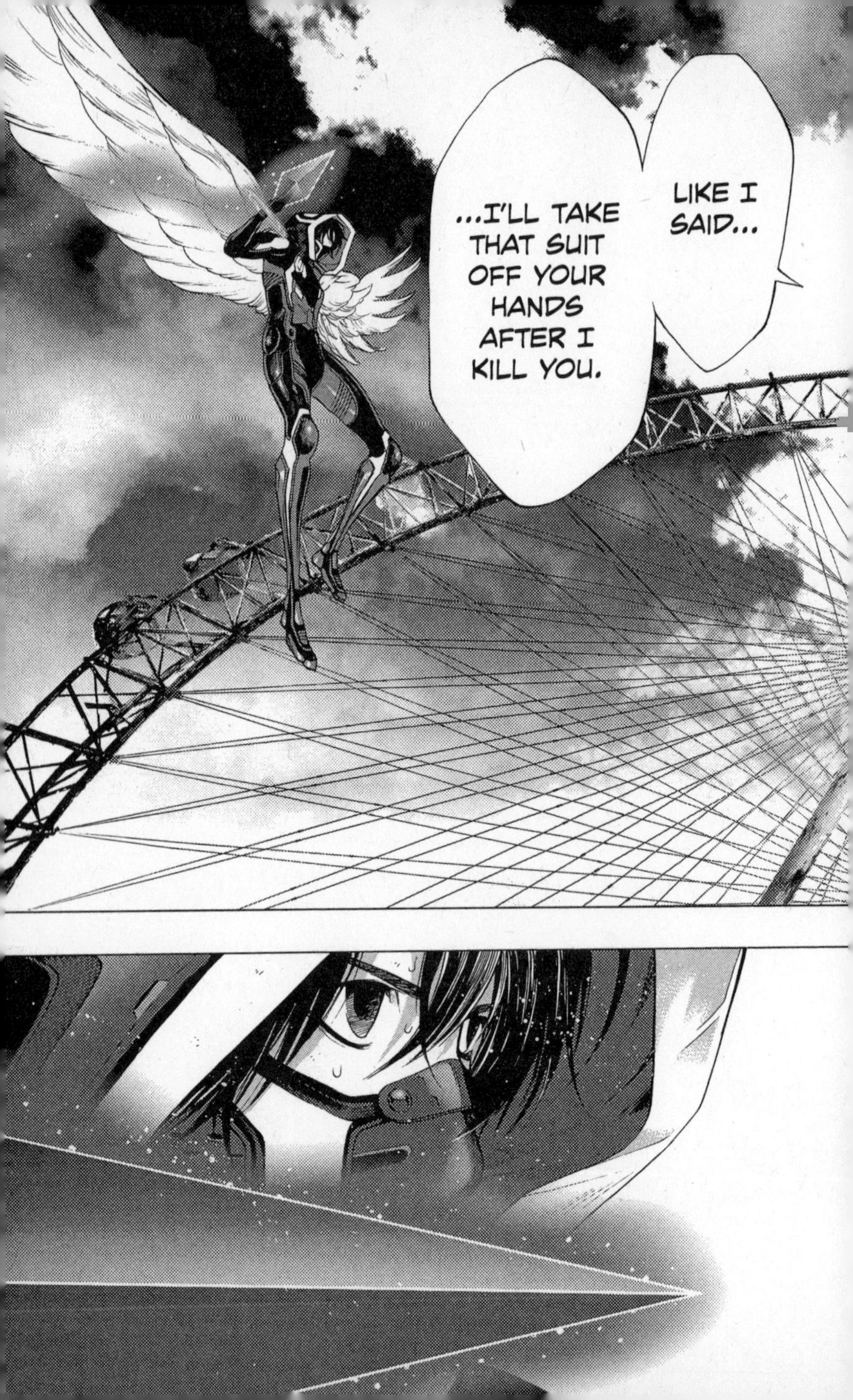
LIKE I SAID...
...I'LL TAKE THAT SUIT OFF YOUR HANDS AFTER I KILL YOU.

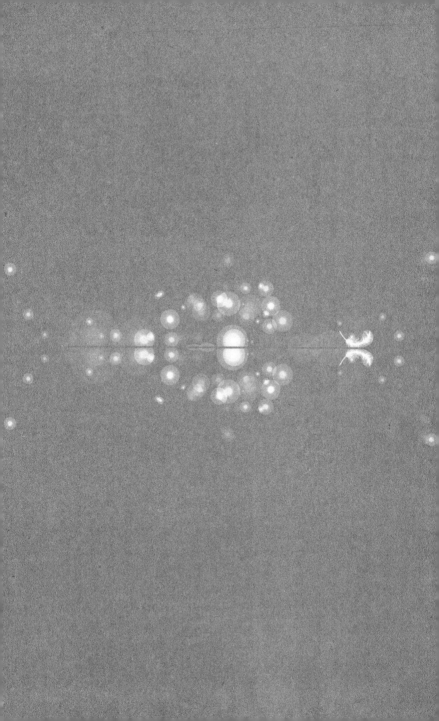

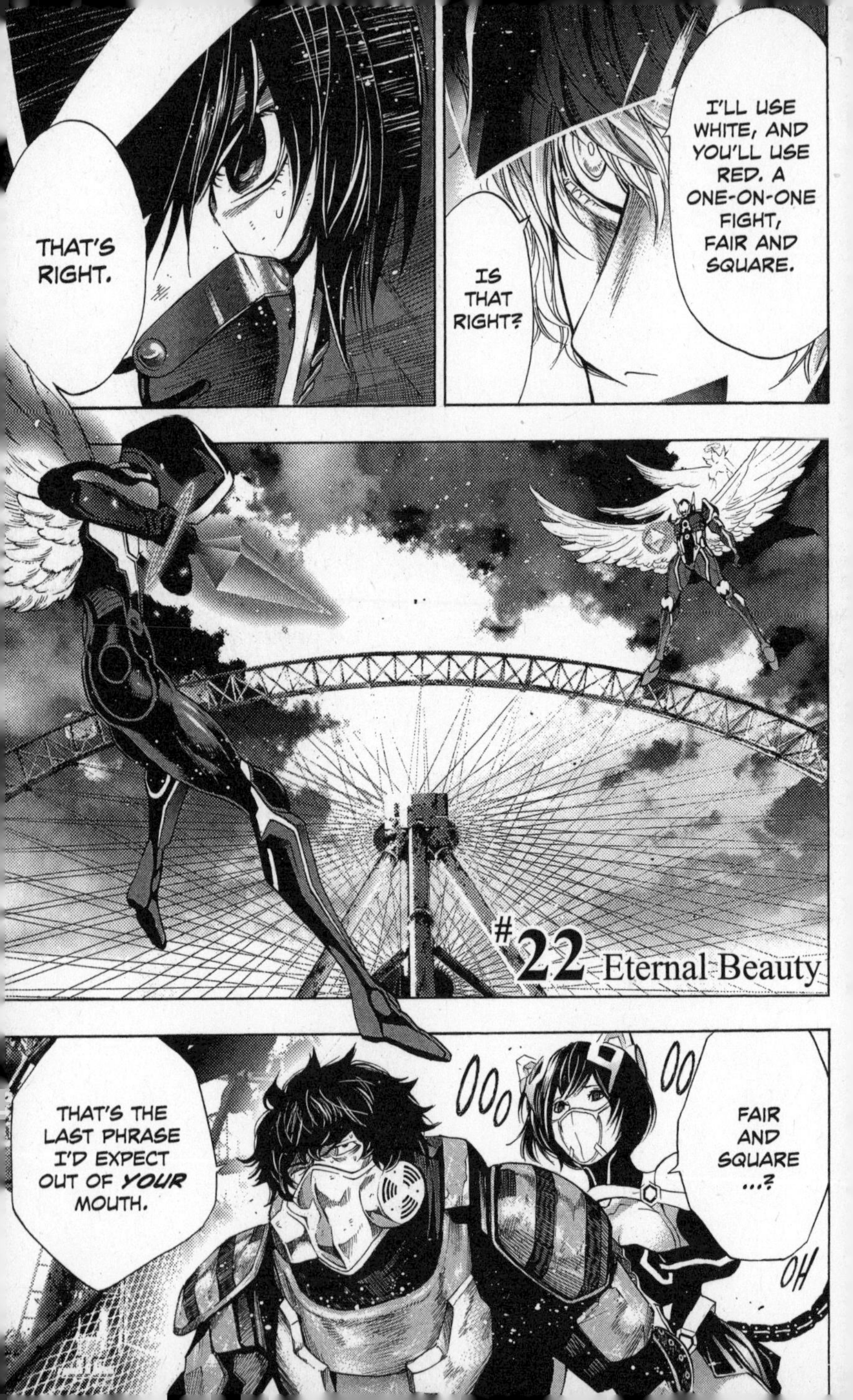
I'LL USE WHITE, AND YOU'LL USE RED. A ONE-ON-ONE FIGHT, FAIR AND SQUARE.
IS THAT RIGHT?
THAT'S RIGHT.
#22 Eternal Beauty
FAIR AND SQUARE ...?
OH
THAT'S THE LAST PHRASE I'D EXPECT OUT OF *YOUR* MOUTH.

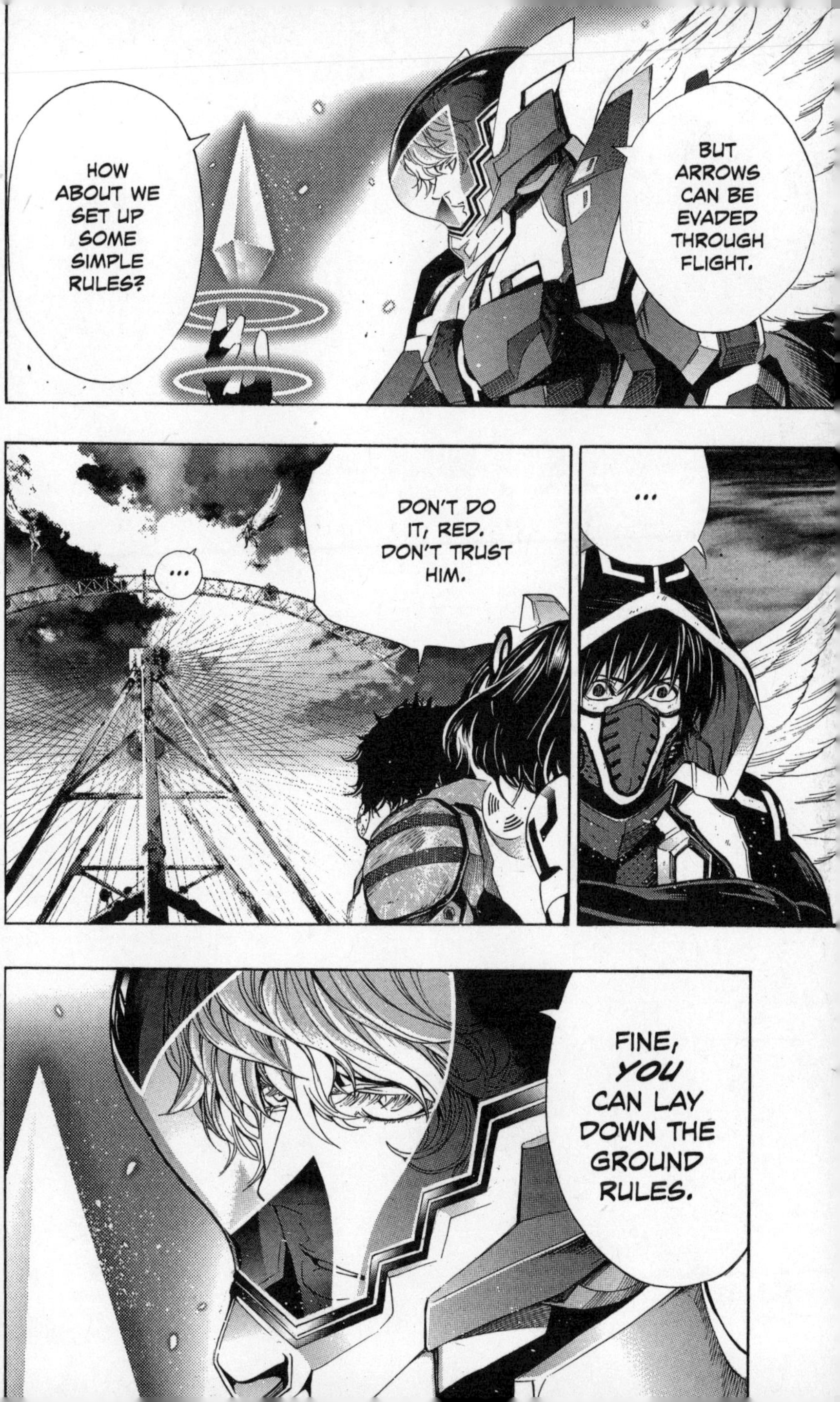
BUT ARROWS CAN BE EVADED THROUGH FLIGHT.
HOW ABOUT WE SET UP SOME SIMPLE RULES?
...
DON'T DO IT, RED. DON'T TRUST HIM.
...
FINE, *YOU* CAN LAY DOWN THE GROUND RULES.

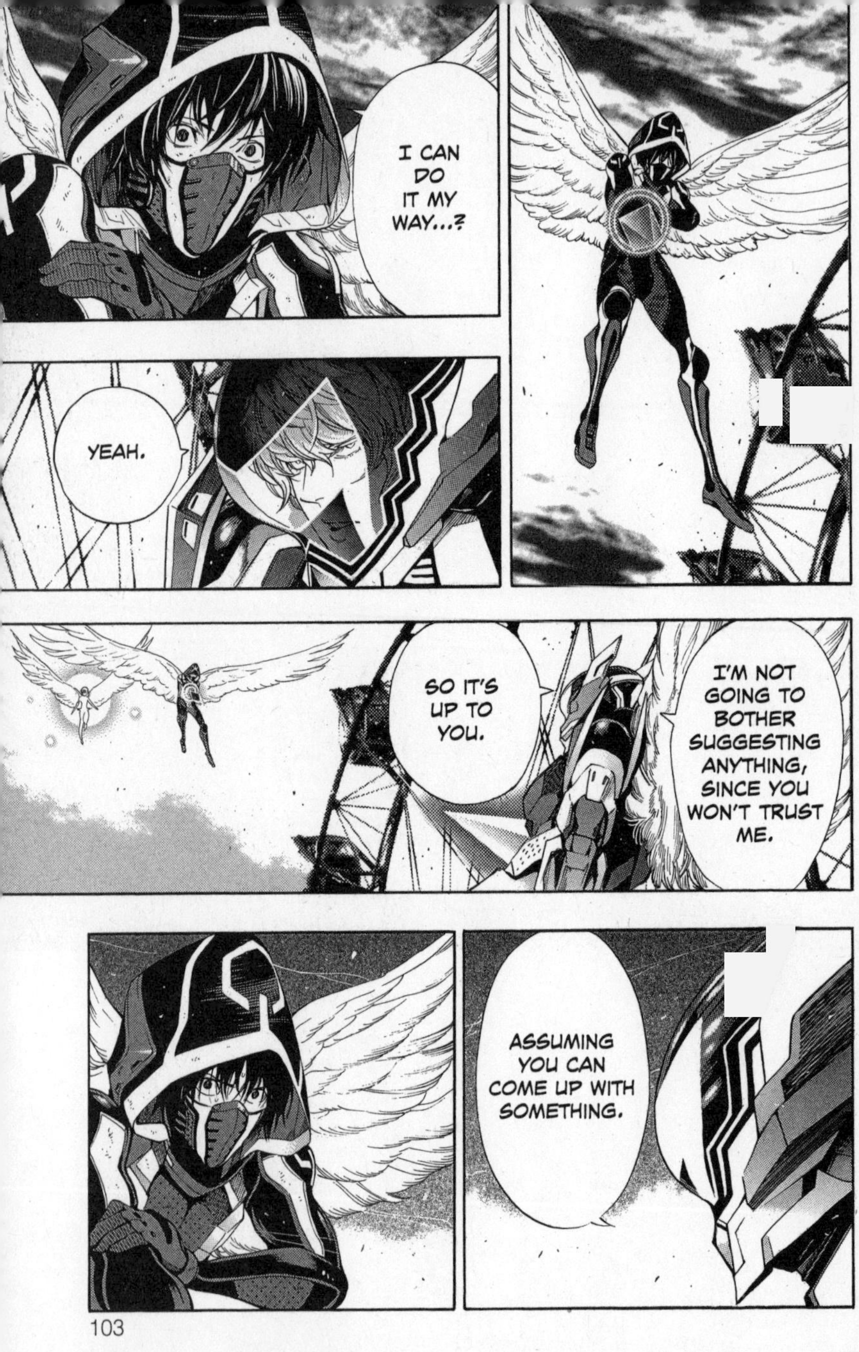
I CAN DO IT MY WAY...?
YEAH.
I'M NOT GOING TO BOTHER SUGGESTING ANYTHING, SINCE YOU WON'T TRUST ME.
SO IT'S UP TO YOU.
ASSUMING YOU CAN COME UP WITH SOMETHING.

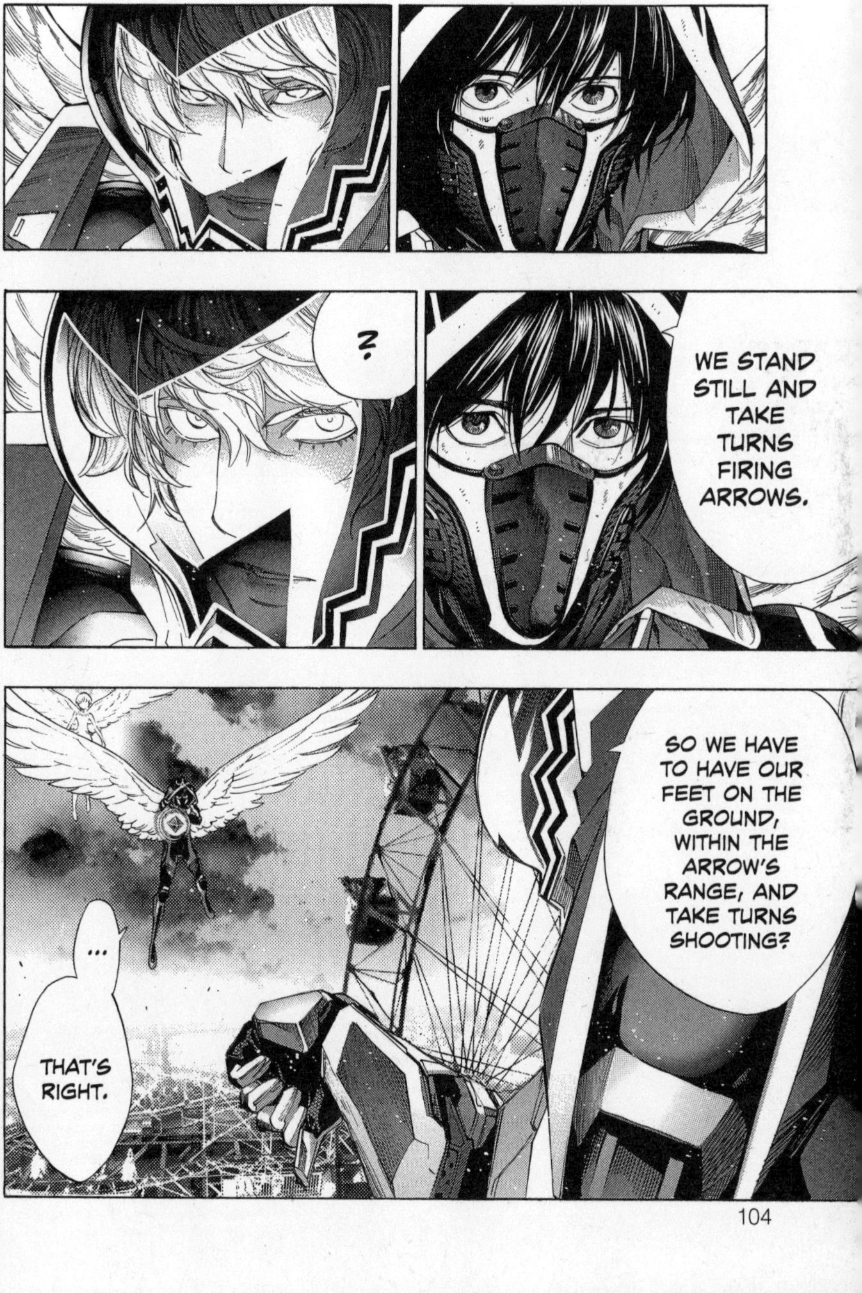
?
WE STAND STILL AND TAKE TURNS FIRING ARROWS.
SO WE HAVE TO HAVE OUR FEET ON THE GROUND, WITHIN THE ARROW'S RANGE, AND TAKE TURNS SHOOTING?
...
THAT'S RIGHT.

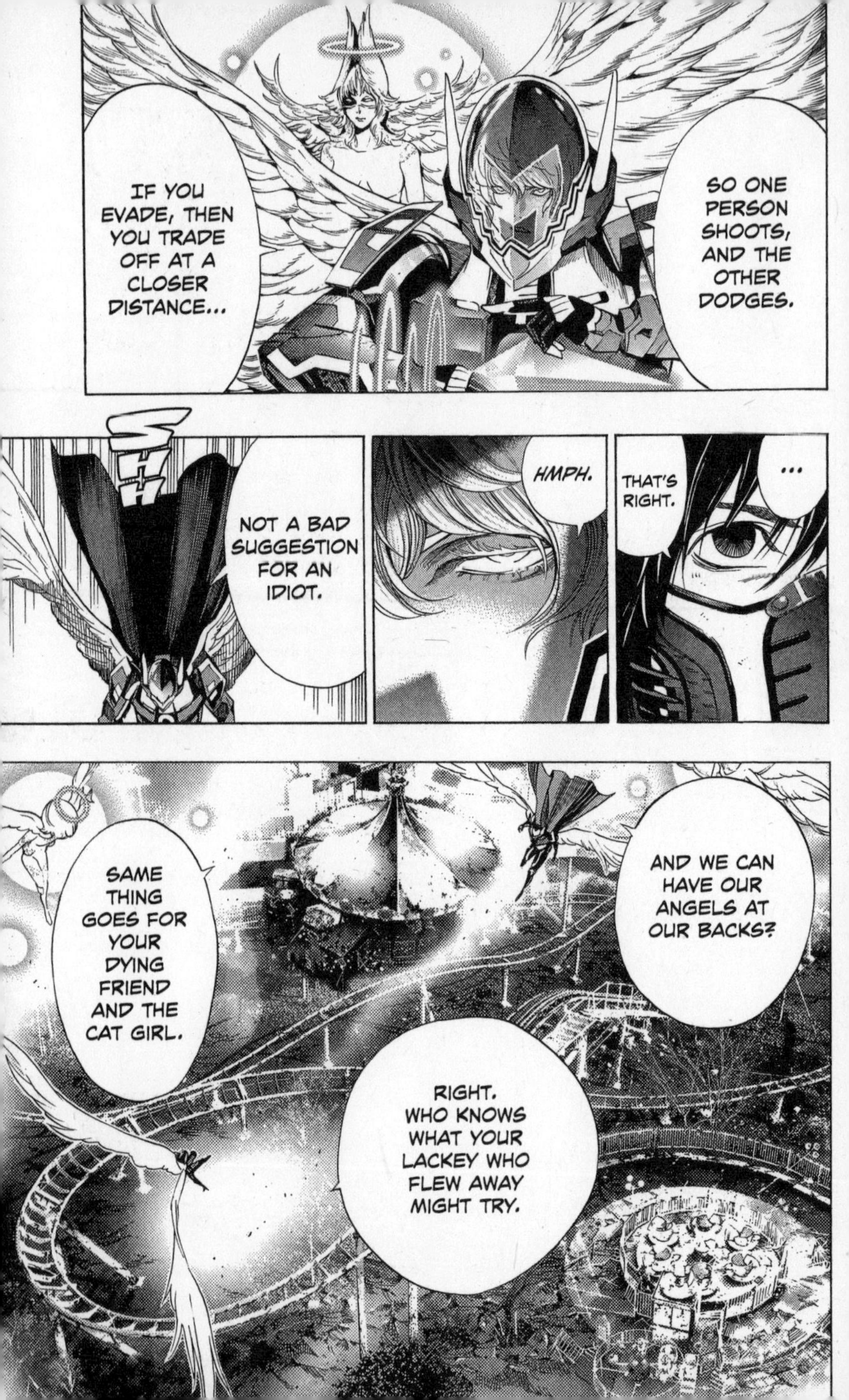
SO ONE PERSON SHOOTS, AND THE OTHER DODGES.
IF YOU EVADE, THEN YOU TRADE OFF AT A CLOSER DISTANCE...
...
THAT'S RIGHT.
HMPH.
NOT A BAD SUGGESTION FOR AN IDIOT.
AND WE CAN HAVE OUR ANGELS AT OUR BACKS?
SAME THING GOES FOR YOUR DYING FRIEND AND THE CAT GIRL.
RIGHT. WHO KNOWS WHAT YOUR LACKEY WHO FLEW AWAY MIGHT TRY.

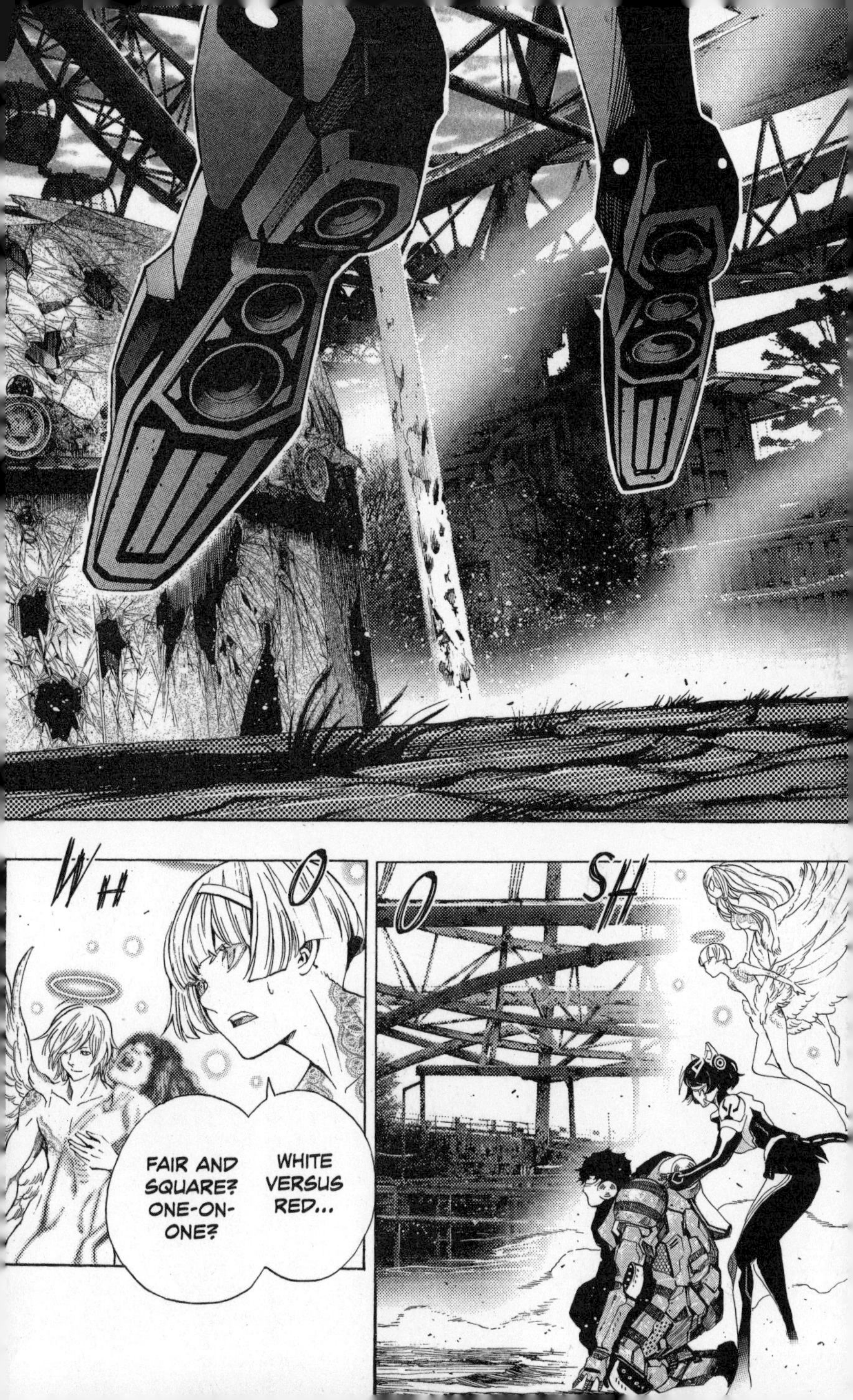
WHOOSH
WHITE VERSUS RED...
FAIR AND SQUARE? ONE-ON-ONE?

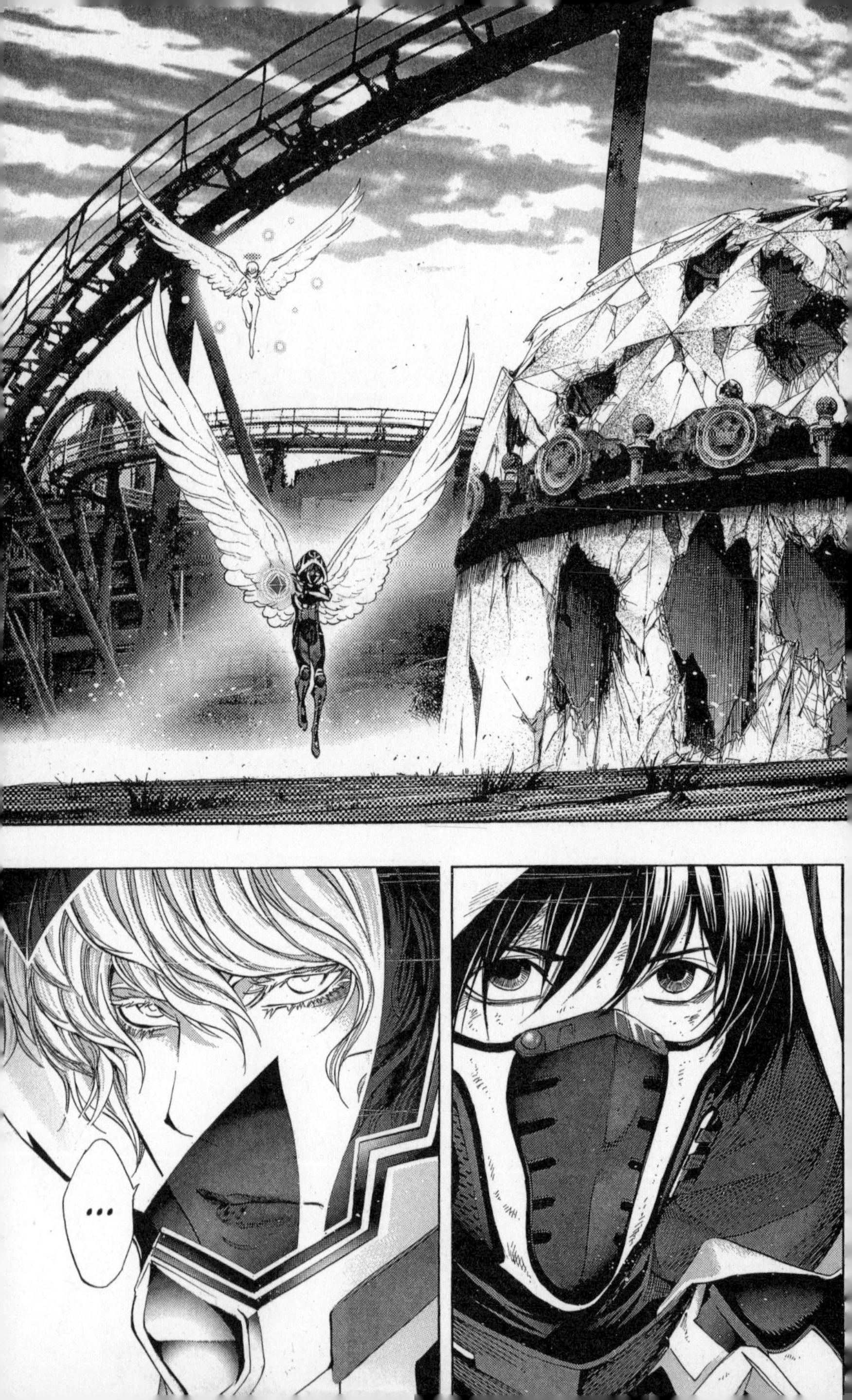
...

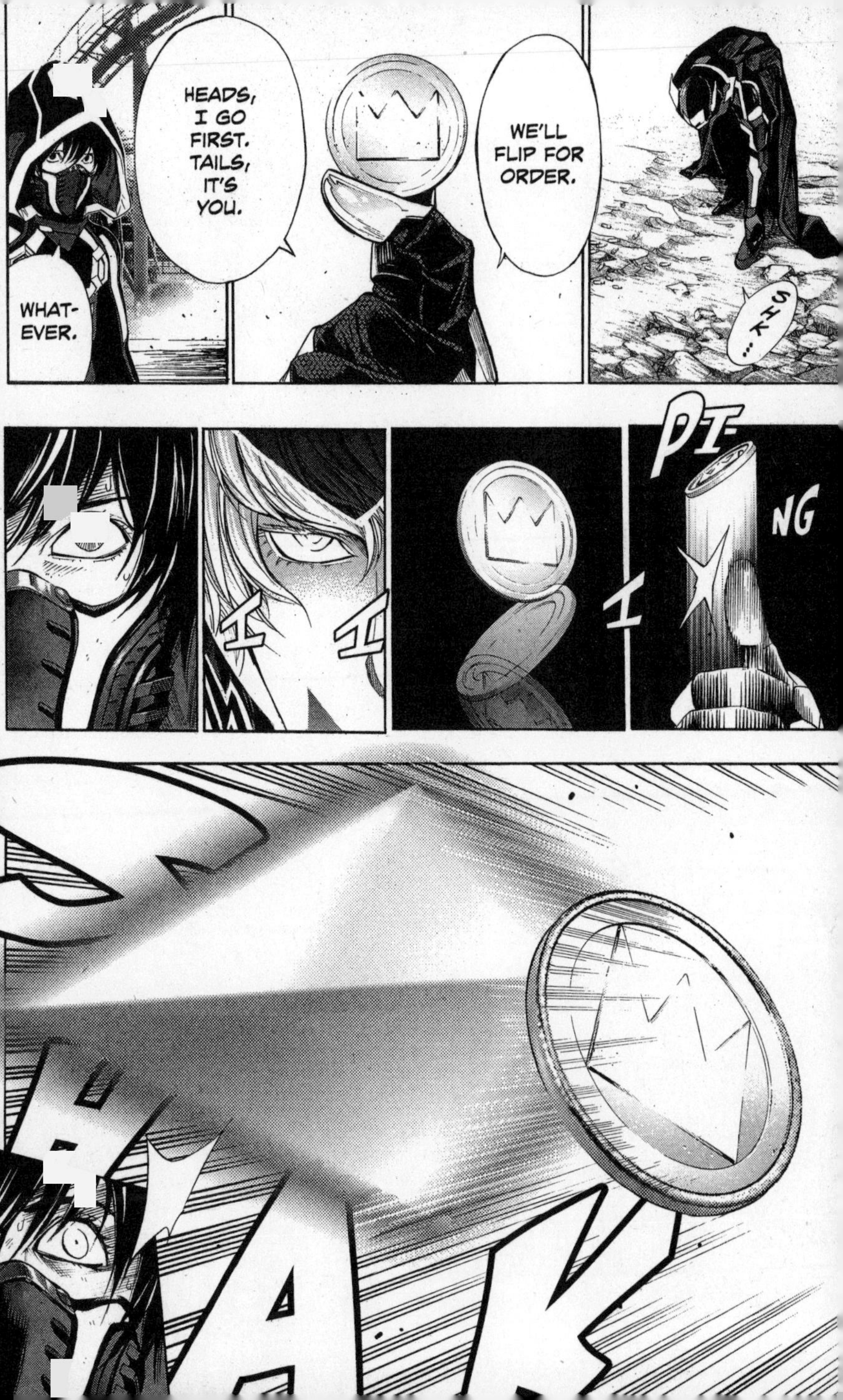
SHK...
WE'LL FLIP FOR ORDER.
HEADS, I GO FIRST. TAILS, IT'S YOU.
WHAT-EVER.
PI-I-NG

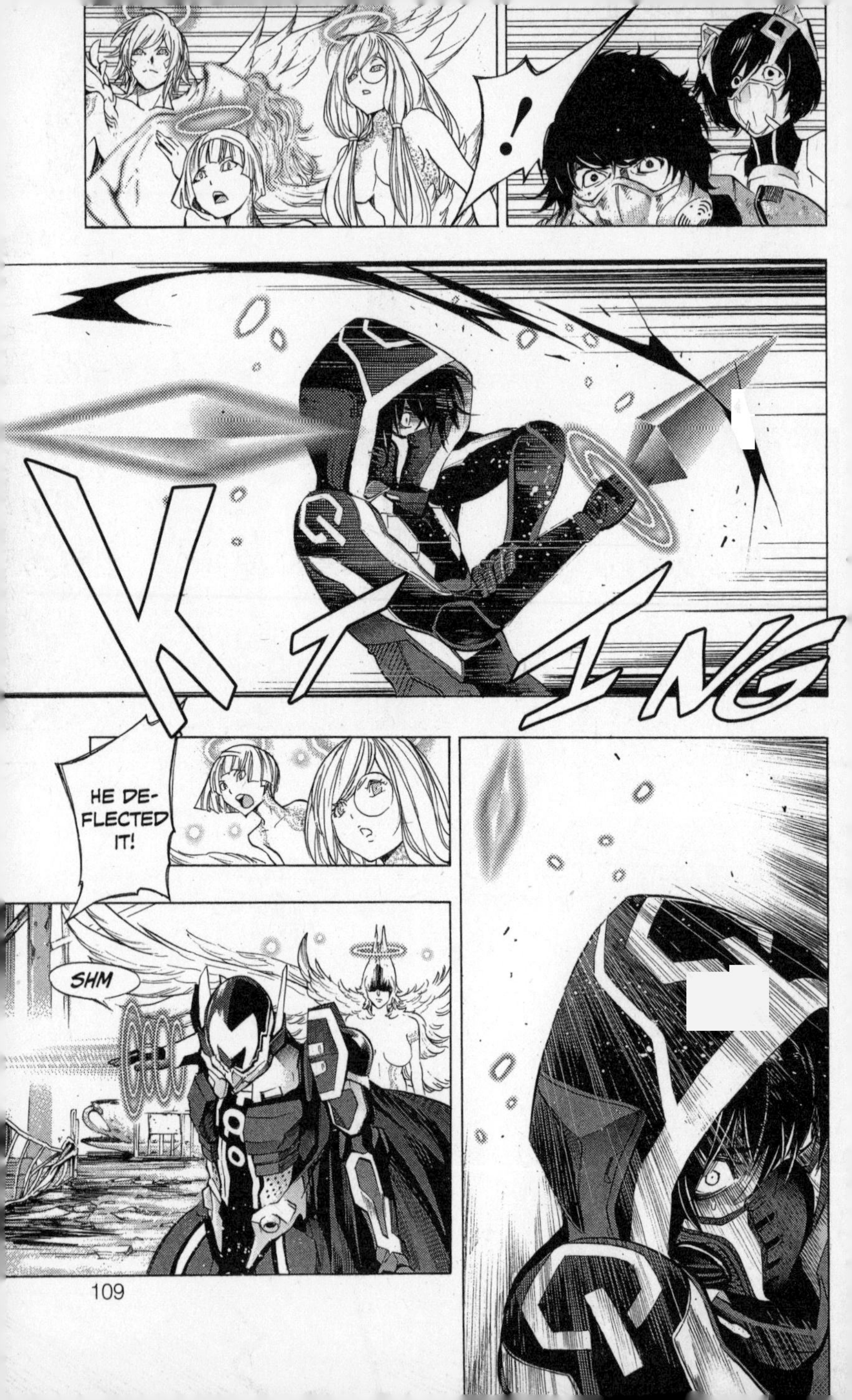
!
KYING
HE DE-
FLECTED
IT!
SHM

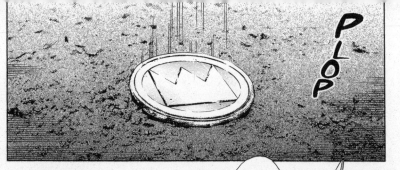

PLOP

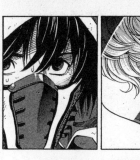

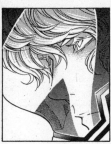

JUST A LITTLE WARM-UP TO TEST YOUR REFLEXES.

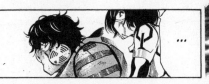

...

GO AHEAD-- YOU FIRST.

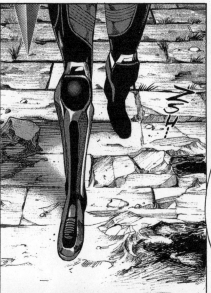

COME THREE METERS CLOSER... NO, BETTER MAKE IT FIVE.

STEP ON UP AND TAKE YOUR SHOT.

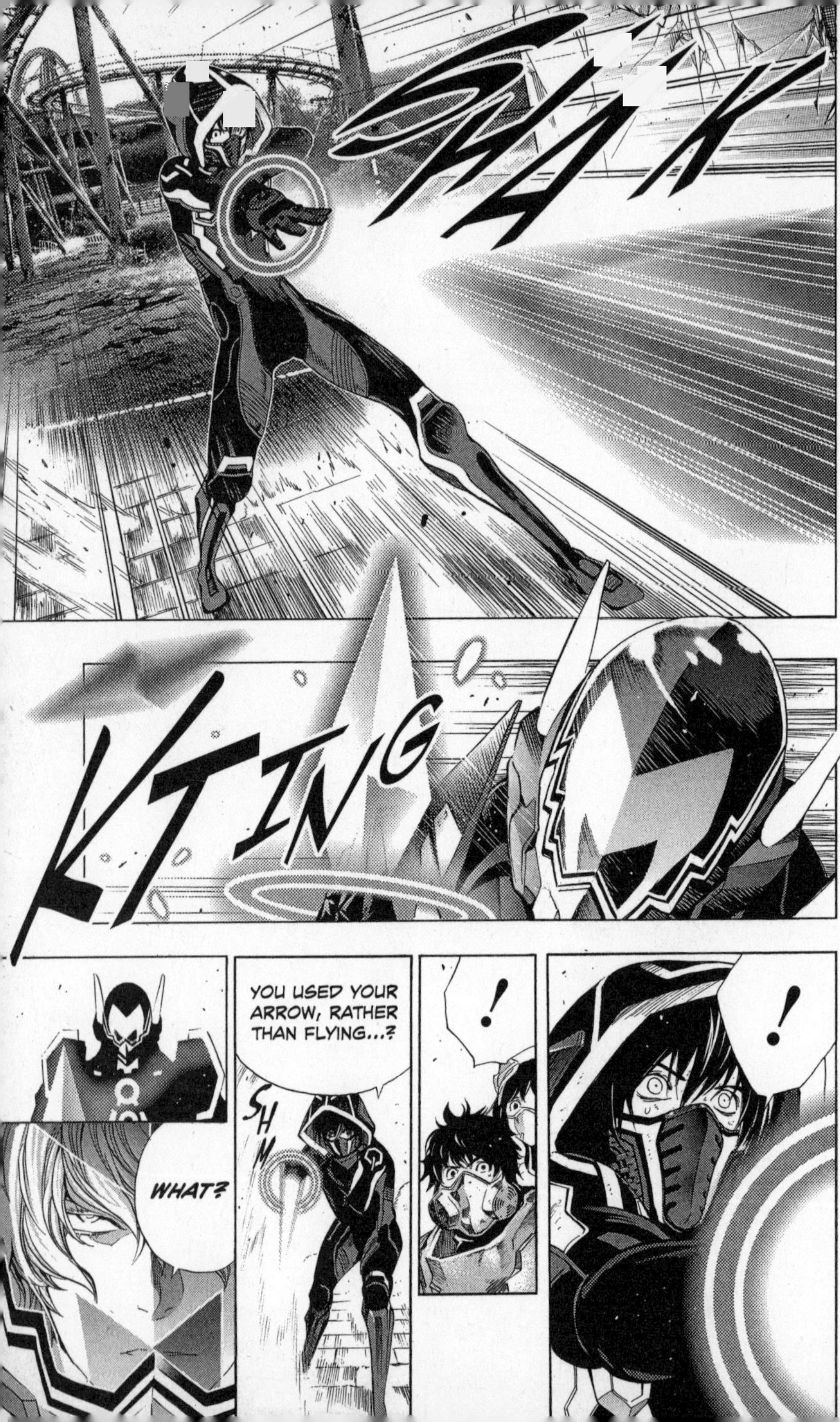
SHAK
KTING
!
!
YOU USED YOUR ARROW, RATHER THAN FLYING...?
SHM
WHAT?

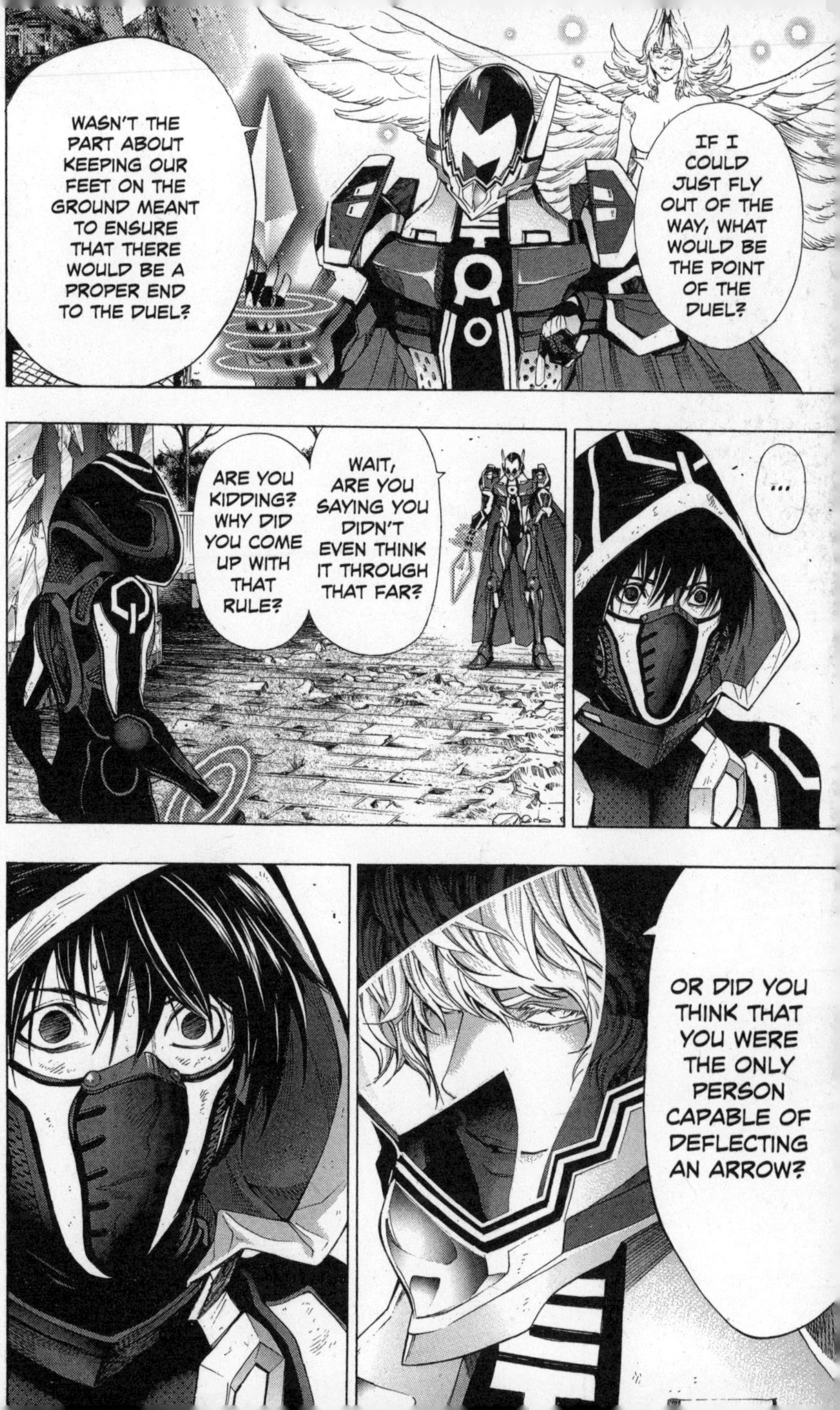
IF I COULD JUST FLY OUT OF THE WAY, WHAT WOULD BE THE POINT OF THE DUEL?
WASN'T THE PART ABOUT KEEPING OUR FEET ON THE GROUND MEANT TO ENSURE THAT THERE WOULD BE A PROPER END TO THE DUEL?
...
WAIT, ARE YOU SAYING YOU DIDN'T EVEN THINK IT THROUGH THAT FAR?
ARE YOU KIDDING? WHY DID YOU COME UP WITH THAT RULE?
OR DID YOU THINK THAT YOU WERE THE ONLY PERSON CAPABLE OF DEFLECTING AN ARROW?

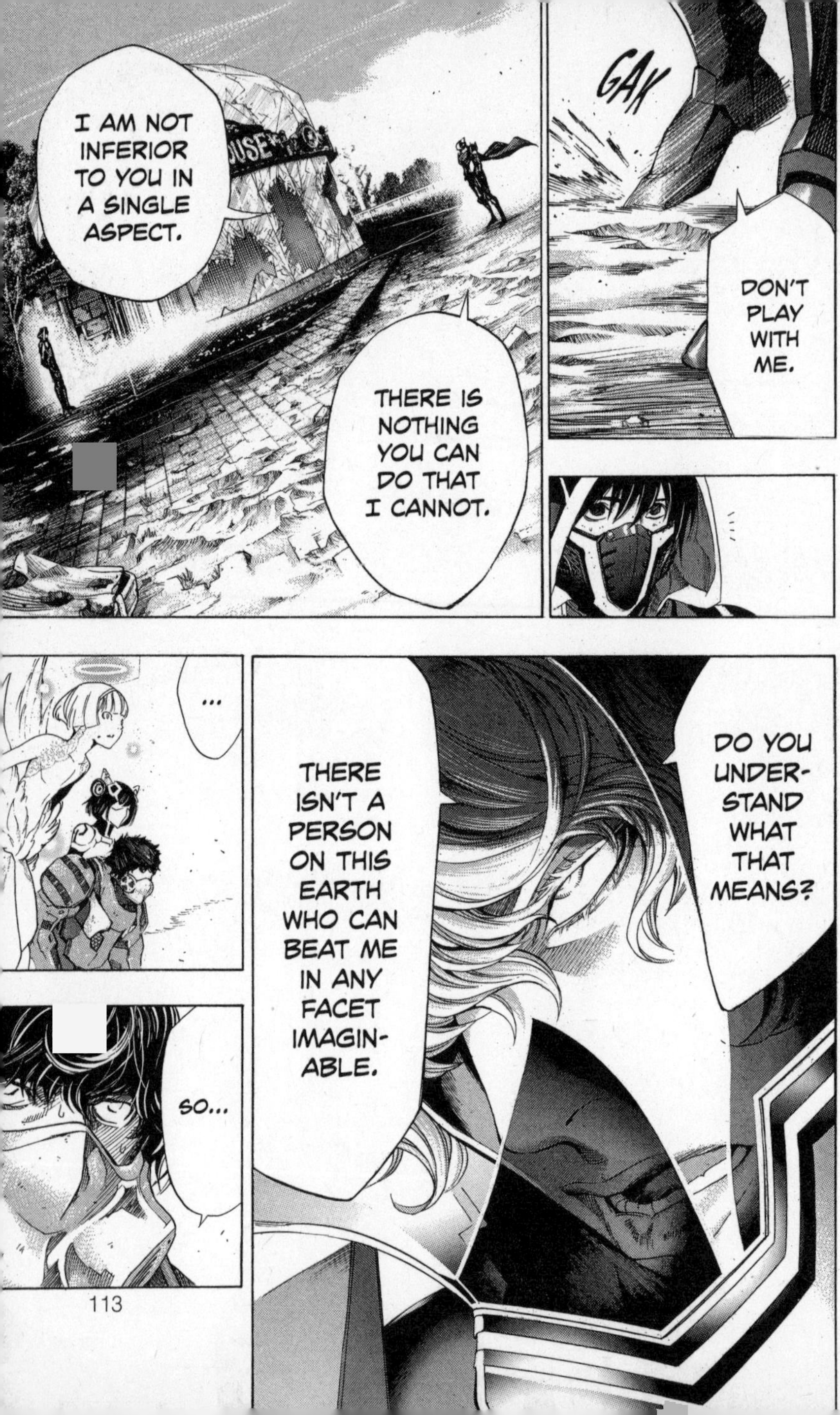
GAK
DON'T PLAY WITH ME.
I AM NOT INFERIOR TO YOU IN A SINGLE ASPECT.
THERE IS NOTHING YOU CAN DO THAT I CANNOT.
DO YOU UNDERSTAND WHAT THAT MEANS?
THERE ISN'T A PERSON ON THIS EARTH WHO CAN BEAT ME IN ANY FACET IMAGINABLE.
...
SO...

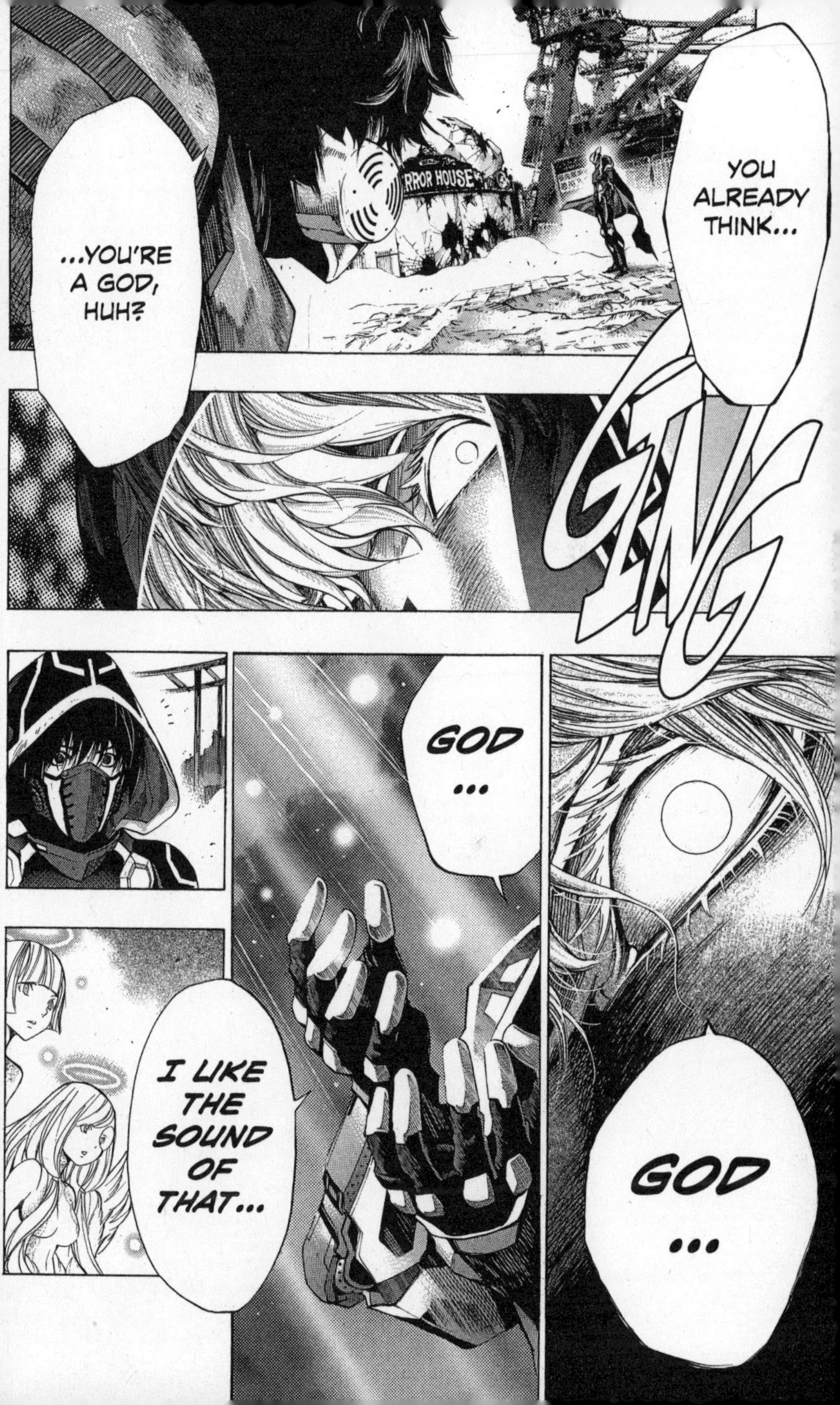
YOU ALREADY THINK...
...YOU'RE A GOD, HUH?
GING
GOD...
GOD...
I LIKE THE SOUND OF THAT...

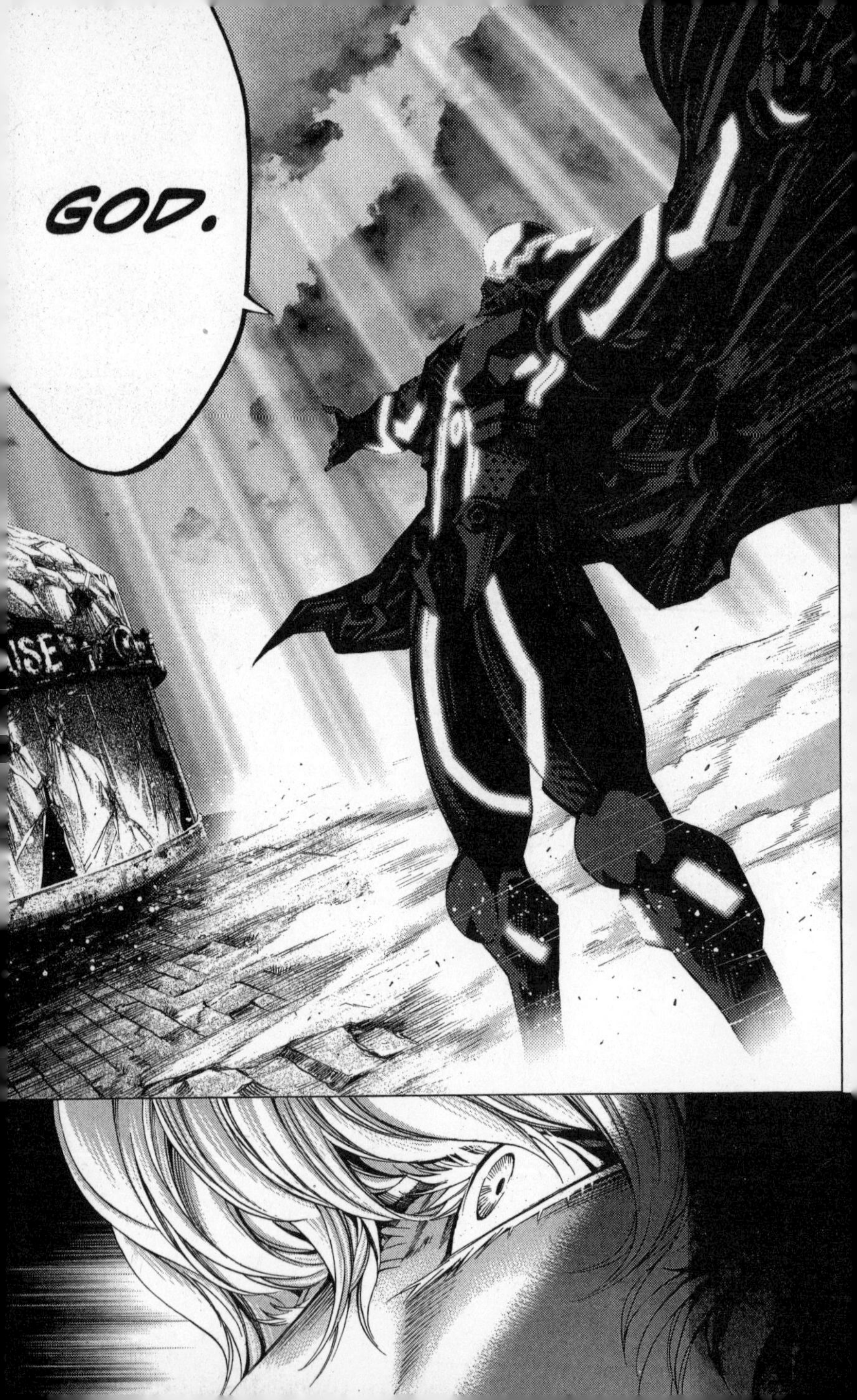
GOD.

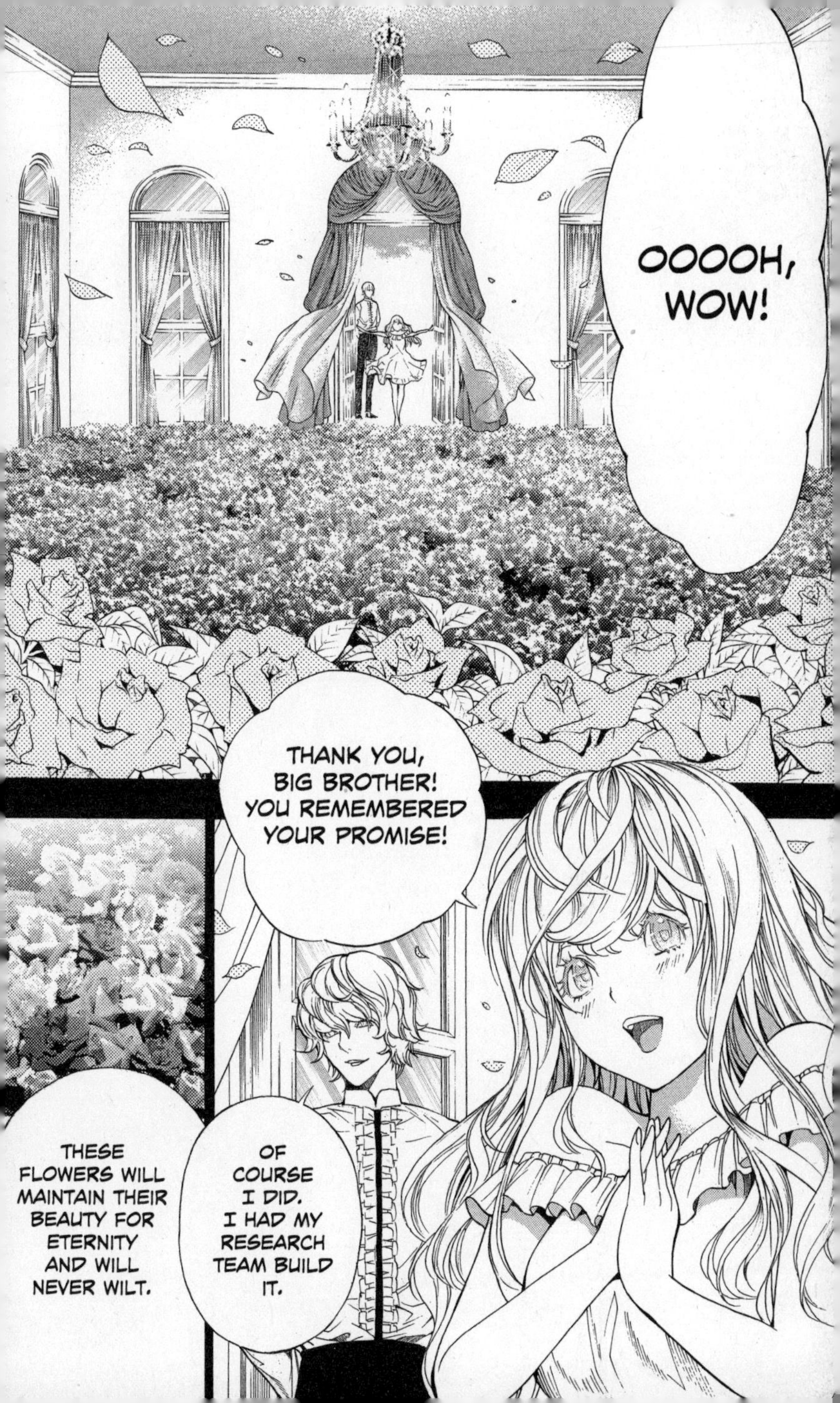
OOOOH, WOW!
THANK YOU, BIG BROTHER! YOU REMEMBERED YOUR PROMISE!
OF COURSE I DID. I HAD MY RESEARCH TEAM BUILD IT.
THESE FLOWERS WILL MAINTAIN THEIR BEAUTY FOR ETERNITY AND WILL NEVER WILT.

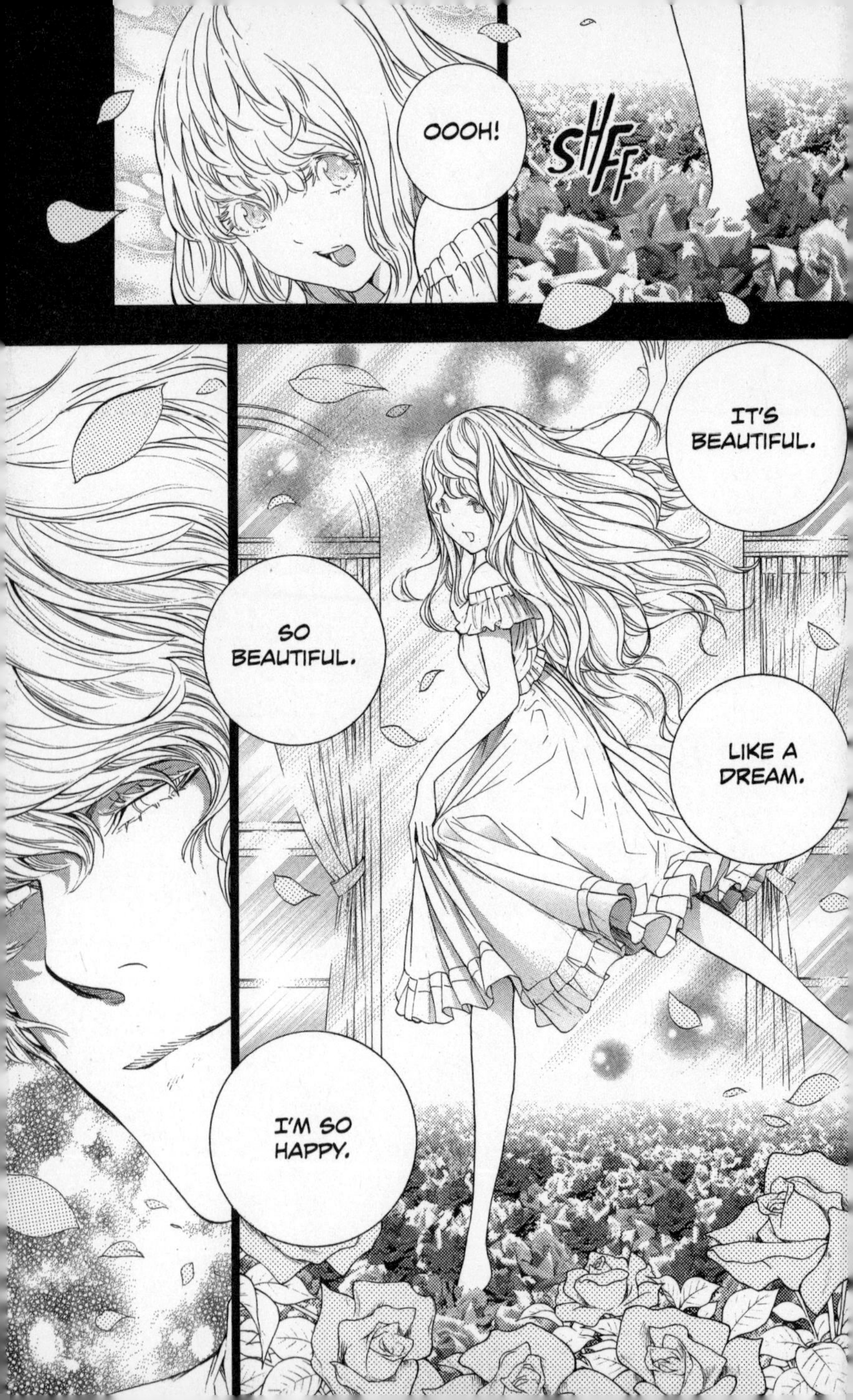
SHFF
OOOH!
IT'S BEAUTIFUL.
SO BEAUTIFUL.
LIKE A DREAM.
I'M SO HAPPY.

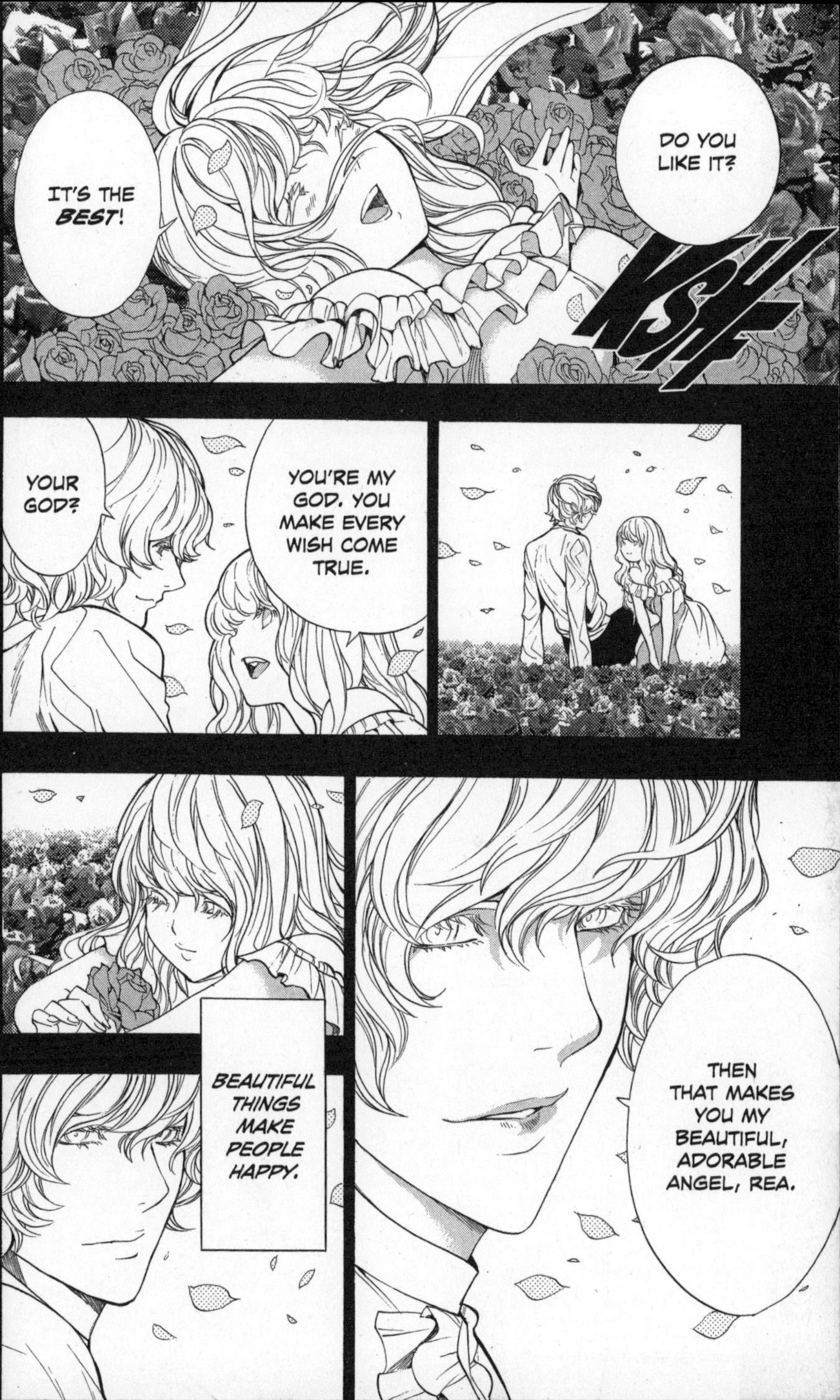
DO YOU LIKE IT?
IT'S THE *BEST*!
WSH
YOU'RE MY GOD. YOU MAKE EVERY WISH COME TRUE.
YOUR GOD?
THEN THAT MAKES YOU MY BEAUTIFUL, ADORABLE ANGEL, REA.
BEAUTIFUL THINGS MAKE PEOPLE HAPPY.

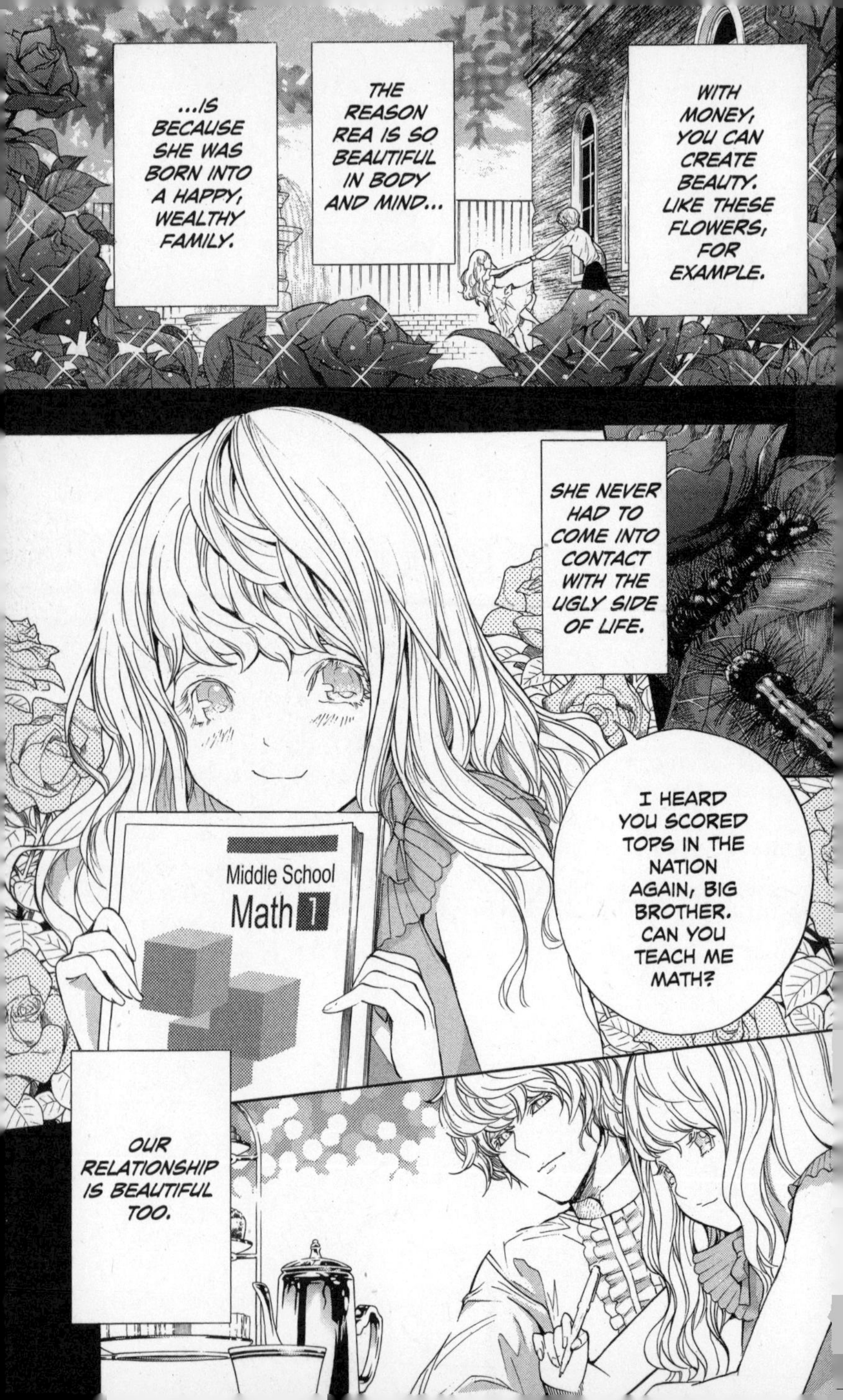
WITH MONEY, YOU CAN CREATE BEAUTY. LIKE THESE FLOWERS, FOR EXAMPLE.
THE REASON REA IS SO BEAUTIFUL IN BODY AND MIND...
...IS BECAUSE SHE WAS BORN INTO A HAPPY, WEALTHY FAMILY.
SHE NEVER HAD TO COME INTO CONTACT WITH THE UGLY SIDE OF LIFE.
I HEARD YOU SCORED TOPS IN THE NATION AGAIN, BIG BROTHER. CAN YOU TEACH ME MATH?
Middle School Math 1
OUR RELATIONSHIP IS BEAUTIFUL TOO.

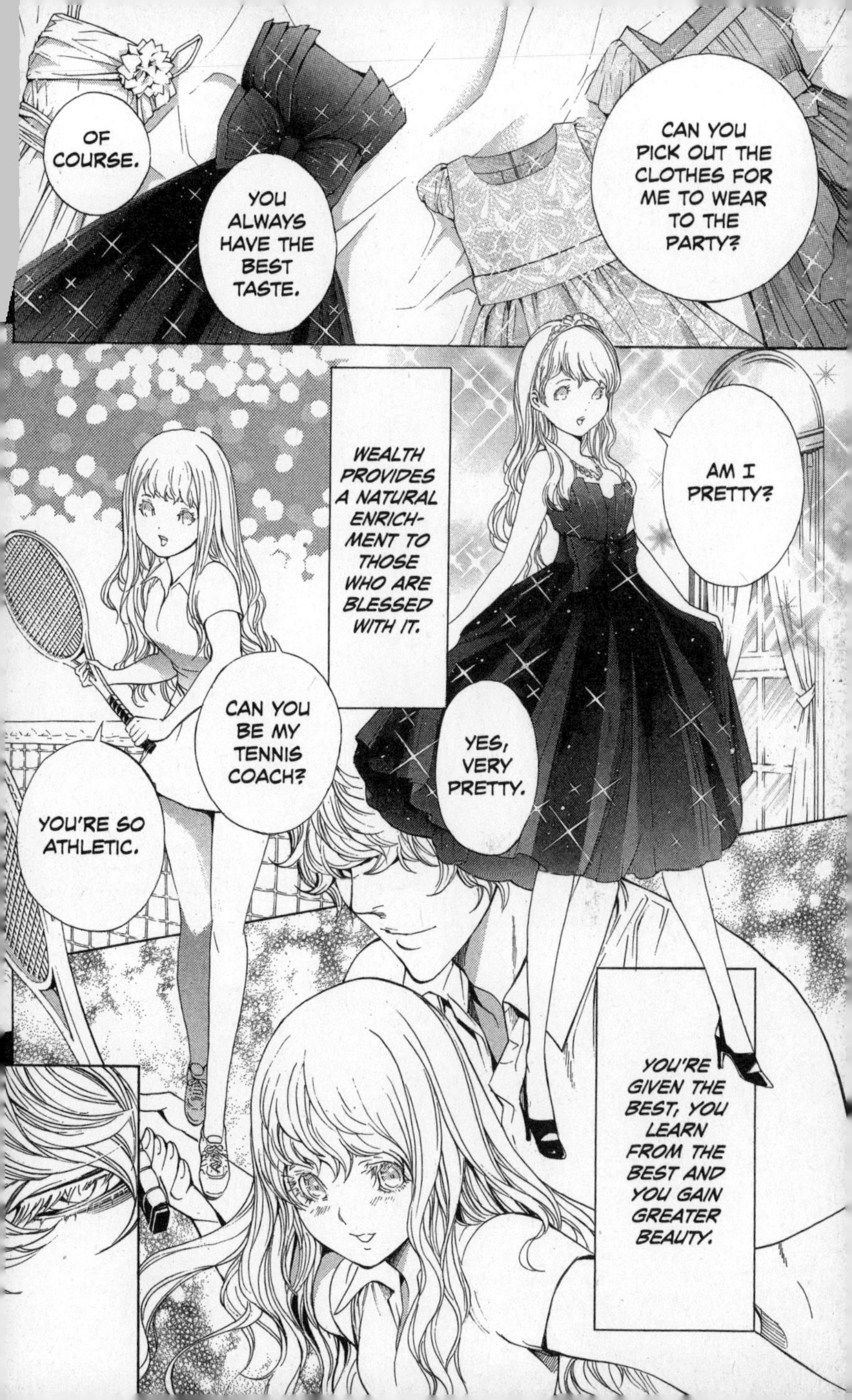
CAN YOU PICK OUT THE CLOTHES FOR ME TO WEAR TO THE PARTY?
YOU ALWAYS HAVE THE BEST TASTE.
OF COURSE.
AM I PRETTY?
YES, VERY PRETTY.
WEALTH PROVIDES A NATURAL ENRICHMENT TO THOSE WHO ARE BLESSED WITH IT.
CAN YOU BE MY TENNIS COACH?
YOU'RE SO ATHLETIC.
YOU'RE GIVEN THE BEST, YOU LEARN FROM THE BEST AND YOU GAIN GREATER BEAUTY.

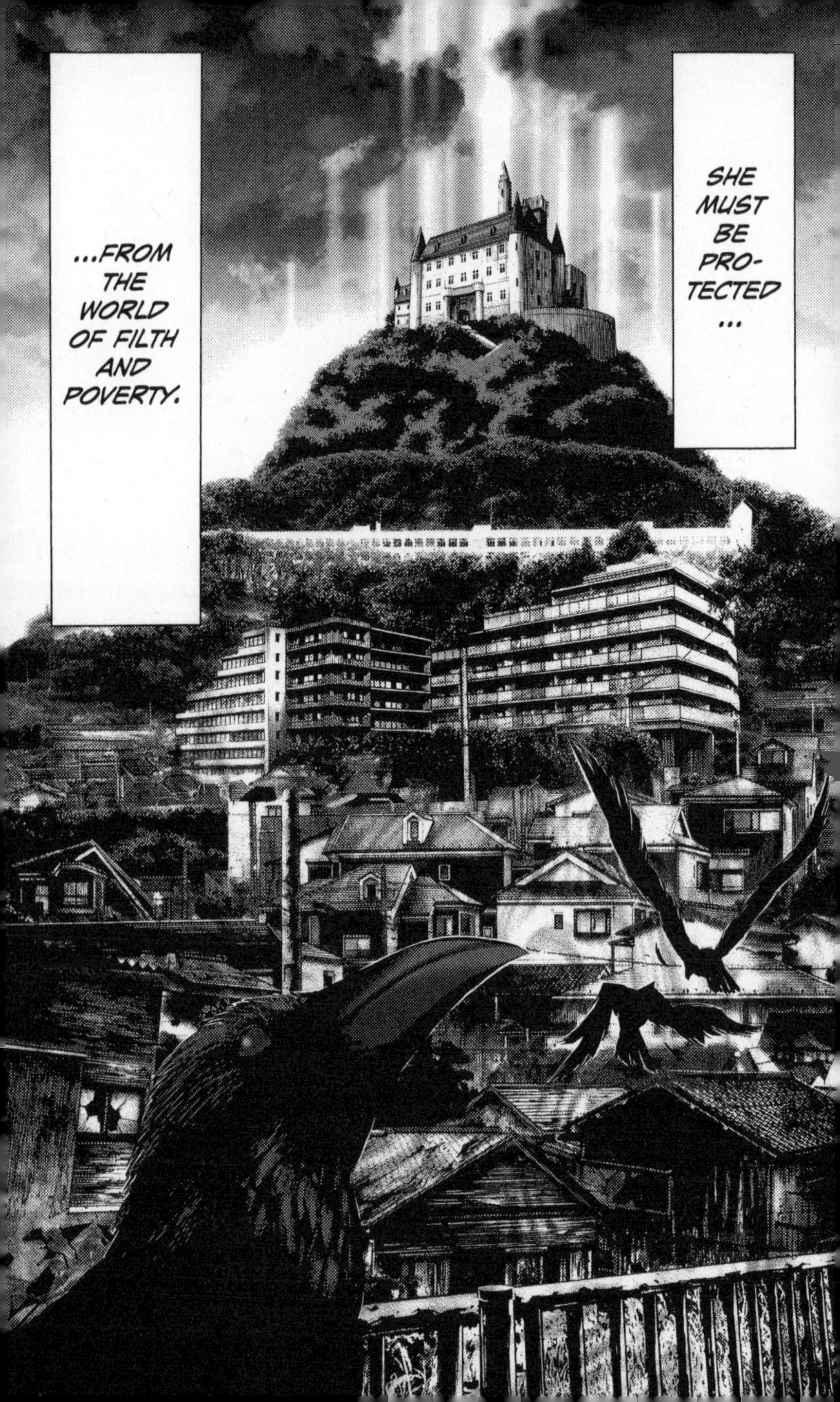
SHE MUST BE PRO-TECTED ...
...FROM THE WORLD OF FILTH AND POVERTY.

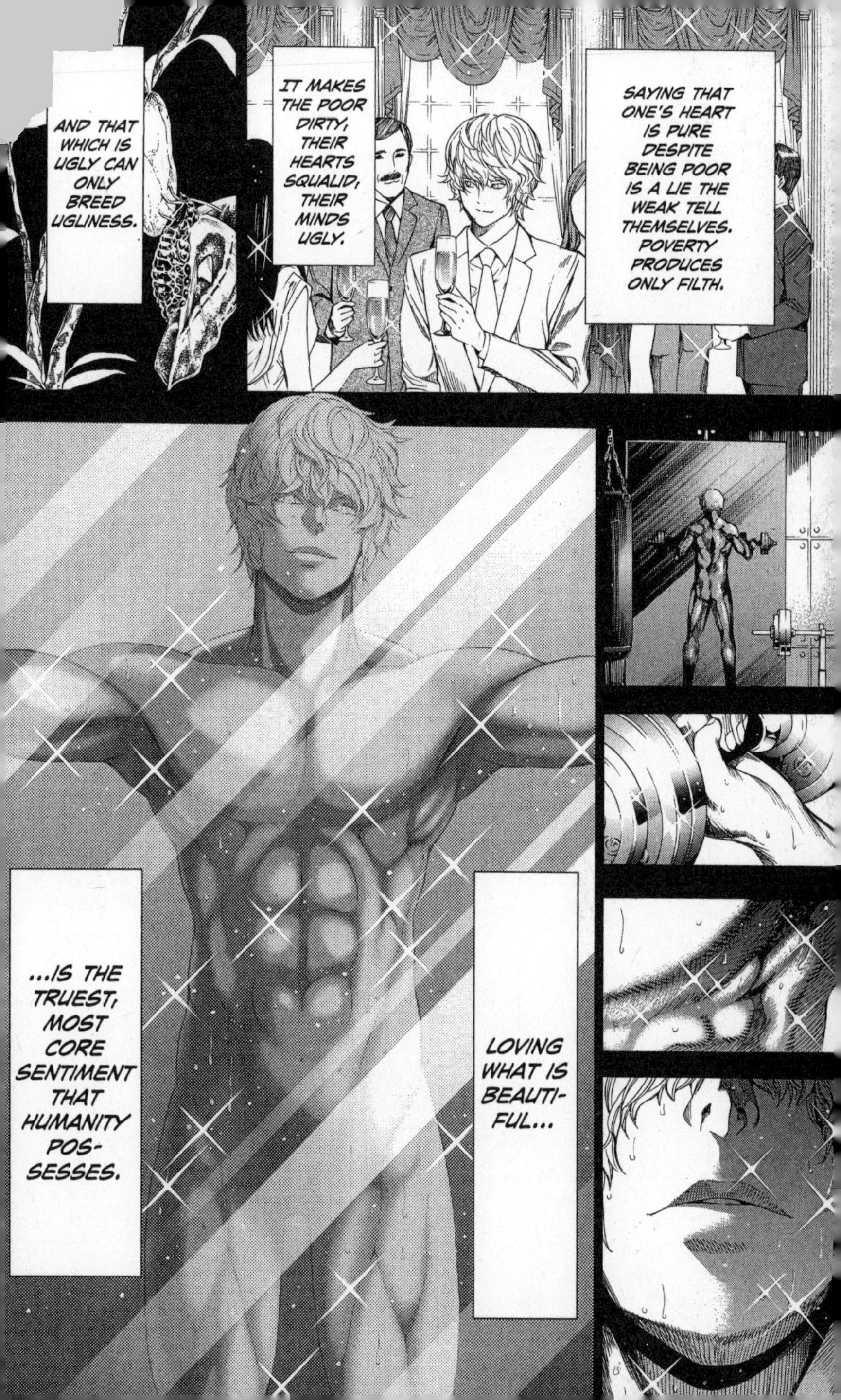
SAYING THAT ONE'S HEART IS PURE DESPITE BEING POOR IS A LIE THE WEAK TELL THEMSELVES. POVERTY PRODUCES ONLY FILTH.
IT MAKES THE POOR DIRTY, THEIR HEARTS SQUALID, THEIR MINDS UGLY.
AND THAT WHICH IS UGLY CAN ONLY BREED UGLINESS.
LOVING WHAT IS BEAUTI-FUL...
...IS THE TRUEST, MOST CORE SENTIMENT THAT HUMANITY POS-SESSES.

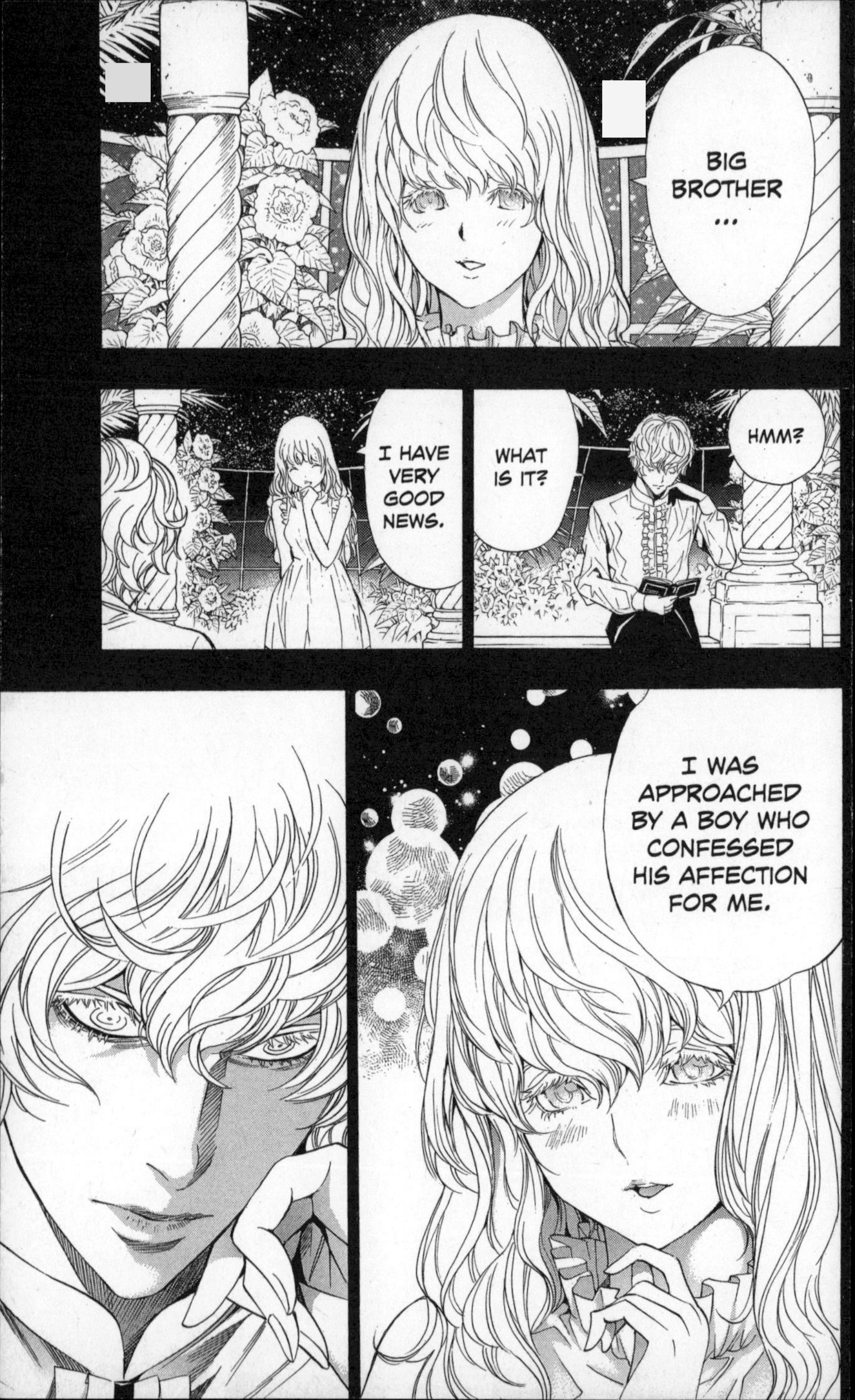
BIG BROTHER ...
HMM?
WHAT IS IT?
I HAVE VERY GOOD NEWS.
I WAS APPROACHED BY A BOY WHO CONFESSED HIS AFFECTION FOR ME.

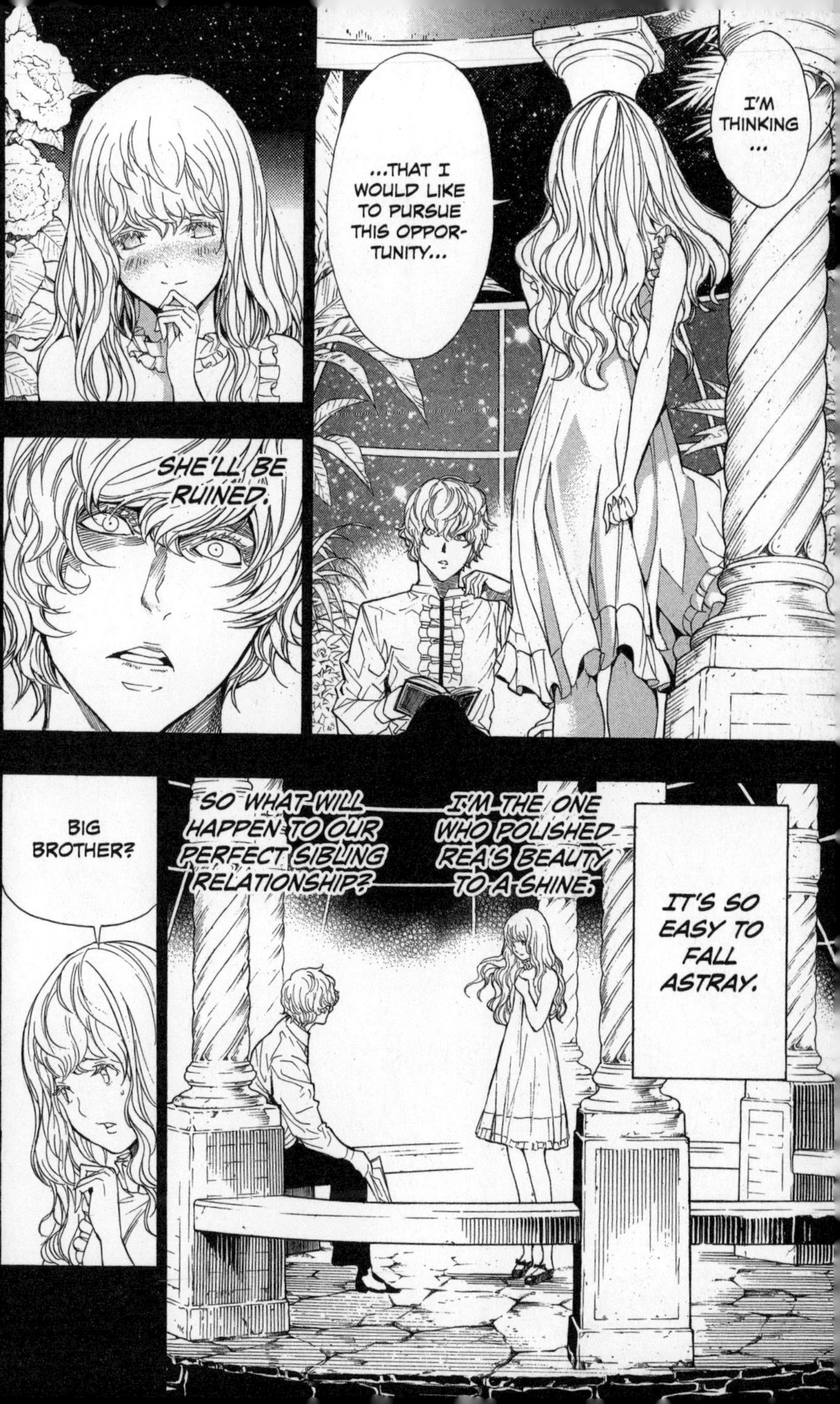
I'M THINKING...
...THAT I WOULD LIKE TO PURSUE THIS OPPORTUNITY...
SHE'LL BE RUINED.
I'M THE ONE WHO POLISHED REA'S BEAUTY TO A SHINE.
IT'S SO EASY TO FALL ASTRAY.
SO WHAT WILL HAPPEN TO OUR PERFECT SIBLING RELATIONSHIP?
BIG BROTHER?

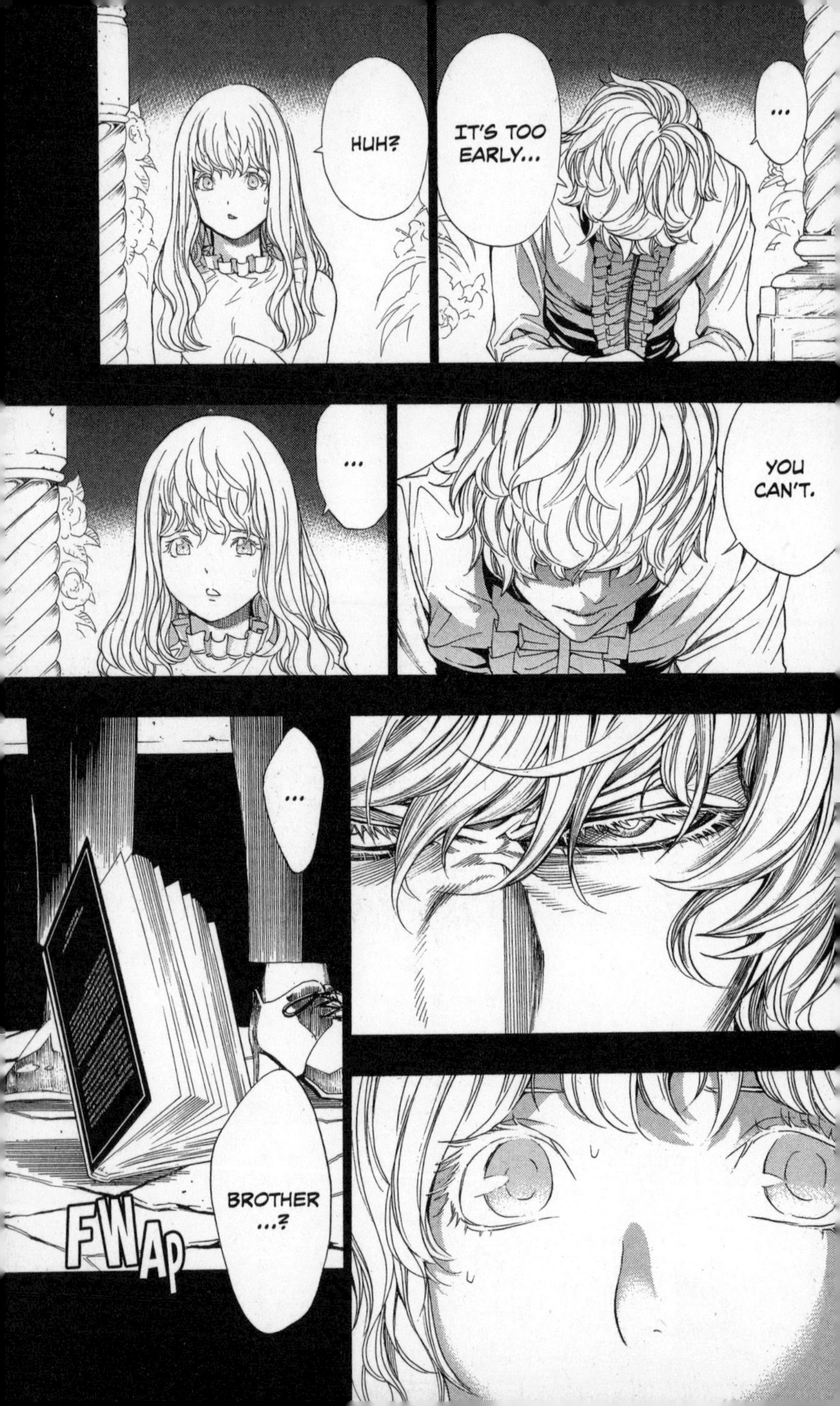
...
IT'S TOO EARLY...
HUH?
YOU CAN'T.
...
...
BROTHER ...?
FWAP

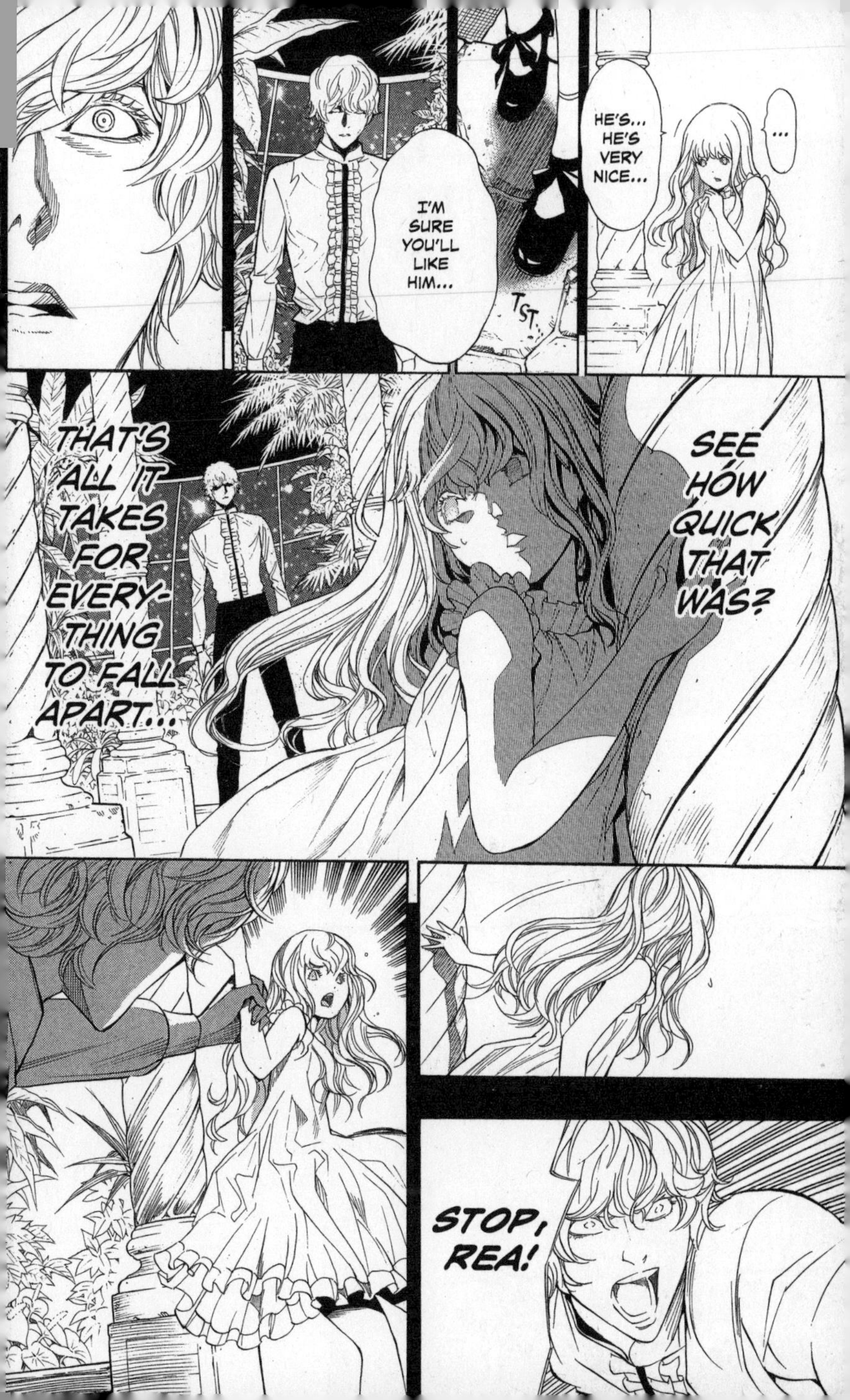
...
HE'S... HE'S VERY NICE...
TST
I'M SURE YOU'LL LIKE HIM...
SEE HOW QUICK THAT WAS?
THAT'S ALL IT TAKES FOR EVERY-THING TO FALL APART...
STOP, REA!

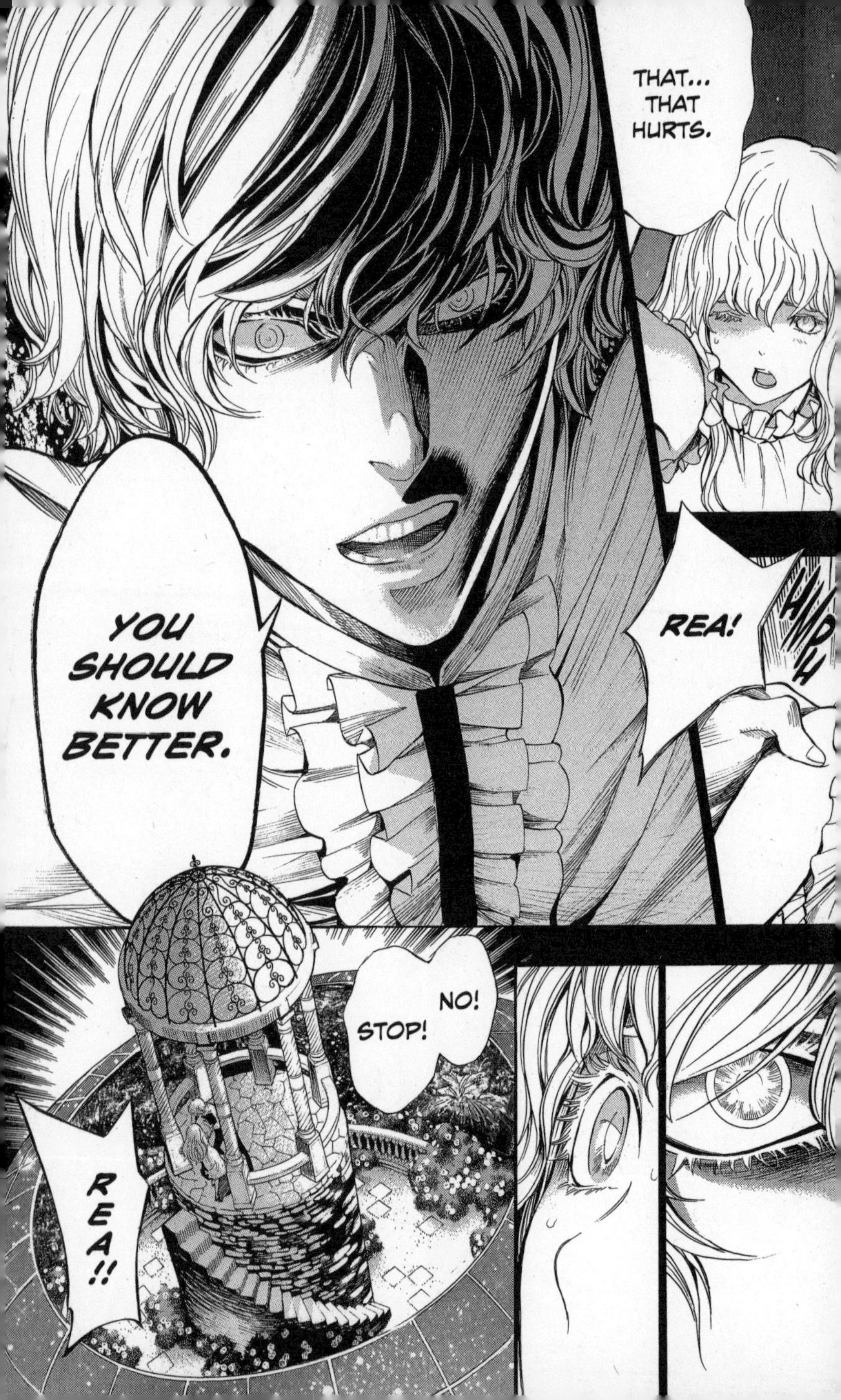
THAT... THAT HURTS.
REA!
YOU SHOULD KNOW BETTER.
NO! STOP!
REA!!

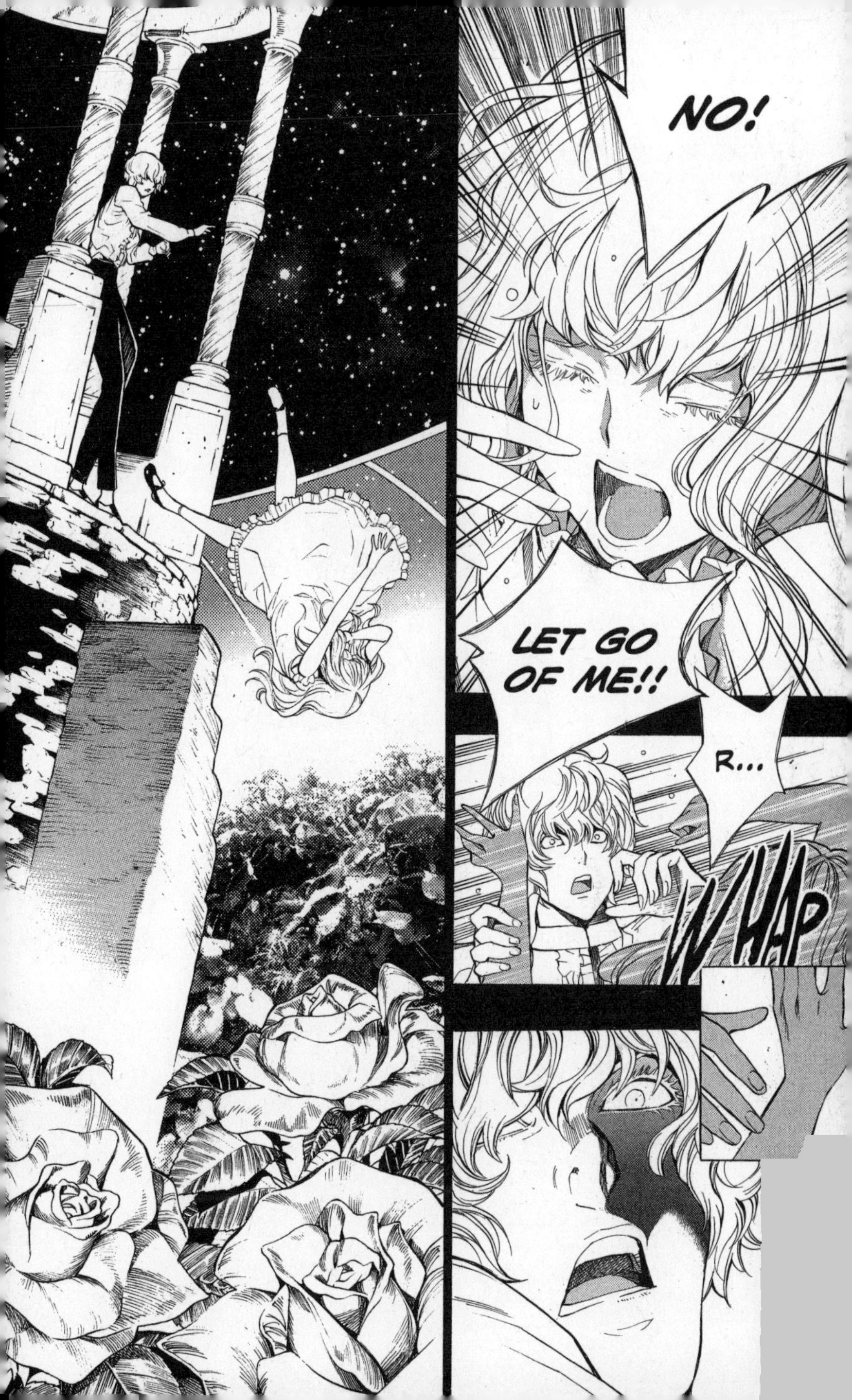
NO!
LET GO OF ME!!
R...
WHAP

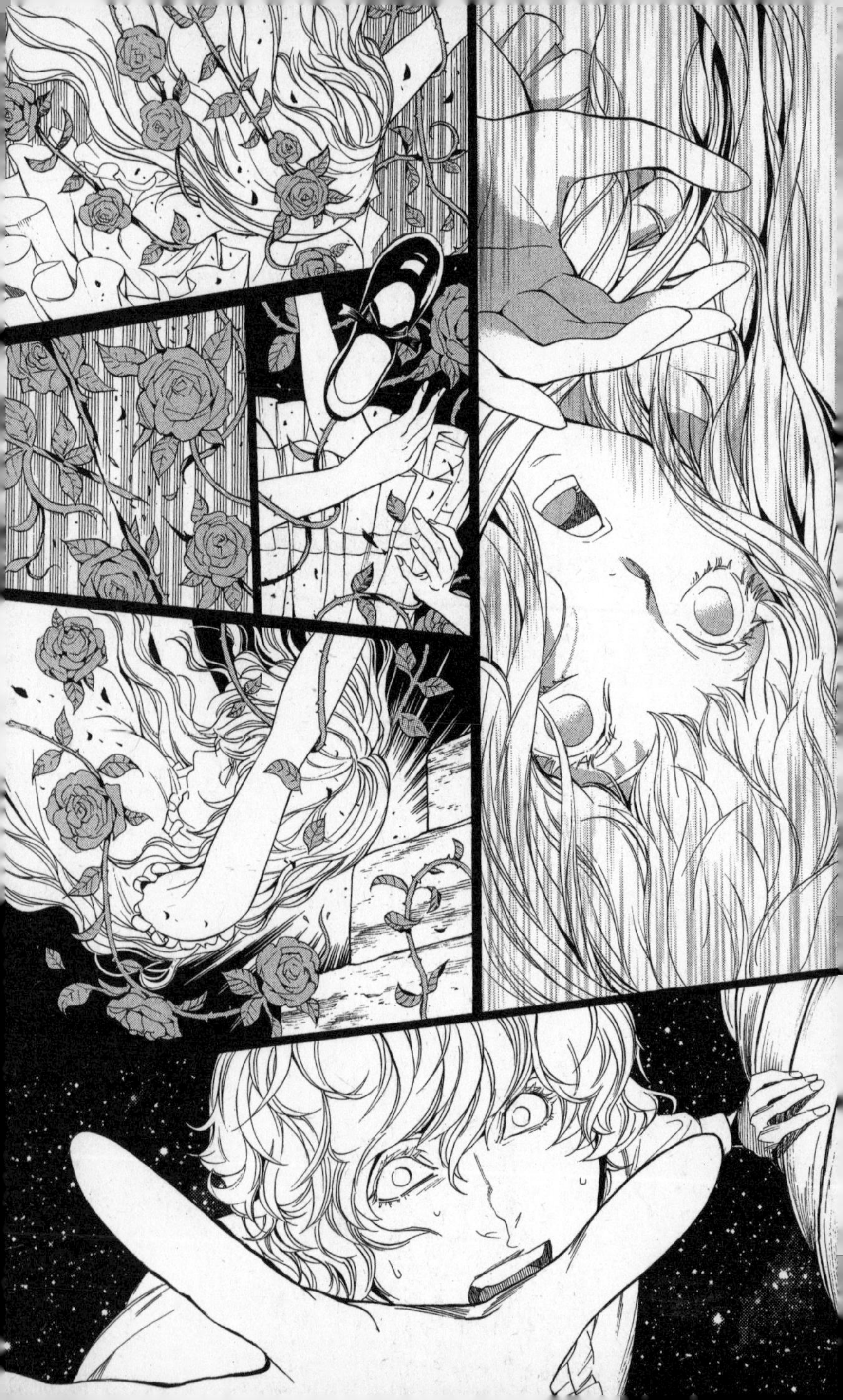

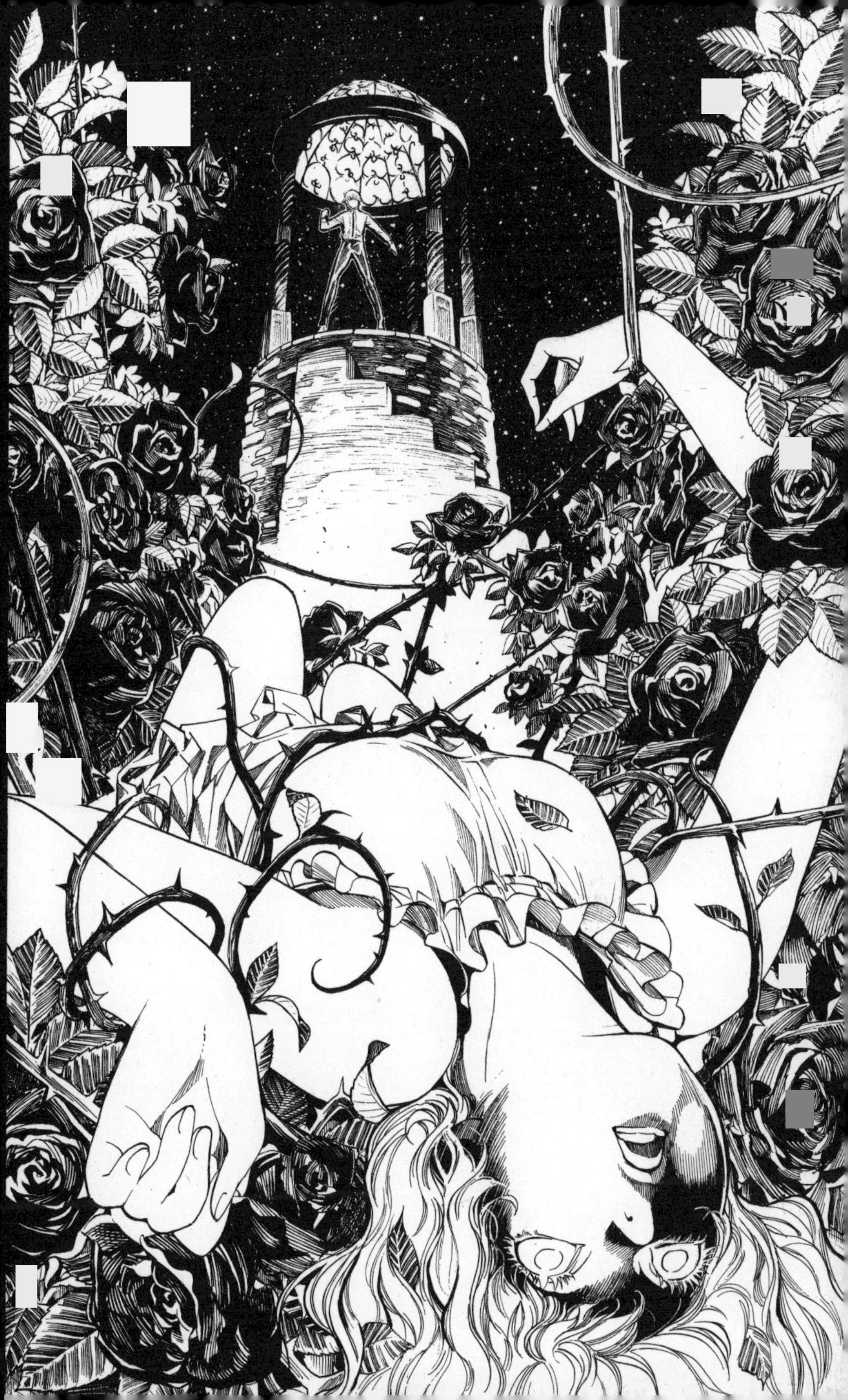

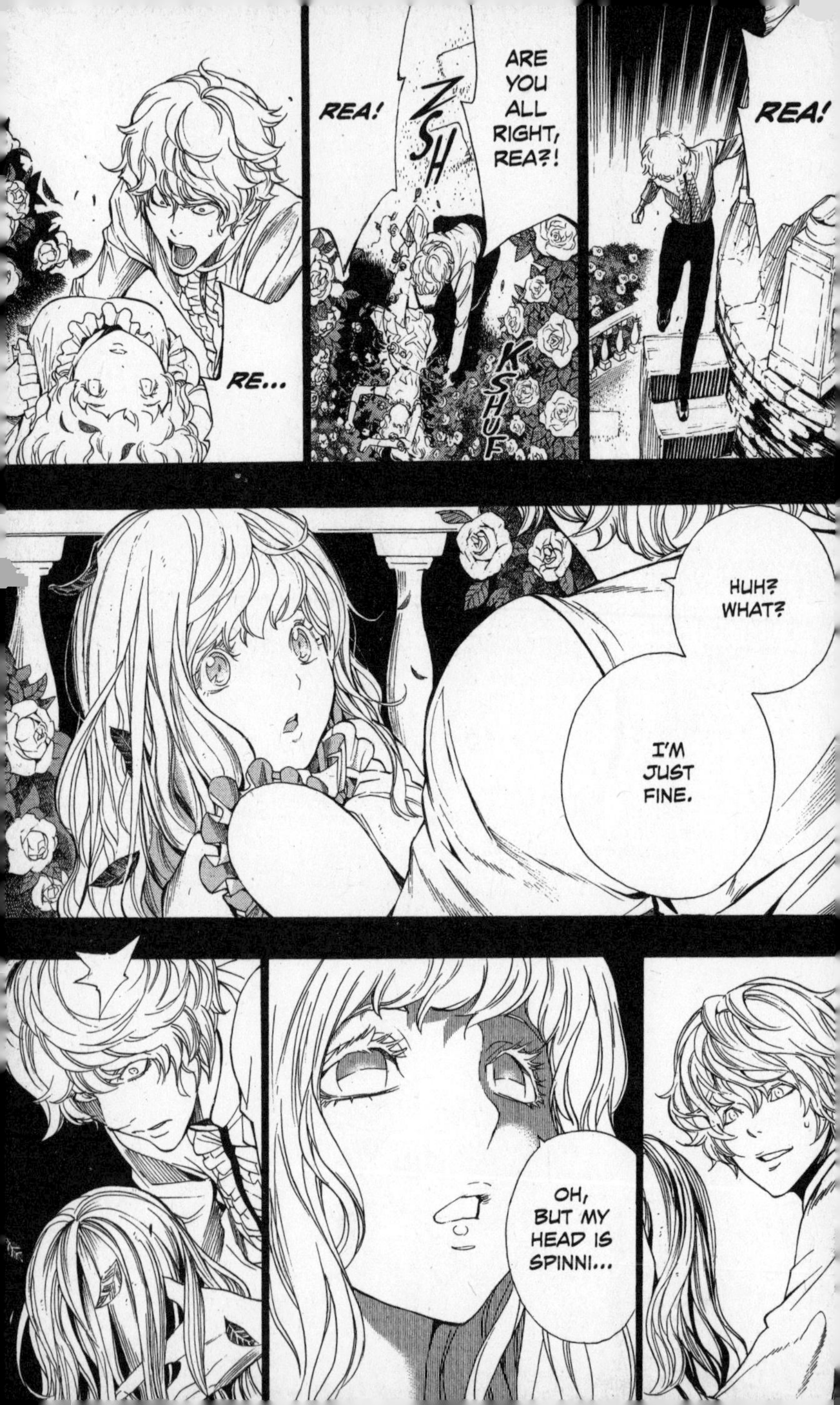
REA!
ARE YOU ALL RIGHT, REA?!
REA!
ZSH
KSHUF
RE...
HUH? WHAT?
I'M JUST FINE.
OH, BUT MY HEAD IS SPINNI...

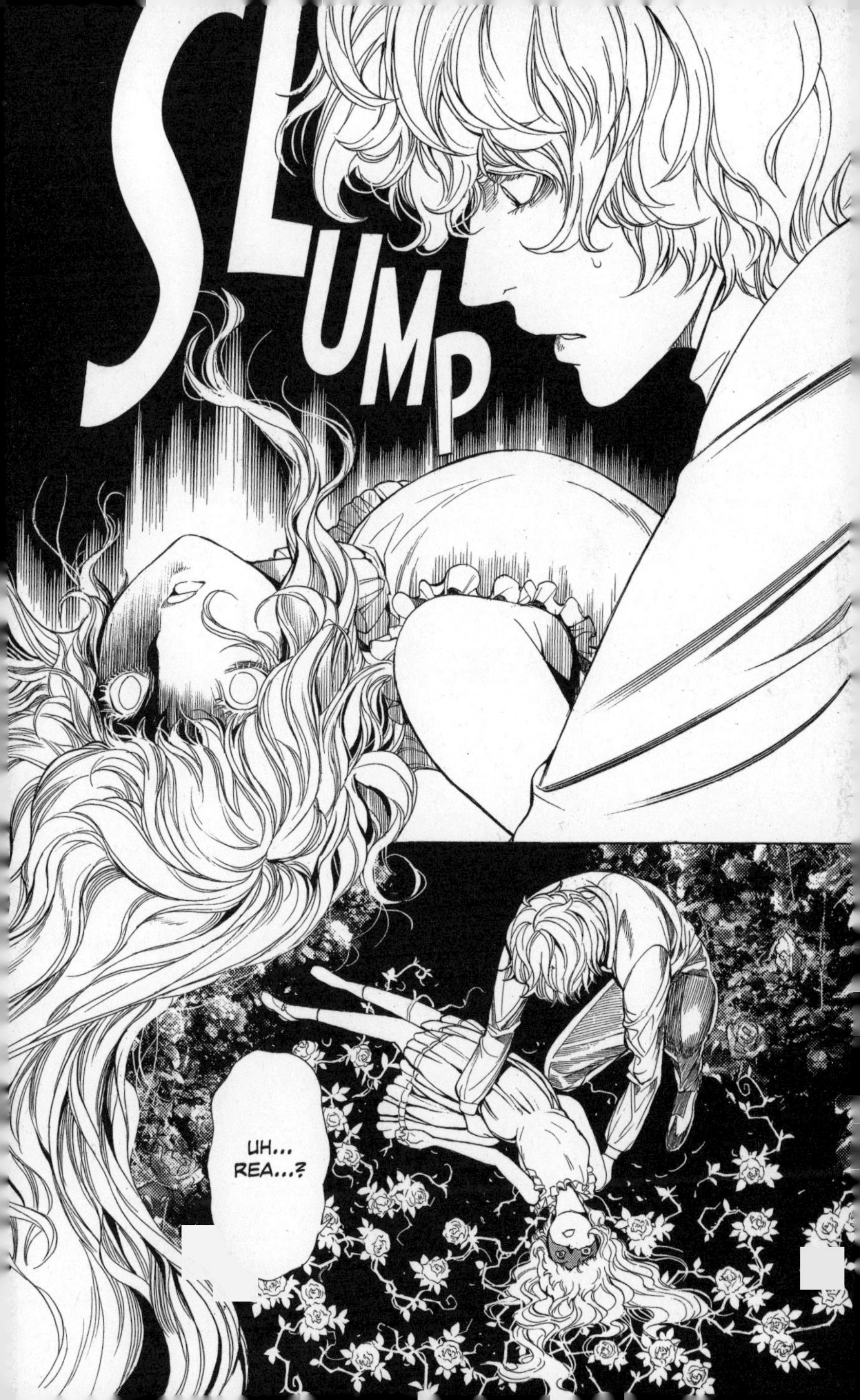
SLUMP
UH... REA...?

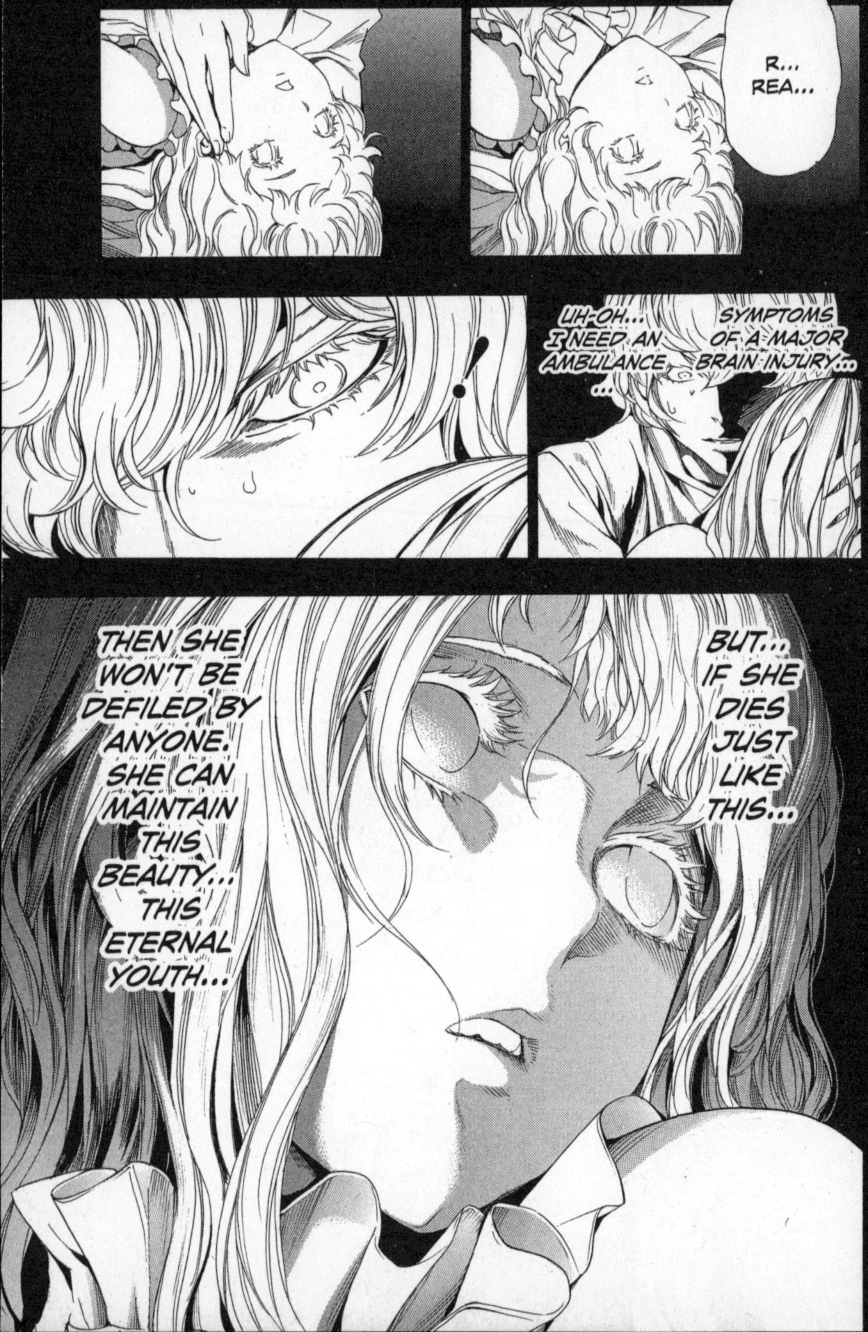
R... REA...
SYMPTOMS OF A MAJOR BRAIN INJURY...
UH-OH... I NEED AN AMBULANCE...
BUT... IF SHE DIES JUST LIKE THIS...
THEN SHE WON'T BE DEFILED BY ANYONE. SHE CAN MAINTAIN THIS BEAUTY... THIS ETERNAL YOUTH...

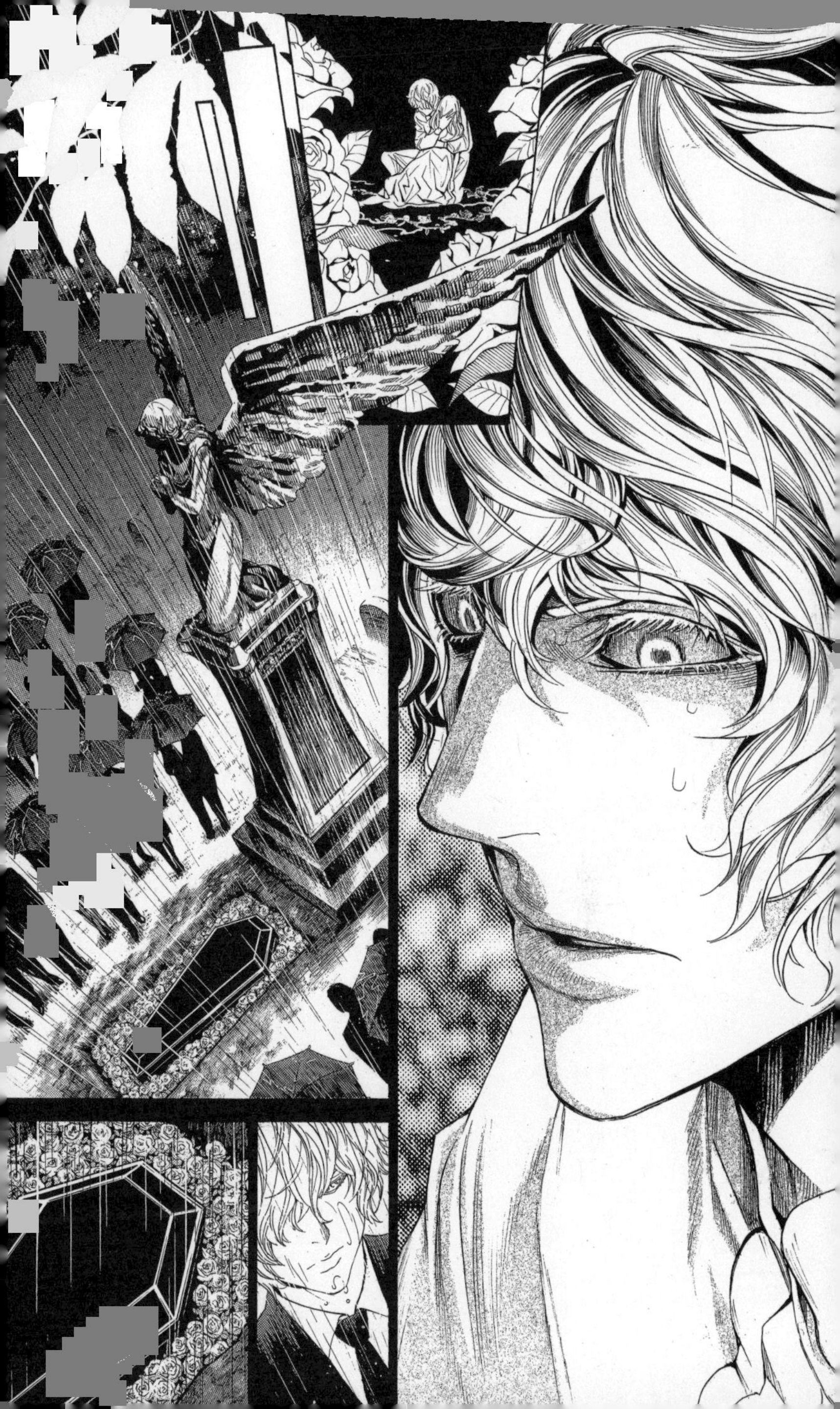

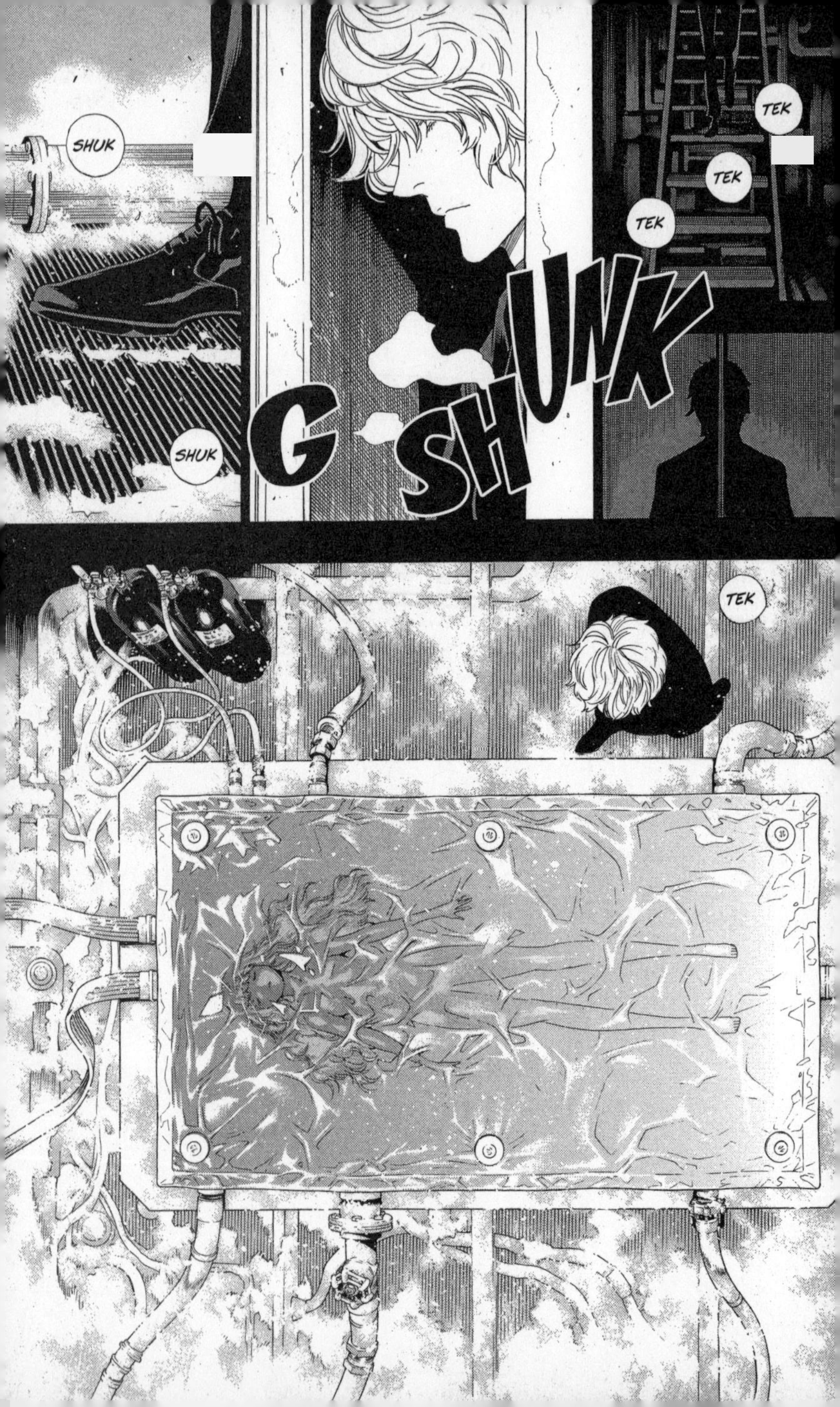
TEK
TEK
TEK
G SHUNK
SHUK
SHUK
TEK

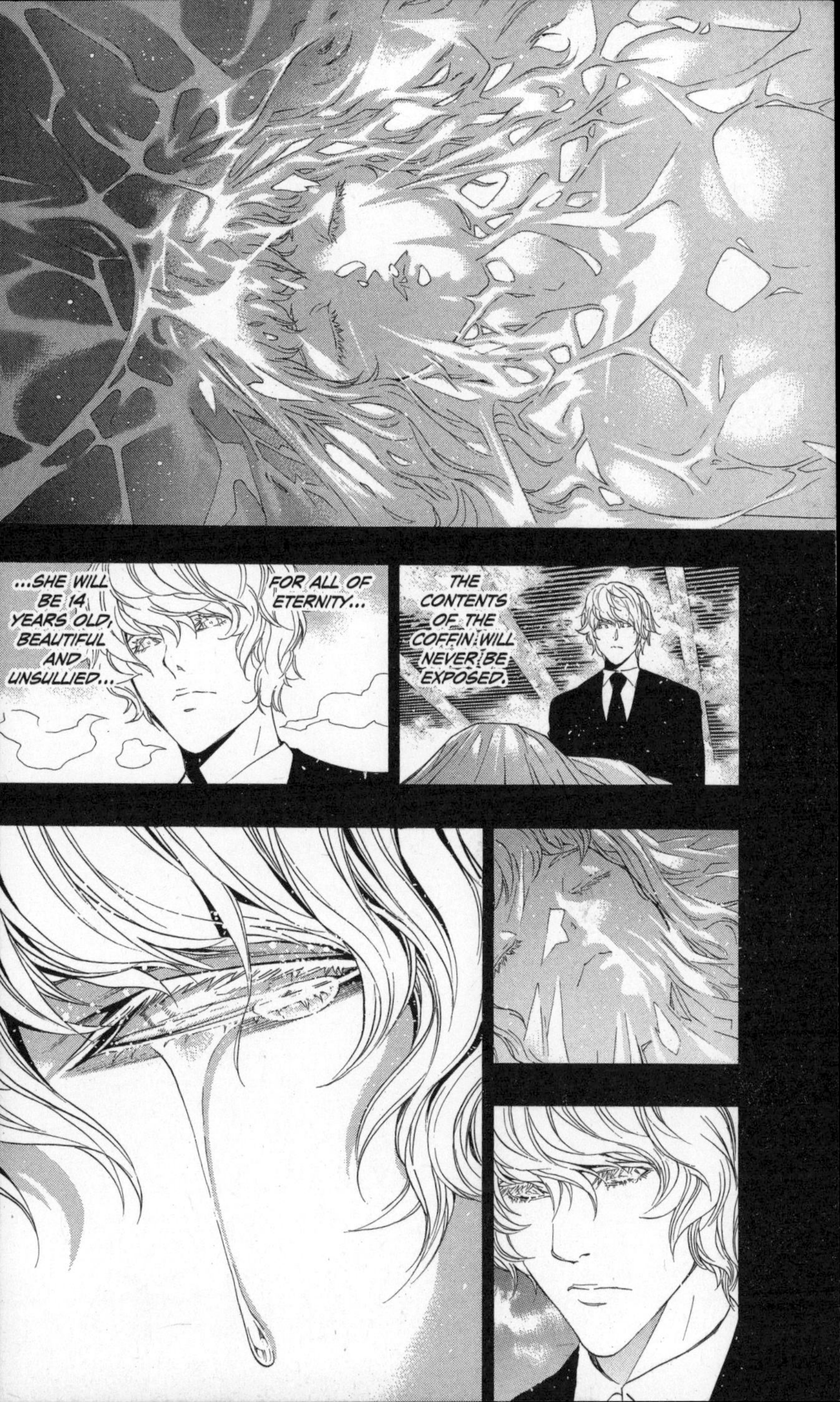
THE CONTENTS OF THE COFFIN WILL NEVER BE EXPOSED.
...SHE WILL BE 14 YEARS OLD, BEAUTIFUL AND UNSULLIED...
FOR ALL OF ETERNITY...

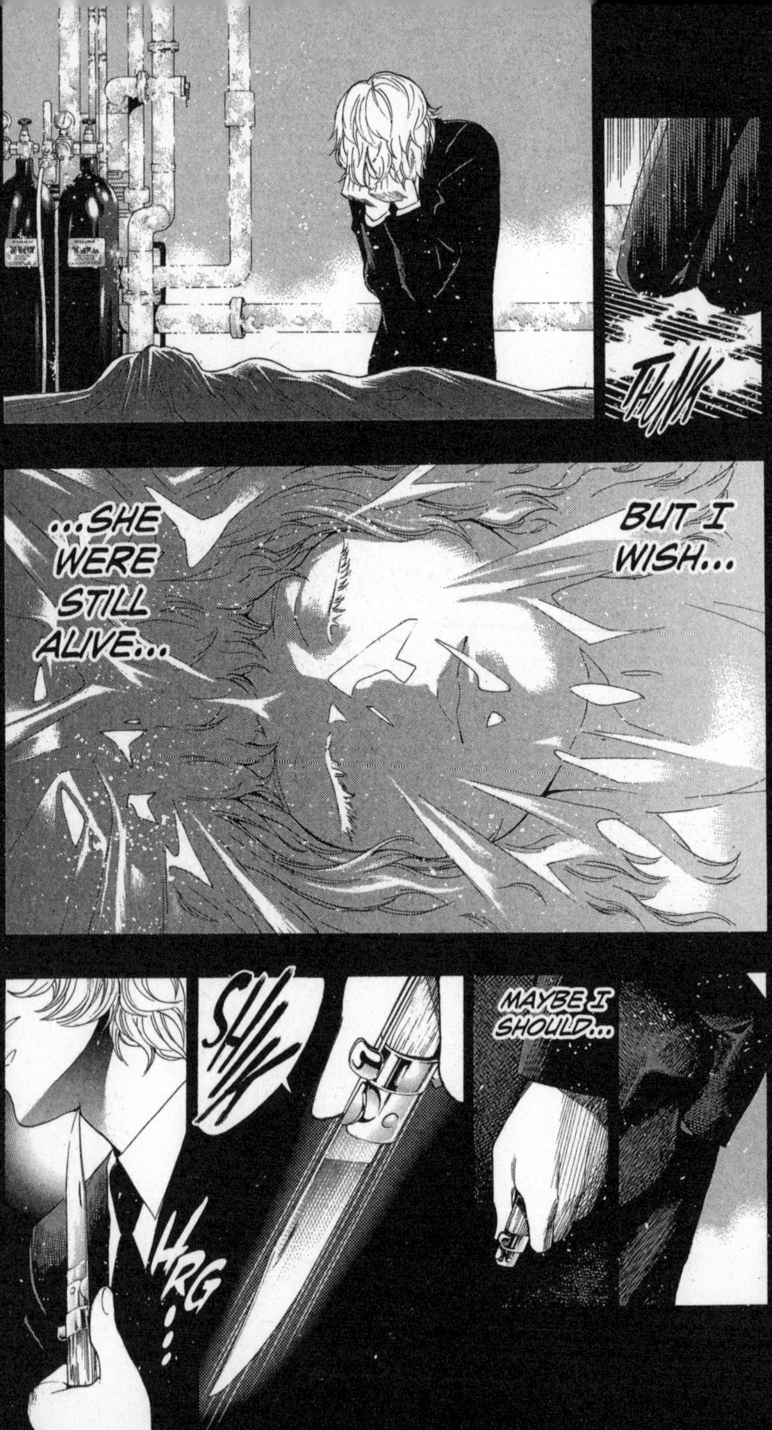
THUNK
BUT I WISH...
...SHE WERE STILL ALIVE...
MAYBE I SHOULD...
SHIK
HRG...

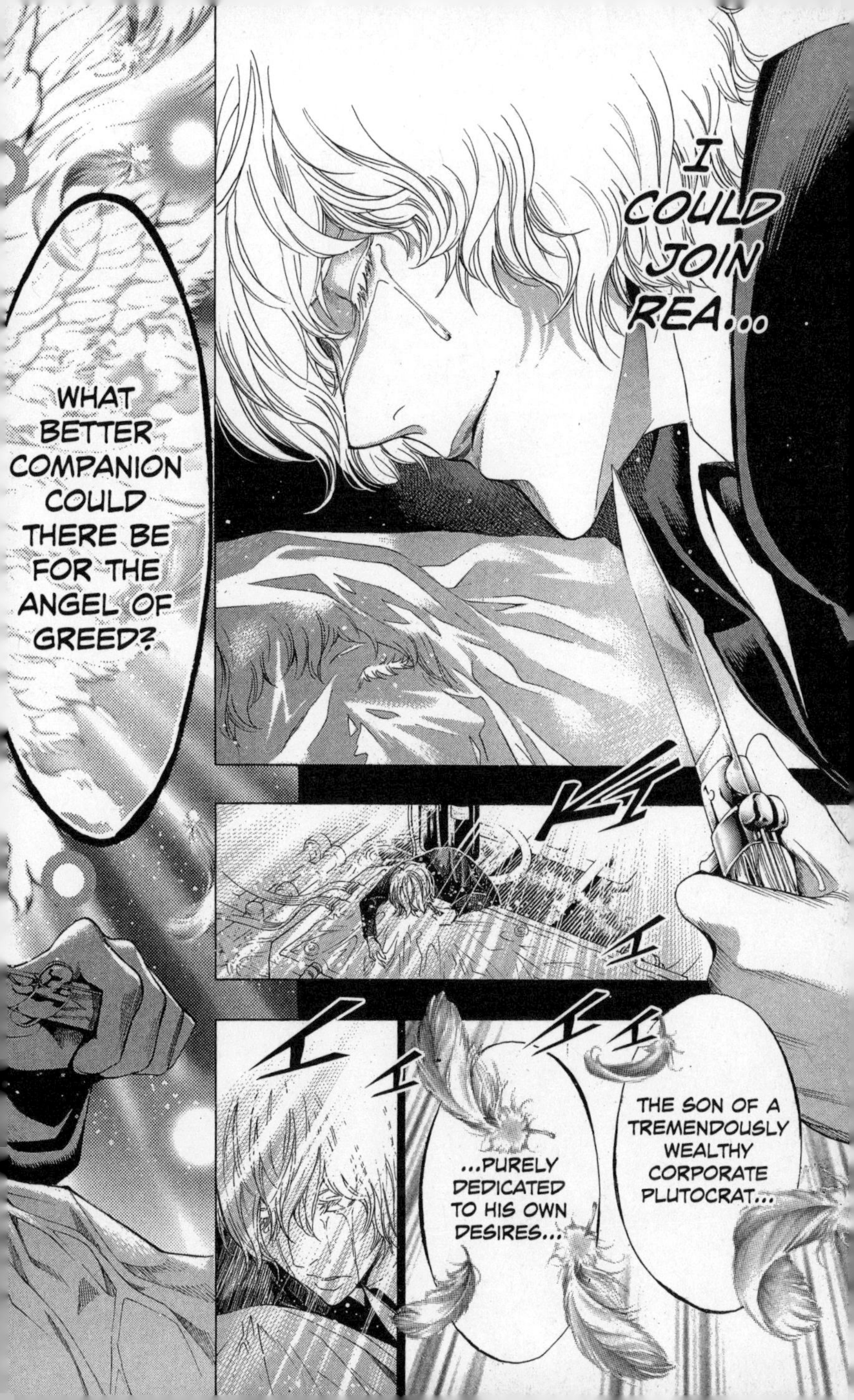
I COULD JOIN REA...
THE SON OF A TREMENDOUSLY WEALTHY CORPORATE PLUTOCRAT...
...PURELY DEDICATED TO HIS OWN DESIRES...
WHAT BETTER COMPANION COULD THERE BE FOR THE ANGEL OF GREED?

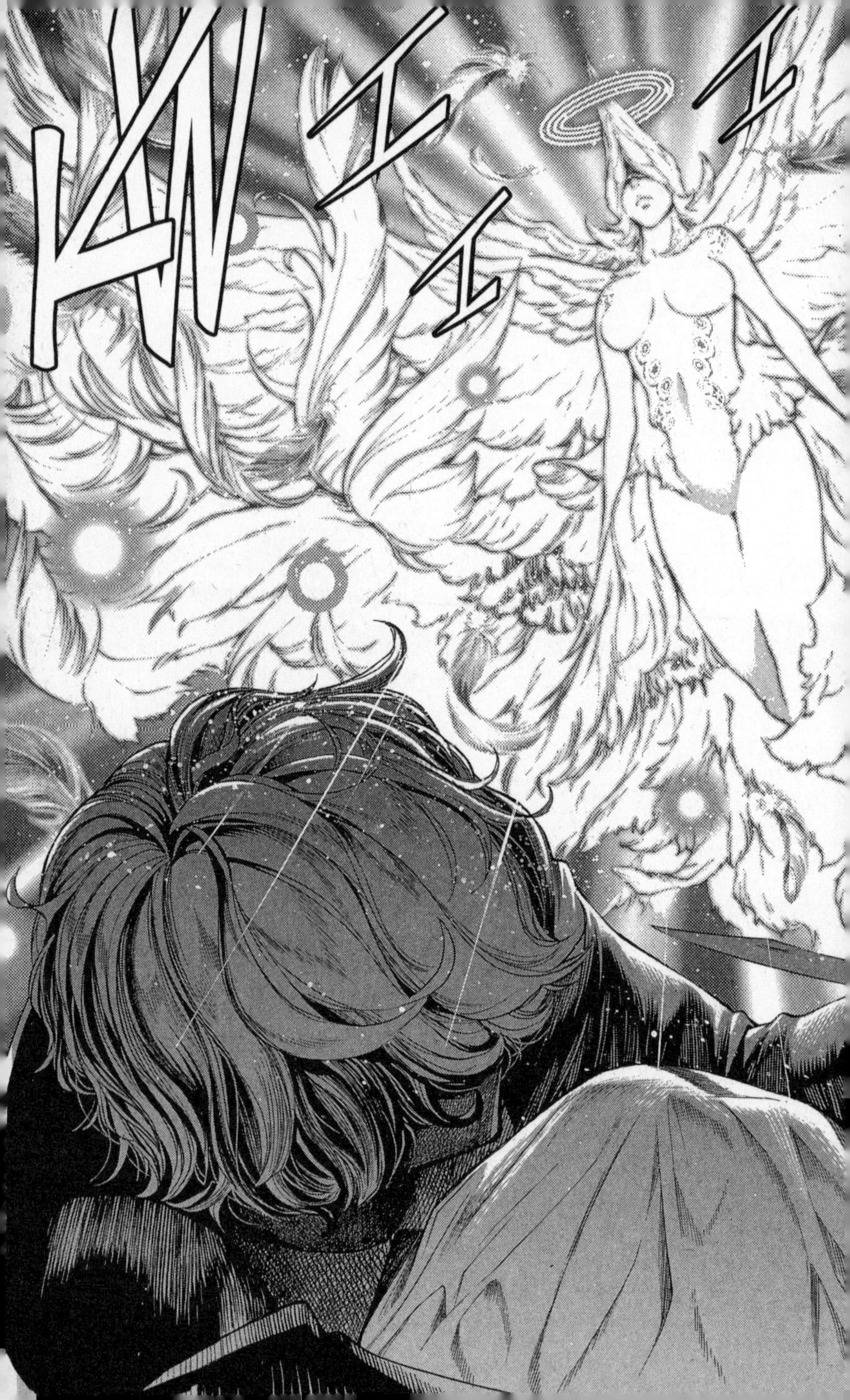

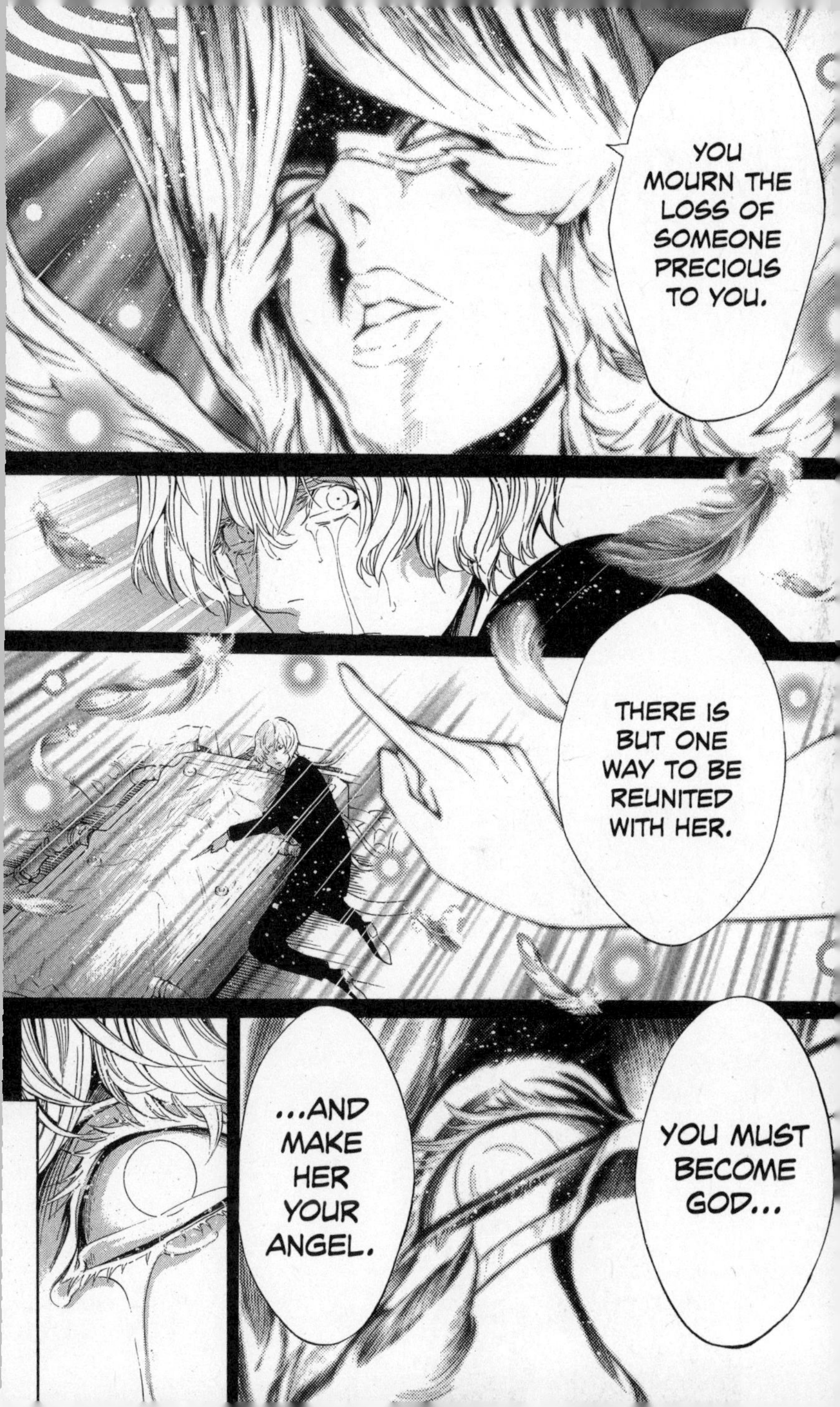
YOU MOURN THE LOSS OF SOMEONE PRECIOUS TO YOU.
THERE IS BUT ONE WAY TO BE REUNITED WITH HER.
YOU MUST BECOME GOD...
...AND MAKE HER YOUR ANGEL.

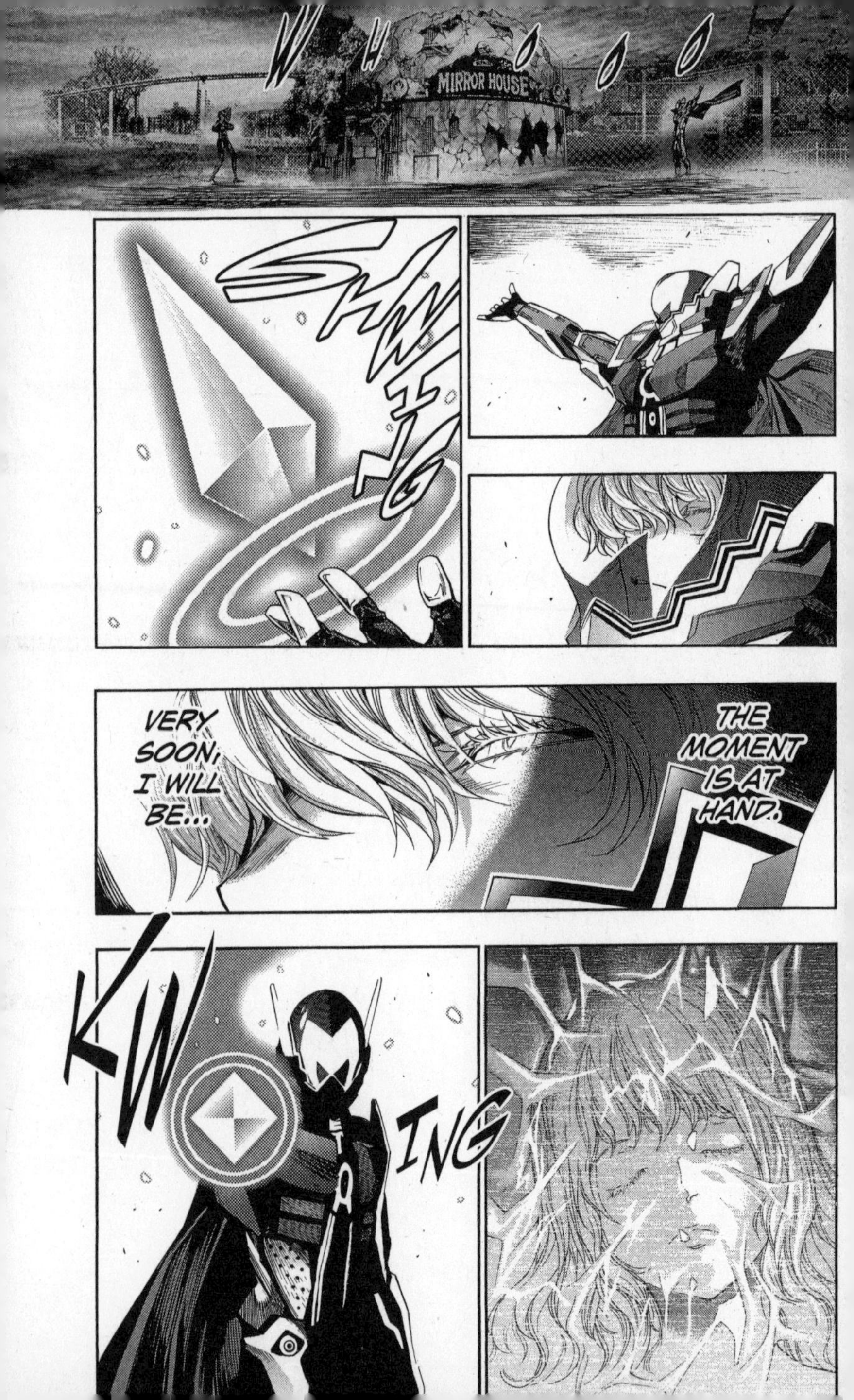
WHOOOO
MIRROR HOUSE
SHING
THE MOMENT IS AT HAND.
VERY SOON, I WILL BE...
KWING

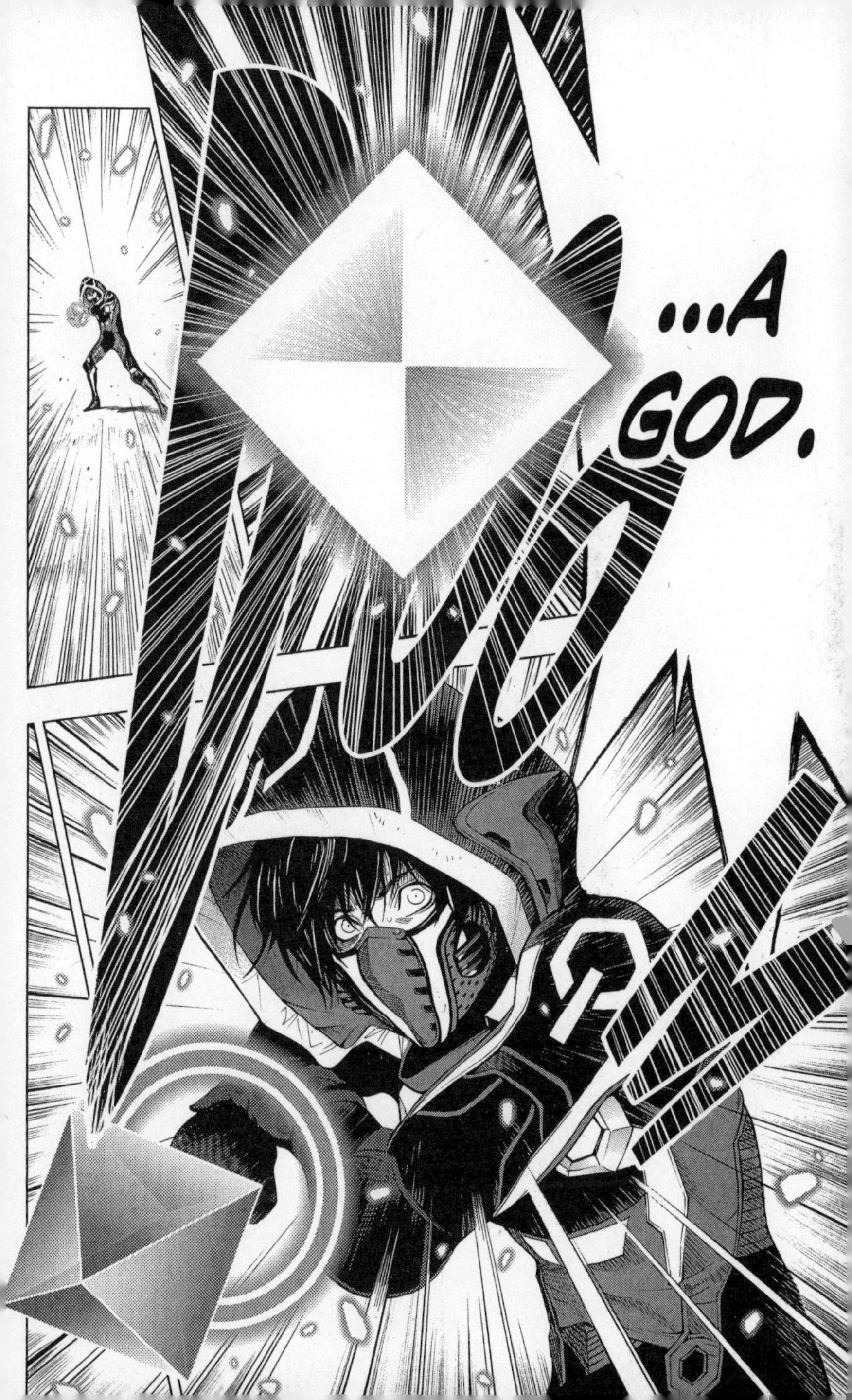
...A GOD.

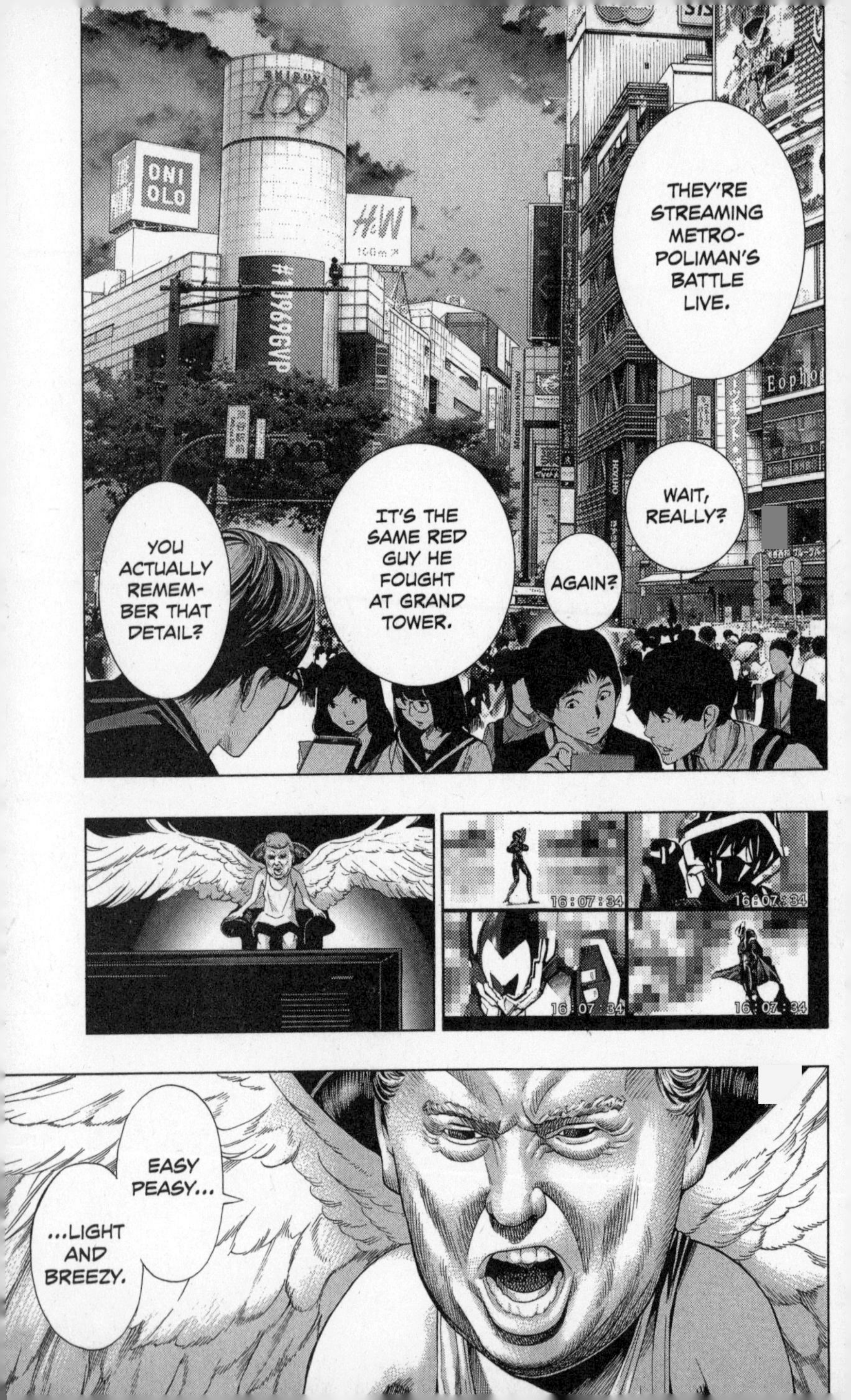
THEY'RE STREAMING METRO-POLIMAN'S BATTLE LIVE.
WAIT, REALLY?
AGAIN?
IT'S THE SAME RED GUY HE FOUGHT AT GRAND TOWER.
YOU ACTUALLY REMEMBER THAT DETAIL?
EASY PEASY...
...LIGHT AND BREEZY.

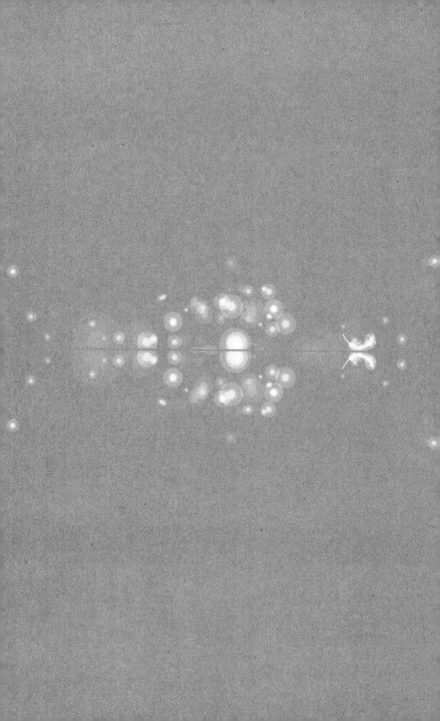

#23 World Peace

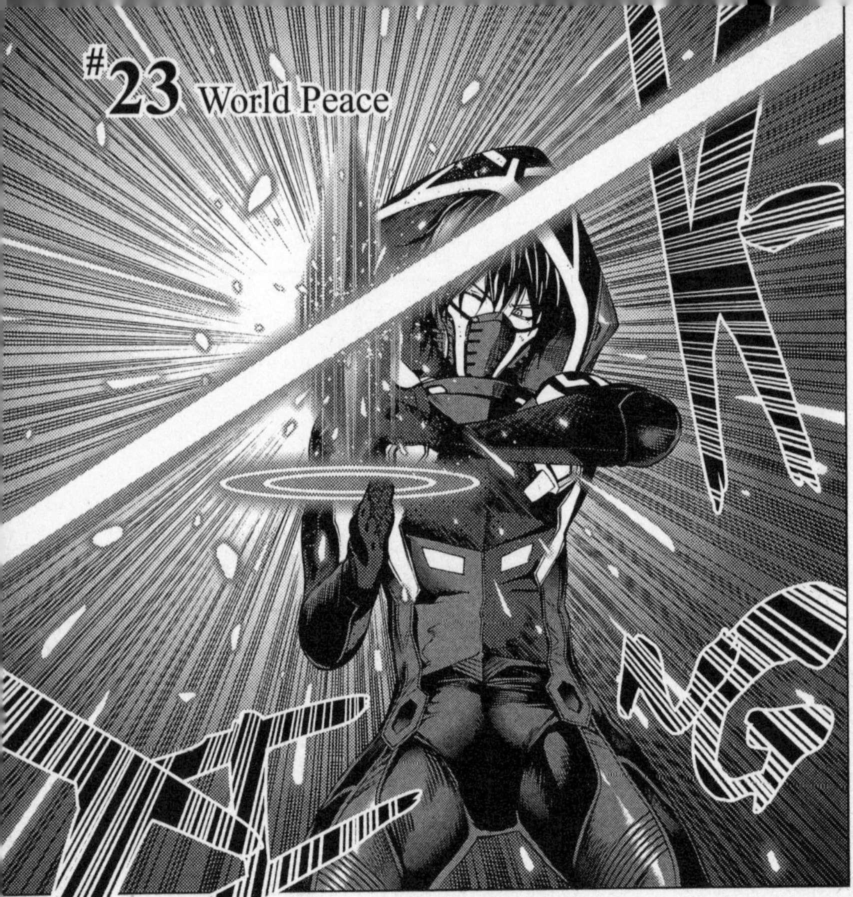

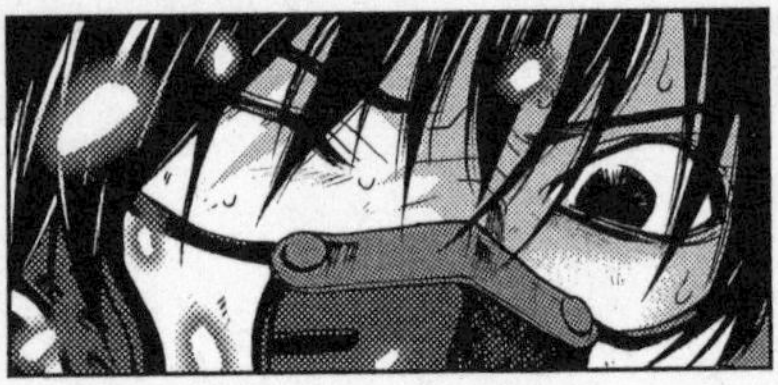

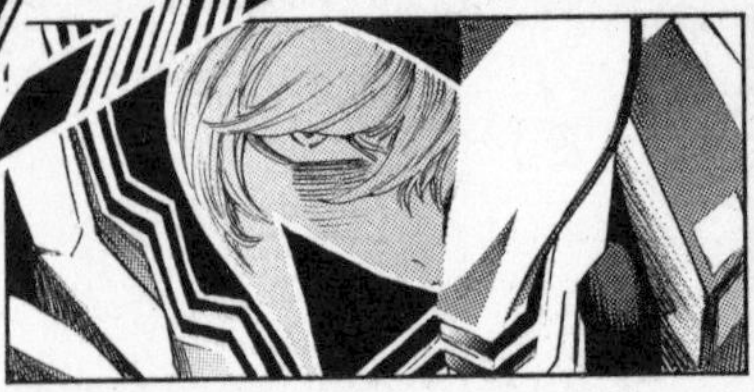

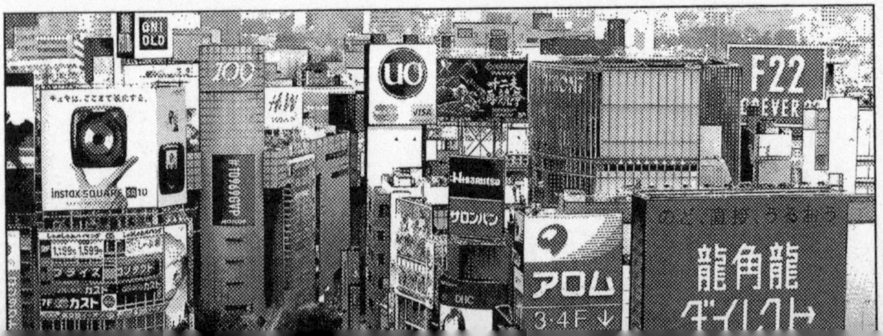
F22
instax SQUARE
アロム

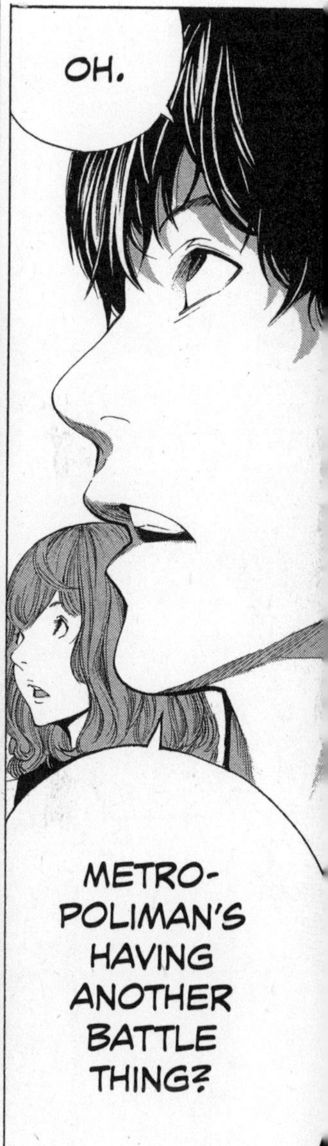

OH.
METRO-POLIMAN'S HAVING ANOTHER BATTLE THING?

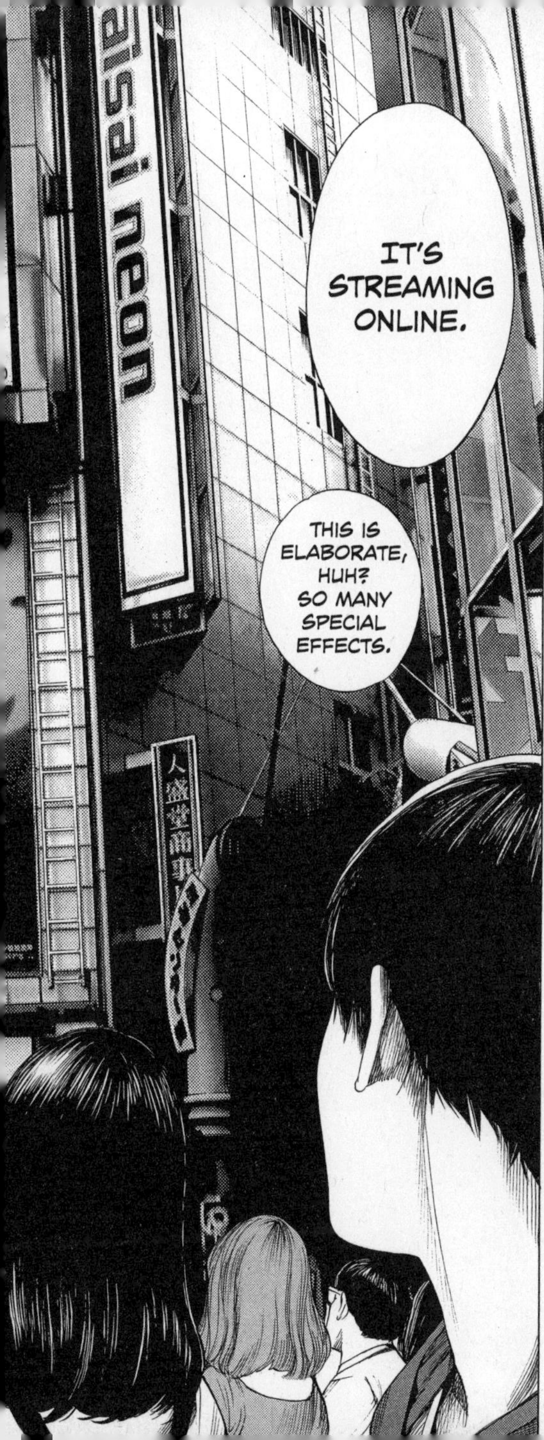

IT'S STREAMING ONLINE.
THIS IS ELABORATE, HUH? SO MANY SPECIAL EFFECTS.

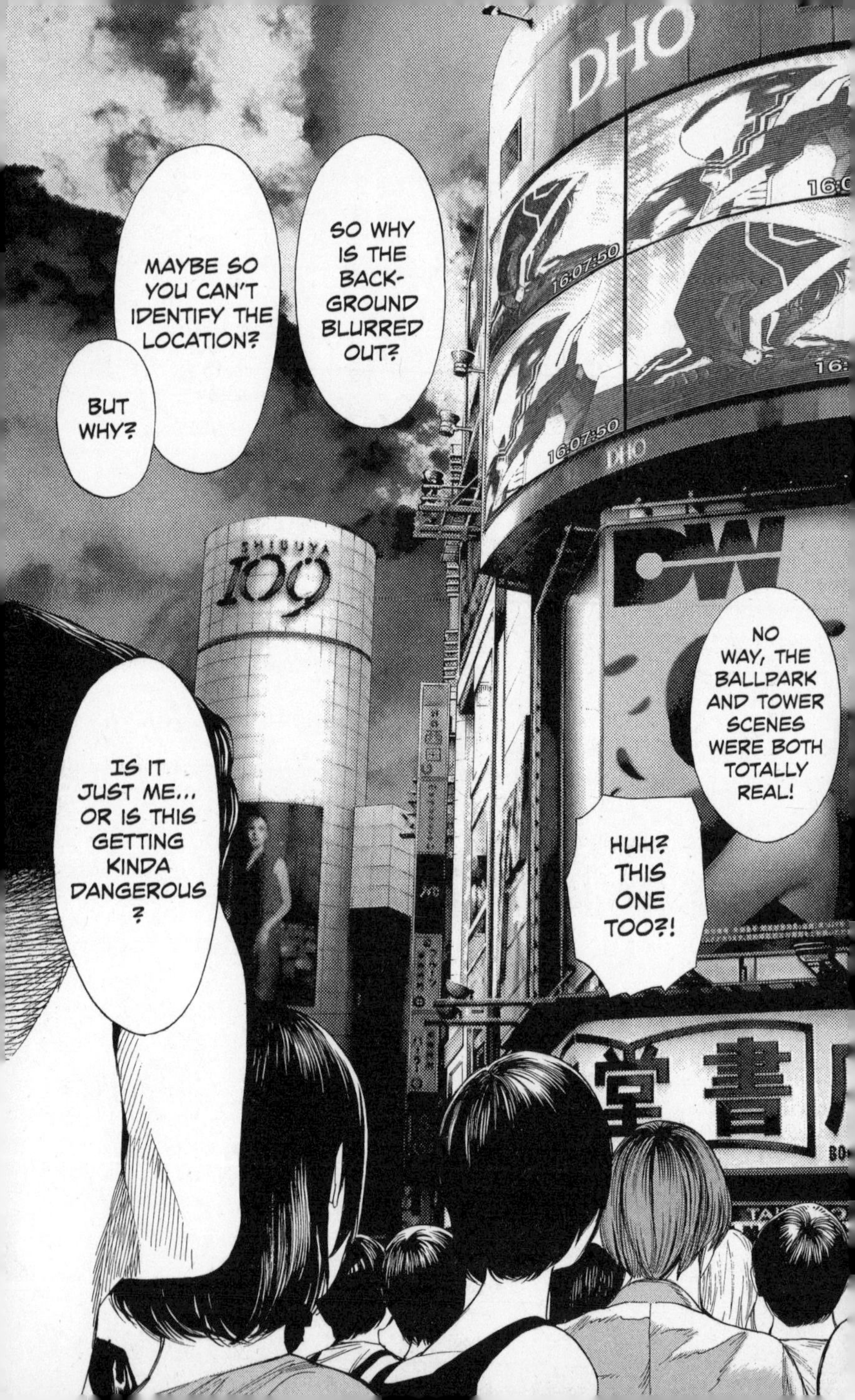
DHO
16:07:50
SO WHY IS THE BACK-GROUND BLURRED OUT?
MAYBE SO YOU CAN'T IDENTIFY THE LOCATION?
BUT WHY?
109
DW
HUH? THIS ONE TOO?!
NO WAY, THE BALLPARK AND TOWER SCENES WERE BOTH TOTALLY REAL!
IS IT JUST ME... OR IS THIS GETTING KINDA DANGEROUS?

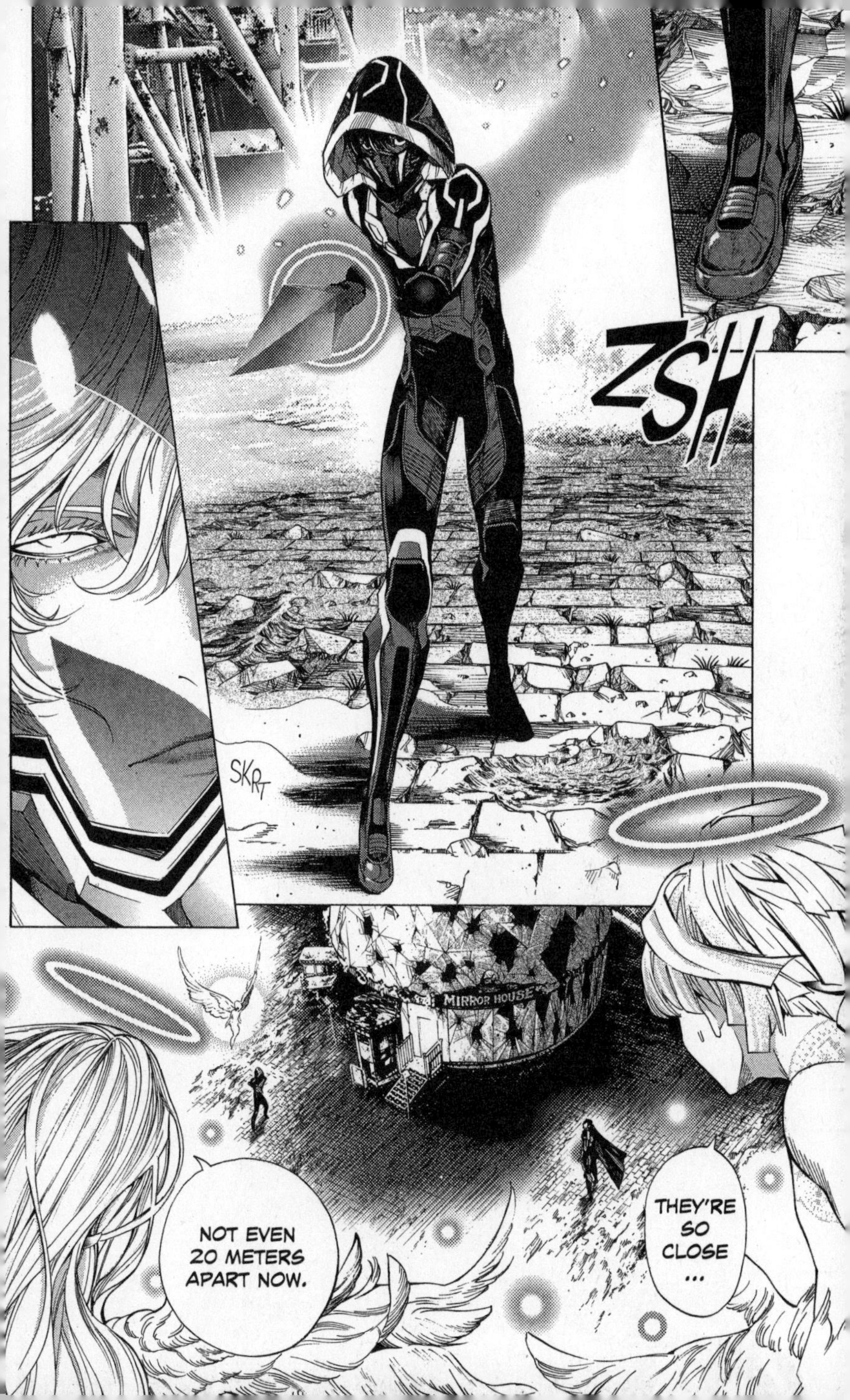
ZSH
SKRT
MIRROR HOUSE
THEY'RE SO CLOSE ...
NOT EVEN 20 METERS APART NOW.

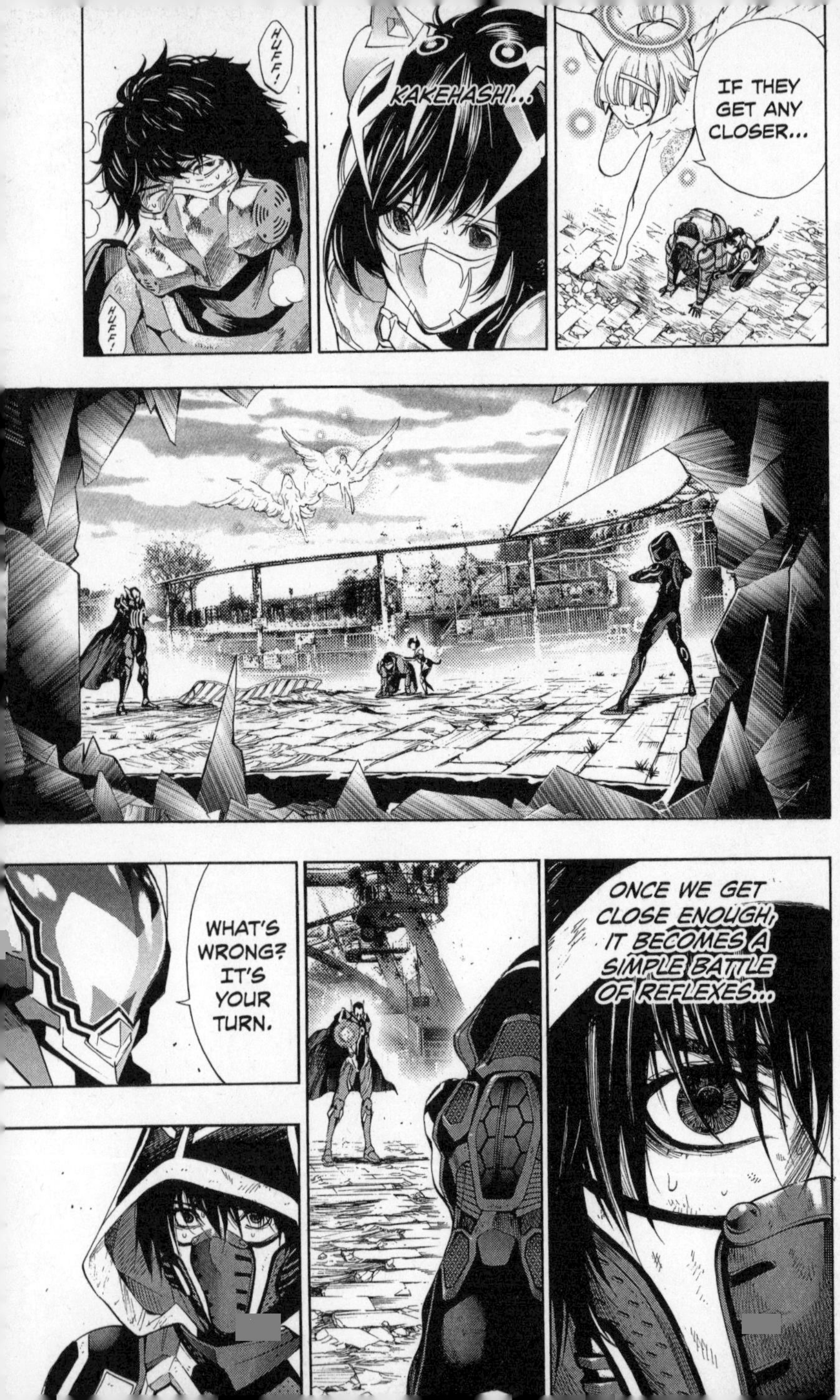

IF THEY GET ANY CLOSER...
KAKEHASHI...
HUFF!
HUFF!
ONCE WE GET CLOSE ENOUGH, IT BECOMES A SIMPLE BATTLE OF REFLEXES...
WHAT'S WRONG? IT'S YOUR TURN.
...

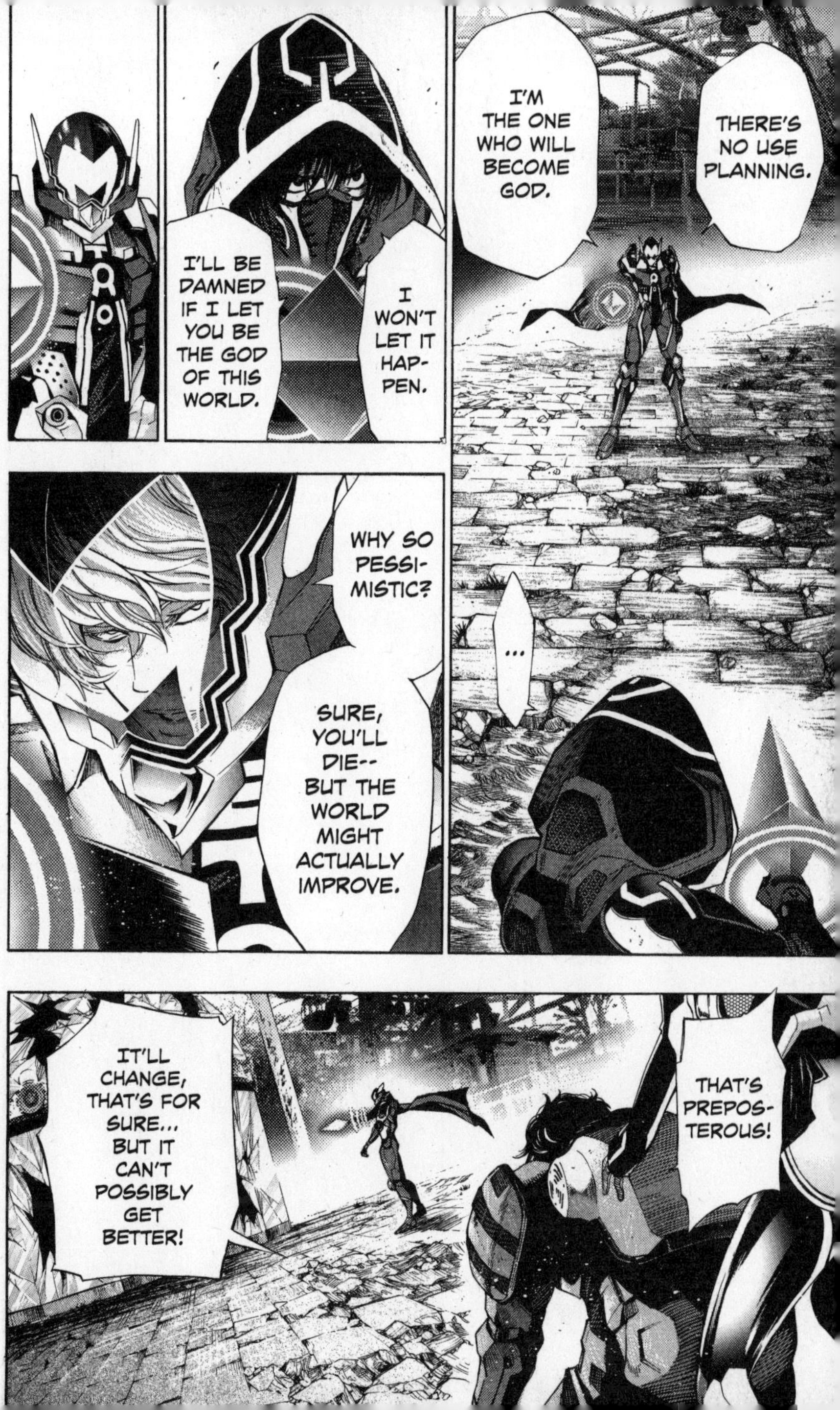
THERE'S NO USE PLANNING.
I'M THE ONE WHO WILL BECOME GOD.
I WON'T LET IT HAP-PEN.
I'LL BE DAMNED IF I LET YOU BE THE GOD OF THIS WORLD.
...
WHY SO PESSI-MISTIC?
SURE, YOU'LL DIE-- BUT THE WORLD MIGHT ACTUALLY IMPROVE.
THAT'S PREPOS-TEROUS!
IT'LL CHANGE, THAT'S FOR SURE... BUT IT CAN'T POSSIBLY GET BETTER!

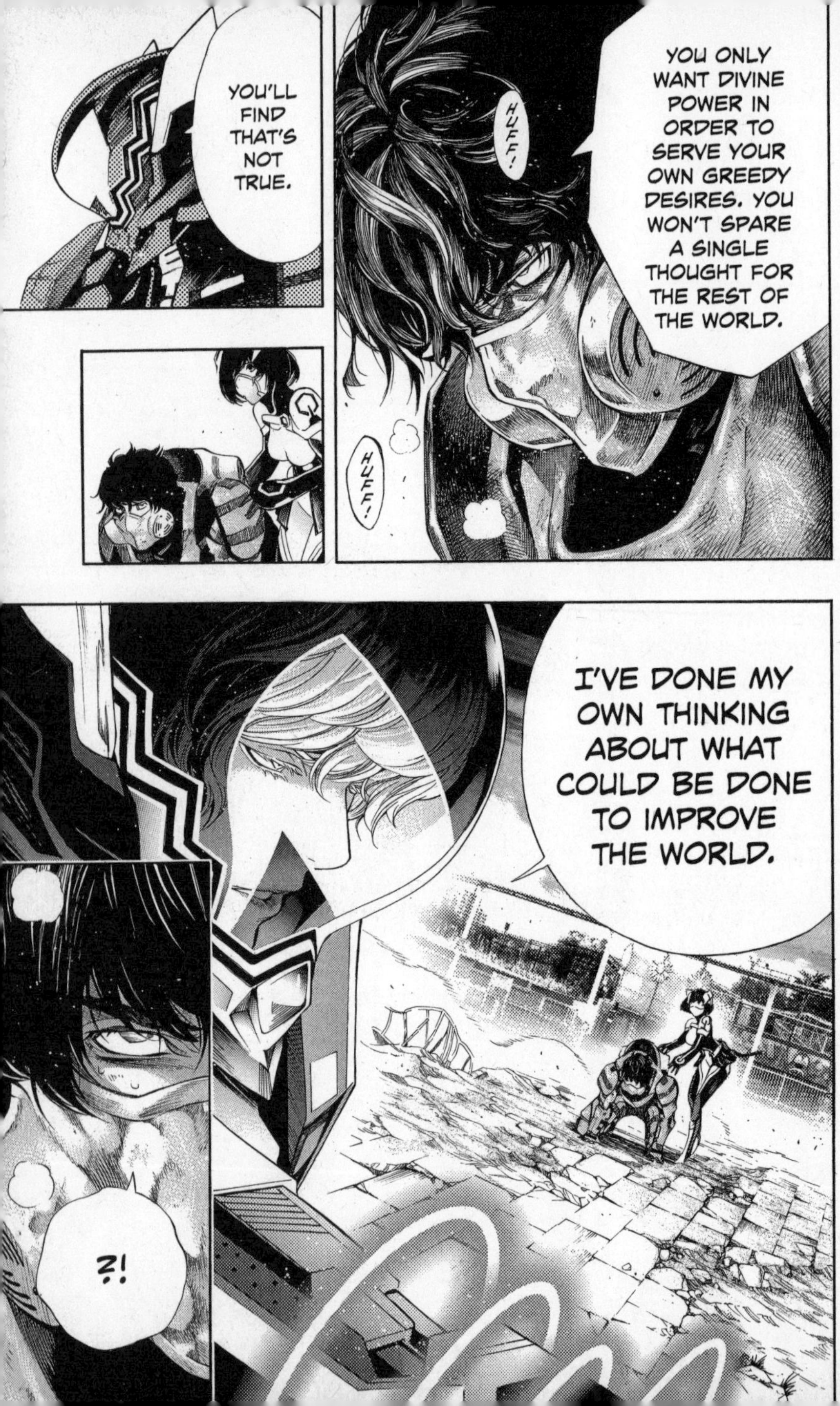
HUFF!
YOU ONLY WANT DIVINE POWER IN ORDER TO SERVE YOUR OWN GREEDY DESIRES. YOU WON'T SPARE A SINGLE THOUGHT FOR THE REST OF THE WORLD.
HUFF!
YOU'LL FIND THAT'S NOT TRUE.
I'VE DONE MY OWN THINKING ABOUT WHAT COULD BE DONE TO IMPROVE THE WORLD.
?!

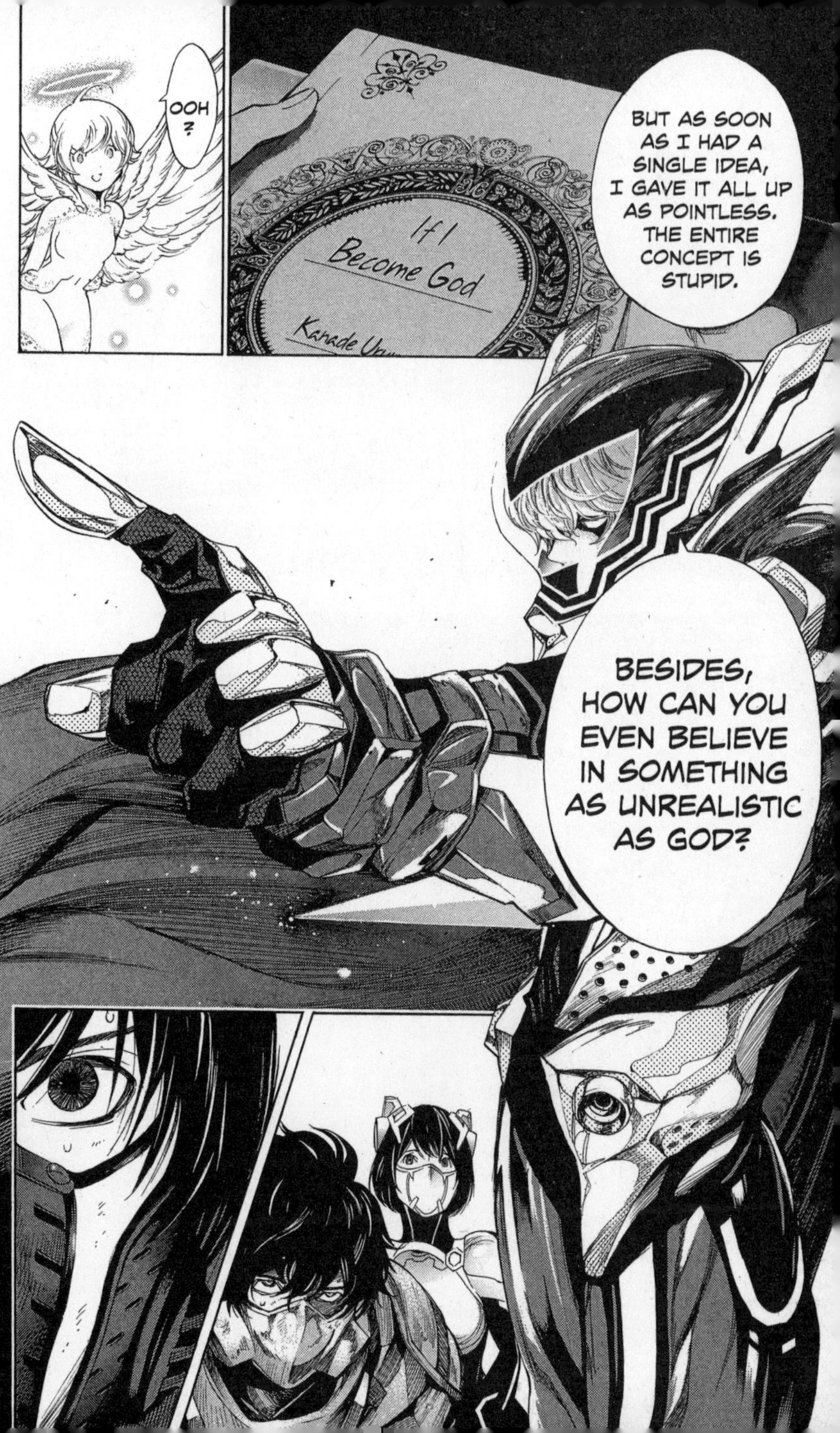
BUT AS SOON AS I HAD A SINGLE IDEA, I GAVE IT ALL UP AS POINTLESS. THE ENTIRE CONCEPT IS STUPID.
If I Become God
Kanade Unu
OOH?
BESIDES, HOW CAN YOU EVEN BELIEVE IN SOMETHING AS UNREALISTIC AS GOD?

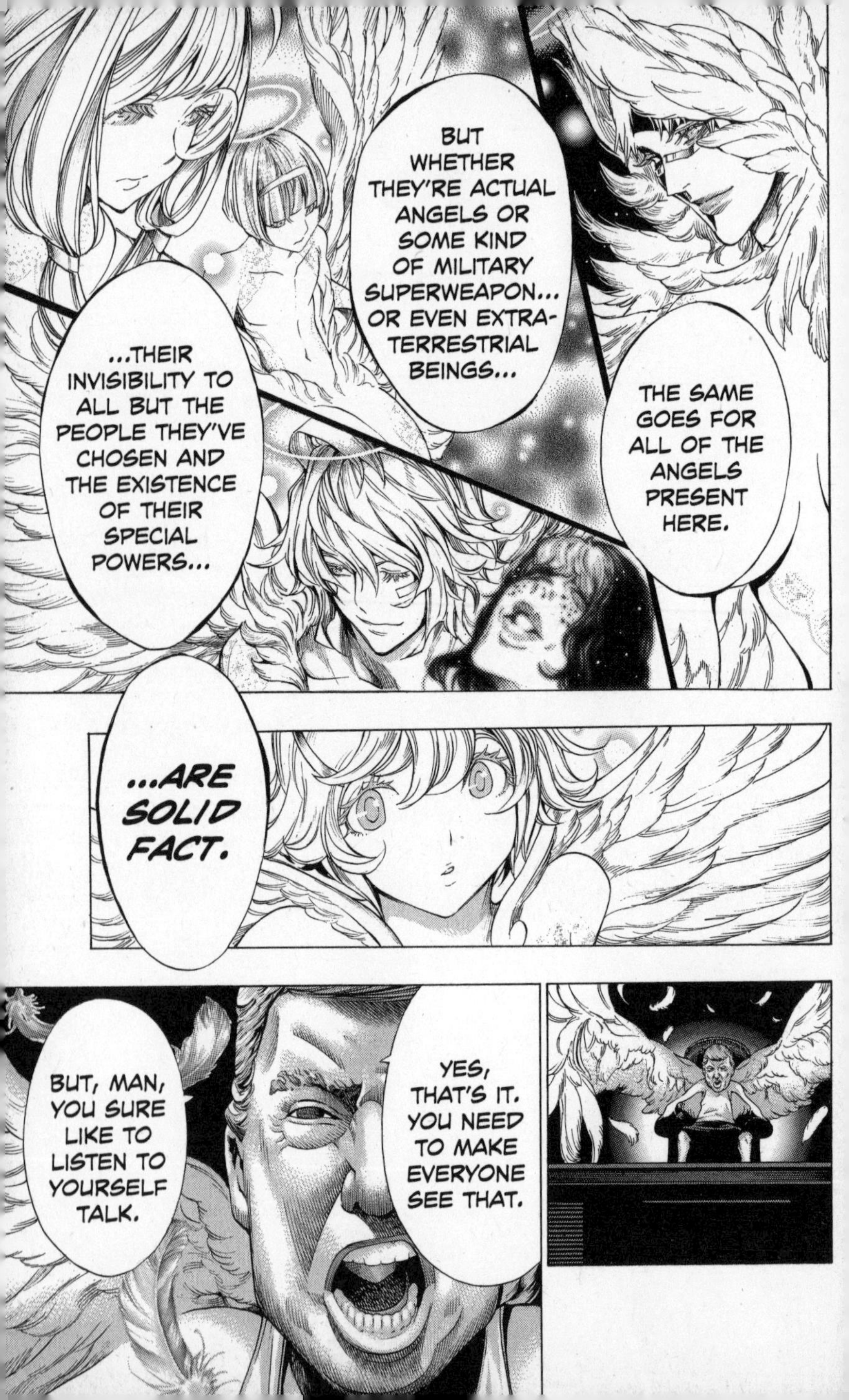
THE SAME GOES FOR ALL OF THE ANGELS PRESENT HERE.
BUT WHETHER THEY'RE ACTUAL ANGELS OR SOME KIND OF MILITARY SUPERWEAPON... OR EVEN EXTRA-TERRESTRIAL BEINGS...
...THEIR INVISIBILITY TO ALL BUT THE PEOPLE THEY'VE CHOSEN AND THE EXISTENCE OF THEIR SPECIAL POWERS...
...ARE SOLID FACT.
YES, THAT'S IT. YOU NEED TO MAKE EVERYONE SEE THAT.
BUT, MAN, YOU SURE LIKE TO LISTEN TO YOURSELF TALK.

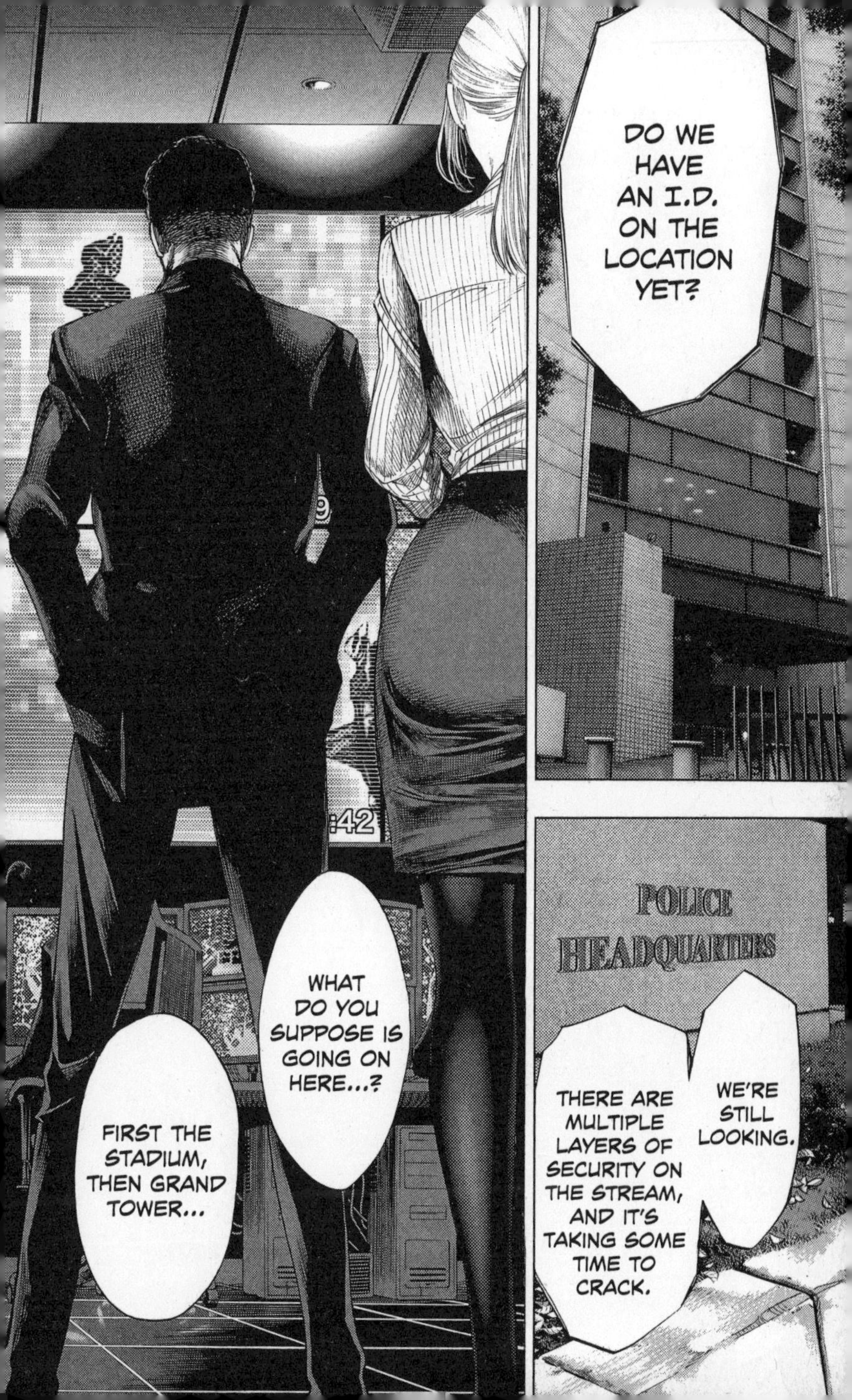
DO WE HAVE AN I.D. ON THE LOCATION YET?
POLICE HEADQUARTERS
WE'RE STILL LOOKING.
THERE ARE MULTIPLE LAYERS OF SECURITY ON THE STREAM, AND IT'S TAKING SOME TIME TO CRACK.
WHAT DO YOU SUPPOSE IS GOING ON HERE...?
FIRST THE STADIUM, THEN GRAND TOWER...

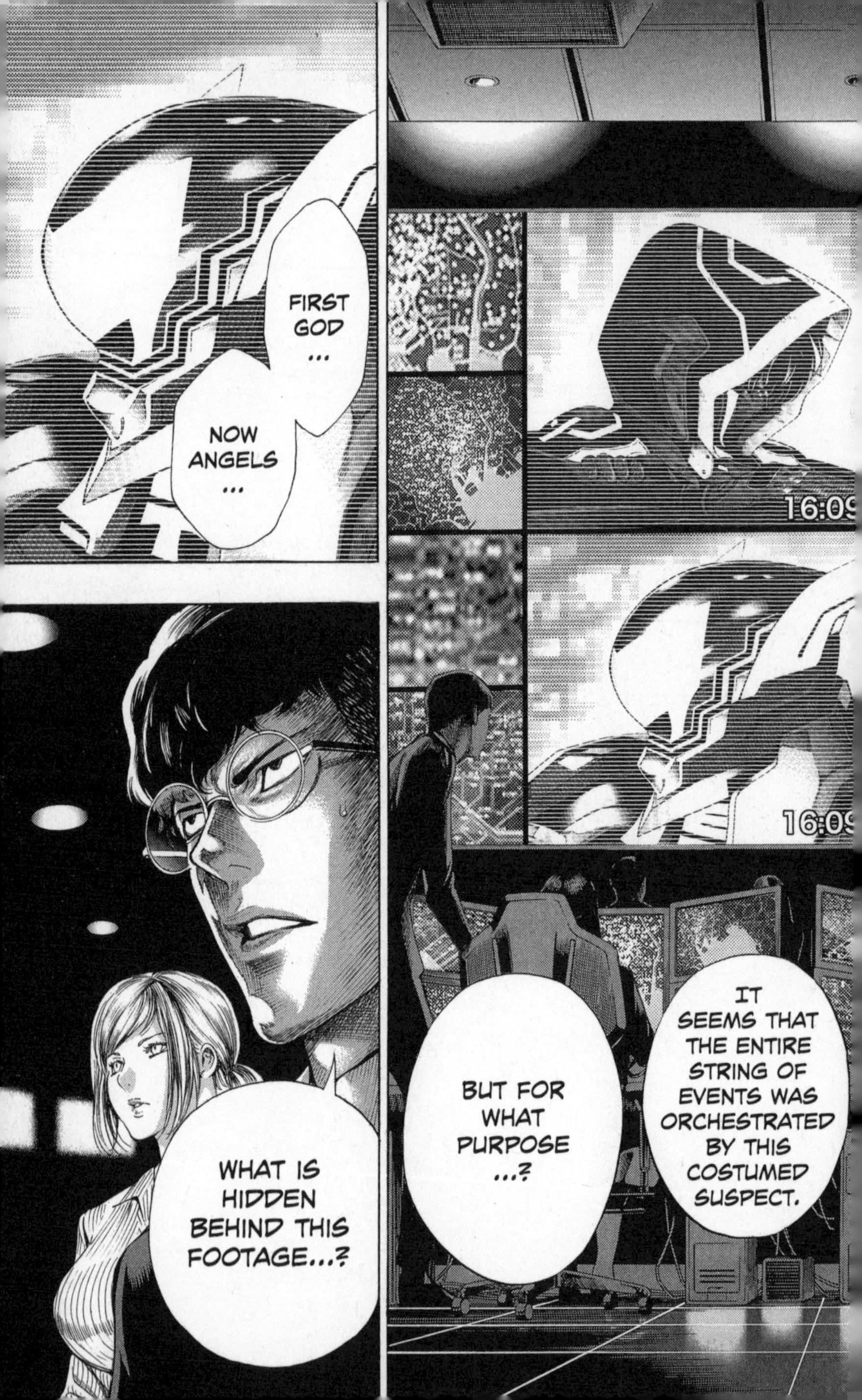
IT SEEMS THAT THE ENTIRE STRING OF EVENTS WAS ORCHESTRATED BY THIS COSTUMED SUSPECT.
BUT FOR WHAT PURPOSE ...?
FIRST GOD ...
NOW ANGELS ...
WHAT IS HIDDEN BEHIND THIS FOOTAGE...?

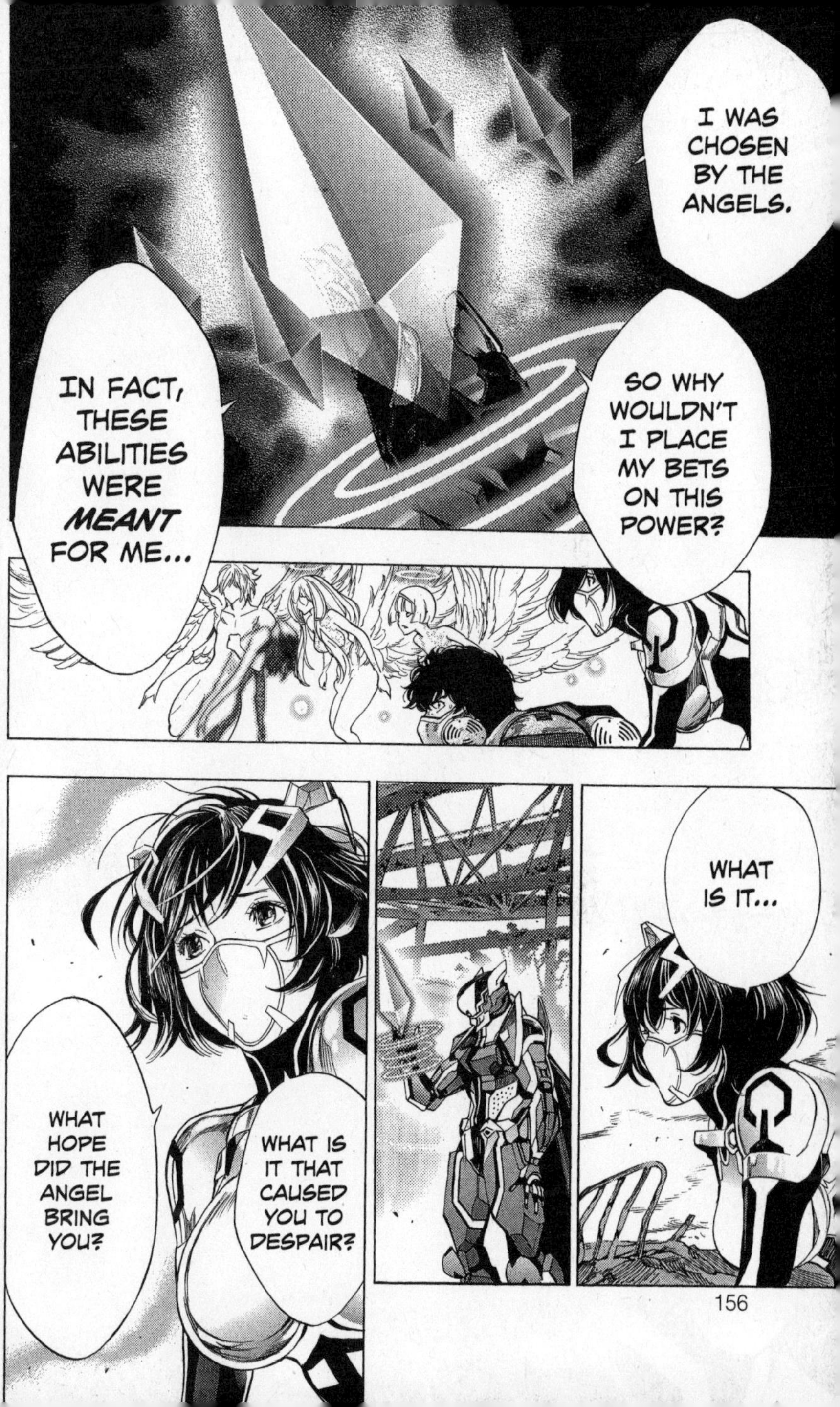
I WAS CHOSEN BY THE ANGELS.
SO WHY WOULDN'T I PLACE MY BETS ON THIS POWER?
IN FACT, THESE ABILITIES WERE *MEANT* FOR ME...
WHAT IS IT...
WHAT IS IT THAT CAUSED YOU TO DESPAIR?
WHAT HOPE DID THE ANGEL BRING YOU?

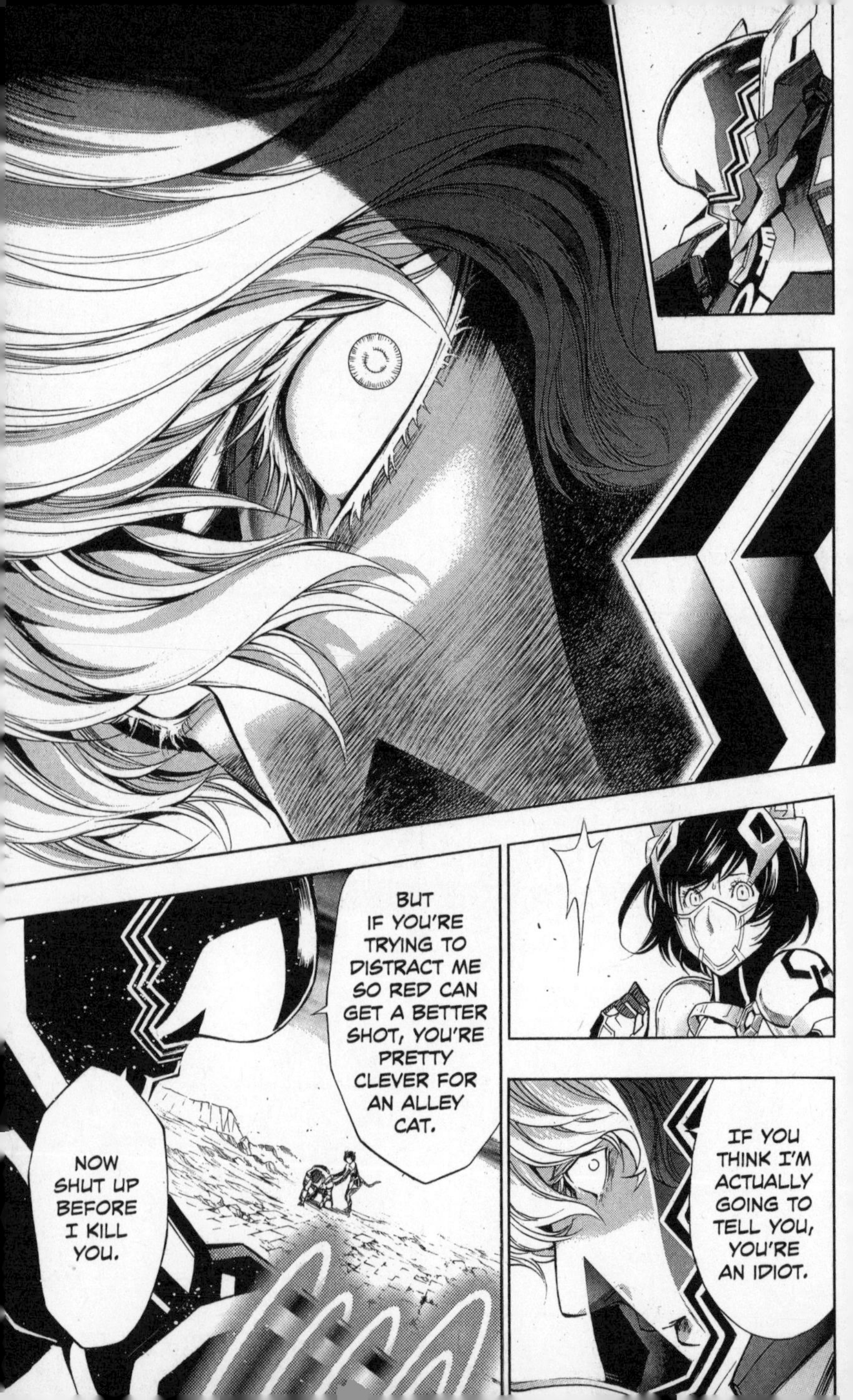
IF YOU THINK I'M ACTUALLY GOING TO TELL YOU, YOU'RE AN IDIOT.
BUT IF YOU'RE TRYING TO DISTRACT ME SO RED CAN GET A BETTER SHOT, YOU'RE PRETTY CLEVER FOR AN ALLEY CAT.
NOW SHUT UP BEFORE I KILL YOU.

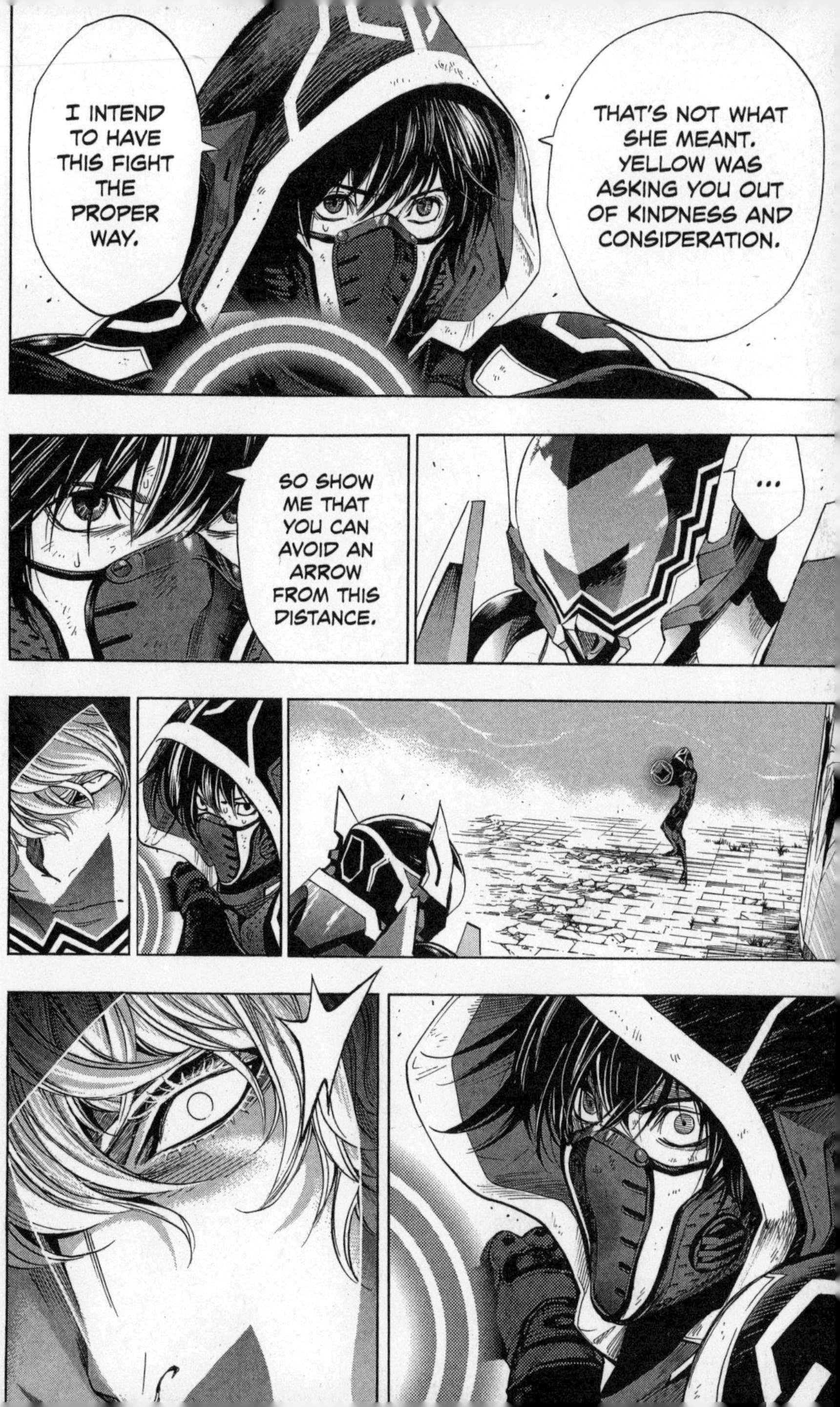
THAT'S NOT WHAT SHE MEANT. YELLOW WAS ASKING YOU OUT OF KINDNESS AND CONSIDERATION.
I INTEND TO HAVE THIS FIGHT THE PROPER WAY.
...
SO SHOW ME THAT YOU CAN AVOID AN ARROW FROM THIS DISTANCE.

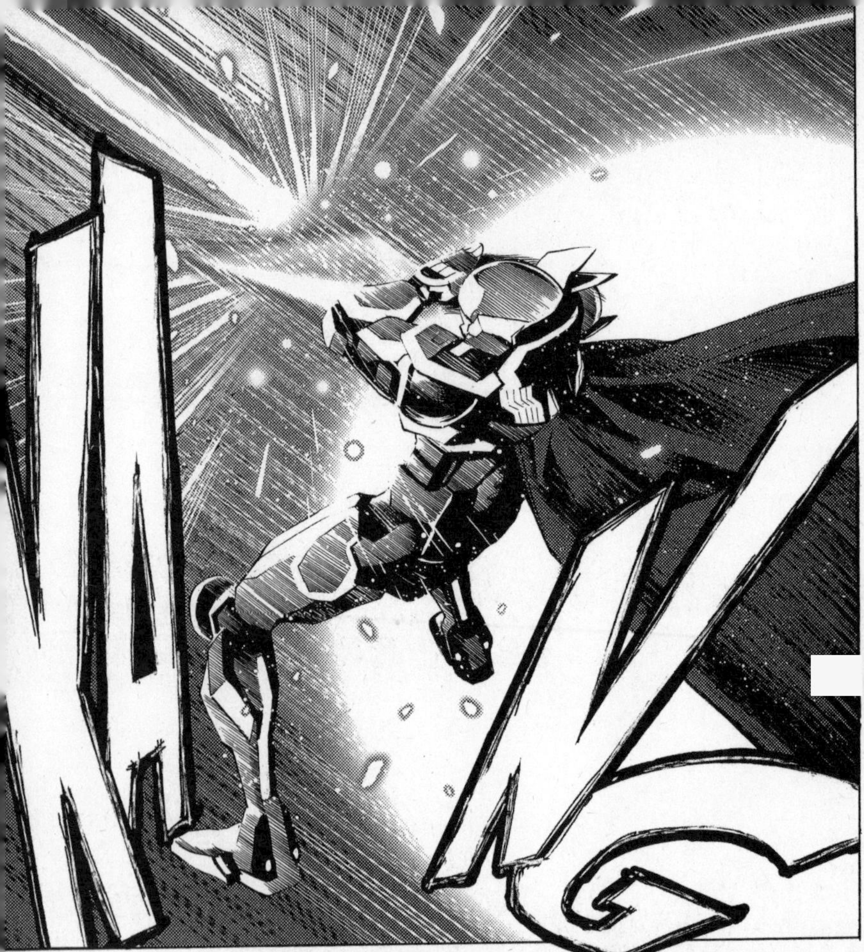
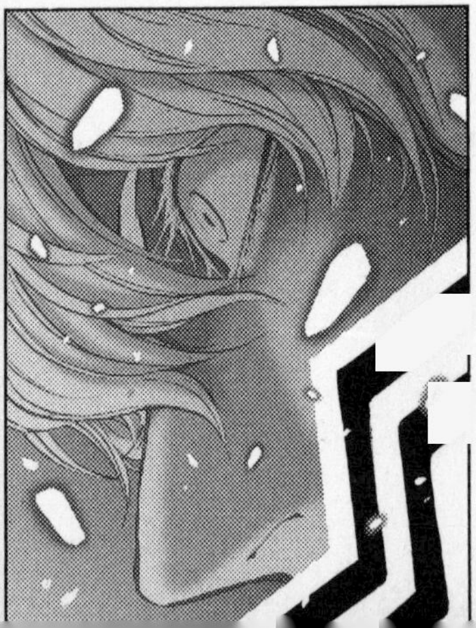
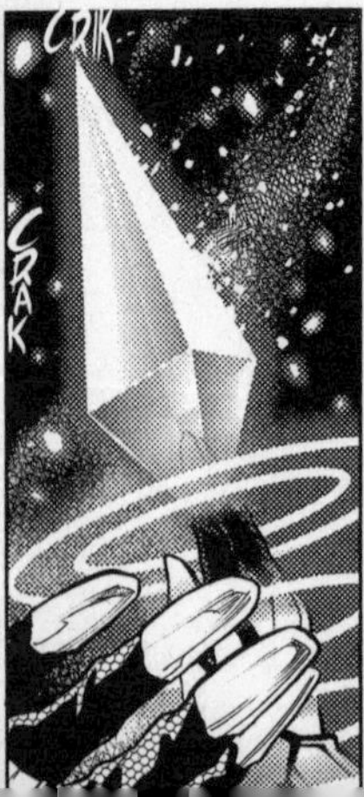
CRIK
CRAK
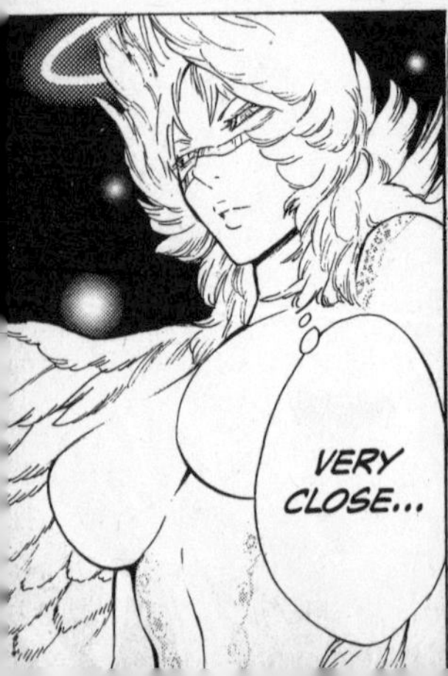
VERY CLOSE...

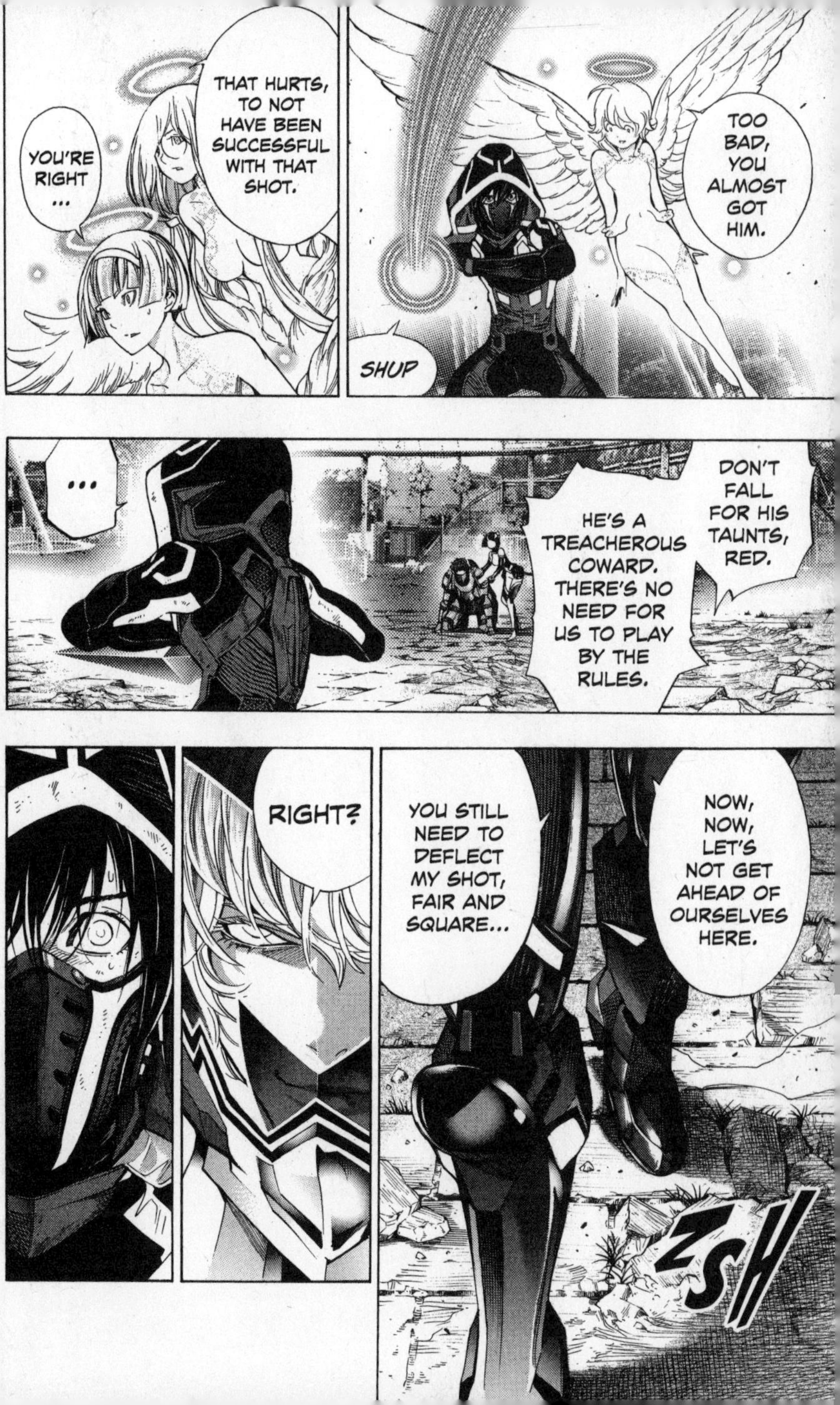
TOO BAD, YOU ALMOST GOT HIM.
SHUP
THAT HURTS, TO NOT HAVE BEEN SUCCESSFUL WITH THAT SHOT.
YOU'RE RIGHT ...
DON'T FALL FOR HIS TAUNTS, RED.
HE'S A TREACHEROUS COWARD. THERE'S NO NEED FOR US TO PLAY BY THE RULES.
...
NOW, NOW, LET'S NOT GET AHEAD OF OURSELVES HERE.
YOU STILL NEED TO DEFLECT MY SHOT, FAIR AND SQUARE...
ZSH
RIGHT?

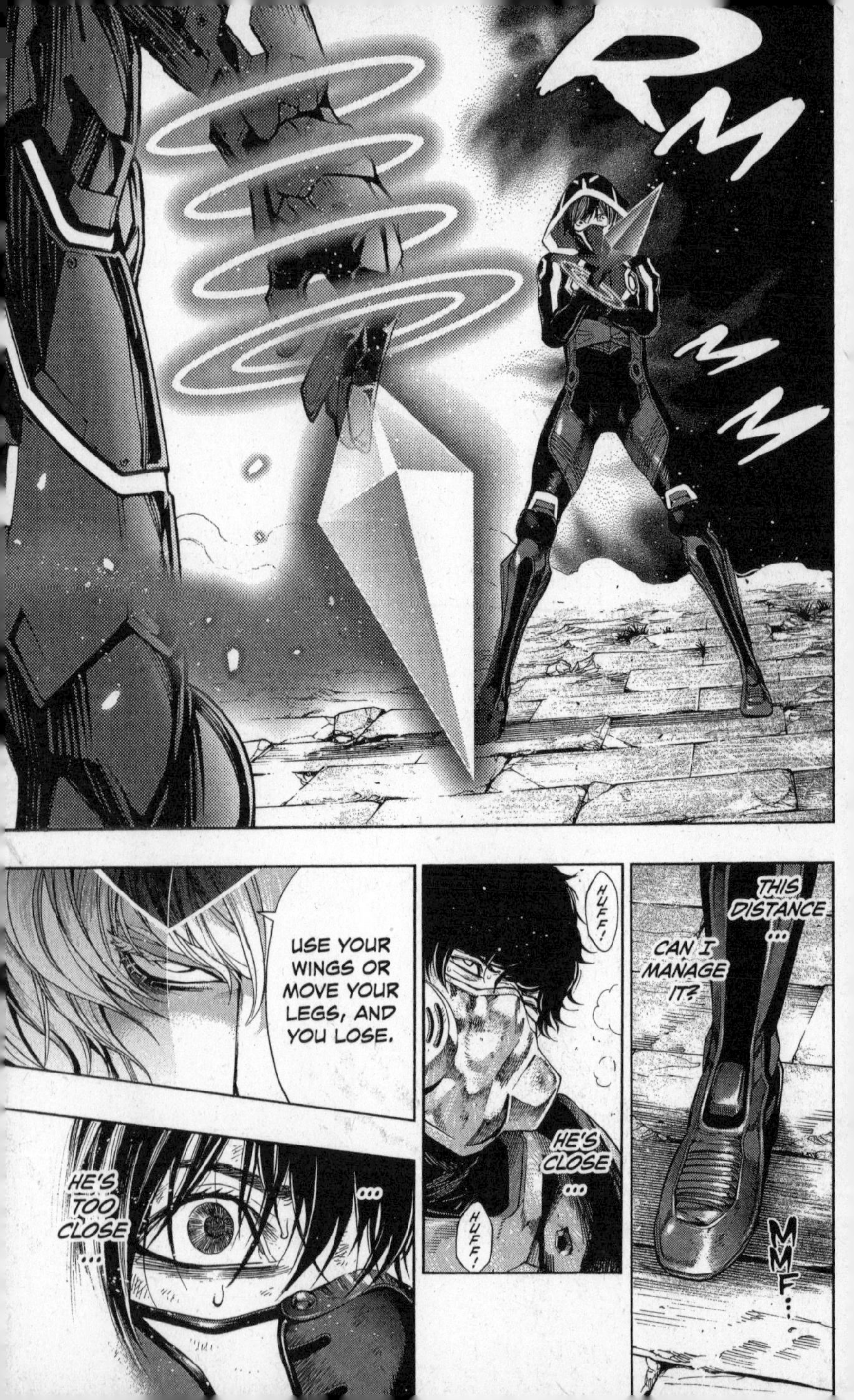
RMMMMM
THIS DISTANCE...
CAN I MANAGE IT?
MMMF...
HUFF!
HE'S CLOSE...
HUFF!
USE YOUR WINGS OR MOVE YOUR LEGS, AND YOU LOSE.
...
HE'S TOO CLOSE...

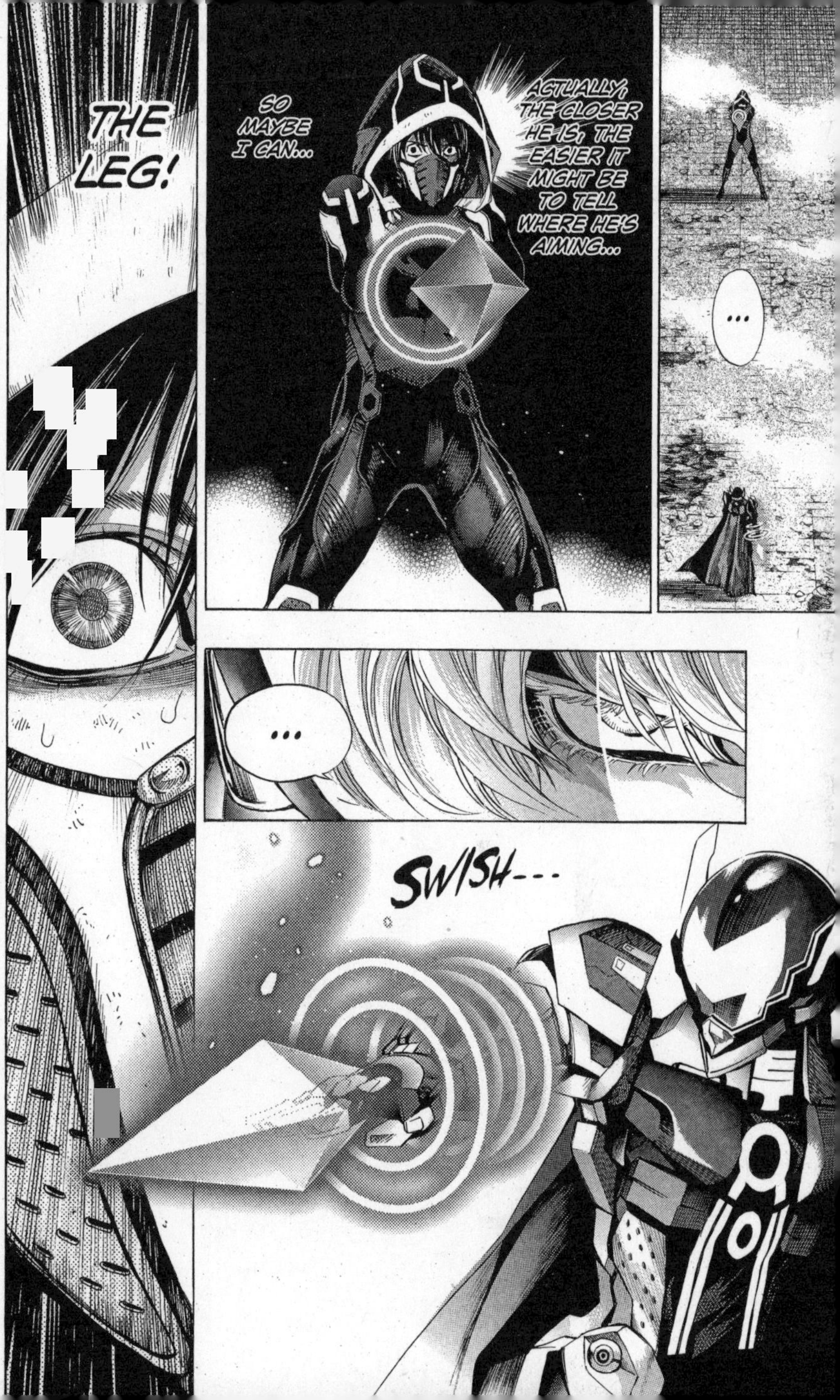
...
ACTUALLY, THE CLOSER HE IS, THE EASIER IT MIGHT BE TO TELL WHERE HE'S AIMING...
SO MAYBE I CAN...
...
SWISH---
THE LEG!

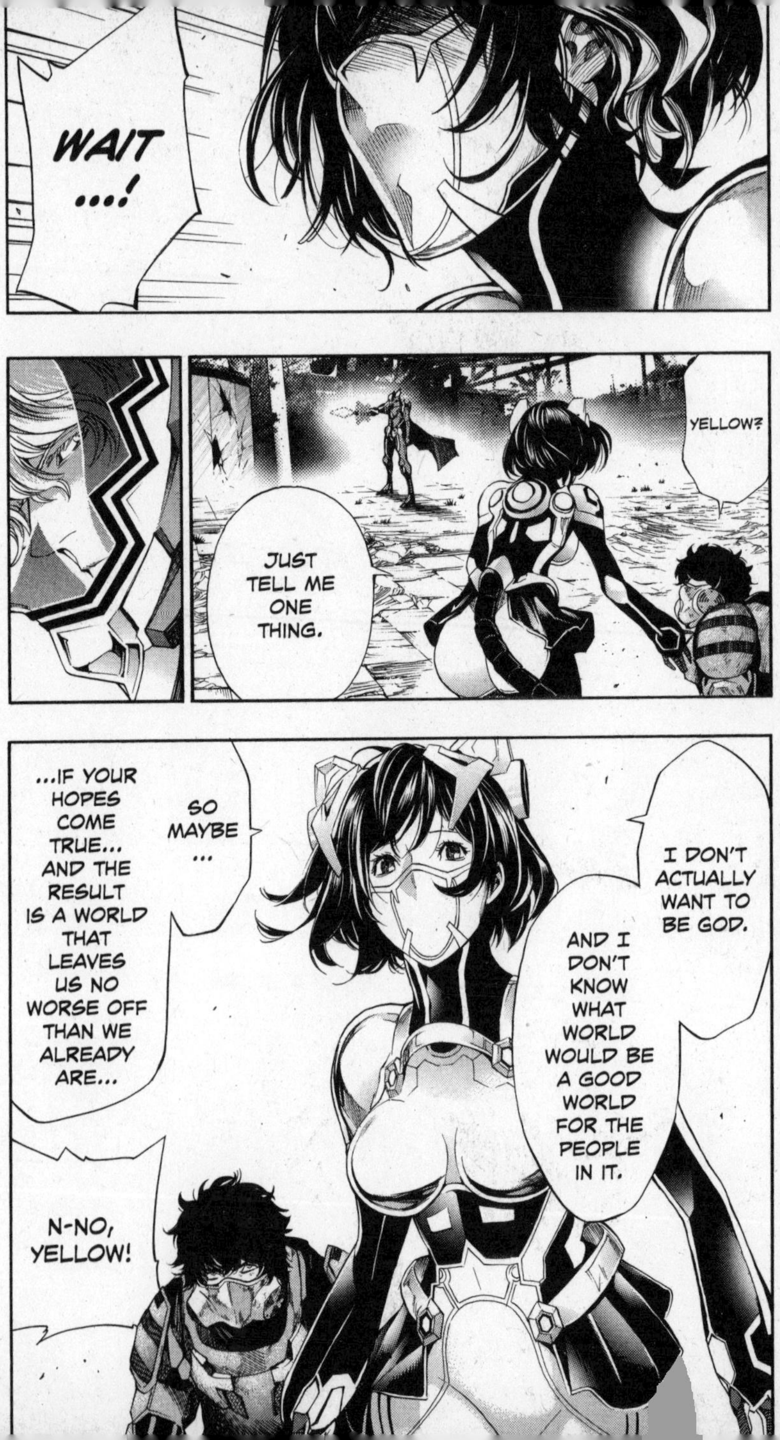
WAIT ...!
YELLOW?
JUST TELL ME ONE THING.
I DON'T ACTUALLY WANT TO BE GOD.
AND I DON'T KNOW WHAT WORLD WOULD BE A GOOD WORLD FOR THE PEOPLE IN IT.
SO MAYBE ...
...IF YOUR HOPES COME TRUE... AND THE RESULT IS A WORLD THAT LEAVES US NO WORSE OFF THAN WE ALREADY ARE...
N-NO, YELLOW!

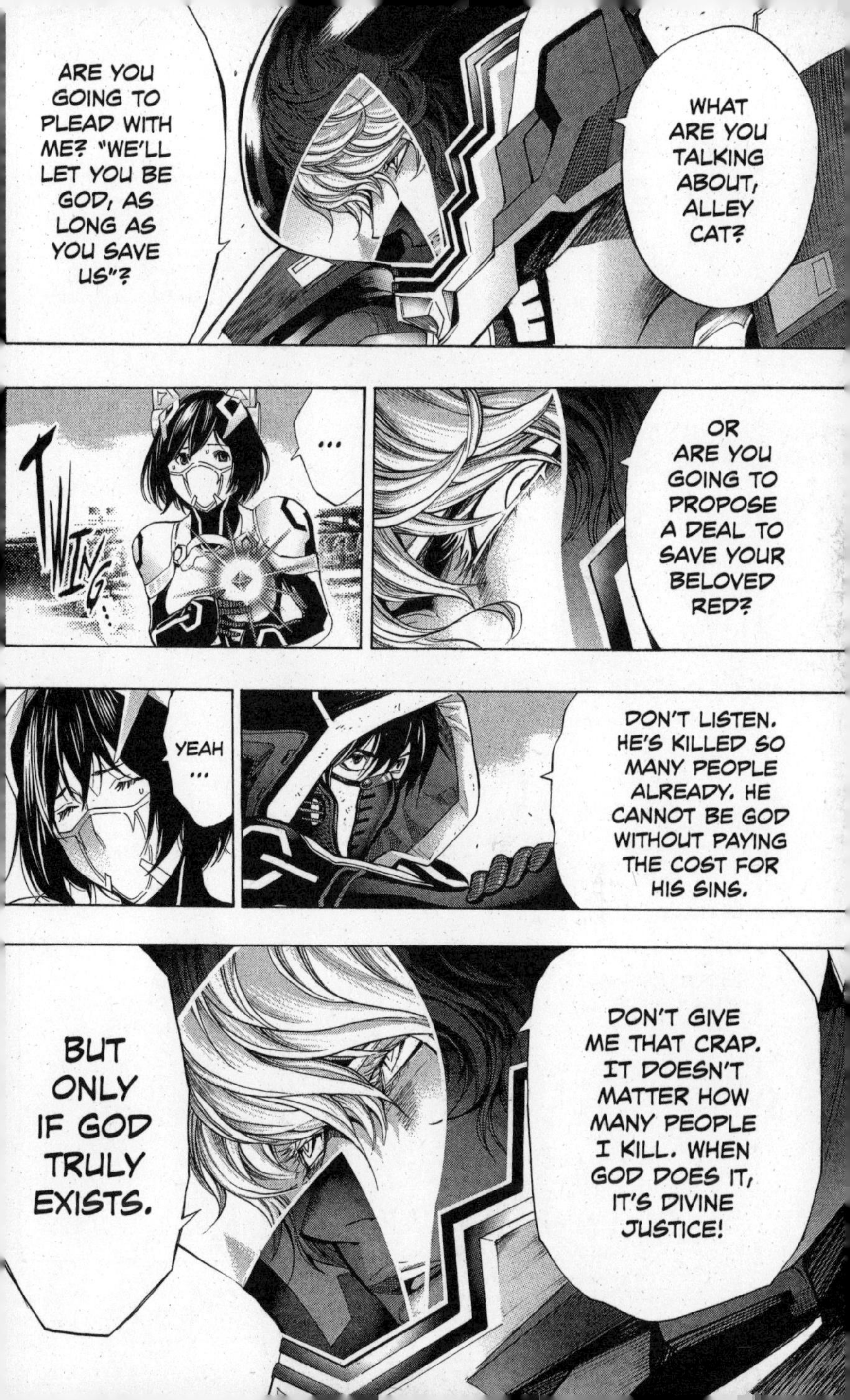
WHAT ARE YOU TALKING ABOUT, ALLEY CAT?
ARE YOU GOING TO PLEAD WITH ME? "WE'LL LET YOU BE GOD, AS LONG AS YOU SAVE US"?
OR ARE YOU GOING TO PROPOSE A DEAL TO SAVE YOUR BELOVED RED?
...
TWING
DON'T LISTEN. HE'S KILLED SO MANY PEOPLE ALREADY. HE CANNOT BE GOD WITHOUT PAYING THE COST FOR HIS SINS.
YEAH ...
DON'T GIVE ME THAT CRAP. IT DOESN'T MATTER HOW MANY PEOPLE I KILL. WHEN GOD DOES IT, IT'S DIVINE JUSTICE!
BUT ONLY IF GOD TRULY EXISTS.

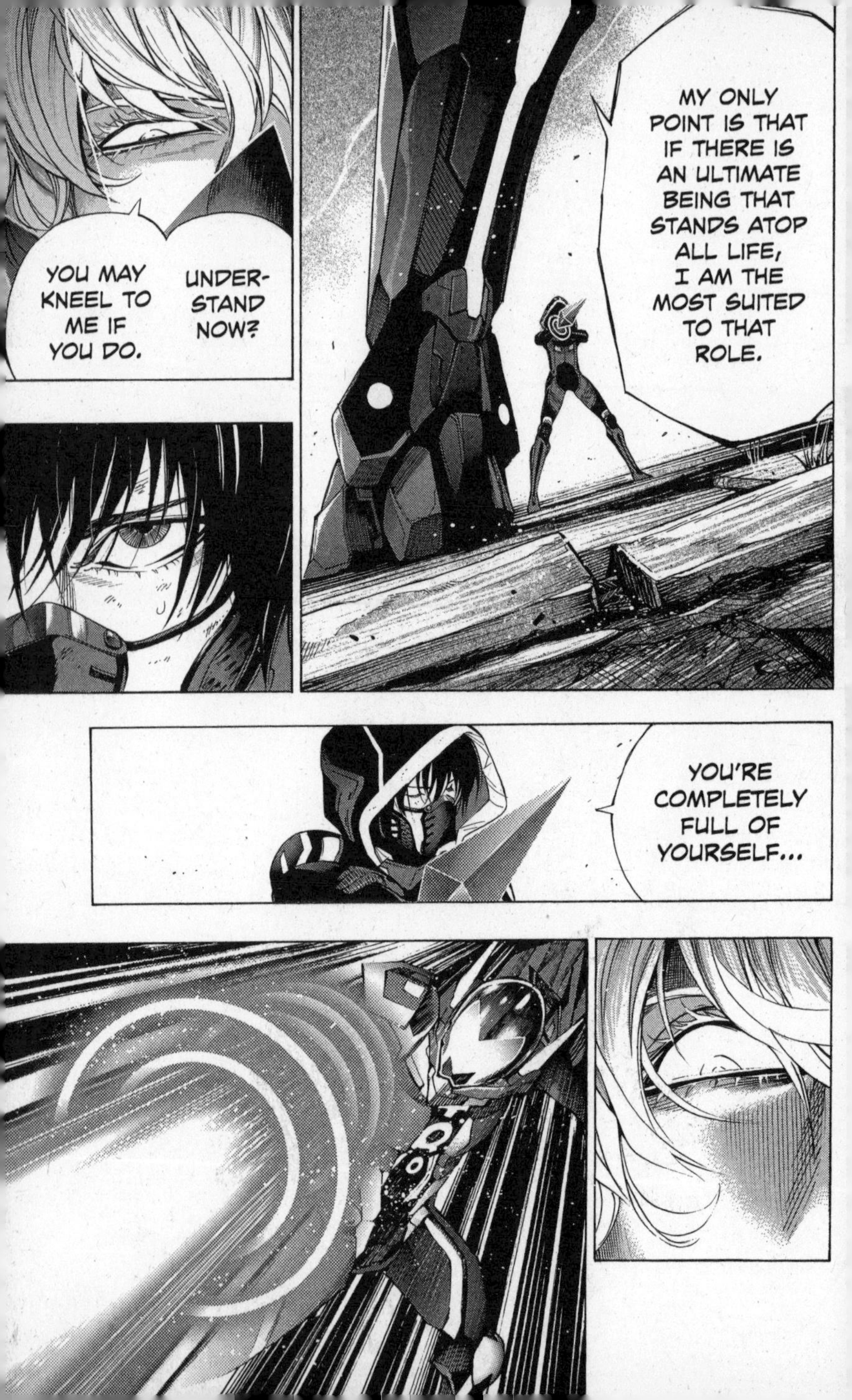
MY ONLY POINT IS THAT IF THERE IS AN ULTIMATE BEING THAT STANDS ATOP ALL LIFE, I AM THE MOST SUITED TO THAT ROLE.
UNDER-STAND NOW?
YOU MAY KNEEL TO ME IF YOU DO.
YOU'RE COMPLETELY FULL OF YOURSELF...

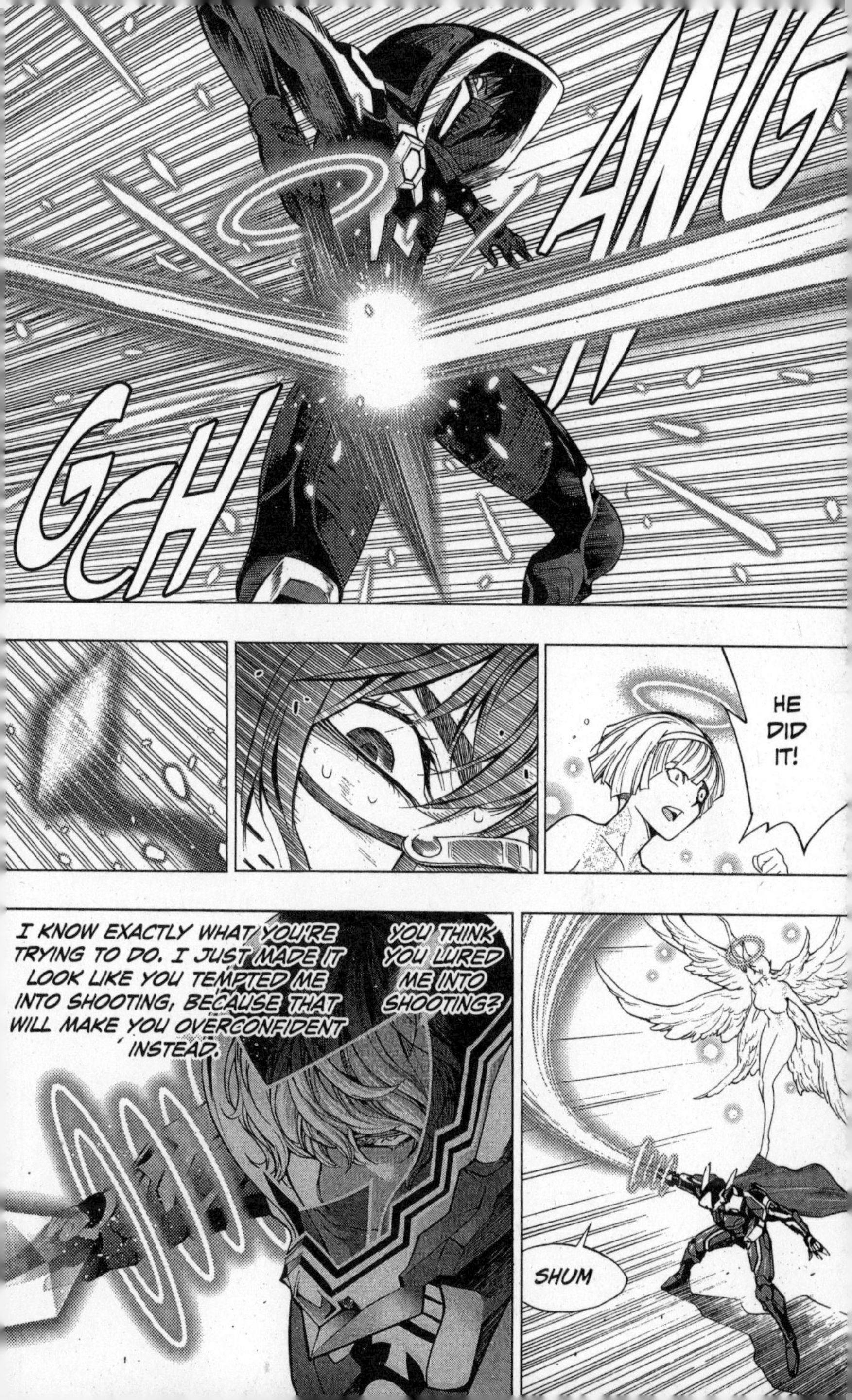
ANG
GCH
HE DID IT!
SHUM
YOU THINK YOU LURED ME INTO SHOOTING?
I KNOW EXACTLY WHAT YOU'RE TRYING TO DO. I JUST MADE IT LOOK LIKE YOU TEMPTED ME INTO SHOOTING, BECAUSE THAT WILL MAKE YOU OVERCONFIDENT INSTEAD.

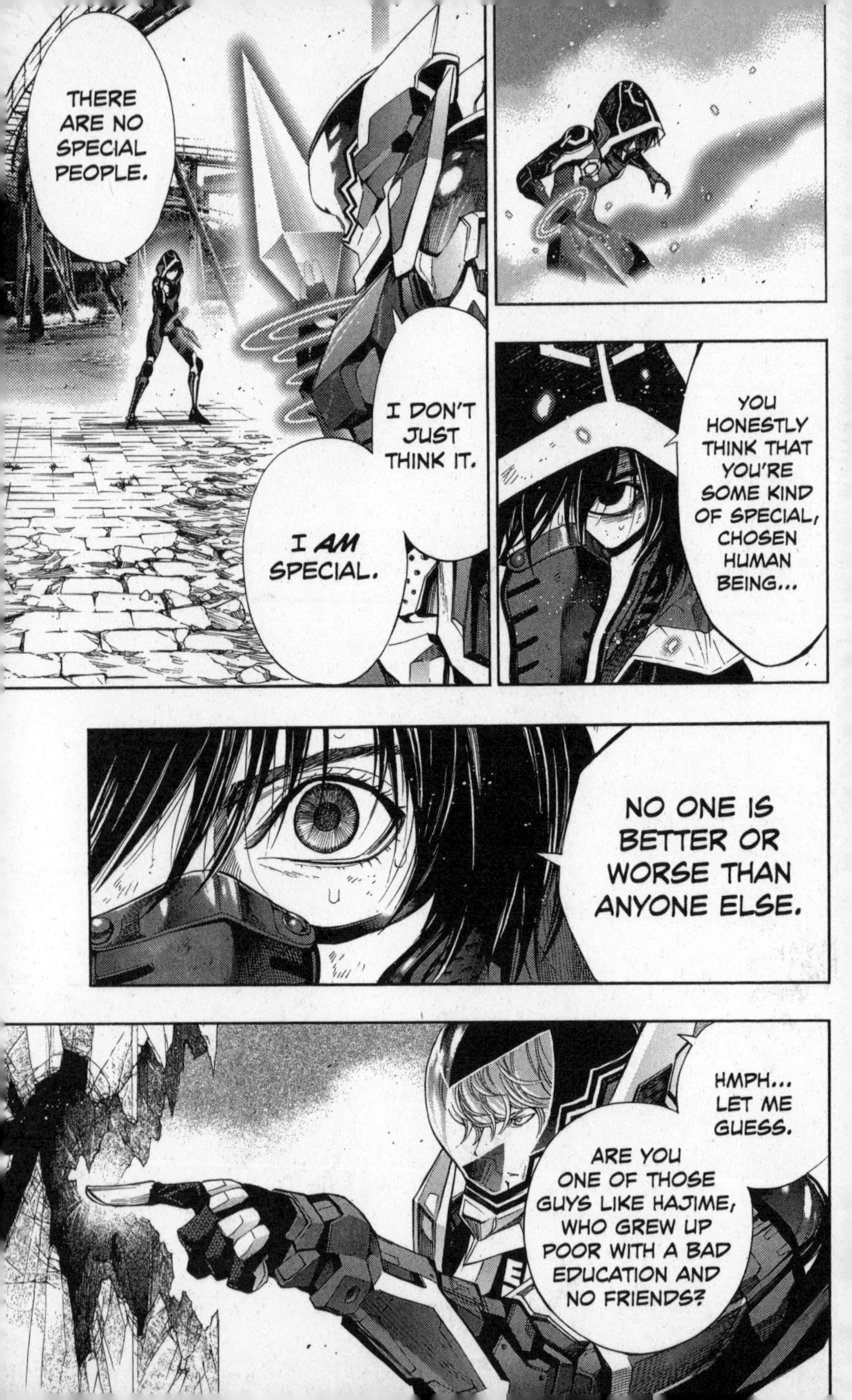
YOU HONESTLY THINK THAT YOU'RE SOME KIND OF SPECIAL, CHOSEN HUMAN BEING...
I DON'T JUST THINK IT.
I *AM* SPECIAL.
THERE ARE NO SPECIAL PEOPLE.
NO ONE IS BETTER OR WORSE THAN ANYONE ELSE.
HMPH... LET ME GUESS.
ARE YOU ONE OF THOSE GUYS LIKE HAJIME, WHO GREW UP POOR WITH A BAD EDUCATION AND NO FRIENDS?

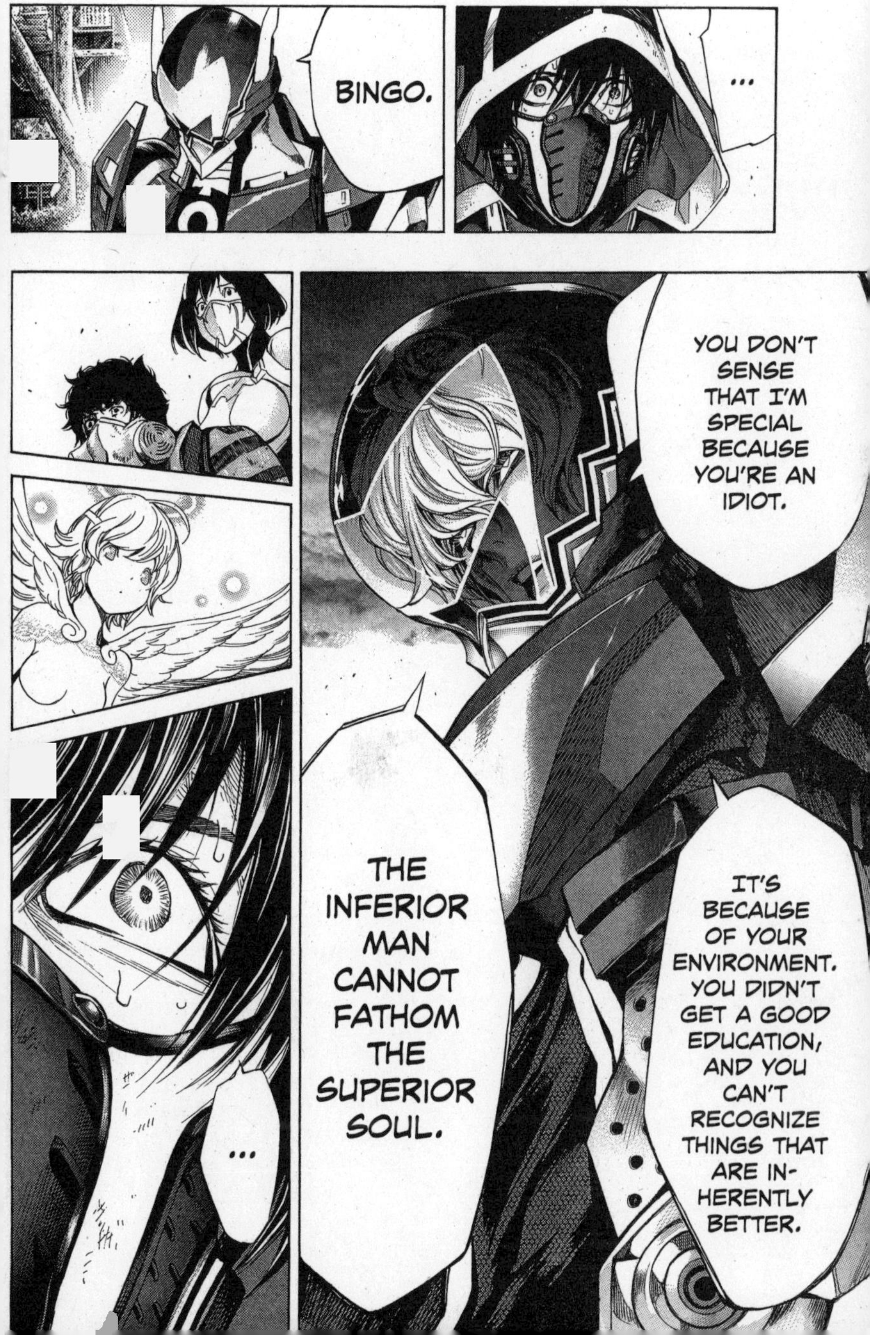
...
BINGO.
YOU DON'T SENSE THAT I'M SPECIAL BECAUSE YOU'RE AN IDIOT.
IT'S BECAUSE OF YOUR ENVIRONMENT. YOU DIDN'T GET A GOOD EDUCATION, AND YOU CAN'T RECOGNIZE THINGS THAT ARE IN-HERENTLY BETTER.
THE INFERIOR MAN CANNOT FATHOM THE SUPERIOR SOUL.
...

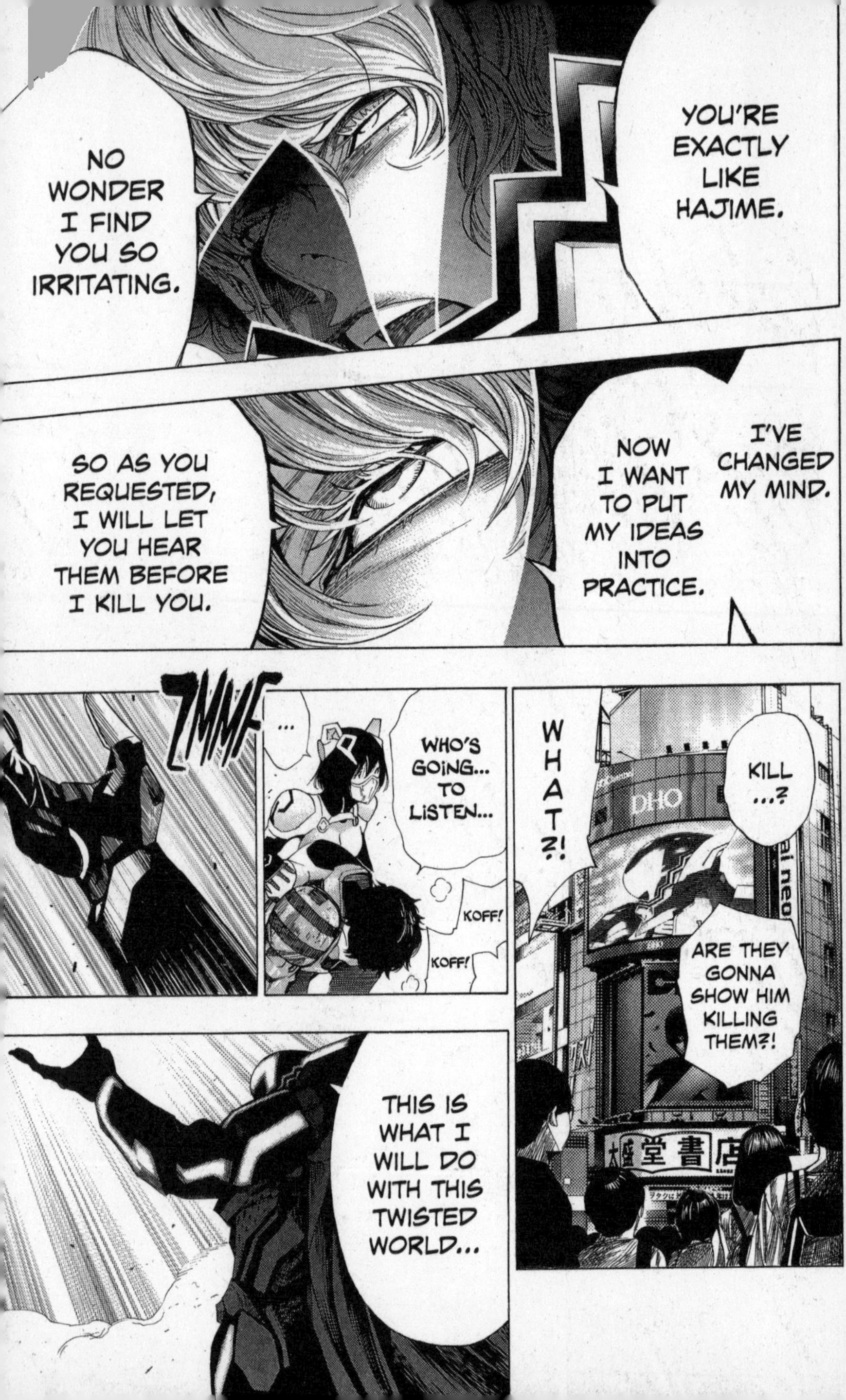
YOU'RE EXACTLY LIKE HAJIME.
NO WONDER I FIND YOU SO IRRITATING.
I'VE CHANGED MY MIND.
NOW I WANT TO PUT MY IDEAS INTO PRACTICE.
SO AS YOU REQUESTED, I WILL LET YOU HEAR THEM BEFORE I KILL YOU.
KILL ...?
WHAT?!
ARE THEY GONNA SHOW HIM KILLING THEM?!
...
WHO'S GOING... TO LISTEN...
KOFF!
KOFF!
ZMMF
THIS IS WHAT I WILL DO WITH THIS TWISTED WORLD...

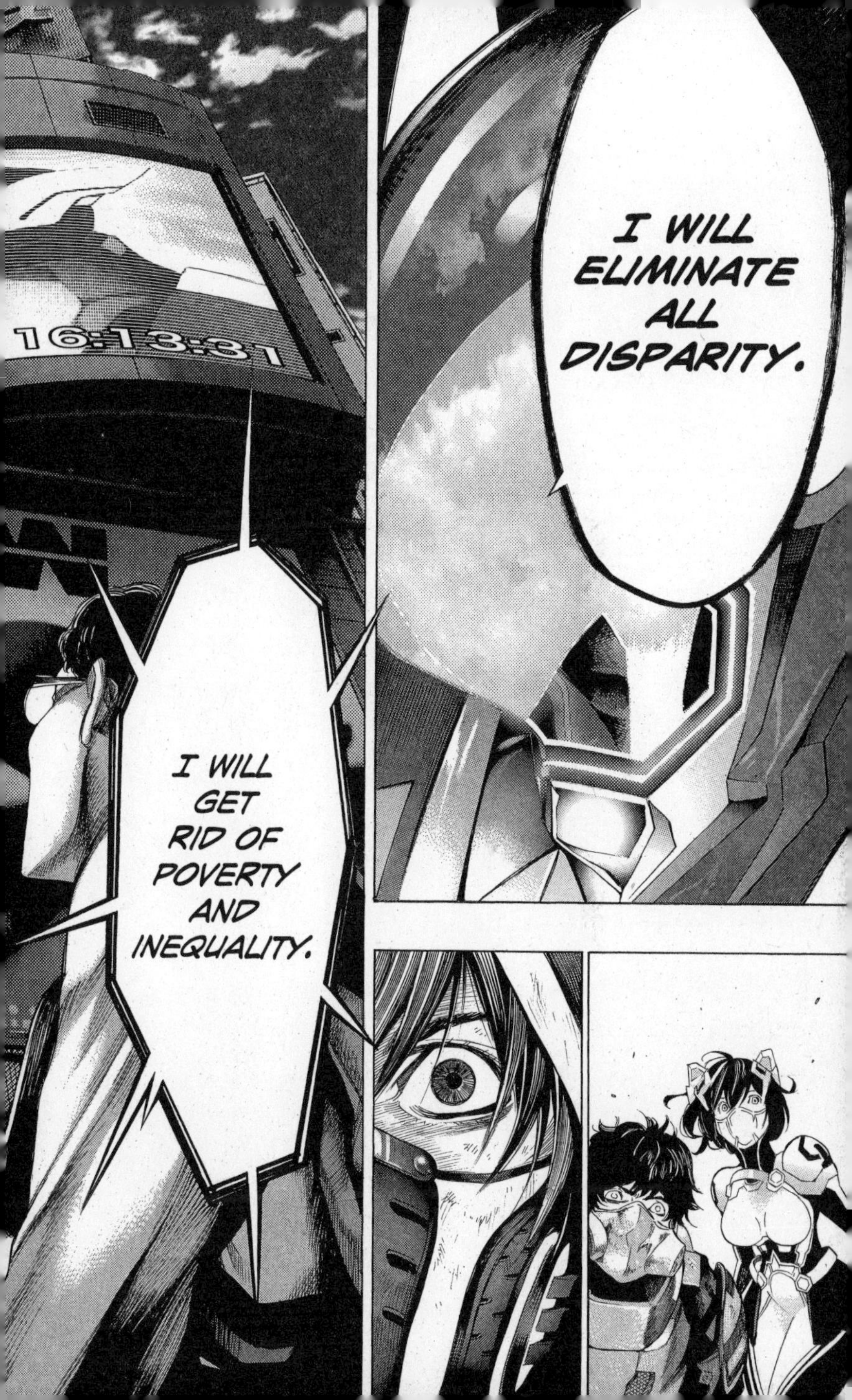
I WILL ELIMINATE ALL DISPARITY.
16:13:31
I WILL GET RID OF POVERTY AND INEQUALITY.

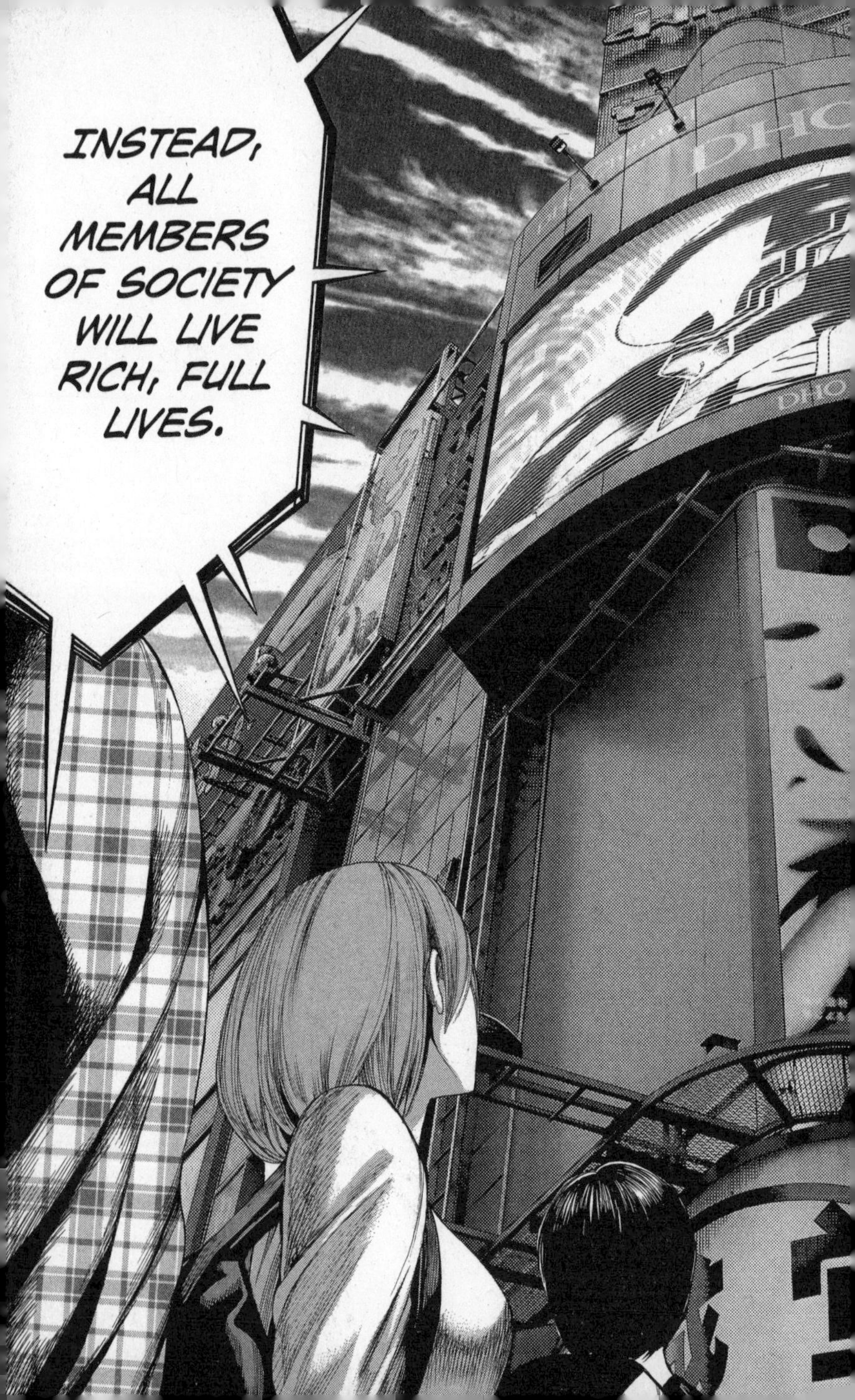
INSTEAD, ALL MEMBERS OF SOCIETY WILL LIVE RICH, FULL LIVES.
DHC

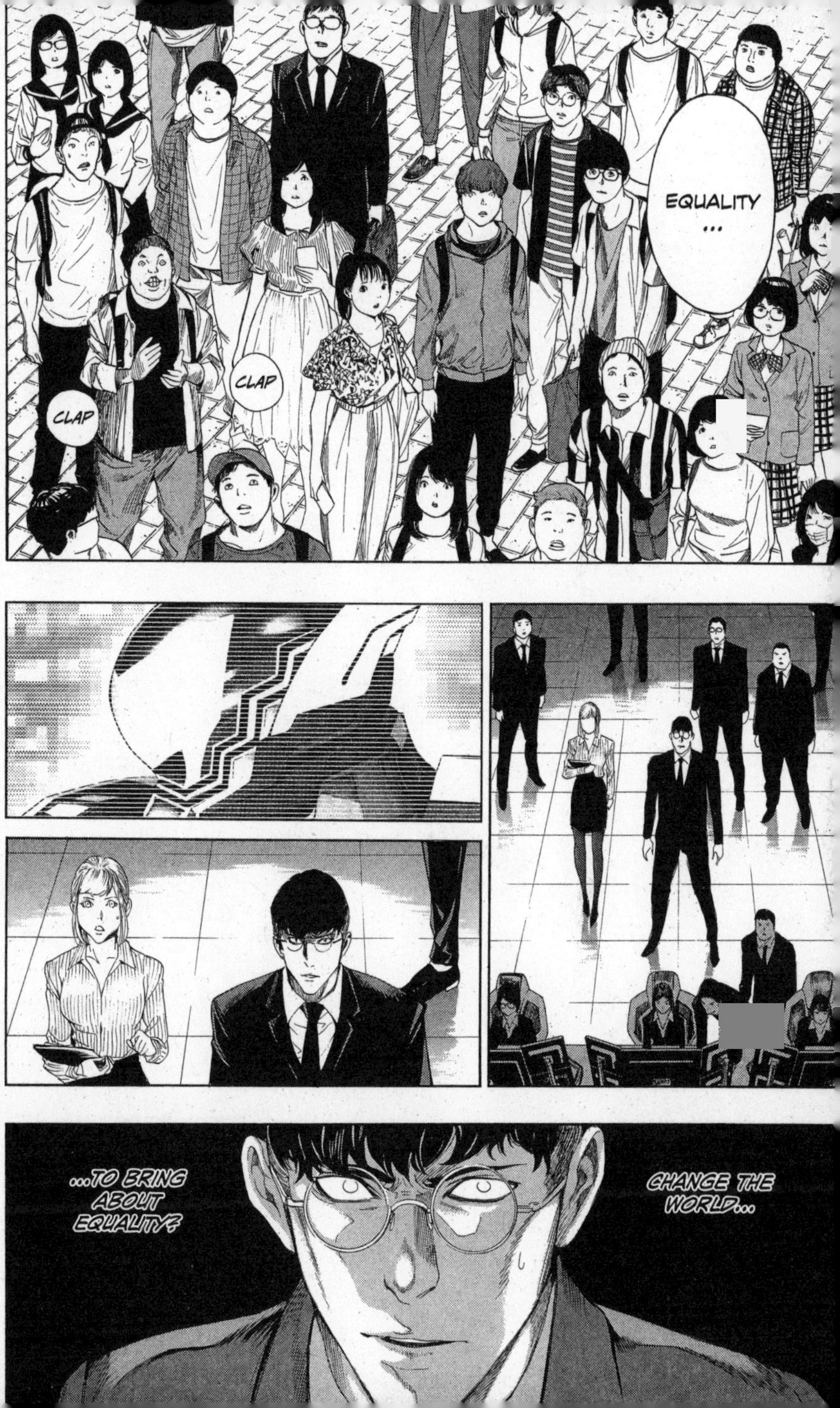
EQUALITY ...
CLAP
CLAP
CHANGE THE WORLD...
...TO BRING ABOUT EQUALITY?

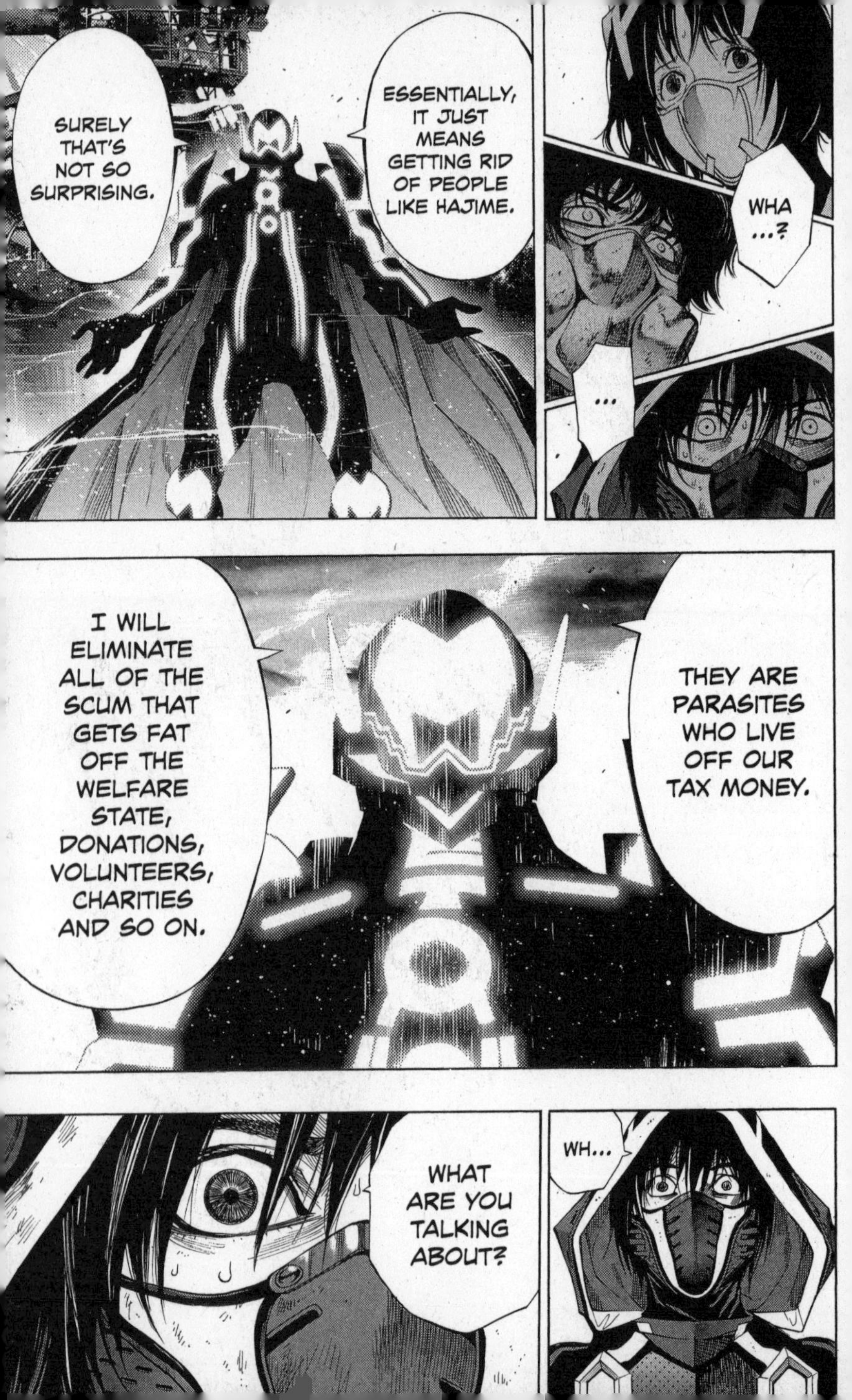
WHA ...?
...
ESSENTIALLY, IT JUST MEANS GETTING RID OF PEOPLE LIKE HAJIME.
SURELY THAT'S NOT SO SURPRISING.
THEY ARE PARASITES WHO LIVE OFF OUR TAX MONEY.
I WILL ELIMINATE ALL OF THE SCUM THAT GETS FAT OFF THE WELFARE STATE, DONATIONS, VOLUNTEERS, CHARITIES AND SO ON.
WH...
WHAT ARE YOU TALKING ABOUT?

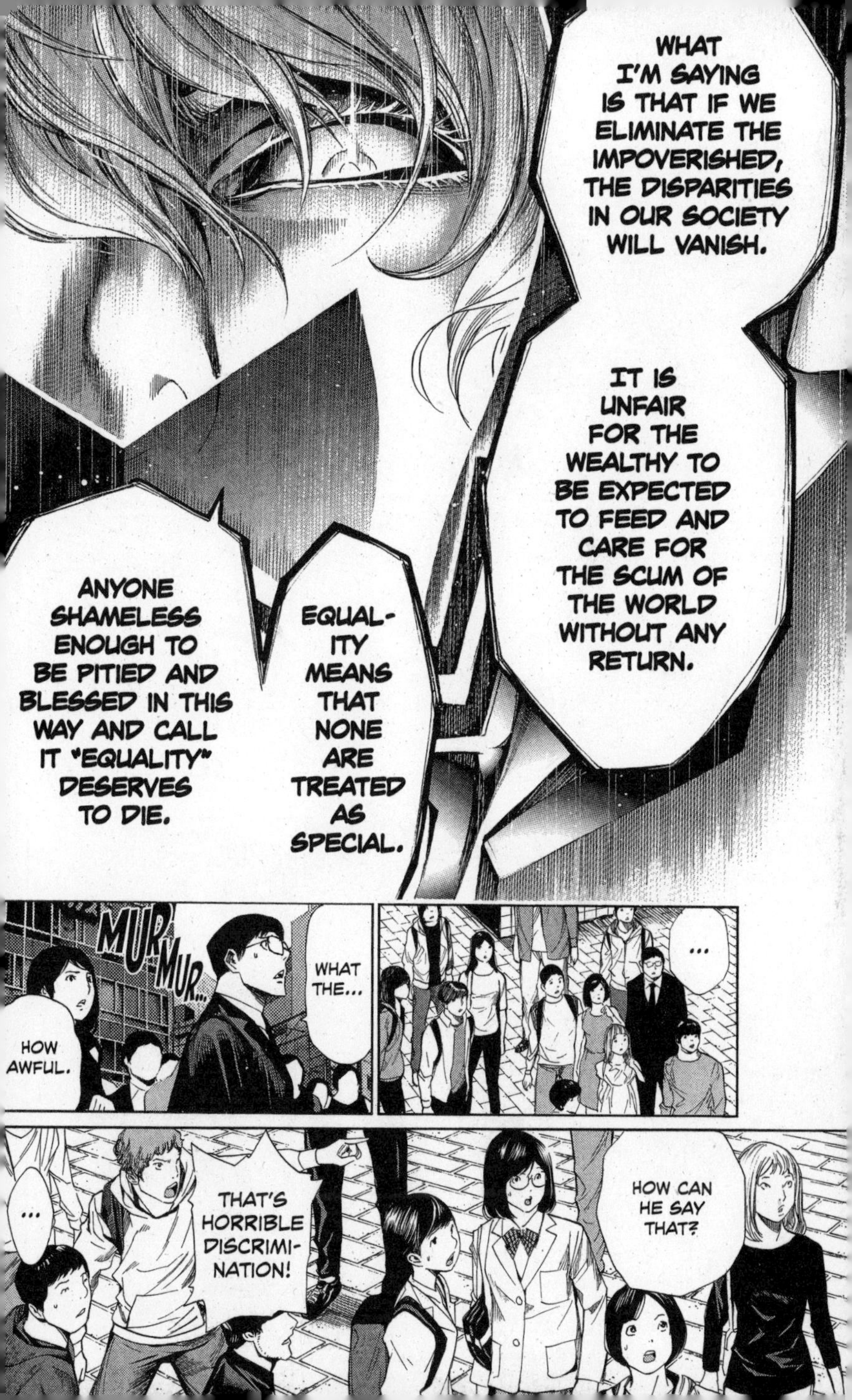
WHAT I'M SAYING IS THAT IF WE ELIMINATE THE IMPOVERISHED, THE DISPARITIES IN OUR SOCIETY WILL VANISH.
IT IS UNFAIR FOR THE WEALTHY TO BE EXPECTED TO FEED AND CARE FOR THE SCUM OF THE WORLD WITHOUT ANY RETURN.
EQUAL-ITY MEANS THAT NONE ARE TREATED AS SPECIAL.
ANYONE SHAMELESS ENOUGH TO BE PITIED AND BLESSED IN THIS WAY AND CALL IT "EQUALITY" DESERVES TO DIE.
...
WHAT THE...
MUR MUR...
HOW AWFUL.
HOW CAN HE SAY THAT?
THAT'S HORRIBLE DISCRIMI-NATION!
...

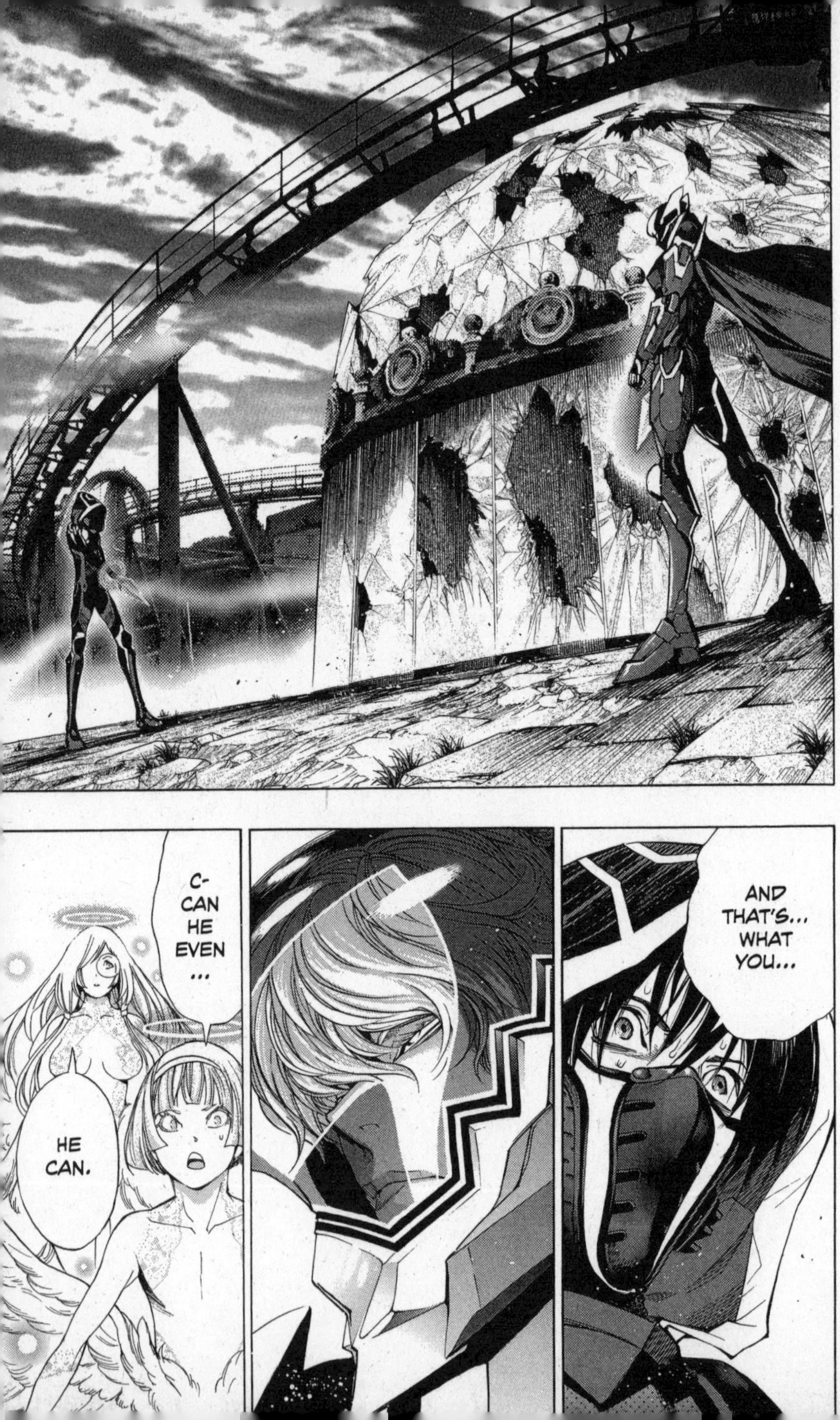
AND THAT'S... WHAT YOU...
C-CAN HE EVEN...
HE CAN.

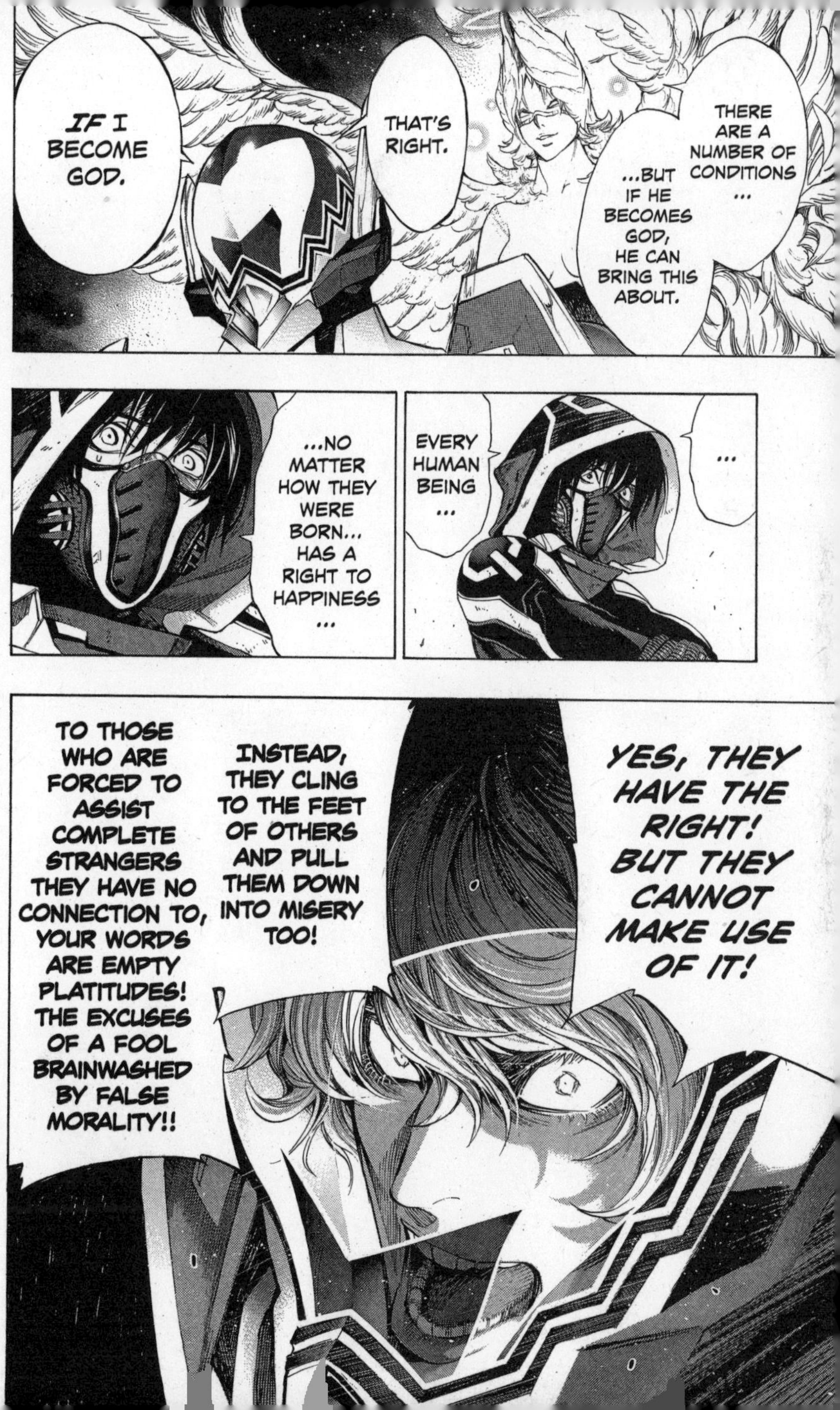
THERE ARE A NUMBER OF CONDITIONS ... ...BUT IF HE BECOMES GOD, HE CAN BRING THIS ABOUT.
THAT'S RIGHT.
IF I BECOME GOD.
...
EVERY HUMAN BEING ...
...NO MATTER HOW THEY WERE BORN... HAS A RIGHT TO HAPPINESS ...
YES, THEY HAVE THE RIGHT! BUT THEY CANNOT MAKE USE OF IT!
INSTEAD, THEY CLING TO THE FEET OF OTHERS AND PULL THEM DOWN INTO MISERY TOO!
TO THOSE WHO ARE FORCED TO ASSIST COMPLETE STRANGERS THEY HAVE NO CONNECTION TO, YOUR WORDS ARE EMPTY PLATITUDES! THE EXCUSES OF A FOOL BRAINWASHED BY FALSE MORALITY!!

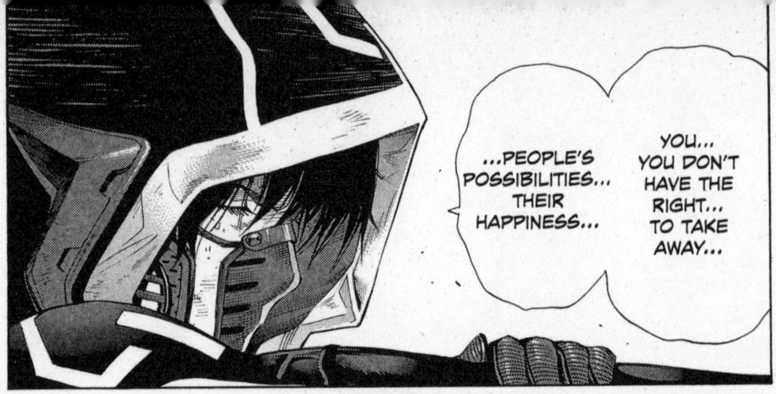
YOU... YOU DON'T HAVE THE RIGHT... TO TAKE AWAY...
...PEOPLE'S POSSIBILITIES... THEIR HAPPINESS...

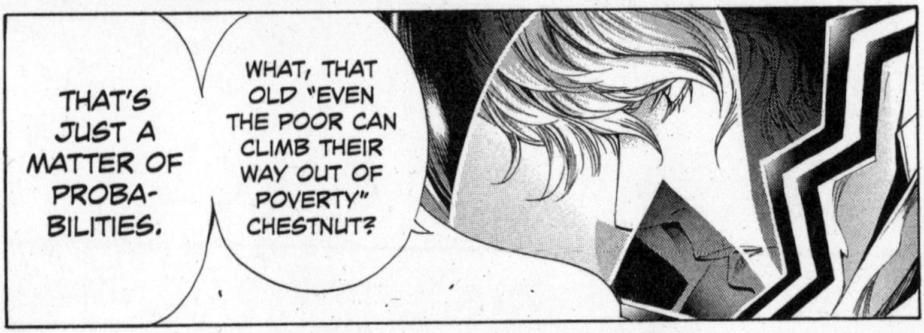
WHAT, THAT OLD "EVEN THE POOR CAN CLIMB THEIR WAY OUT OF POVERTY" CHESTNUT?
THAT'S JUST A MATTER OF PROBA-BILITIES.

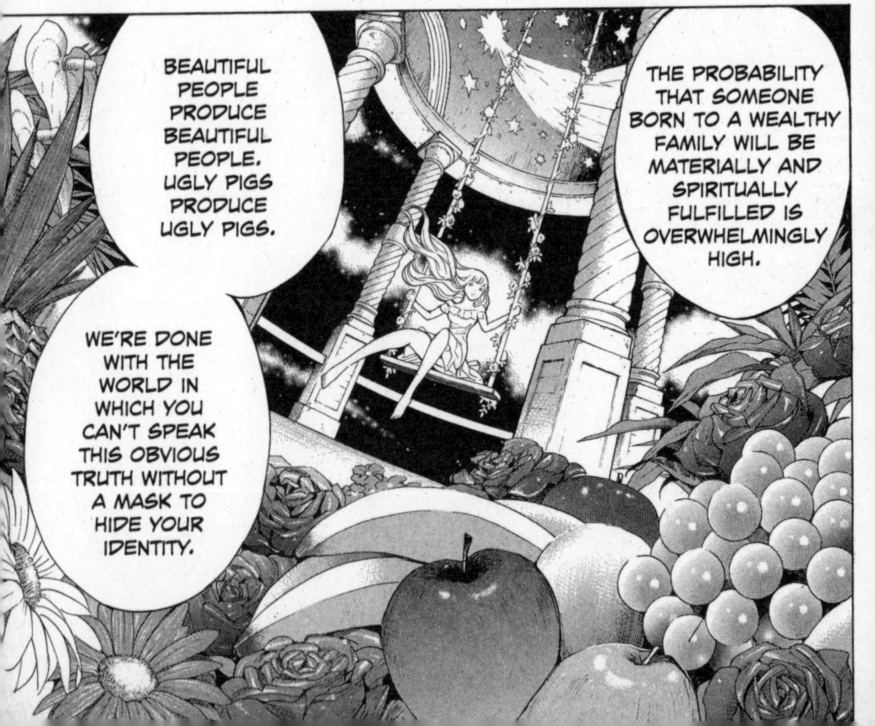
THE PROBABILITY THAT SOMEONE BORN TO A WEALTHY FAMILY WILL BE MATERIALLY AND SPIRITUALLY FULFILLED IS OVERWHELMINGLY HIGH.
BEAUTIFUL PEOPLE PRODUCE BEAUTIFUL PEOPLE. UGLY PIGS PRODUCE UGLY PIGS.
WE'RE DONE WITH THE WORLD IN WHICH YOU CAN'T SPEAK THIS OBVIOUS TRUTH WITHOUT A MASK TO HIDE YOUR IDENTITY.

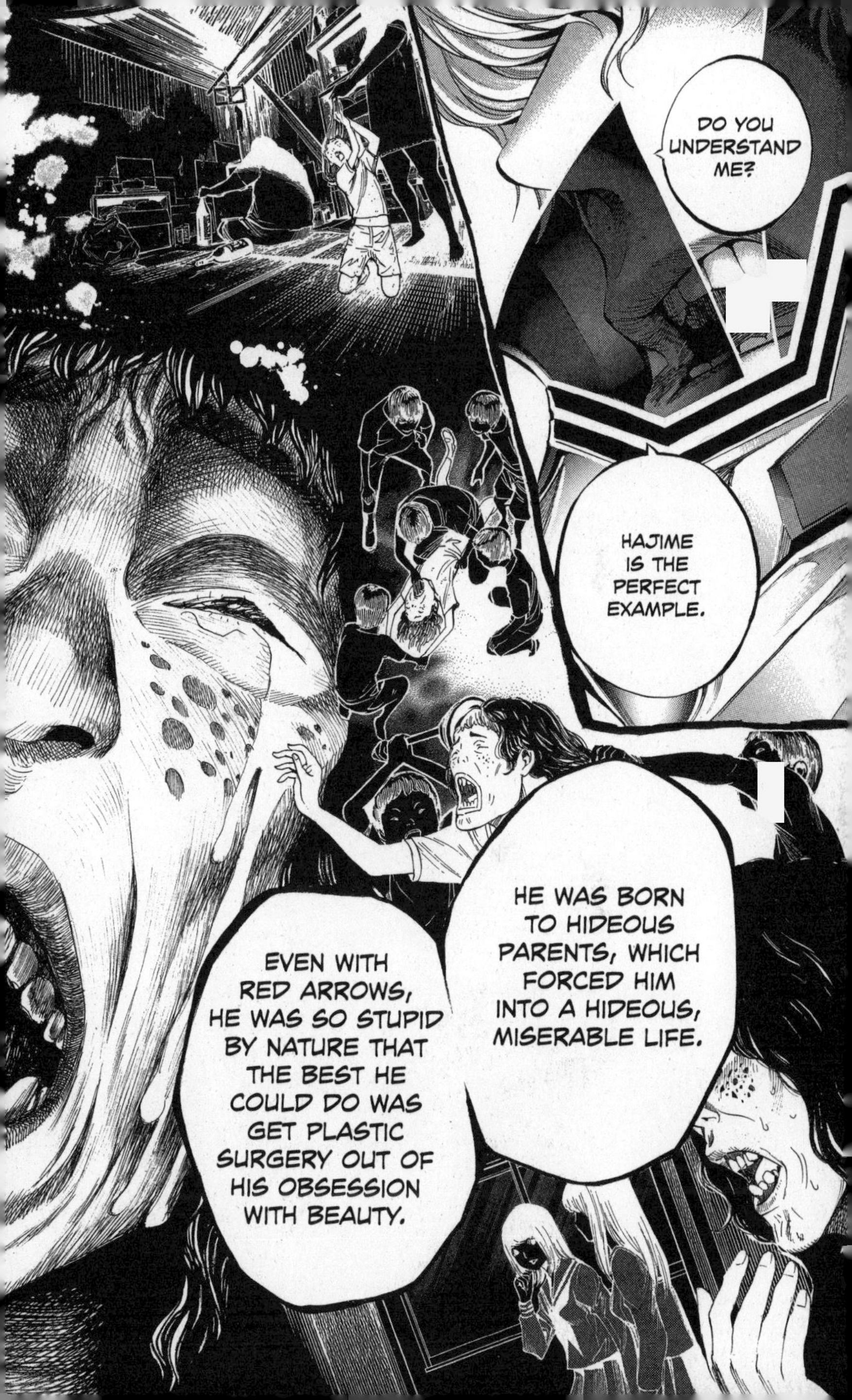
DO YOU UNDERSTAND ME?
HAJIME IS THE PERFECT EXAMPLE.
HE WAS BORN TO HIDEOUS PARENTS, WHICH FORCED HIM INTO A HIDEOUS, MISERABLE LIFE.
EVEN WITH RED ARROWS, HE WAS SO STUPID BY NATURE THAT THE BEST HE COULD DO WAS GET PLASTIC SURGERY OUT OF HIS OBSESSION WITH BEAUTY.

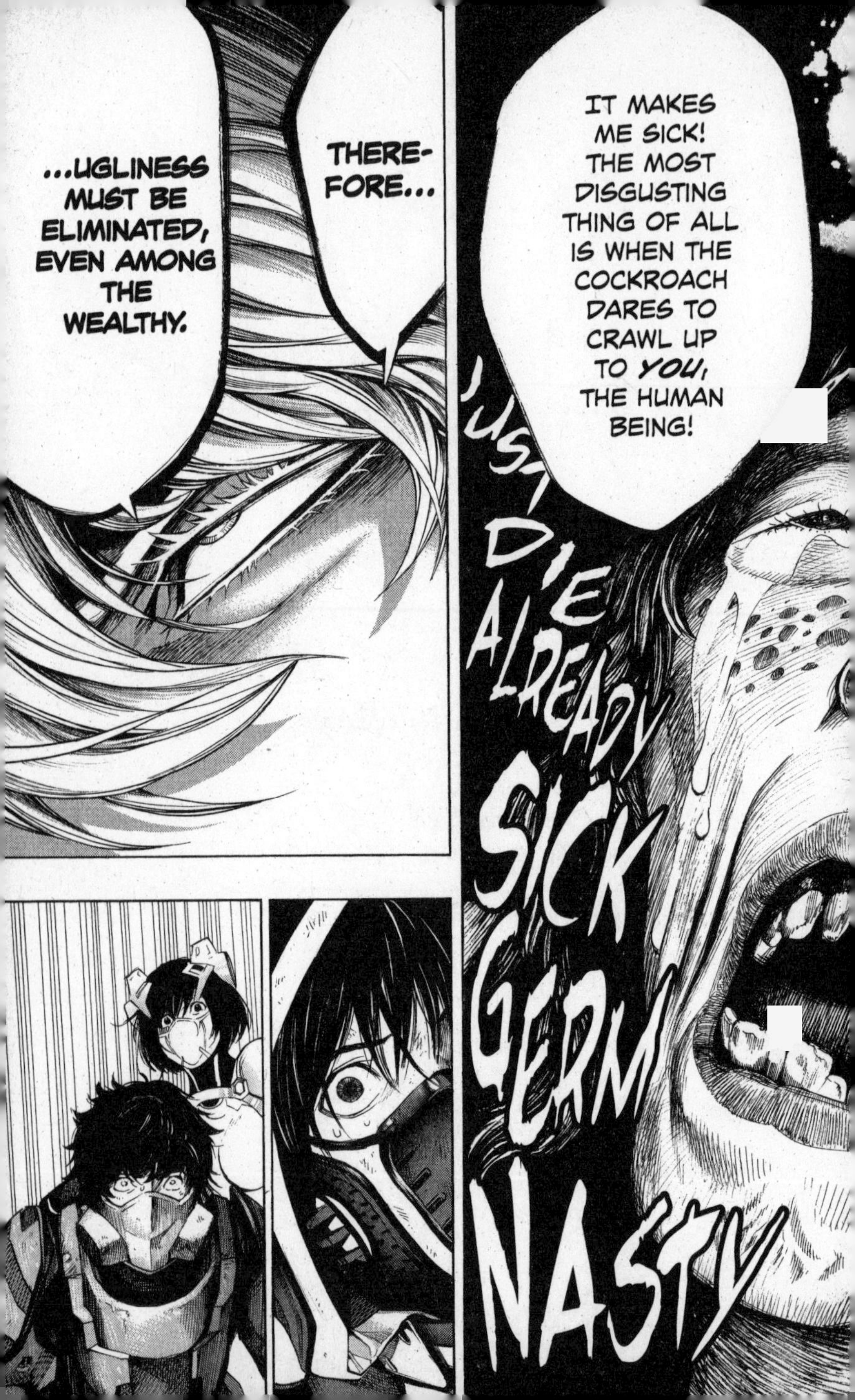
IT MAKES ME SICK! THE MOST DISGUSTING THING OF ALL IS WHEN THE COCKROACH DARES TO CRAWL UP TO *YOU*, THE HUMAN BEING!
JUST DIE ALREADY
SICK
GERM
NASTY
THERE-FORE...
...UGLINESS MUST BE ELIMINATED, EVEN AMONG THE WEALTHY.

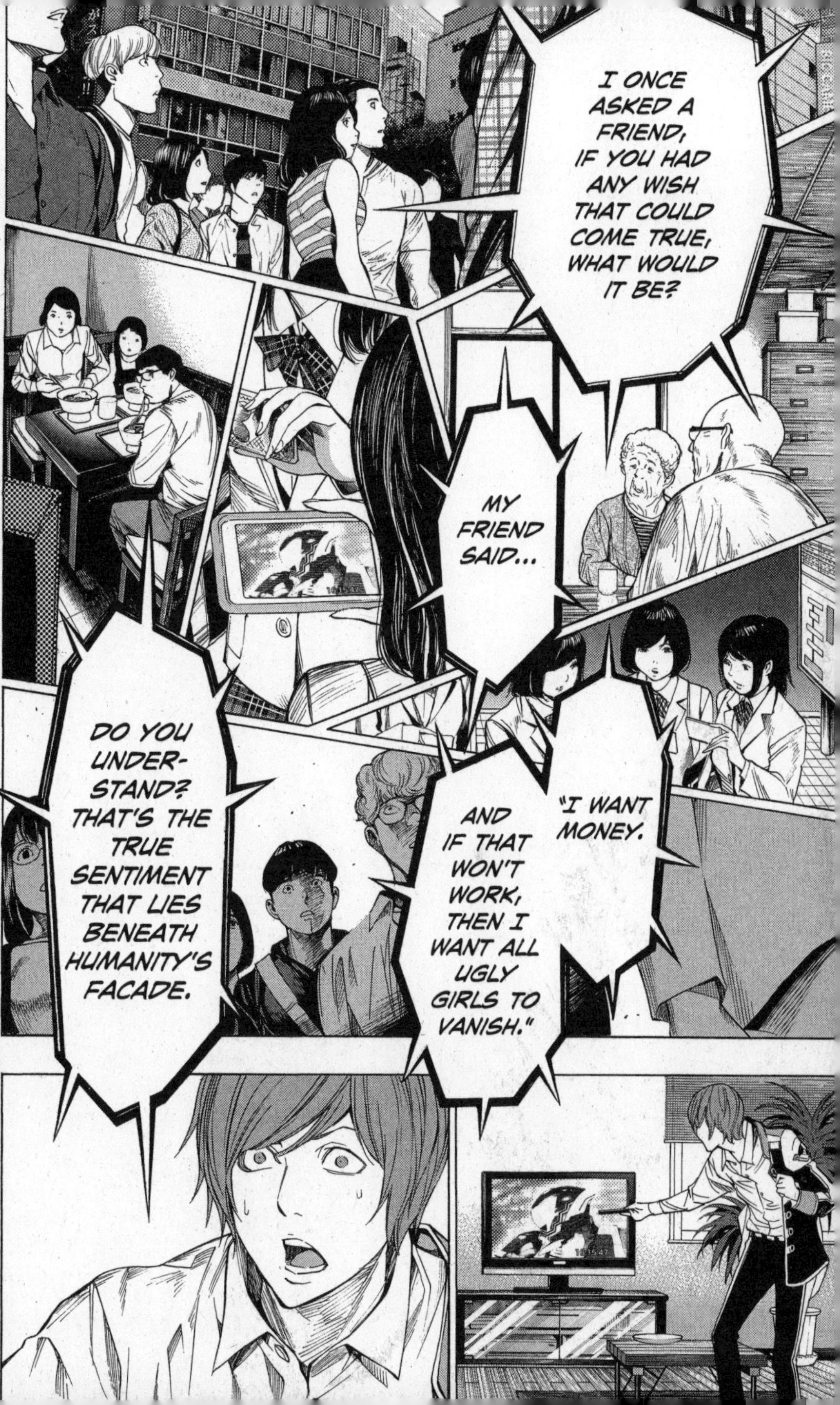
I ONCE ASKED A FRIEND, IF YOU HAD ANY WISH THAT COULD COME TRUE, WHAT WOULD IT BE?
MY FRIEND SAID...
"I WANT MONEY.
AND IF THAT WON'T WORK, THEN I WANT ALL UGLY GIRLS TO VANISH."
DO YOU UNDER-STAND? THAT'S THE TRUE SENTIMENT THAT LIES BENEATH HUMANITY'S FACADE.

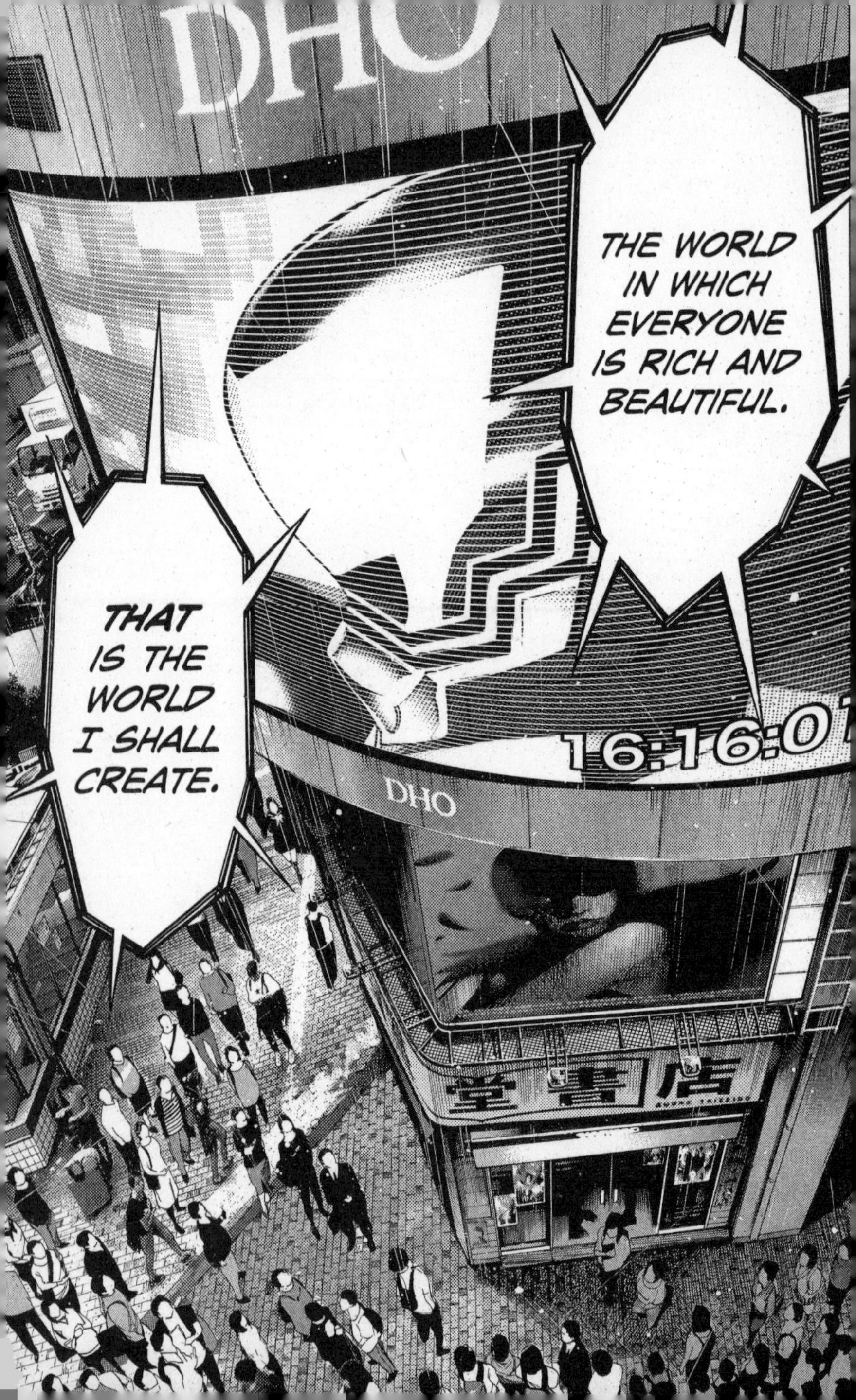
DHO
THE WORLD IN WHICH EVERYONE IS RICH AND BEAUTIFUL.
THAT IS THE WORLD I SHALL CREATE.
16:16:0
DHO
堂書店

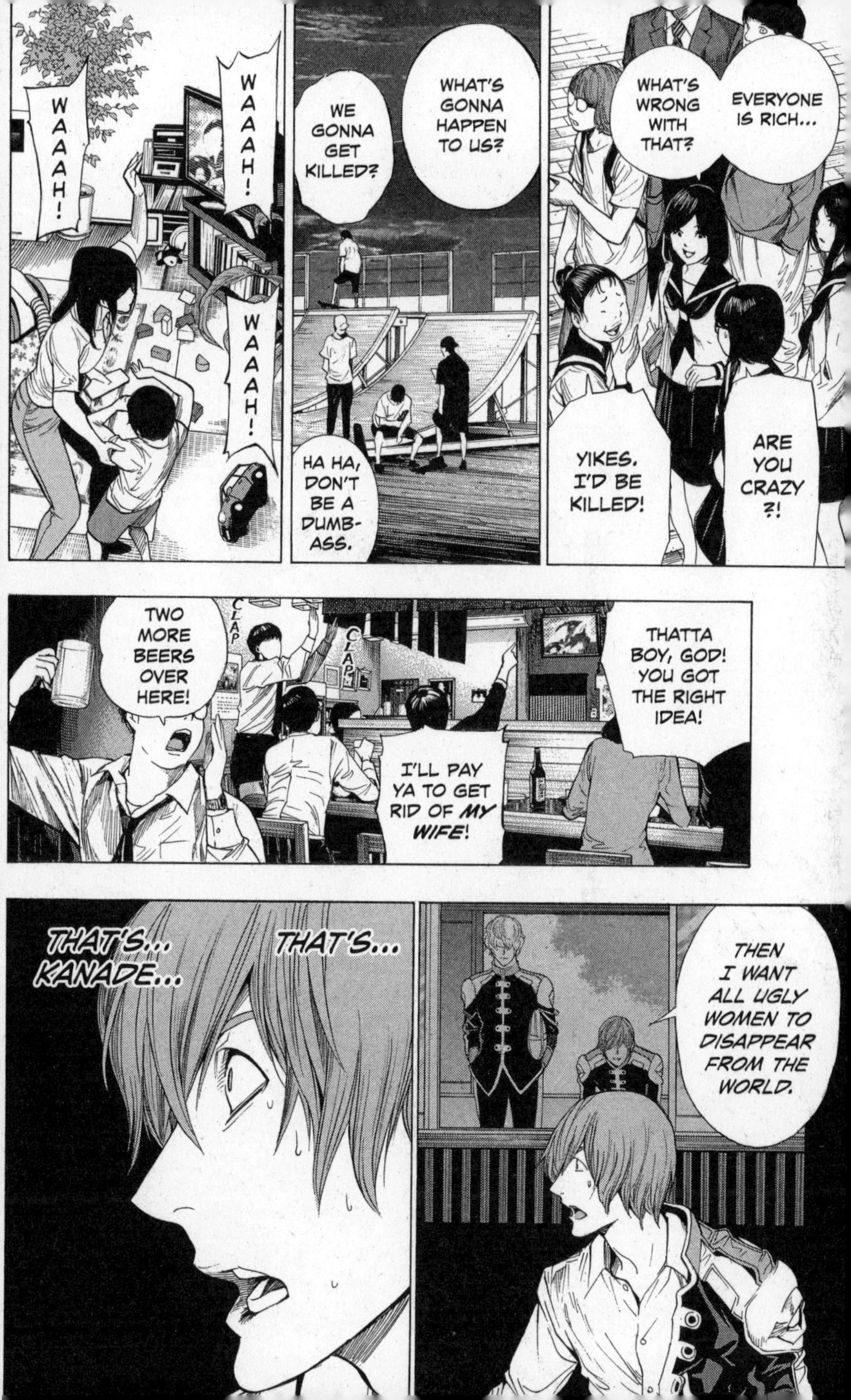
EVERYONE IS RICH...
WHAT'S WRONG WITH THAT?
ARE YOU CRAZY ?!
YIKES. I'D BE KILLED!
WHAT'S GONNA HAPPEN TO US?
WE GONNA GET KILLED?
HA HA, DON'T BE A DUMB-ASS.
WAAAAH!
WAAAAH!
WAAAAH!
THATTA BOY, GOD! YOU GOT THE RIGHT IDEA!
I'LL PAY YA TO GET RID OF *MY WIFE*!
CLAP
CLAP
TWO MORE BEERS OVER HERE!
THEN I WANT ALL UGLY WOMEN TO DISAPPEAR FROM THE WORLD.
THAT'S...
THAT'S... KANADE...

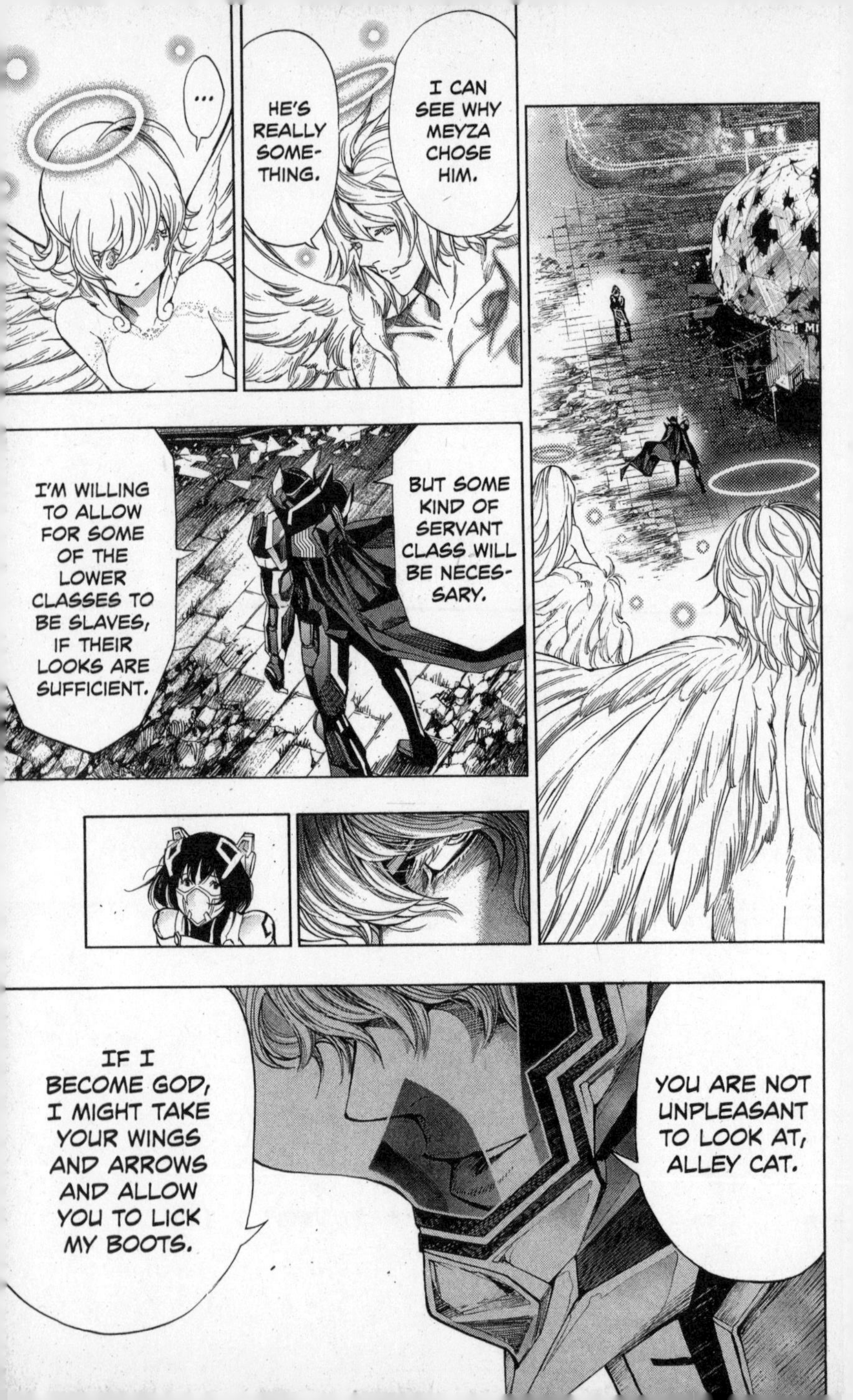
I CAN SEE WHY MEYZA CHOSE HIM.
HE'S REALLY SOME-THING.
...
BUT SOME KIND OF SERVANT CLASS WILL BE NECES-SARY.
I'M WILLING TO ALLOW FOR SOME OF THE LOWER CLASSES TO BE SLAVES, IF THEIR LOOKS ARE SUFFICIENT.
YOU ARE NOT UNPLEASANT TO LOOK AT, ALLEY CAT.
IF I BECOME GOD, I MIGHT TAKE YOUR WINGS AND ARROWS AND ALLOW YOU TO LICK MY BOOTS.

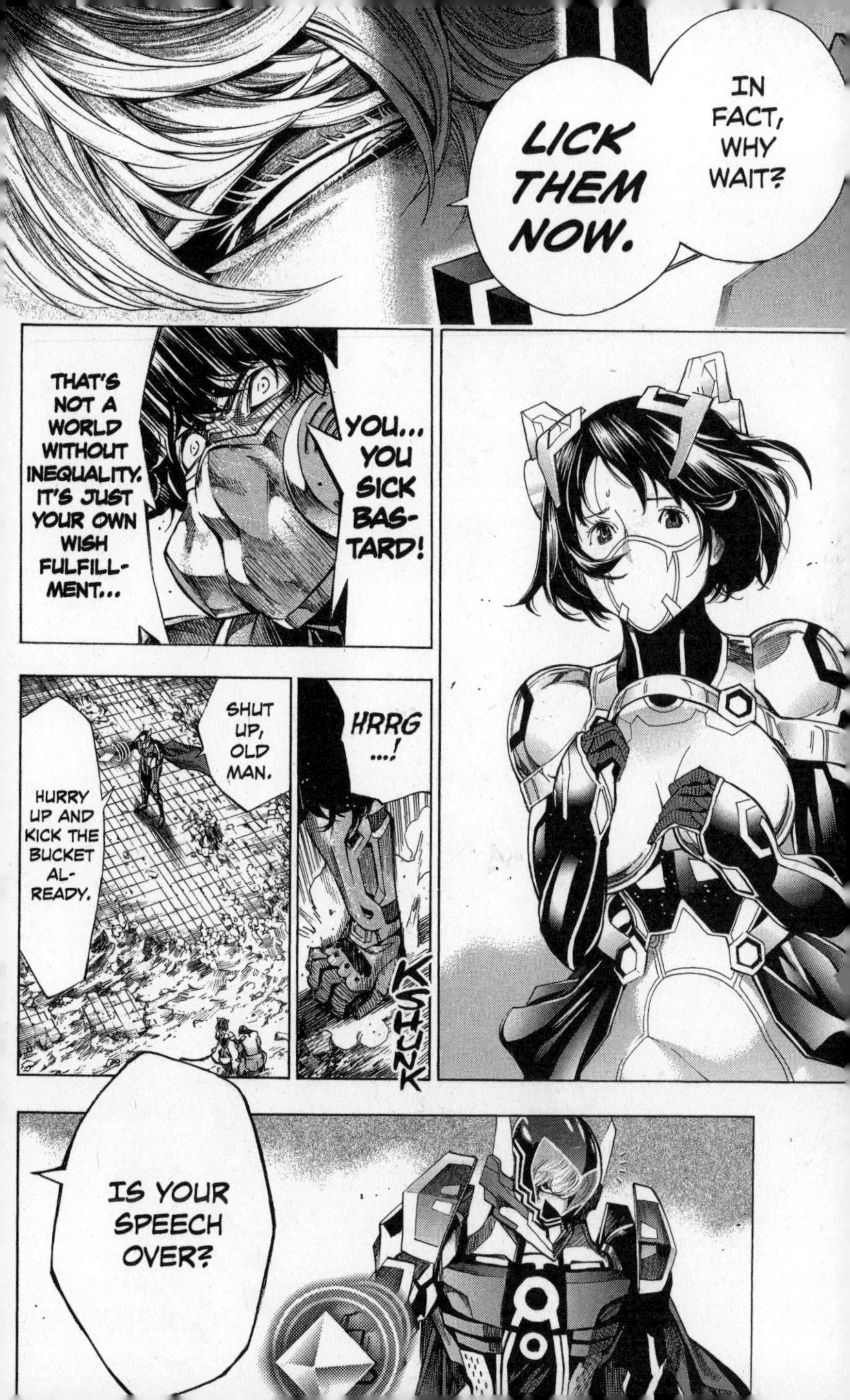
IN FACT, WHY WAIT?
LICK THEM NOW.
YOU... YOU SICK BAS-TARD!
THAT'S NOT A WORLD WITHOUT INEQUALITY. IT'S JUST YOUR OWN WISH FULFILL-MENT...
HRRG...!
KSHUNK
SHUT UP, OLD MAN.
HURRY UP AND KICK THE BUCKET AL-READY.
IS YOUR SPEECH OVER?

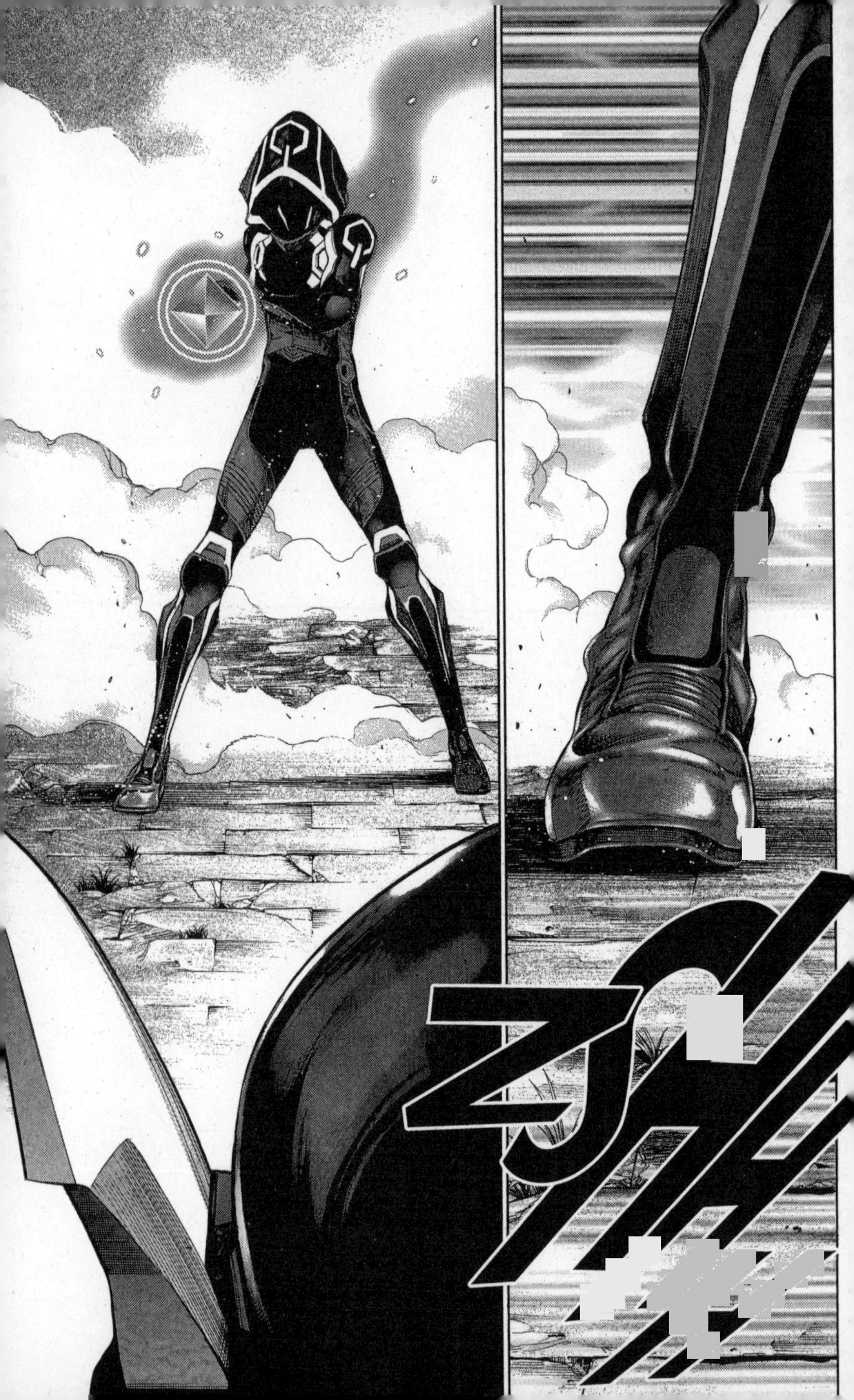

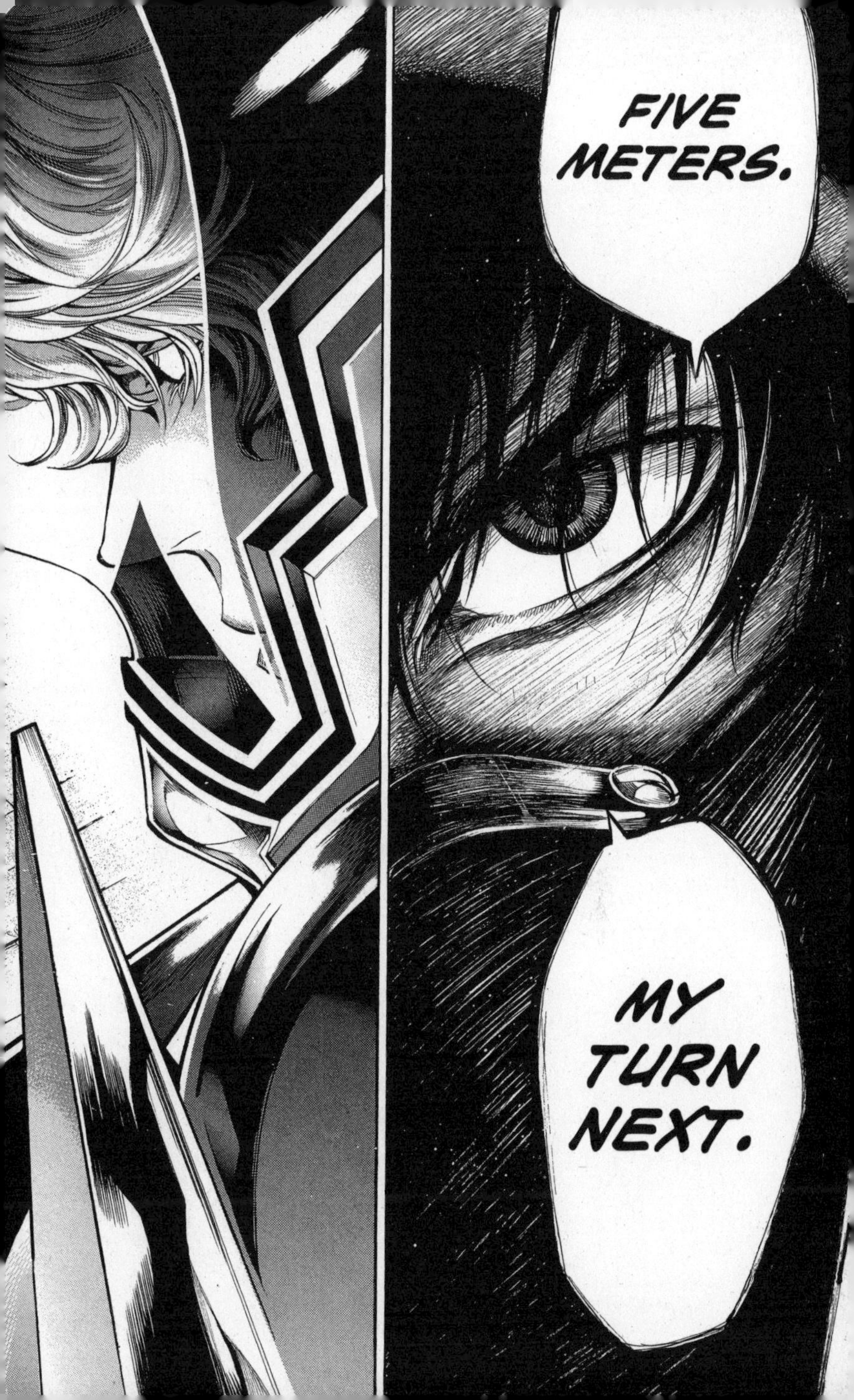
FIVE METERS.
MY TURN NEXT.

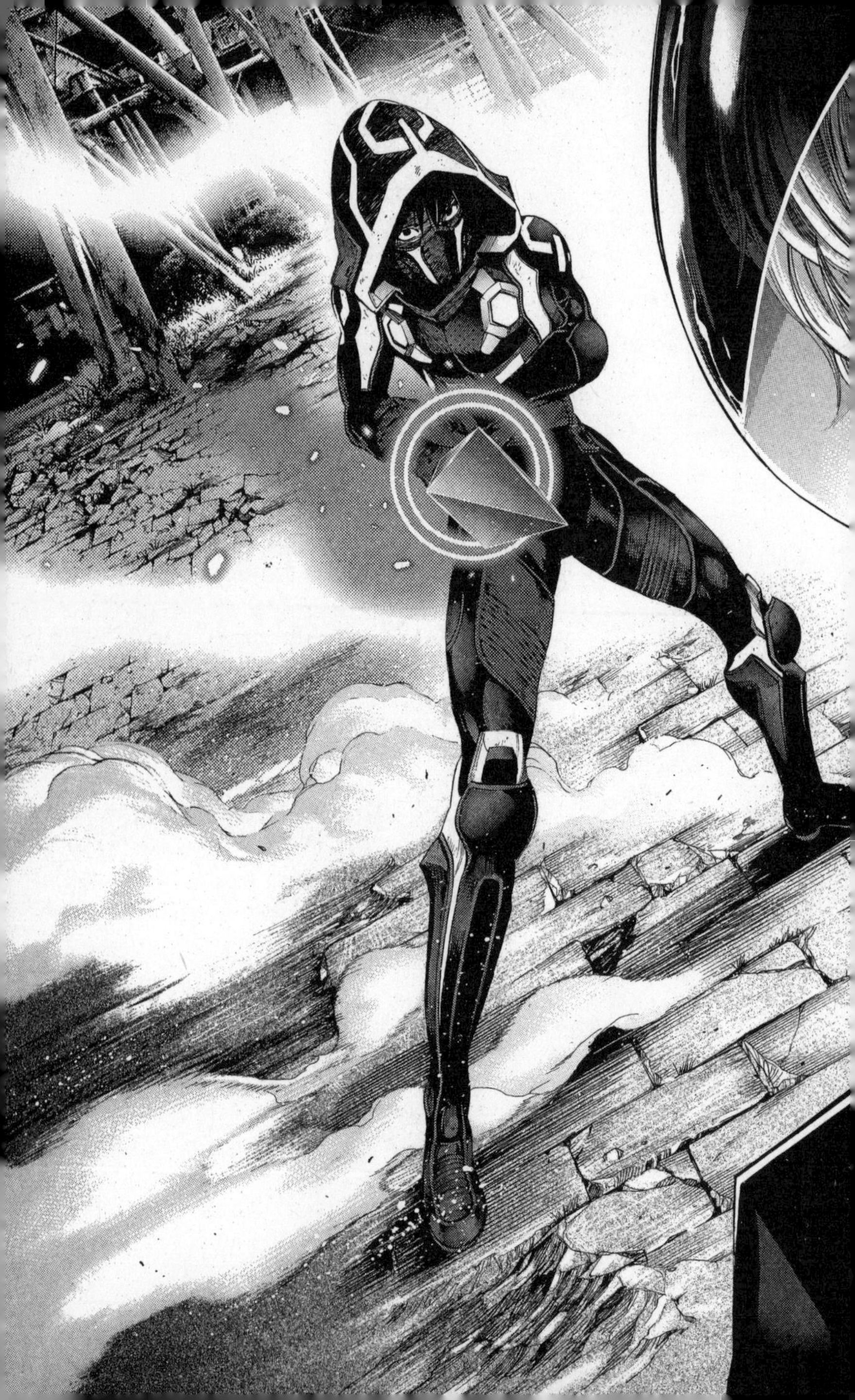

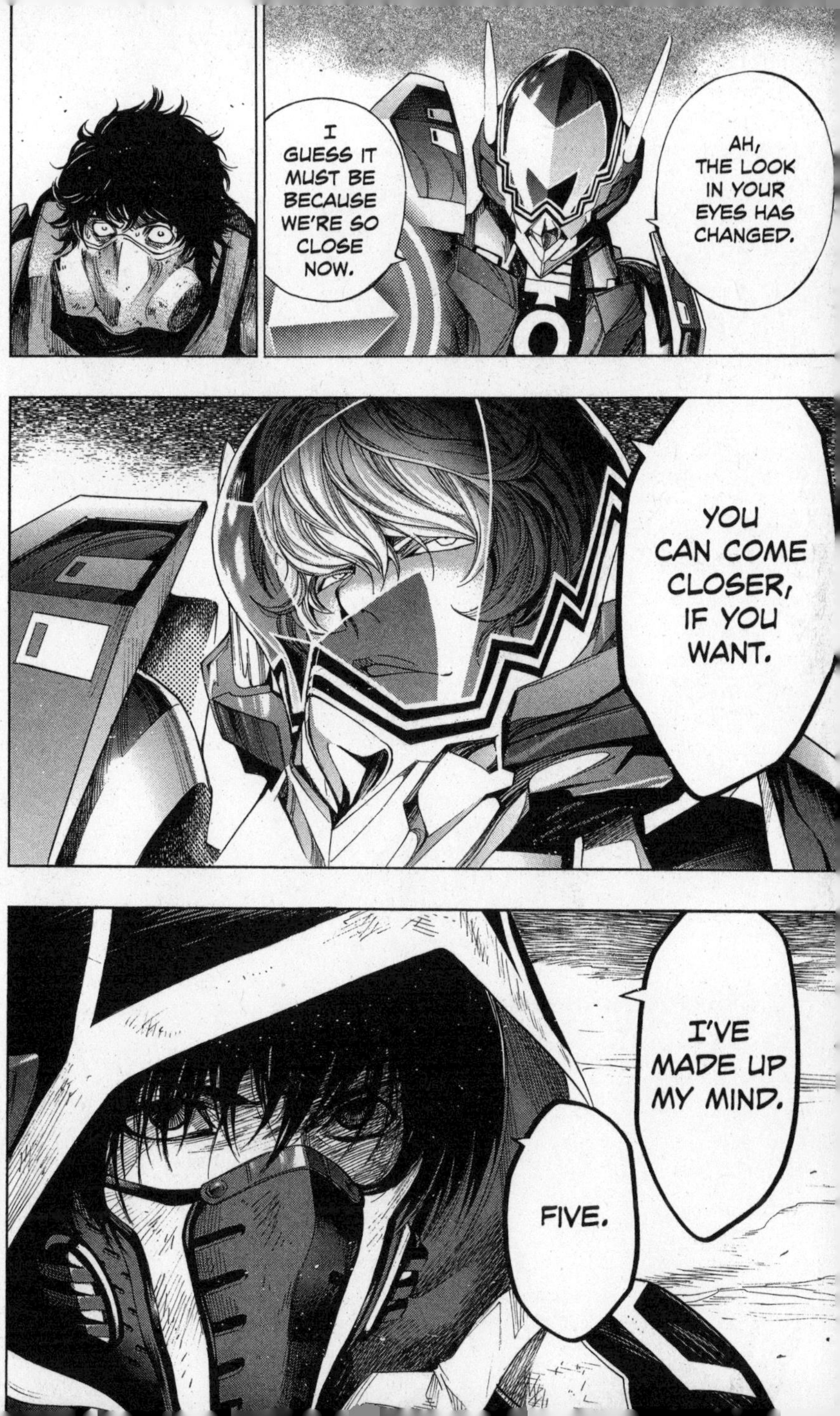
AH, THE LOOK IN YOUR EYES HAS CHANGED.
I GUESS IT MUST BE BECAUSE WE'RE SO CLOSE NOW.
YOU CAN COME CLOSER, IF YOU WANT.
I'VE MADE UP MY MIND.
FIVE.

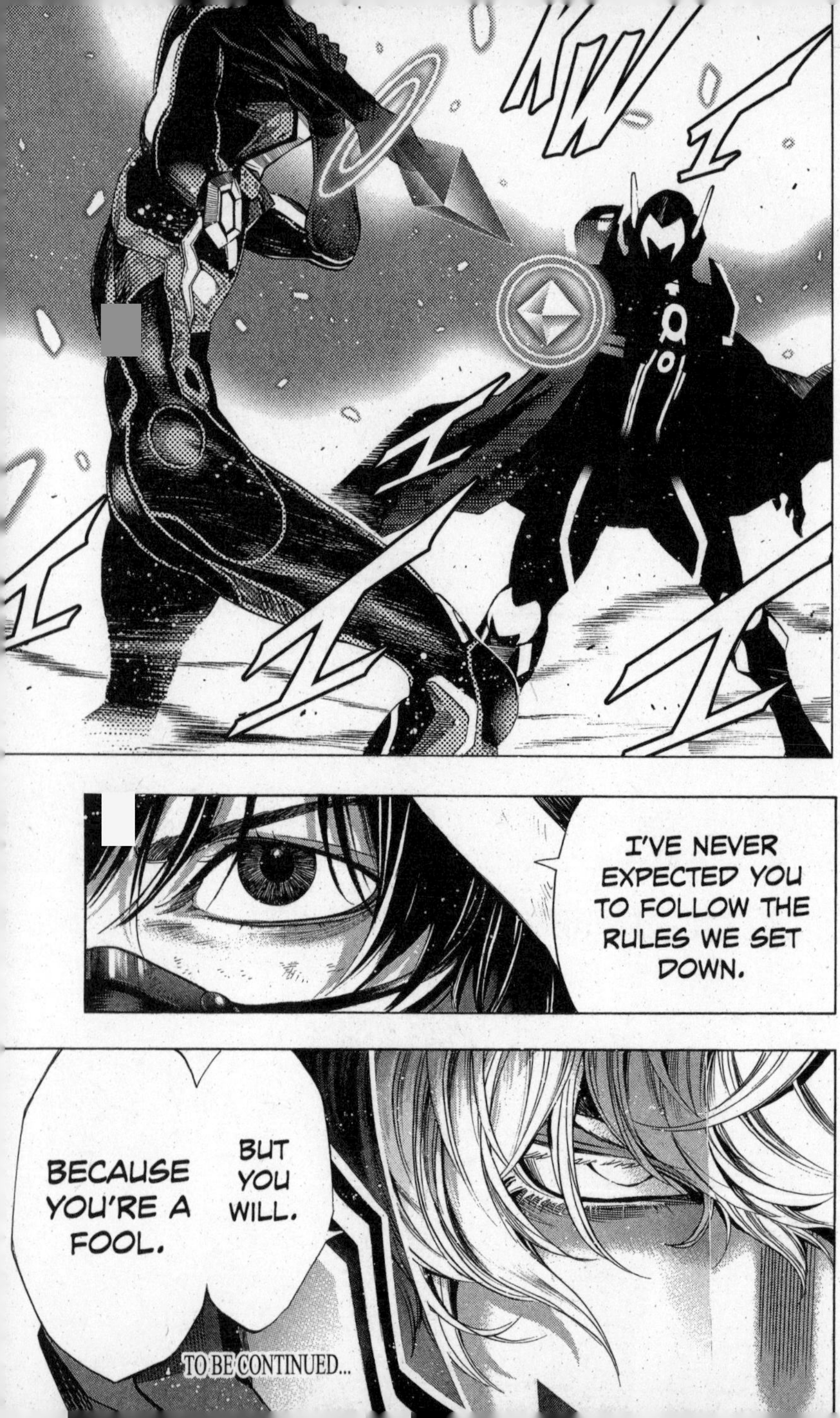
I'VE NEVER EXPECTED YOU TO FOLLOW THE RULES WE SET DOWN.
BUT YOU WILL.
BECAUSE YOU'RE A FOOL.
TO BE CONTINUED...

T s u**g**u mi **Oh** b **a**

Born in Tokyo, Tsugumi Ohba is the author
of the hit series *Death Note* and *Bakuman。*.

Ta **k** e s**h** i Oba **ta**

Takeshi Obata was born in 1969 in Niigata,
Japan, and first achieved international
recognition as the artist of the wildly popular
Shonen Jump title *Hikaru no Go*, which won the
2003 Tezuka Osamu Cultural Prize: Shinsei
"New Hope" Award and the 2000 Shogakukan
Manga Award. He went on to illustrate the smash
hit *Death Note* as well as the hugely successful
manga *Bakuman。* and *All You Need Is Kill*.

PLATINVM END

VOLUME 7
SHONEN JUMP Manga Edition

STORY **Tsugumi Ohba**

ART **Takeshi Obata**

TRANSLATION Stephen Paul
TOUCH-UP ART & LETTERING James Gaubatz
DESIGN Shawn Carrico
EDITOR Alexis Kirsch

ORIGINAL COVER DESIGN Narumi Noriko

Printed in the U.S.A.

Published by VIZ Media, LLC
P.O. Box 77010
San Francisco, CA 94107

10 9 8 7 6 5 4 3 2 1
First printing, December 2018

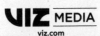

viz.com

shonenjump.com

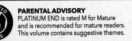

YOU'RE READING THE
WRONG WAY!

PLATINUM END reads from right to left, starting in the upper-right corner. Japanese is read from right to left, meaning that action, sound effects and word-balloon order are completely reversed from English order.

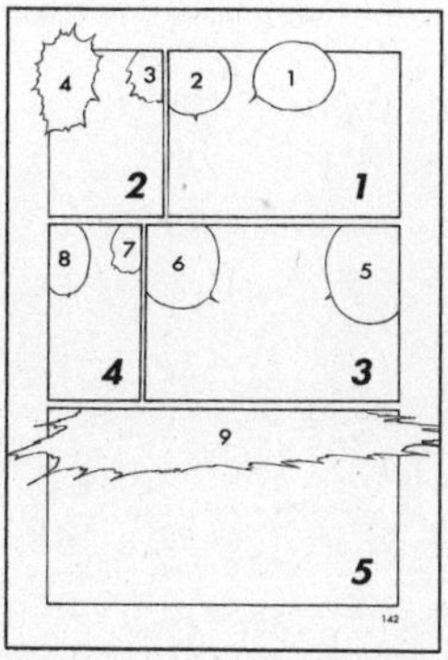

1
2
3
4
1
2
5
6
7
8
3
4
9
5
142

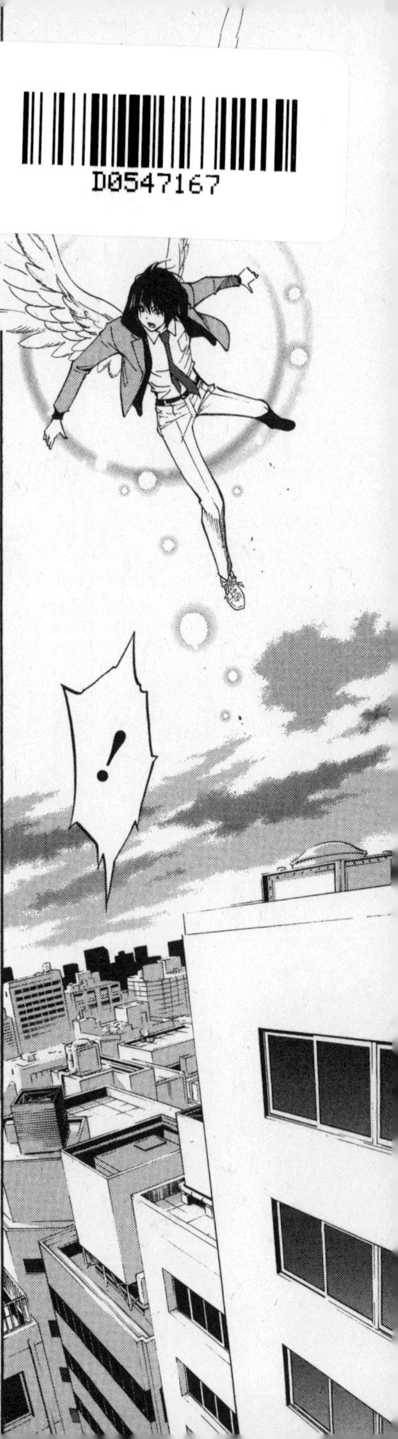

!